# IFIP Advances in Information and Communication Technology 430

# IFIP – The International Federation for Information Processing

IFIP was founded in 1960 under the auspices of UNESCO, following the First World Computer Congress held in Paris the previous year. An umbrella organization for societies working in information processing, IFIP's aim is two-fold: to support information processing within its member countries and to encourage technology transfer to developing nations. As its mission statement clearly states,

> *IFIP's mission is to be the leading, truly international, apolitical organization which encourages and assists in the development, exploitation and application of information technology for the bene t of all people.*

IFIP is a non-profitmaking organization, run almost solely by 2500 volunteers. It operates through a number of technical committees, which organize events and publications. IFIP's events range from an international congress to local seminars, but the most important are:

- The IFIP World Computer Congress, held every second year;
- Open conferences;
- Working conferences.

The flagship event is the IFIP World Computer Congress, at which both invited and contributed papers are presented. Contributed papers are rigorously refereed and the rejection rate is high.

As with the Congress, participation in the open conferences is open to all and papers may be invited or submitted. Again, submitted papers are stringently refereed.

The working conferences are structured differently. They are usually run by a working group and attendance is small and by invitation only. Their purpose is to create an atmosphere conducive to innovation and development. Refereeing is also rigorous and papers are subjected to extensive group discussion.

Publications arising from IFIP events vary. The papers presented at the IFIP World Computer Congress and at open conferences are published as conference proceedings, while the results of the working conferences are often published as collections of selected and edited papers.

Any national society whose primary activity is about information processing may apply to become a full member of IFIP, although full membership is restricted to one society per country. Full members are entitled to vote at the annual General Assembly, National societies preferring a less committed involvement may apply for associate or corresponding membership. Associate members enjoy the same benefits as full members, but without voting rights. Corresponding members are not represented in IFIP bodies. Affiliated membership is open to non-national societies, and individual and honorary membership schemes are also offered.

Jianying Zhou   Nurit Gal-Oz   Jie Zhang
Ehud Gudes (Eds.)

# Trust
# Management VIII

8th IFIP WG 11.11
International Conference, IFIPTM 2014
Singapore, July 7-10, 2014
Proceedings

Springer

Volume Editors

Jianying Zhou
Institute for Infocomm Research, Infocomm Security Department
1 Fusionopolis Way, #21-01 Connexis, South Tower, Singapore 138632, Singapore
E-mail: jyzhou@i2r.a-star.edu.sg

Nurit Gal-Oz
Sapir Academic College, Department of Computer Science
7916500 D.N. Hof Ashkelon, Israel
E-mail: galoznurit@gmail.com

Jie Zhang
Nanyang Technological University, School of Computer Engineering
Block N4 #02C-100, Nanyang Avenue, Singapore 639798, Singapore
E-mail: zhangj@ntu.edu.sg

Ehud Gudes
Ben-Gurion University, Department of Computer Science
84105 Beer-Sheva, Israel
E-mail: ehud@cs.bgu.ac.il

ISSN 1868-4238      e-ISSN 1868-422X
ISBN 978-3-662-51562-4      e-ISBN 978-3-662-43813-8
DOI 10.1007/978-3-662-43813-8
Springer Heidelberg New York Dordrecht London

*Typesetting:* Camera-ready by author, data conversion by Scientific Publishing Services, Chennai, India

Printed on acid-free paper

Springer is part of Springer Science+Business Media (www.springer.com)

# Preface

This volume contains the proceedings of IFIPTM 2014, the 8th IFIP WG 11.11 International Conference on Trust Management, held in Singapore, during July 7–10, 2014.

IFIPTM provides a truly global platform for the reporting of research, development, policy, and practice in the interdependent areas of privacy, security, and trust. Following the tradition established by the previous successful IFIPTM conferences since 2007, IFIPTM 2014 focused on the following main areas: trust and reputation models, privacy issues and social and behavioral models of trust, the relationship between trust and security, trust under attacks, and trust in the cloud environment. This variety of topics, and the fact the authors and the participants come from different organizations around the world, show the relevance of IFIPTM as the focus of international research on trust and its related areas.

IFIPTM 2014 was an open IFIP conference. The program of the conference featured both theoretical research papers and reports of real-world case studies. IFIPTM 2014 received 36 submissions from 23 different countries, including: Australia, Belgium, Canada, France, Germany, Greece, Hong Kong, India, Ireland, Israel, Italy, Japan, Luxembourg, Malaysia, The Netherlands, New Zealand, Norway, Saudi Arabia, Singapore, Switzerland, Tunisia, UK, and USA. The Program Committee selected 12 full papers and five short papers for presentation and inclusion in the proceedings after a very careful review process in which all papers received three to four reviews. Only the top papers were accepted as full papers to maintain the high quality of the IFIPTM conference.

The program of IFIPTM 2014 included two invited keynote presentations by academic experts in the fields of trust management including the recipient of the 2014 Winsborough Award for service and research in the fields of trust and trust management, Prof. Christian Damsgaard Jensen from the Technical University of Denmark. The proceedings include an invited paper by Prof. Jensen. In addition the program included a panel organized by Prof. Stephen Marsh on "Trust and Security" and a session of posters and demonstrations, which is reported in a separate volume.

In the IFIPTM 2014 conference, as well as in previous IFIPTM conferences, we had an accompanying workshop that enabled the presentation of truly new ideas including ongoing PhD research. In addition we offered two tutorials on relevant and current research on trust management. We believe the deep and wide profiles of the events will solidify IFIPTM as an international, multidisciplinary trust conference.

Running an international conference requires an immense effort from all parties involved. We would like to thank the Program Committee members and external referees for having provided timely and in-depth reviews of the submitted papers. We would also like to thank the workshop, tutorial, poster and demonstration, publication, local organization, registration, publicity, liaison, and website chairs, and the Advisory Committee, for their great help in organizing the conference. Thanks to the authors who submitted papers and the participants for their support to the conference. We are also grateful to Nanyang Technological University for providing the venue for IFIPTM 2014.

We hope you enjoy the proceedings.

April 2014

Jianying Zhou
Nurit Gal-Oz
Jie Zhang
Ehud Gudes

# IFIP Trust Management VIII

## 8th IFIP WG 11.11 International Conference on Trust Management, 2014

### Singapore
### 7–10 July 2014

## General Chairs

Jie Zhang       Nanyang Technological University, Singapore
Ehud Gudes      Ben Gurion University, Israel

## Program Chairs

Jianying Zhou      Institute for Infocomm Research, Singapore
Nurit Gal-Oz      Sapir Academic College, Israel

## Workshop and Tutorial Chairs

Christian Jensen     Technical University of Denmark, Denmark
Theo Dimitrakos     BT Research, UK

## Poster and Demonstration Chairs

Yuko Murayama     Iwate Prefectural University, Japan
Sjouke Mauw      University of Luxembourg, Luxembourg

## Panel/Special Session Chairs

Sandip Sen      University of Tulsa, USA
Stephen Marsh     University of Ontario Institute of Technology, Canada

## Graduate Symposium Chairs

Rehab Alnemr     Hewlett Packard Bristol, UK
Audun Josang     University of Oslo, Norway

## Publication Chair

Ying Qiu       Institute for Infocomm Research, Singapore

## Publicity Chairs

Murat Sensoy                          Ozyegin University, Turkey
Zeinab Noorian                        University of Saskatchewan, Canada
Fang Hui                              Nanyang Technological University, Singapore

## Local Organization Chairs

Chunyan Miao                          Nanyang Technological University, Singapore
Yang Liu                              Nanyang Technological University, Singapore
Joseph Teo Chee Ming                  Institute for Infocomm Research, Singapore

## Web Chairs

Anirban Basu                          KDDI R&D Laboratories, Japan
Tim Muller                            Nanyang Technological University, Singapore

## Program Committee

Rehab Alnemr                          HP Labs Bristol, UK
Man Ho Au                             University of Wollongong, Australia
Anirban Basu                          Tokai University, Japan
Elisa Bertino                         Purdue University, USA
David Chadwick                        University of Kent, UK
Frédéric Cuppens                      Telecom Bretagne, France
Theo Dimitrakos                       BT Research, UK
Rino Falcone                          Institute of Cognitive Sciences and
                                       Technologies, Italy
Carmen Fernández-Gago                 University of Malaga, Spain
Josep Ferrer                          University of the Balearic Islands, Spain
Simone Fischer-Hübner                 Karlstad University, Sweden
Sara Foresti                          The University of Milan, Italy
Nurit Gal-Oz                          Sapir Academic College, Israel
Dieter Gollmann                       Hamburg University of Technology, Germany
Stefanos Gritzalis                    University of the Aegean, Greece
Ehud Gudes                            Ben Gurion University, Israel
Omar Hasan                            INSA Lyon, France
Peter Herrmann                        Norwegian University of Science and
                                       Technology, Norway
Xinyi Huang                           Deakin University, Australia
Roslan Ismail                         Tenaga National University, Malaysia
Christian D. Jensen                   Technical University of Denmark, Denmark
Audun Jøsang                          University of Oslo, Norway
Yuecel Karabulut                      VMware, USA
Costas Lambrinoudakis                 University of Piraeus, Greece
Joseph Liu                            Institute for Infocomm Research, Singapore

| | |
|---|---|
| Javier Lopez | University of Malaga, Spain |
| Stephen Marsh | University of Ontario Institute of Technology, Canada |
| Fabio Martinelli | IIT-CNR, Italy |
| Sjouke Mauw | University of Luxembourg, Luxembourg |
| Yuxin Meng | City University of Hong Kong, Hong Kong, SAR China |
| Chunyan Miao | Nanyang Technological University, Singapore |
| Yuko Murayama | Iwate Prefectural University, Japan |
| Wee Keong Ng | Nanyang Technological University, Singapore |
| Masakatsu Nishigaki | Shizuoka University, Japan |
| Dhiren Patel | Sardar Vallabhbhai National Institute of Technology, India |
| Günther Pernul | University of Regensburg, Germany |
| Sini Ruohomaa | University of Helsinki, Finland |
| Pierangela Samarati | University of Milan, Italy |
| Ketil Stoelen | SINTEF, Norway |
| Mahesh Tripunitara | The University of Waterloo, Canada |
| Claire Vishik | Intel Corporation, UK |
| Ian Wakeman | University of Sussex, UK |
| Shouhuai Xu | University of Texas at San Antonio, USA |
| Jie Zhang | Nanyang Technological University, Singapore |
| Jianying Zhou | Institute for Infocomm Research, Singapore |

## External Reviewers

Diener, Michael
Geneiatakis, Dimitris
Jonker, Hugo
Lazouski, Aliaksandr
Liu, Yuan
Meng, Guozhu
Omerovic, Aida
Pitropakis, Nikolaos
Reisser, Andreas
Saracino, Andrea

Seehusen, Fredrik
Seng, Stéphane
Solhaug, Bjørnar
Sänger, Johannes
Tsohou, Aggeliki
Wang, Dongxia
Wu, Wei
Xu, Chang
Yu, Han
Zhang, Aston

# Table of Contents

## Short Papers

# The Importance of Trust in Computer Security

Christian Damsgaard Jensen

Department of Applied Mathematics & Computer Science
Technical University of Denmark
DK-2800 Kgs. Lyngby, Denmark
Christian.Jensen@imm.dtu.dk

**Abstract.** The computer security community has traditionally regarded security as a "hard" property that can be modelled and formally proven under certain simplifying assumptions. Traditional security technologies assume that computer users are either malicious, e.g. hackers or spies, or benevolent, competent and well informed about the security policies. Over the past two decades, however, computing has proliferated into all aspects of modern society and the spread of malicious software (malware) like worms, viruses and botnets have become an increasing threat. This development indicates a failure in some of the fundamental assumptions that underpin existing computer security technologies and that a new view of computer security is long overdue.

In this paper, we examine traditional models, policies and mechanisms of computer security in order to identify areas where the fundamental assumptions may fail. In particular, we identify areas where the "hard" security properties are based on trust in the different agents in the system and certain external agents who enforce the legislative and contractual frameworks.

Trust is generally considered a "soft" security property, so building a "hard" security mechanism on trust will at most give a spongy result, unless the underlying trust assumptions are made first class citizens of the security model. In most of the work in computer security, trust assumptions are implicit and they will surely fail when the environment of the systems change, e.g. when systems are used on a global scale on the Internet. We argue that making such assumptions about trust explicit is an essential requirement for the future of system security and argue why the formalisation of computational trust is necessary when we wish to reason about system security.

## 1 Introduction

Most security models and policies, and the technologies needed to support these models and enforce these policies, are based on security abstractions that have emerged in the context of military security or centralized (corporate) computing environments. Common for these environments is that there is a single authority to define and enforce security policies and to punish transgressions. During the past 20 – 30 years, these abstractions have been extended to cover local area networks, corporate intranets, virtual private networks and virtual organisations, but most of these extensions only work in environments where there is a single explicit root of authority for security enforcement. This authority is rooted in criminal-, civil- or military law, which requires appropriate

J. Zhou et al. (Eds.): IFIPTM 2014, IFIP AICT 430, pp. 1–12, 2014.
© IFIP International Federation for Information Processing 2014

and effective enforcement agencies or in the local security organisation within a corporation or a joint entity, as part of a virtual organisation, where the scope and responsibilities of this entity is governed by a contract and where conflicts will be resolved through an agreed legal framework.

In general, the root of authority is responsible for defining security policies that are interpreted by security mechanisms according to the underlying security model. These security policies can be interpreted as both explicit and implicit statements of trust in the different entities in the system. Moreover, the security mechanisms that enforce these security policies implemented in software and hardware and frequently rely on information from other subsystems, which raises further trust issues. In order to understand the importance of trust in computer security, we need to examine the relationships between the root of authority and all other entities in the system as they are enforced by security mechanisms that interpret security policies according to the underlying security model. We therefore need to understand the most common security models, policies and mechanisms and the way that they are implemented and enforced in practice.

The notions of security models and policies are used inconsistently in the literature, so, in order to facilitate our discussion, we start by presenting our definition of a security model, -policy, and -mechanism. A *security model* is an abstract specification of the desired security properties of a system, which defines abstract representations of all security relevant entities and specifies the rules that govern their relationships. A *security policy* defines a mapping between the (abstract) security model and the (concrete) entities in a given system, either directly through permissions, e.g. specifying allowed operations for user $u$ on file $f$, or indirectly through inference rules, e.g. defining dynamic rules that will resolve to *allow* or *deny*, when instantiated with the specific values of user $u$ and file $f$. Finally, a *security mechanism* is the set of functions in the underlying system that is responsible for interpreting and enforcing the security policy according to the security model.

Security models are commonly divided into two main classes: information flow models and access control models. The information flow models aim to control the flow of information inside a system, so that protected information will only be able to flow to authorised locations (a location may be a variable, a subsystem, or a specific device, depending on the granularity of the information flow analysis). Information flow models are commonly used with formal methods to prove that the system consisting of software and protocols conform to the formally specified security policy [9]. These formal proofs generally require complete knowledge about all possible information flows (variable assignments, method invocations, message transmissions, etc.) in the system, which requires access to the source code of all the software and all the tools that have ever been used to build and verify the system.[1] The access control model aims to control the way that passive entities, such as information and other resources (e.g. input from external devices) managed by the system, can be accessed by active entities, such as running programs, subsystems or external processes. The access control model needs the ability to enumerate all active and passive entities in the system and to associate policies with all requests by the former to perform operations on the latter. The first

---

[1] In his 1984 Turing Award lecture, Ken Thompson illustrates how tools, such as a compiler, can be abused to generate malicious code from well behaved source code [20].

requirement is trivial because the system needs identifiers to correctly manage all system entities anyway. The second requirement can be met in a number of different ways, but the conceptually simplest way to do this is through an access control matrix [15] that defines a row $r_i$ for each active entity $i$ and a column $c_j$ for each entity $j$, which includes both active and passive entities in the system, and where the authorised operations, such as read, write, append, call, etc., for active entity $i$ on entity $j$ is encoded in the access control matrix in position $(i,j)$ – if there are no authorised operations for entity $i$ on entity $j$ the position is simply left empty. This access matrix model has some limitations, [14] and it is cumbersome and error prone to specify security policies, so higher level access control models, such as the Bell & LaPadula confidentiality model [5], the Biba integrity model [6] and Role-Based Access Control [11,18], have emerged to facilitate the specification and evolution of access control policies. Access control policies are normally enforced by a special component, called a *guard* or a *reference monitor*, implemented in each of the subsystems that manage the entities, e.g. in each of the file servers that manage the files in a distributed file system. It is important to note that the access control model specify policies that control the interaction between entities, which means that the security properties are profoundly different from those obtained through the information flow model. On the one hand, the access control model requires no knowledge about the implementation or the internal state of any of the components in the system, which means that it can be much more generally applied, but on the other hand, it provides no guarantees about the confidentiality or integrity of data once access has been granted, e.g. any entity that has been authorised to perform certain operations on another entity according to the access control policy may, in principle, provide a proxy service for this operation to all other entities (both authorised and unauthorised). Security properties achieved through the access control model are therefore contingent on the behaviour of all authorised entities, i.e. that all active entities can be trusted to help enforce the security policy.

In practice, the necessary access to source code or formal specifications for all software and hardware used to implement a system as well as formal proofs that the running system conforms to specifications, means that information flow models are primarily used in high security systems, such as military information systems, or some parts of avionics and automotive control systems. The common need to dynamically install and update software without access to source code or complete specification, means that most commercial computer systems are protected by policies and mechanisms based on the access control model.

In the rest of this paper, we examine the access control model in more detail and discuss some of the trust issues that arise when this model is used. Section 2 examines the access control model and identifies some of the implicit trust assumptions that emerge as a consequence of the way that we specify and enforce access control policies in computer systems. In Section 3, we examine some of the fundamental trust issues that relate to the technical components in the system. This is followed, in Section 4, by an examination of the implicit trust assumptions relating to societal factors in the environment where the system operates. Finally, we present a summary of our discussions, present our conclusions and outline interesting directions for future work in Section 5.

## 2   Access Control

Access control mechanisms are designed to prevent unauthorised users from accessing resources managed by the system and to limit the access of authorised users to exactly those operations allowed by the access control policy. Access control policies are normally divided into two main classes, mandatory- and discretionary access control policies. The mandatory access control policies define system wide rules that cover all entities in the system and are normally centrally defined, i.e. it is not possible for an active entity to make any modification to the system that violates these policies. Discretionary access control policies allow active entities to define or change certain aspects of the access control policies, e.g. a user $u_i$ may grant access rights to a file $f$ that $u_i$ has created to another user $u_j$. The objective of most mandatory access control policies are to provide strong security guarantees, similar to the ones that can be obtained through the information flow model, and they are often quite restrictive and cumbersome to use. In practice, this means that most current computer systems used outside high security environments are protected by discretionary access control policies. As the specification of discretionary access control policies are, at least in part, left as an exercise to the users, there is an obvious element of trust vested in those users.

The enforcement of an access control policy relies on a *reference monitor*, which is a central component that mediates all access to entities managed by the system – the active entities are normally called *subjects* and the passive entities are normally called *objects*.[2] When objects reside on several nodes in a distributed system, then the access control mechanism must have a reference monitor on each of these nodes. A simplified view of the access control mechanism is shown in Figure 1.

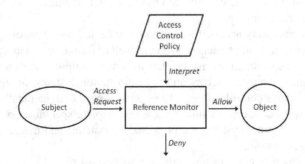

**Fig. 1.** Access Control Model

The figure shows a subjects which requests to access an object in a particular way. The reference monitor verifies that the requested operation conforms to the access control policy and allows the operation to proceed if it does; otherwise the request is denied. This presentation of the access control model is fairly simple and easy to understand,

---

[2] Subjects may also be considered objects in operations by other subjects, e.g. when one process starts or stops another process.

but it omits several important details. First of all, there are a number of technical issues that must be considered; we refer to these as technical trust issues. The reference monitor is a system entity, which is only able to interact with other system entities, such as processes running on the same computer. Access control policies, however, normally employ a higher level of abstraction, e.g. access rights are granted to human users or roles within an organisation, so the system needs an unambiguous way to represent this information and associate it with specific system entities. This is typically achieved by requiring users to "log in" to systems which associates their unique identifier (UID) with all processes that they run. The access request and the user credentials, e.g. the UID, must be communicated to the reference monitor using a secure channel that ensures the integrity and authenticity of the request. Similarly, the reference monitor must have a secure channel to read the access control policy, which must be correctly managed as a protected object in the system. We examine these technical issues in greater detail in Section 3. Second, the access control mechanism has little power to constrain the authorised subject's use of the object resources once access has been granted. Such constraints are generally imposed by elements outside the system, which we, for lack of a better word, refer to as social trust issues. These issues are examined in greater detail in Section 4.

## 3   Technical Trust in Security

Traditional access control policies rely on the authenticated identity of the user requesting to access a particular resource. This means that the system has to establish the identity of the user (this is known as identification) and verify that the user really is who he claims to be (this is known as authentication). The identification and authentication is normally done through the "log in" process mentioned above, where the user provides a username (identification) and a password (authentication). When the user has logged in, the UID will be associated with all processes that the user runs and can be transmitted to other systems that manage objects that the user wishes to access. Before the user can log in to the system, he has to be enrolled, i.e. an account has to be created for the user. The enrolment serves two purposes, it allocates a unique UID for the user and records the information (password or biometrics) that will be used to authenticate the user, and it defines the initial access control policy for the user; this second step is known as authorisation.

When the user has been enrolled and and has logged in to the system, he can start programs that may eventually request to access protected resources in the system. This requires the subject to forward its credentials along with the access request to the reference monitor. If the object resides on the same host as the subject, access requests are normally made through the system call interface, but when the object resides on a different computer, the subject normally submit credentials that have been protected by some cryptographic mechanism to the reference monitor. In the latter case, the verification of the cryptographic credentials normally require the help of a trusted third party, such as a key distribution center (KDC), like the authentication- and ticket granting service employed in Kerberos [16], or a Public Key Infrastructure (PKI), e.g. based on X.509 [17] or SPKI [10] certificates or even anonymous credentials [8].

These technical issues are illustrated in Figure 2 and will be discussed in greater details in the following.

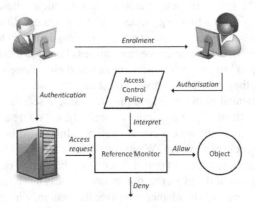

**Fig. 2.** Access Control in Practice

## 3.1   Enrolment

There are two types of enrolment, enrolment in the system, i.e. the account creation mentioned above, and enrolment in the organisation. Enrolment in the system is normally the only type of enrolment necessary for personal or stand-alone systems, while some form of enrolment in the organisation is necessary when users register on a website, subscribe to services or get hired by an organisation – in most cases, successful enrolment in the organisation is followed by enrolment into the systems managed by the organisation.

Part of the enrolment process is to verify the identity of the user and to establish whether the user is sufficiently trusted to be enrolled at the desired level in the organisation. If we consider the case of a new employment, the human resources (HR) department will examine the user's degree diplomas and diplomas from other courses along with the user's employment history in order to determine whether the user is competent. The HR department will also perform a background check, which may include the user's financial situation, affiliation with contentious organisations, a possible criminal record and frequently also a psychological assessment, in order to determine the trustworthiness of the potentially new employee. This illustrates an interesting point about the enrolment in organisations. In most cases, a comprehensive and meticulous trust evaluation is performed by the HR department, which help select the most suitable applicant. The final decision, to hire a person is binary, i.e. the trust evaluation is only used to decide whether a person should be allowed to pass the security perimeter and become part of the insiders.

## 3.2   Authorisation

Once the user has been enrolled in the organisation, the HR department will initiate the enrolment into the system and define the authorisations of the user, i.e. specify the initial access control policy for the user. This policy is primarily based on the functions that the person is hired to perform and will grant necessary access to all objects that the user may need to function in his new job. This illustrates an interesting point about the enrolment process and the authorisation of users. Despite the comprehensive and meticulous trust evaluation is performed by the HR department, the authorisation is primarily based on the functions that the person is hired to perform.

## 3.3 Authentication

Authentication is a binary process that, if it succeeds associates the user's UID with the subject. While the authentication community accepts that there may be some uncertainty associated with the authentication, e.g. passwords may be easy to guess [7,1] and biometric authentication operates with explicit notions of false acceptances and false rejections, the access control community generally assumes that the authentication mechanism is perfect, i.e. the access control mechanism has blind trust in the authentication mechanism.

In a distributed system, where users are authenticated on remote computers, the user credentials must be transported securely from the host where the user has authenticated to the host where the object resides and where the reference monitor will be invoked to grant or deny access to the object. As mentioned above. this is typically done using a trusted third party (TTP), such as a KDC or a PKI. In the case of a KDC, the party that authenticates the user will typically also manage the keys required to secure the credentials, i.e. the reference monitor only need to consider a single TTP. In the case of a PKI, the reference monitor has to trust the local authentication server and the hierarchy of certificate authorities (CAs) that are necessary to validate the signature of the local authentication server. Moreover, the subject and the object need to share a common trusted root CA, which raises interesting problems in large-scale open dynamic systems. In particular, the failure of the Dutch national CA DigiNotar [19] has demonstrated the brittleness of PKI based authentication infrastructures.

## 3.4 Access Request Verification

Access requests from the local node are normally passed to the reference monitor in system calls, which can be considered a secure mechanism. If subject and object reside on different hosts, it is not only necessary to consider the security of the credential transport mechanism, as discussed above, it is also possible that the host where the subject runs has been compromised while the host where the object resides remains secure. We therefore need to examine the different elements that determine the security status of the subject.

First of all, the computer hardware must comply exactly to specification. While incorrect implementation or missing functionality will impact all process and therefore quickly be discovered, but there is a rising concern about extra functionality, such as back doors, being built into computer and network equipment hardware [22]. Second, the operating system must not be compromised, which requires both the protection of the BIOS, the boot loader and the entire operating system code and the boot process to have executed correctly. While there have been some efforts to guarantee the integrity of the bootstrap process [21,2,4], these efforts have had little impact on common computer systems. Moreover, recent leaks by Edward Snowden suggest that the U.S. National Security Agency (NSA) is able to corrupt parts of the computing industry [12], which raises important issues about the trustworthiness of the underlying computing platforms. Finally, the user program must be correct in the sense that they do only request the necessary resources and preserve the confidentiality and integrity properties defined in the security policy.

This means that, when the reference monitor grants a subject access to an object, it has to trust the hardware of the subject host, the integrity of the BIOS, boot loader and operating system on that host, the system administration procedures, including the boot sequence, software updates etc., of the subject host and the software that the user executes and which requests the access on behalf of the user. Moreover, the reference monitor must trust all the same elements of all the hosts in the transitive closure of the chain of trusted third parties used to attest and certify security properties in the systems. These trust aspects are not adequately covered by current security models, where the security of external components are generally implicitly assumed. Research has been carried out to address some of these issues, but this work is fragmented and there is no comprehensive model that captures all relevant trust aspects.

Finally, the behaviour of users is normally considered external to the system security models, which makes it difficult to reason about the practical security of a computer systems. The importance of considering human behaviour as part of the system security model is probably best illustrated by the recent leaks of classified information by Chelsea (Bradley) Manning and Edward Snowden. When the U.S. Army and the NSA, considered two of the most security conscious organisations in the world, fail to accurately assess the trustworthiness of enrolled users, what can smaller organisations with fewer resources and less attention to security hope to achieve.

## 4   Social Trust in Security

In the previous sections, we examined many of the current security abstractions and identified a number of areas, where the security of the system depends on trust vested in different system components and, more importantly, in the users. In the following, we examine some of the factors that really constrains users and prevent them from violating the security policy and compromise the security of the system. The factors that we believe are among the most important constrains on human users are: Management, influences from colleagues and social norms in the society, the prevalent morals, ethics and sometimes religion in a society, legislation and the effective enforcement of laws, these factors are shown in Figure 3.

A more intricate understanding of the effects of these factors must draw a broad set of disciplines including psychology, sociology, philosophy, religion, economics and law. In the following, we present a brief outline of some of these effects as we understand them.

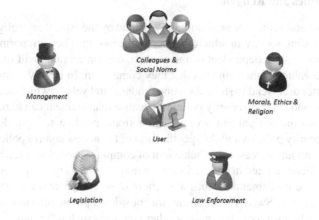

**Fig. 3.** Real Constraints on Human Behaviour

## 4.1   Management

Management is the root of authority for the work on security in the organisation, i.e. it defines the overall security policies, determines the consequences for policy violations and allocates resources for the enforcement of the security policies. By specifying the security policies and communicating them to all users of the system, management defines the boundaries for acceptable behaviour, which most users will respect. In many cases, the authority of management is derived from some form of contract, such as an employment or service provision contract, between the management and the user. If the user violates the terms of this contract, different forms of sanctions may be put in place, ranging from an admonition to termination of the contract. Fear of possible sanctions will constrain users and help promote desired behaviour in the user population only when the enforcement is seen as effective, i.e. the risk of discovery is high and the sanctions are carried out indiscriminately.

## 4.2   Colleagues and Social Norms

Humans are social animals, so most users will try to adapt their behaviour to the social norms in the environment. When other users set good examples, most users will do the same from a desire to "fit in". If, on the other hand, there is a common disregard for management and disrespect for the rules and policies, many people will pay less attention to those rules and policies. The pressures exercised through social norms are often situational, which means that changes in the environment may result in changes of what is seen as accepted behaviour. This means that organisations with a high churn rate can rely less on organisational culture and positive reinforcement from the behaviour of other users. The contextual effects of social norms are in many ways common to the more long term constraints imposed by morals, ethics and in many cases religion.

### 4.3  Morals, Ethics and Religion

A person's morals and values are predominantly shaped by the ethical and religious values of the surrounding society in which that person grows up. They are normally long lived and in many cases independent of the context, e.g. immigrants will often retain many of the core values of the countries that they come from. In largely homogeneous societies, computer users tend to share the same fundamental values, which often makes it easier to define and explain security policies, because management can harness commonly accepted notions of right and wrong. Such notions are often, to some degree, encoded into the security policies and the specification of the access control policies. Such tacit assumptions about the reasonable behaviour of computer users, however, mean that access control policies defined in one environment may work poorly in another environment, because some fundamental values are different, so computer users may behave in different ways, e.g. in Sweden, tax returns are considered public information and are therefore readable by everyone, but in most other countries such information would be considered private and therefore kept confidential.

In increasingly open and global societies, security/policies will be defined in one environment, but the objects may be accessed by subjects that execute in a completely different environment. This makes it challenging to define security policies, because it becomes necessary to reason about the context in which the policy is interpreted as well as the context in which it is defined.

### 4.4  Legislation

Similar to the effects of morals and ethics, different societies have developed different laws to deal with many of the same issues. Security policies are normally extensions of the legal framework, i.e. they specify rules that are not explicitly covered by legislation, but this relationship between legislation and security policy is often implicit.

Tacit notions of what is legal and illegal are often important when security policies are defined, but particular legislation, such as copyright protection, data protection and criminal law, may be very different in different countries, e.g. charges had to be dropped against the Philippine authors of the "I Love You" virus in 2000, because there were no laws in the Philippines against writing malware at the time [3].

The differences in legislation makes it necessary to thoroughly understand the legal framework in which the security policy is to be enacted and the provisions in law that facilitate the enforcement of security policies.

Legislation and security policies defines the limits of acceptable behaviour, so well-behaved users will know when they behave well, but the full effect of the law is only achieved through credible enforcement and effective sanctions.

### 4.5  Enforcement

Laws and policies that are not effectively enforced become declaration of intent that people observe when it is convenient. Effective enforcement of policies requires that the enforcement agency is equipped with sufficient resources and powers to carry out this task. It is, however difficult to quantify security and to demonstrate the direct benefits of spending on security, so many security agencies operate with fewer resources than they feel that they need.

It is generally simple for a well resourced security agency to enforce policies inside an organisation, but all security agencies are limited by jurisdiction, which often prevents them from directly pursuing outside threats, e.g. trace hackers across multiple networks in different countries.

Unless the agencies that are put in place to enforce the security policies offer a credible threat of detection and unless violations are rigorously sanctioned, users tend to ignore rules and policies that they do not understand and which get in the way of the immediate task.

## 5    Conclusions

In his thought provoking keynote at the First ERCIM Workshop on Security and Trust Management, Dieter Gollmann explained "why trust is bad for security".[3] The main thrust of his argument is that the concept of trust is extremely broad and ambiguous. In particular, he pointed out that the word "trust" has often been misappropriated by the computer security community to describe technologies that provide neither trust nor security in any great way, e.g. trusted computing base, trusted third parties, trusted computing, etc. As such, his arguments are very similar to the critique of technical trust technologies that we presented in Section 3, but we argue that most existing "hard" security abstractions are really founded in trust. This may be trust in the implementations of hardware and software, the technical staff that maintain the systems, the users who run programs, the staff that enrol and provision these users or external factors, such as societal norms, legislation or "the system's" ability to enforce rules and sanction violations.

In our view, we need to make trust a first class citizen of our security models if we are to successfully reason about the security of global computing systems. This requires development of formal models of trust, both qualitative and quantitative, and new ways of reasoning about security which take these models into account.

## References

1. Password recovery speeds, http://www.lockdown.co.uk/?pg=combi (visited April 15, 2014)
2. Arbaugh, W.A., Farber, D.J., Smith, J.M.: A Secure and Reliable Bootstrap Architecture. Tech. Rep. MS-CIS-96-35, University of Pennsylvania,, School of Engineering and Applied Science, Computer and Information Science Department, Philadelphia, Pennsylvania, U.S.A (1996)
3. Arnold, W.: Technology; Philippines to Drop Charges on E-Mail Virus. The New York Times (August 22, 2000),
http://www.nytimes.com/2000/08/22/business/
technology-philippines-to-drop-charges-on-e-mail-virus.html
(visited April 15, 2014)

---

[3] A paper summarizing these thoughts are published in ENTCS [13].

4. Balacheff, B., Chen, L., Pearson, S., Plaquin, D., Proudler, G.: Trusted Computing Platforms - TCPA Technology in Context. Prentice Hall (2003)
5. Bell, D.E., LaPadula, L.J.: Secure Computer Systems, Vol. I. Mathematical Foundations and Vol. II. A Mathematical Model. Tech. Rep. MTR-2547, The MITRE Corporation (1973)
6. Biba, K.J.: Integrity Considerations for Secure Computer Systems. Tech. Rep. MTR-3153, The MITRE Corporation (1977)
7. Bonneau, J.: The science of guessing: analyzing an anonymized corpus of 70 million passwords. In: IEEE Symposium on Security and Privacy, San Francisco, CA, USA (May 2012)
8. Brands, S.A.: Rethinking Public Key Infrastructures and Digital Certificates: Building in Privacy. MIT Press, Cambridge (2000)
9. Denning, D.E.: A lattice model of secure information flow. Commun. ACM 19(5), 236–243 (1976)
10. Ellison, C., Frantz, B., Lampson, B., Rivest, R., Thomas, B., Ylonen, T.: SPKI Certificate Theory. Tech. Rep. RFC 2693, Internet Engineering Task Force (IETF) (September 1999)
11. Ferraiolo, D., Kuhn, R.: Role-based access control. In: In 15th NIST-NCSC National Computer Security Conference, pp. 554–563 (1992)
12. Ferranti, M.: Report on NSA 'secret' payments to RSA fuels encryption controversy. PC World (December 23, 2013),
    http://www.pcworld.com/article/2082720/report-on-nsa-secret-payments-to-rsa-fuels-encryption-controversy.html
    (visited April 15, 2014)
13. Gollmann, D.: Why trust is bad for security. Electron. Notes Theor. Comput. Sci. 157(3), 3–9 (2006)
14. Harrison, M.A., Ruzzo, W.L., Ullman, J.D.: Protection in operating systems. Commun. ACM 19(8), 461–471 (1976)
15. Lampson, B.W.: Protection. In: Proceedings of the 5th Princeton Conference on Information Sciences and Systems (1971)
16. Neuman, C., Yu, T., Hartman, S., Raeburn, K.: The Kerberos Network Authentication Service (V5), RFC 4120 (July 2005)
17. Neuman, C., Yu, T., Hartman, S., Raeburn, K.: Information technology – Open Systems Interconnection – The Directory: Public-key and attribute certificate frameworks, Recommendation X.509 (October 2012)
18. Sandhu, R.S., Coyne, E.J., Feinstein, H.L., Youman, C.E.: Role-based access control models. Computer 29(2), 38–47 (1996)
19. The Dutch Ministry of the Interior and Kingdom Relations: DigiNotar CA certificates will be revoked on September 28 2011 (September 2011),
    http://www.logius.nl/english/news-message/titel/diginotar-ca-certificates-will-be-revoked-on-september-28-2011/,
    (visited April 15, 2014)
20. Thompson, K.: Reflections on trusting trust. Commun. ACM 27(8), 761–763 (1984)
21. Wobber, E., Abadi, M., Burrows, M., Lampson, B.: Authentication in the taos operating system. ACM Trans. Comput. Syst. 12(1), 3–32 (1994)
22. Wolf, J.: U.S. lawmakers seek to block China Huawei, ZTE U.S. inroads. Reuters (October 8, 2012), http://www.reuters.com/article/2012/10/08/us-usa-china-huawei-zte-idUSBRE8960NH20121008
    (visited April 15, 2014)

# TrustMUSE: A Model-Driven Approach
# for Trust Management

Mark Vinkovits, René Reiners, and Andreas Zimmermann

Fraunhofer FIT
User Centered Ubiquitous Computing
Schloss Birlinghoven, 53754 Sankt Augustin, Germany
{mark.vinkovits,rene.reiners,andreas.zimmermann}@fit.fraunhofer.de

**Abstract.** With the increasing acceptance of Trust Management as a building block of distributed applications, the issue of providing its benefits to real world applications becomes more and more relevant. There are multiple Trust Management frameworks ready to be applied; however, they are either unknown to developers or cannot sufficiently be adapted to applications' use cases. In our research, we have defined a meta model to modularize Trust Management, where each element in the model has clearly defined dependencies and responsibilities – also enforced by a complete API. Based on this model, we were able to develop a process supported by a number of tools that enables non-security expert users to find an applicable Trust Management solution for their specific problem case. Our solution – collectively called the TrustMUSE system – has evolved over an iterative user-centered development process: starting with multiple focus group workshops to identify requirements, and having multiple prototypes to conduct usage observations. Our user evaluation has shown that our system is understandable for system designers, and is able to support them in their work.

**Keywords:** Trust Management, Model-Driven Architecture, User-Centered Design, Meta Model, Usable Security.

# 1    Introduction

During recent years, Trust Management has gained increasing attention and is becoming more and more accepted as an essential building block of distributed systems, especially for the Internet of Things [18]. There is a vast number of research results in the field, and a variety of use cases is covered by these. However, these solutions rarely find their way into real-world applications. One possible explanation for this, as already identified by others, is the general lack of security expertise present during the development of applications [19]. As a result, even though Trust Management frameworks provide sound procedures for common threats, they are not integrated into systems, because developers simply are not aware of them. To avoid this problem, two basic steps are necessary: first, we need to ensure that designers of these applications have a general understanding of Trust Management and of available solutions; secondly, developers need support with regard to developing or integrating Trust Management frameworks. These are the points we address with our research by

J. Zhou et al. (Eds.): IFIPTM 2014, IFIP AICT 430, pp. 13–27, 2014.

developing a model-driven process that helps selecting and integrating applicable Trust Management solutions into specific application use-cases.

We organized our research according a user-centered design methodology [1]: first, we identified our users to be non-security expert developers. Focusing on this user group, we arranged a number of requirement sessions with focus groups using different scenarios as presented in [2, 3]; this way we gained a broad view on the challenges developers had. During the development of our approach, we concentrated on regularly evaluating also intermediate results to ensure that we did not lose focus of our target end users. Within this user-centered design process, this paper presents the state at the end of the first large iteration, where all intermediate results of the individual components have already been evaluated once, and the first evaluation of the whole integrated system took part.

From the first requirements workshops, that were the first step of our user-centered process, we found that there already was a general understanding of Trust Management [2] and that a structured, hierarchical view was requested to gain an overview of available solutions. Therefore, we chose to develop model-driven approach for working with Trust Management, called the TrustMUSE system (Trust Management Usable Software suitE). By applying grounded theory, we first composed a meta model of Trust Management as underlying structure of our system (The definition process, a first version and a validation of the elements of the model have already been presented in [4]). This meta model identified common aspects of different Trust Management frameworks; thereby, it enabled a more structured and focused view on the benefits and characteristics of distinct realizations. To be able to use the conceptual elements of the meta model in a more specified model-driven approach, we improved the concept into the TrustMUSE Model by defining the APIs of each element; these APIs not just abstract the functionality of the individual elements, but also concentrate on integration and implementation issues.

Looking at the TrustMUSE Model as the shaping structure of our approach, as next step towards our complete TrustMUSE system, we defined the TrustMUSE Process as an easily understandable process for interacting with the model. The TrustMUSE Process, as specified in [3], provides the means to systematically browse Trust Management state of the art. It enables developers to think in terms of their application, and in return be provided with a Trust Management framework. The software part of our system is the TrustMUSE Builder, which guides our target users through the TrustMUSE system and automates its processes.

With having a first integrated prototype of the whole TrustMUSE system available, we executed a first evaluation where target end users not just provided feedback about the intermediate concepts, but were asked to solve a specific application design task with our integrated approach. All of our test users were able to find an appropriate Trust Management framework based on TrustMUSE, and also understood what had been suggested to them. Even if this was only a first evaluation, its results were significant as they provided a first valid indication of whether TrustMUSE was able to solve the previously mentioned challenges.

The remaining paper is structured as follows: section 2 contains state of the art in the areas of modelling and usable security; section 3 describes the TrustMUSE Model and presents its APIs; section 4 deals with the TrustMUSE Process and TrustMUSE Builder implementation, which is then evaluated in section 5. Section 6 concludes the paper and outlines future work.

## 2    State of the Art

There is a large number of Trust Management frameworks available - all designed for different specific domains [5–7]. Similarly, there exist multiple surveys collecting and categorizing Trust and Reputation Management frameworks and identifying common aspects [8, 9]. As evident from these examples, Trust Management has thoroughly been researched, and there are many approaches ready to be used for finding trustworthy service providers in distributed environments. A consequence of this vivid research is the recent attempt to standardize Trust Management, and achieve interoperability between individual frameworks. There are multiple aspects where such standardization has started: common taxonomy [10], generic models [11], meta models [4, 12] and identification of common procedures [13]. However, these standardization approaches are still at their start and are barely applied – also because of their lack of formal application method.

Even if standardization of Trust Management were at its full extent, developers of distributed applications, who are less acquainted with security, would still have a hard time in knowing which solutions are the most appropriate for their challenges. On the one hand, this is due to the well-known problem of users having difficulties understanding security concepts [14]; on the other hand, this is caused by the lack of well-defined processes for finding a Trust Management solution applicable to a problem [3]. In order to solve the first problem, the field of user-centered security had risen [15]. It identifies the need to approach users, and support them in securely using software. This is generally achieved by applying an iterative user-centered design methodology [1], as we also did for our own approach. For achieving the desired understanding of security at the developers, Model-Driven Security (MDS) is one potential solution [16]. MDS aims at creating clear and understandable models of applied security procedures: this helps to clearly separate aspects of the software, improving overview and understanding of functionality. Additionally, during development, MDS enables code to be better structured and stay in accordance with specification and documentation.

Individual smaller steps of our approach had been presented previously: we presented the requirements from the initial workshops in [2]; in [4], we presented the conceptual meta model which is further improved into the TrustMUSE Model in this paper; the TrustMUSE Process that enables non-security experts to find an appropriate Trust Management solution for an application has been shown in [3].

## 3    TrustMUSE Model

The TrustMUSE Model is a meta model with accompanying APIs for Trust Management frameworks. It is based on the original TrustFraMM concept that has been published in [4]. Over the past years, we have continued to work with this model: we implemented specific Trust Management frameworks based on the model's elements, we have defined generic interfaces over which services can be consumed and interchanged, and we defined design patterns for the integration of the system into arbitrary applications. The experience gained through this process has matured the TrustMUSE Model into the version we present in this chapter. First, we provide an overview of the meta model – a detailed description of the elements can be found in [4] – and the accompanying APIs as seen in Fig. 1; after that, we briefly describe two systems we implemented in accordance with the model.

## 3.1    Description of the Model

There is no proper way to describe Trust Management functionality in a sequential way; therefore our sequential presentation of the TrustMUSE Model should not be considered as a restriction on the operation of describable frameworks. We start our description from *Trust Evidence*: the raw pieces of data – like observations, recommendations and certificates – that guide the system in deciding whom to trust. *Trust Evidences* have assigned *Trust Scopes* – used similarly at other places of the system – to distinguish received data according to aspects or contexts of entities' behavior. *Trust Discovery and Distribution* defines where, how to search for and eventually also share evidences, and it places them into the *Evidence Storage*: a typed database providing querying functionality to the rest of the system. *Trust Evaluation* takes this data, filtered by entities, and passes it to the associated *Trust Model*. This model describes the rules and procedures that turn raw data into assessed *Trust Values*. The output from this step is placed into the *Trust Storage*, which is the counterpart of the *Evidence Storage*, just for interpreted information. This information is then used by *Trust Enforcement* – the act of trusting: deciding if for a given service an entity is to be trusted, selecting a fitting provider for an action, or simply notifying the application about changes in someone's trust. Compared to using pure assessed *Trust Values*, this act includes considering contexts, risks, alternatives and priorities. After an interaction with another entity, it is possible to provide feedback into the system by the means of *Interaction Evaluation*. It places any feedback into the *Evidence Storage* and additionally, depending on its implementation, initiates *Trust Update*: the procedures that keep the status of the system fresh.

The APIs of the elements introduced so far represented the services of the underlying functionality; for this reason we did not discuss them in detail. However, the next element requires more introduction as its behavior is more bound to a specific design pattern: *Trust Representation* is the element holding information related to the formats applied in any of the TrustMUSE Model's elements. We did not indicate this in the class diagram, but almost every component may be dependent on it. It is needed to enable the integration of different procedures with their accompanying formats – as is intended by TrustMUSE. To implement this, *Trust Representation* is a repository for factory objects[1] where every element can register a class that is able to parse its respective formats; these factories are then used by other elements when required. The API of *Trust Representation* reflects this role as it provides methods to find specific factories based on input data, constructor parameters or names.

---

[1]  http://www.oodesign.com/factory-pattern.html
Last visited 22nd January 2014.

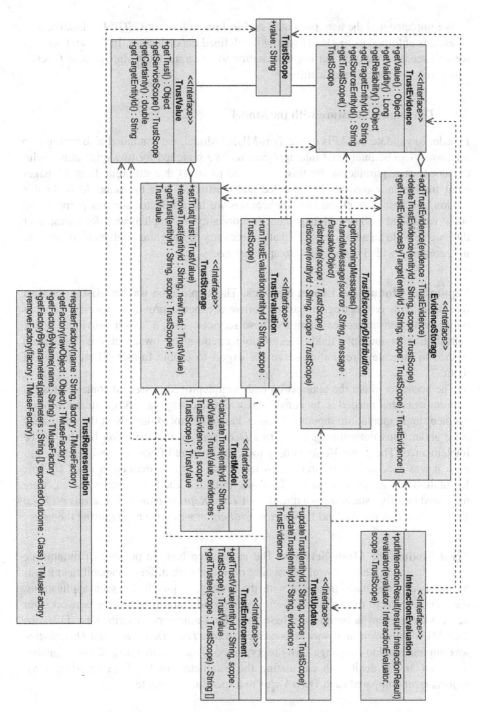

**Fig. 1.** UML class diagram of the TrustMUSE Model

We implemented the here presented API in Java in form of OSGi[2] Declarative Services; this enforced us to clearly follow the defined dependencies. In the next section, we will see how we used our implementation to integrate Trust Management functionality into two specific applications.

## 3.2    Developing Software with the Model

In order to validate the APIs of the TrustMUSE Model, we continued elaborating it to see how it can be integrated into applications. We searched for two applications with distinct trust requirements: by this, we aimed to stress that different Trust Management implementations can be modeled and consumed over the same APIs. In this section, we first present the two applications we have selected for this purpose and show what kind of Trust Management functionality we implemented for them; after this, we provide an additional API that is necessary to integrate implementations done in accordance with TrustMUSE into applications.

**Reputation Module for Expert Network.** This application was an existing product that dealt with connecting human or software experts, providing specific services online, with consumers searching for those services – e.g. a lawyer providing online consultation in multiple fields for possible clients. The owner of this application wished to indicate a reputation score per expert to enable further differentiation of them.

The scenario where the application had been deployed possessed some interesting requirements that needed to be considered while selecting an appropriate Trust Management implementation: reputation scores had to be stored directly at the entity they were about, thus determining how *Trust Discovery and Distribution* had had to be implemented. The *Trust Model* simply took the average of positive and negative ratings; it was executed every time a new rating came in – as defined in *Trust Update*. Reputation scores, as well as the feedback provided about received services, were presented as a five-star scale – a question of *Trust Representation*. There was no *Trust Enforcement* component, and *Interaction Evaluation* was done by enquiring the user.

**Trust Module for Mesh Network.** The application had the purpose of monitoring and debugging a mesh network consisting of nodes with different capabilities; it was not intended to actually intervene with the routing. Typically for such applications, our solution was to run on each device, sharing observations across the network. Our Trust Management solution was based on the framework described by [17]; the TrustMUSE division of it was as presented in [4]: *Trust Discovery and Distribution* was implemented to exchange own observations, *Trust Update* initiated this regularly, the *Trust Model* dealt with calculating the parameters of the Beta function, *Trust Enforcement* compared each *Trust Value* to a specified threshold.

---

[2]  http://www.osgi.org/Main/HomePage Last visited 22nd January 2014.

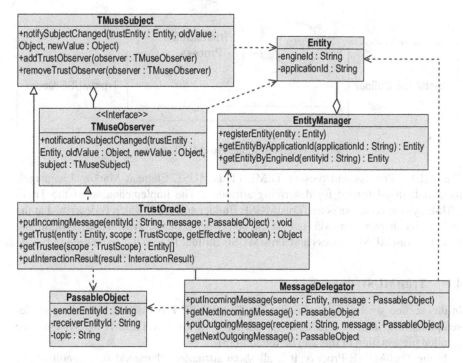

**Fig. 2.** TrustMUSE integration layer class diagram

**Integrating TrustMUSE Based Solutions into Applications.** As identified during the requirements process [2], developers would like to mainly build on a basic set of services in their applications – only when required, did they want to customize Trust Management functionality. Therefore we created the TrustMUSE integration layer as seen in Fig. 2: a set of interfaces and utility classes that wrap the Trust Management implementation, and simplify it for the user to consume trust information. The main interface an application works with is the *Trust Oracle*: it consists of the four main methods that a user expects to receive and that are necessary for the framework to operate.

# 4    TrustMUSE Process and TrustMUSE Builder

The TrustMUSE Model enables separation of concerns within the Trust Management domain; it helps non-security experts to gain an understanding of its functionalities, and benefit from different implementations. What the TrustMUSE Model cannot provide on its own, however, is the ability to know what implementations work in what environments or for which problems. To provide support in this task, we developed the TrustMUSE Process. In this chapter, we first briefly provide an overview of the

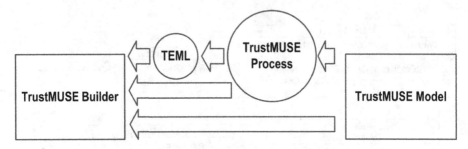

**Fig. 3.** Overview of the TrustMUSE system

TrustMUSE Process and present TEML (TrustMUSE Element Markup Language): the standardized format for describing attributes. The implementation of the Trust-MUSE system concepts is the TrustMUSE Builder software, which is described at the end of this chapter. An overview of the components of the TrustMUSE system, and how the TrustMUSE Process and TrustMUSE Builder fit into it, can be seen in Fig. 3.

### 4.1   TrustMUSE Process

In this section we briefly summarize the TrustMUSE Process, and show how its development fits into the methodology used for the overall TrustMUSE system. The detailed presentation of this can be found in [3].

In the TrustMUSE Process, it is all about attributes: characteristics, conditions or services of Trust Management implementations. For the process, each author providing an implementation, defines the attributes that apply for the developed solution. When executing the process, the user is presented with the set of all author defined attributes, sorted by TrustMUSE Model elements. Developers are now able to focus on one element at a time, select and exclude attributes that seem relevant for the application's scenario – thereby actually selecting between Trust Management implementations that are applicable for it. After having finished the selection of attributes, the TrustMUSE Process suggests those implementations that have the largest overlap with the attributes selected by the user.

The benefit in the TrustMUSE Process is that developers receive a Trust Management solution without having read the whole state of the art in the field. Even if the first suggestion does not fit completely, developers can quickly change the attributes to receive an alternative candidate; this still significantly reduces the number of frameworks necessary to be read, before finding a fitting one. An example of possible attributes for different TrustMUSE Model elements can be seen in Table 1.

The definition of the TrustMUSE Process had been based on requirements we collected beforehand in focus group workshops. From the requirements, we developed two paper prototypes and compared them during multiple user interviews using a specific development scenario, and manually simulating the process's operation with

**Table 1.** Example attributes for the TrustMUSE Process

| TrustMUSE Model element | Example standard attributes |
|---|---|
| Trust Discovery and Distribution | Trusted third party; Personalized view on entities; Requires continuous Internet connectivity. |
| Trust Model | Trusted third party; Uncertainty handling; Continuous forgetting. |
| Trust Enforcement | Weighted aggregation. |
| Interaction Evaluation | Rule based feedback; multi-level feedback. |
| Trust Update | Calendar based; Number of interactions based. |

multiple sheets of prepared paper templates. The feedback collected from these user interviews than finalized the process, and guided the implementation of the TrustMUSE Builder.

## 4.2   Standardization and Tooling

To achieve the model-driven process we aim for, a certain level of standardization of Trust Management has been necessary; this includes the APIs we have seen but it also includes formats and tools that are presented in this section. As described in the previous section, to enable the TrustMUSE Process, Trust Management experts have to provide attributes for their developed solutions; additionally, these attributes have to be in the same format for all solutions to be able to integrate them into one tool. To enable this uniform representation of attributes we defined the TrustMUSE Element Markup Language (TEML), based on which attributes and their dependencies can be provided, sorted by TrustMUSE Model elements, in machine readable XML format.

A TEML document is composed as follows: the author starts with defining a *trustMUSEElement* with a freely chosen *name* attribute and the *className* of the TrustMUSE Model element the solution is for. As a next step, the characterizing attributes are given to the solution through a number of *attribute* XML elements. In case the solution has no collisions with other elements, the TEML document is finished; else these collisions also have to be defined in the same document. To do so, it is necessary to define further *trustMUSEElements*: these will have no *name* but only a *className* attribute. The attributes, which are placed into these latter *trustMUSEElements*, define the collisions of the solution. Finally, the identifiers of the colliding *trustMUSEElements* have to be provided as dependencies to the original solution's XML element. The DTD of TEML can be seen in Fig. 4.

In order to facilitate the cumbersome process of creating correct XML documents by hand, we developed a GMF[3] based utility in which TEML documents can be generated automatically: the author simply pulls the respective TrustMUSE Model elements onto the canvas, and types attributes into them. Collisions can also be defined by simply connecting two elements. When saved, the utility generates two files: one file containing the diagram layout and one containing the TEML document.

---

[3]  http://www.eclipse.org/modeling/gmp/ Retrieved 27th January 2014.

```
<?xml version="1.0">
<!DOCTYPE TrustMUSE [
<!ELEMENT TrustMUSE (trustMUSEElement+)>
<!ELEMENT trustMUSEElement (attribute+)>
<!ELEMENT attribute EMPTY>

<!ATTLIST trustMUSEElement name CDATA #IMPLIED>
<!ATTLIST trustMUSEElement className (Scope | TrustEvi-
dence | TrustValue | EvidenceStorage | TrustStorage |
TrustDiscoveryDistribution | TrustUpdate | TrustEvalua-
tion | TrustEnforcement | InteractionEvaluation | Tru-
stRepresentation) #REQUIRED>
<!ATTLIST trustMUSEElement dependencies IDREFS
#IMPLIED>
<!ATTLIST attribute name CDATA #REQUIRED>
]>
```

**Fig. 4.** DTD of TEML

### 4.3    TrustMUSE Builder Prototype

With the presented concepts at hand, we are able to create the tool that automates the execution of the TrustMUSE Process: the TrustMUSE Builder, implemented as a standalone .NET WPF[4] desktop application. At start-up, it reads its working directory for stored TEML documents and additional informative text files – short descriptions, lists of references and implementation libraries. Parsing these files, the application builds up its model of possible TrustMUSE Model element implementations, their attributes and dependencies; then it prepares and shows the GUI as it has been specified in [3].

The first view of the GUI is called the composition state: this is the state where the user can select and exclude attributes by clicking the checkboxes next to the attributes. After each selection, the application logic checks which candidate implementations are to be excluded, based on the defined collisions, and disables them. For each TrustMUSE Model element, the user can view a short help description; also for each attribute there is a tool tip providing an explanation of the presented term. A screenshot of this view can be seen in Fig. 5. If the user feels happy with the selection and has nothing more to add, she can go to the next view – called the composed state.

The composed state has the same layout as the previous one; the difference is that instead of showing attributes, it shows specific implementations for the elements. An implementation suggestion consists of a name, as specified in the TEML, a short description, and a list of additional references. The user can review whether the suggested framework looks sane for the application's purpose, and decide whether to go back to the composing state and change the attributes, or to acknowledge the framework.

---

[4]  http://msdn.microsoft.com/en-us/library/ms754130(v=vs.110).aspx
Retrieved 27th January 2014.

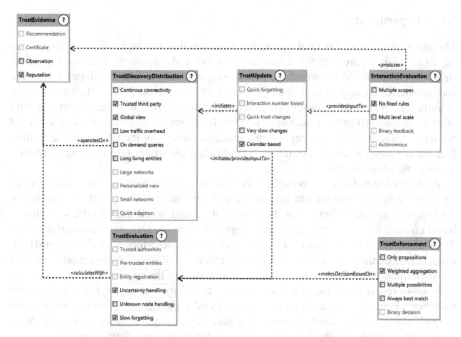

**Fig. 5.** Screenshot of the composition state of TrustMUSE Builder

If the suggested framework is acknowledged, which is done by clicking a button in the GUI, TrustMUSE Builder copies the implementation libraries from the respective elements into one specified folder. From this point on, the development process for the user, building on OSGi, looks as follows: as first step, the folder with the implementation libraries has to be set as target platform; second, missing code has to be filled in – like the TMuseFactory for the used trust representation, the network and communication handling, and the consumption of the API's integration layer; finally, the configurations for the different implementations have to be set. If all this is done, the Trust Management framework will be ready to be used.

## 5    First Qualitative User Evaluation and Threads to Validity

We evaluated the implementation of the integrated prototypic TrustMUSE system with application developers in a final set of interviews. Our aim was to find out whether our solution is able to support our target users finding a Trust Management solution when given a specific problem: that is, can users based on our system do the transition from specification to solution. Although our system was still in a very early stage of implementation, the evaluation held great significance as it had the potential of providing first valid feedback about the usefulness of the TrustMUSE approach. In this section we present our interview set up and present the collected responses; at the end of the section we interpret the results, and identify lessons learnt and future work.

## 5.1    Experiment

The main question of the final evaluation was, whether our target users, non-security expert developers, are able find an appropriate Trust Management framework with the support of TrustMUSE. Accordingly, for the evaluation, we first developed a scenario and produced an application specification with very clear Trust Management requirements: our scenario described a company that signed half year contracts with other companies to provide access to its distributed services. To ensure that users did not try to solve the task with regular requests to a server, we included a clause, stating that the company's server was not to be contacted too often, into the specification – out of scalability reasons.

With this scenario, we approached five users: each of them had multiple years of software design experience but little to no security qualification. At the beginning of the test, we presented them with the specification and asked them to draft a solution based on their knowledge, without any support. Following this, we presented them the TrustMUSE Builder software: we provided a brief description of the TrustMUSE Process and explained that the presented software is not fully implemented; therefore the participants were allowed to ask questions during the experiment, however, we only answered if the misunderstanding was caused by the prototypic nature of the tool. For a better understanding of the developers' mindset, we asked our participants to think aloud, explain their decisions and state any ambiguities they encounter. Also, after they received the framework suggestion from the tool, they were asked to describe how they interpret the proposed solutions, and whether they think it is appropriate for their original problem. In the experiment, they were only asked to go as far as to click the framework generation button; we did not intend to evaluate the code integration aspects of the TrustMUSE system at that moment. Finally, we did a structured interview consisting of twelve statements with five-point Likert scale – strongly disagree, disagree, undecided, agree, strongly agree – responses, categorized into three topics: how clear were the components and dependencies of the model, how well was the process able to help them, how much did they benefit from the tool. Additionally, we also collected some open feedback for future extensions of the tool.

**Table 2.** Results of the user evaluation

| Statement | Mean answer | P-Value |
|---|---|---|
| You understand the concept of Trust Management. | Agree | 0.0002 |
| You understand the sub-processes present in Trust Management. | Undecided | 0.0332 |
| You understand the connection between the Trust Management components. | Agree | 0.0001 |
| You think the concept of attributes is a good way to describe your scenario. | Undecided | 0.0004 |
| You understand the Trust Management solution that has been proposed. | Agree | 0.0002 |
| You think the proposed framework is appropriate for your problem. | Agree | 0.0001 |
| You could explain the proposed framework to someone else. | Agree | 0.0002 |

## 5.2     Results

The participants, when asked to provide a solution for the specification based on their own knowledge, all foresaw a certificate based system – except for one user who could not come up with a solution; however, they were not able to provide any more details regarding the realization of their idea. Subsequently, with the support of TrustMUSE, each user was able to find an appropriate solution for the problem, and understood how the proposed framework solved the specification. Additionally, our users stated to have gained a deeper understanding of Trust Management, and to have understood the relations defined in the TrustMUSE Model.

While the above statements remain valid for the overall experiment, there were statements in the interviews where the responses were much diffused and often had outliers. To be able to make sense and exclude invalid results, we applied statistical evaluation methods to the response sets: we checked the interquartile ranges (IQR) and made statistical hypothesis tests. First, we excluded all statements where the responses' IQR was more than 2; this step excluded four statements out of the twelve. Afterwards, for the remaining statements, we made the null hypothesis that our participants disagreed with them; testing our data against this null hypothesis excluded one additional statement. The statements remaining valid after our tests, with accompanying p-values, are presented in Table 2.

## 5.3     Lessons Learnt and Future Work

Reviewing our results from the evaluation, we found that our approach started on a sound track: developers were able to solve the task with the support of TrustMUSE that they could not properly handle before. Additionally, a very important benefit of TrustMUSE, as stated by the test participants, was the gained information about elemental components within Trust Management, their relations, and their applicability. However, TrustMUSE still showed to be too technical and users had difficulties dealing with all the new terminology; also, clarity and usability of attributes' terminology in the TrustMUSE Process caused misunderstandings.

The difficulty in defining attributes is that they have to be detailed enough to describe fine operational details of implementations; however, they should not be too technical, so that our target users still understand them. Additionally, as we have learnt from our user tests, attributes have to be unambiguous: even if we provide explanations, users tend to interpret terms to accommodate their own beliefs. Therefore, it will be necessary to execute a separate user-centered design process, where the appropriate set of attributes shall be found through multiple iterations. The overall process shall consist of analyzing multiple frameworks, dividing them by TrustMUSE Model elements, attributing them, and then talking to developers about their understanding.

Our users expressed some additional wishes towards the TrustMUSE Builder tool: they wished to see what effects their decisions had on the final framework suggestion. They sometimes felt lost during the use of the tool, and did not know whether what they did made sense; they could not clearly see the relation between their input and the application's output. Therefore, future developments should address these issues: find visual features that could tackle the lack of transparency, provide better indication of what the tool is doing currently, and generally better involve the user into the decision process.

# 6    Conclusions

In this paper we presented TrustMUSE (Trust Management Usable Software suitE): a model-driven approach for integrating Trust Management into applications. Building on the experience from the state of the art in user-centered security and model-driven security, our approach aims at supporting non-security expert application designers to find appropriate Trust Management frameworks for their application domains. We first presented the TrustMUSE Model: a meta model for Trust Management with accompanying APIs. Based on OSGi based implementation experience, we also provided an API for an integration layer that wraps Trust Management functionality, and only exposes main services that are needed by the relying distributed application.

Built on top of the TrustMUSE Model, we presented the concept of the Trust-MUSE Process and its implementation: the TrustMUSE Builder. This tool first reads different Trust Management implementations that are described using TEML (Trust-MUSE Element Markup Language) documents; these implementations are then presented in an abstract format to the users of the tool. They can then describe their application specification by means of attributes, and subsequently receive a Trust Management framework suggestion tailored to their needs.

We closed this paper with the evaluation of our system, where users were asked to solve a Trust Management task based on the TrustMUSE Builder software. Each user was able, within a limited time span, to come up with an appropriate solution; additionally, they felt confident in the validness of the proposed framework for their problem. Based on the collected user feedback after the experiment, we conclude, that we should further increase the abstraction level of the representations used in Trust-MUSE. Future work needs to address the design of a more straight forward process that better supports our target end users in incorporating Trust Management into their application designs.

**Acknowledgements.** This work has been performed within the ALMANAC project, co-funded by the EC within the FP7, theme ICT-2014.1.4 Future Internet and smart Internet of Things, grant agreement No. 609081. Possible inaccuracies of information are under the responsibility of the project. This report reflects solely the views of its authors. The European Commission is not liable for any use that may be made of the information contained therein.

# References

1. Gould, J.D., Lewis, C.: Designing for usability: key principles and what designers think. Commun. ACM. 28, 300–311 (1985)
2. Vinkovits, M.: Towards requirements for trust management. In: Privacy, Security and Trust (PST) 2012, pp. 159–160. IEEE Comput. Soc., Paris (2012)
3. Vinkovits, M., Zimmermann, A.: Defining a trust framework design process. In: Furnell, S., Lambrinoudakis, C., Lopez, J. (eds.) TrustBus 2013. LNCS, vol. 8058, pp. 37–47. Springer, Heidelberg (2013)

4. Vinkovits, M., Zimmermann, A.: TrustFraMM: Meta Description for Trust Frameworks. In: ASE/IEEE International Conference on Privacy, Security, Risk and Trust, Amsterdam, Netherlands, pp. 772–778 (2012)
5. Marti, S., Garcia-Molina, H.: Limited reputation sharing in P2P systems. In: Proceedings of the 5th ACM Conference on Electronic Commerce, EC 2004, pp. 91–101. ACM Press, New York (2004)
6. Zouridaki, C., Mark, B.L., Hejmo, M.: Byzantine robust trust establishment for mobile ad hoc networks. Telecommun. Syst. 35, 189–206 (2007)
7. Blaze, M., Feigenbaum, J., Lacy, J.: Decentralized trust management. In: Proceedings 1996 IEEE Symposium on Security and Privacy, pp. 164–173. IEEE Comput. Soc. Press (1996)
8. Josang, A., Ismail, R., Boyd, C.: A survey of trust and reputation systems for online service provision. Decis. Support Syst. 43, 618–644 (2007)
9. Artz, D., Gil, Y.: A survey of trust in computer science and the Semantic Web. Web Semant. Sci. Serv. Agents World Wide Web 5, 58–71 (2007)
10. Viljanen, L.: Towards an ontology of trust. In: Katsikas, S.K., López, J., Pernul, G. (eds.) TrustBus 2005. LNCS, vol. 3592, pp. 175–184. Springer, Heidelberg (2005)
11. Kinateder, M., Baschny, E., Rothermel, K.: Towards a Generic Trust Model – Comparison of Various Trust Update Algorithms. In: Herrmann, P., Issarny, V., Shiu, S.C.K. (eds.) iTrust 2005. LNCS, vol. 3477, pp. 177–192. Springer, Heidelberg (2005)
12. Saadi, R., Rahaman, M.A., Issarny, V., Toninelli, A.: Composing trust models towards interoperable trust management. In: Wakeman, I., Gudes, E., Jensen, C.D., Crampton, J. (eds.) IFIPTM 2011. IFIP AICT, vol. 358, pp. 51–66. Springer, Heidelberg (2011)
13. Gómez Mármol, F., Martínez Pérez, G.: Towards pre-standardization of trust and reputation models for distributed and heterogeneous systems. Comput. Stand. Interfaces 32, 185–196 (2010)
14. Whitten, A., Tygar, J.D.: Why Johnny Can 't Encrypt: A Usability Evaluation of PGP 5.0. In: Proceedings of the 8th USENIX Security Symposium (1999)
15. Zurko, M.E., Simon, R.T.: User-centered security. In: Proceedings of the 1996 Workshop on New Security Paradigms, NSPW 1996, pp. 27–33. ACM Press, New York (1996)
16. Basin, D., Doser, J., Lodderstedt, T.: Model driven security: From UML models to access control infrastructures. ACM Trans. Softw. Eng. Methodol. 15, 39–91 (2006)
17. Buchegger, S., Le Boudec, J.-Y.: A Robust Reputation System for P2P and Mobile Ad-hoc Networks. In: Proceedings of the Second Workshop on the Economics of Peer-to-Peer Systems (2004)
18. IoT-A FP7 Project: Final Architectural Reference Model for the IoT. (2013), http://www.iot-a.eu/public/public-documents/d1.5/view (last visited January 27, 2014)
19. CISCO: Cisco 2014 Annual Security Report (2014), http://www.cisco.com/web/offers/lp/2014-annual-security-report/index.html (last visited February 6, 2014)

# Reusability for Trust and Reputation Systems

Johannes Sänger and Günther Pernul

Department of Information Systems
University of Regensburg
Regensburg, Germany
{johannes.saenger,guenther.pernul}@wiwi.uni-regensburg.de
http://www-ifs.uni-regensburg.de

**Abstract.** Reputation systems have been extensively explored in various disciplines and application areas. A problem in this context is that the computation engines applied by most reputation systems available are designed from scratch and rarely consider well established concepts and achievements made by others. Thus, approved models and promising approaches may get lost in the shuffle. In this work, we aim to foster reuse in respect of trust and reputation systems by providing a hierarchical component taxonomy of computation engines which serves as a natural framework for the design of new reputation systems. In order to assist the design process we, furthermore, provide a component repository that contains design knowledge on both a conceptual and an implementation level.

**Keywords:** trust, reputation, reusability, trust pattern.

## 1 Introduction

In the last decade, trust and reputation have been extensively explored in various disciplines and application areas. Thereby, a wide range of metrics and computation methods for reputation-based trust has been proposed. While most common systems have been introduced in eCommerce, such as eBay's reputation system[1] that allows to rate sellers and buyers, considerable research has also been done in the context of peer-to-peer networks, mobile ad hoc networks, social networks or ensuring data accuracy, relevance and quality in several environments [1]. Computation methods applied range from simple arithmetic over statistical approaches up to graph-based models involving multiple factors such as context information, propagation or personal preferences. A general problem is that most of the new introduced trust and reputation models use computation methods that are designed from scratch and rely on one novel idea which could lead to better solutions [2]. Only a few authors built on proposals of others. Therefore, approved models and promising approaches may get lost in the shuffle.

In this work, we aim to encourage reuse in the development of reputation systems by providing a framework for creating reputation systems based on reusable

---

[1] http://www.ebay.com

J. Zhou et al. (Eds.): IFIPTM 2014, IFIP AICT 430, pp. 28–43, 2014.

components. Design approaches for reuse have been given much attention in the software engineering community. The research in trust and reputation systems could also profit from benefits like effective use of specialists, accelerated development and increased reliability. Toward this goal, we propose a *hierarchical taxonomy* for components of computation engines used in reputation systems. We, thereto, decompose the computation phase of common reputation models to derive single building blocks. The classification based on their functions serves as a natural framework for the design of new reputation systems. To facilitate the reuse of the identified components we, moreover, set up a *component repository* containing artifacts on both a conceptual and an implementation level. On the conceptual level, we describe each building block as a design pattern-like solution. On the implementation level, we provide already implemented components by means of web-services.

The rest of this paper is based on the design science research paradigm involving the guidelines for conducting design science research by Hevner et al. [3] and organized as follows: Firstly, we give an overview of the general problem context, the relevance and motivation of our work. We, thereby, identify the research gap and define the objectives of our research. In the following section, we introduce our hierarchical component taxonomy of computation engines used in reputation systems. Subsequently, we point out how our component repository is conceptually designed and implemented. Finally, we summarize the contribution and name our plans for future work.

## 2 Problem Context and Motivation

With the success of the Internet and the increasing distribution and connectivity, trust and reputation systems have become important artifacts to support decision making in network environments. To impart a common understanding, we firstly provide a definition of the notion of trust. At the same time, we explain the properties of trust that are important with regard to this work. Then, we point out how trust can be established applying computational trust models. Focusing an reputation-based trust, we explain how and why the research in reputation models could profit from reuse. We, thereby, identify the research gap and define the objectives of this work.

### 2.1 The Notion of Trust and Its Properties

The notion of trust is a topic that has been discussed in research for decades. Although it has been intensively examined in various fields, it still lacks a uniform, generally accepted definition. Reasons for this circumstance are the multifaceted terms trust is associated with like credibility, reliability or confidence as well as the multidimensionality of trust as an abstract concept that has a cognitive, an emotional and a behavioral dimension. As pointed out by [4], trust has been described as being structural in nature by sociologists while psychologists viewed trust as an interpersonal phenomenon. Economists, however, interpreted trust as rational choice mechanism. The definition often cited in literature regarding trust and reputation online that is referred to as *reliability trust* was proposed by Gambetta in 1988 [5]:

"*Trust (or, symmetrically, distrust) is a particular level of the subjective probability with which an agent assesses that another agent or group of agents will perform a particular action, both before he can monitor such action (or independently of his capacity ever to be able to monitor it) and in a context in which it affects his own action.*"

Multiple authors furthermore include security and risk which can lead to more complex definitions. Anyway, it is generally agreed that trust is multifaceted and dependent on a variety of factors. Trust is *dynamical, context specific, subjective, propagative, non-transitive, composable* and *event sensitive* as Sherchan et al. [6] point out. These properties are important with respect to this work, since they form the basis for many applied computation techniques in trust and reputation systems described in section 3.2. Reusable components could extend current models by the ability to gradually include these properties.

## 2.2   Reputation-Based Trust

In the recent years, several trust models have been developed to establish trust. Thereby, two common ways can be distinguished, namely policy-based and reputation-based trust establishment [7]. Policy-based trust is often referred to as a *hard security mechanism* due to the exchange of hard evidence (e.g. credentials). Reputation-based trust, in contrast, is derived from the history of interactions. Hence, it can be seen as an estimation of trustworthiness (*soft security*). In this work, we focus on reputation-based trust. Reputation is defined as follows:

"*Reputation is what is generally said or believed about a person's or thing's character or standing.*" [8]

It is based on referrals, ratings or reviews from members of a community and can, therefore, be considered as a collective measure of trustworthiness [8]. Trustworthiness as a global value is objective. The trust an agent puts in someone or something as a combination of personal experience and referrals, however, is subjective.

## 2.3   Research Gap: Design of Reputation Systems with Reuse

It has been argued (e.g. by [2]) that most reputation-based trust models proposed in the academic community are built from scratch and do not rely on existing approaches. Only a few authors continue their research on the ideas of others. Thus, many approved models and promising thoughts go unregarded. The benefits of reuse, though, have been recognized in software engineering for years. However, there are only very few works that proposed single components to enhance existing approaches. Rehak et al. [9], for instance, introduced a generic mechanism that can be combined with existing trust models to extend their capabilities by efficiently modeling context. The benefits of such a component that can easily be combined with existing systems are obvious. Nonetheless, research in trust and reputation still lacks in sound and accepted principles to foster reuse.

To gradually close this gap, we aim to provide a framework for the design of new reputation systems with reuse. As described above, we thereto propose a hierarchical component taxonomy of computation engines used in reputation systems. Based on this taxonomy, we set up a repository containing design knowledge on both a conceptual and an implementation level. The uniform and well-structured artifacts collected in this repository can be used by developers to select, understand and apply existing concepts on the one hand, as well as encourage researchers to provide novel components on a conceptual and an implementation level, on the other hand. In this way, the reuse of ideas, concepts and implemented components as well as the communication of reuse knowledge should be achieved.

## 3  A Hierarchical Component Taxonomy for Computation Methods in Reputation Systems

To derive a taxonomy from existing models, our research includes two steps: (1) the analysis of the generic process of reputation systems and (2) the identification of logical components of the computation methods used in common trust and reputation models. A critical question is how to determine and classify single components. We thereto follow an approach to function-based component classification, where the taxonomy is derived from the functions identified components fulfill.

### 3.1  The Generic Process of Reputation Systems

The generic process of reputation systems, as depicted in Figure 1, can be divided into three steps: (1) *collection & preparation*, (2) *computation* and (3) *storage & communication*. Those steps were adapted from the three fundamental phases of reputation systems identified by [10] and [11]: feedback generation/collection, feedback aggregation and feedback distribution. Feedback aggregation as the central part of every trust and reputation system was furthermore divided into three process-steps *filtering*, *weighting* and *aggregation* taken together as computation. The context setting consists of a trustor who wants to build a trust relation toward a trustee by providing context and personalization parameters and receiving a trustee's reputation value.

**Collection and Preparation.** In the collection and preparation phase, the reputation system gleans information about the past behavior of a trustee and prepares it for subsequent computing. Although personal experience is the most reliable, it is often not sufficiently available or nonexistent. Therefore, data from other sources needs to be collected. These can be various, ranging from public or personal collections of data centrally stored to data requested from different

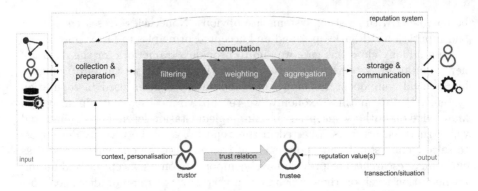

**Fig. 1.** Generic process of a reputation system, inspired by [10]

peers in a distributed network. After all available data is gathered, it is prepared for further use. Preparation techniques include, for instance, a normalization. Once the preparation is completed, the reputation data serves as input for the computation phase.

**Computation.** The computation phase is the central part of every reputation system which takes the reputation information collected as input and generates a trust/reputation value as output. This phase can be divided into the three generic process-steps *filtering, weighting* and *aggregation*. Depending on the computation engine, not all steps have to be implemented. The first two steps, filtering and weighting preprocess the data for the subsequent aggregation. The need for these steps is obvious: The first question to be answered is *which* information is useful for further processing (filtering). The second process-step concerns the question of *how relevant* the information is for the specific situation (weighting). In line with this, Zhang et al. [12] pointed out that current trust models can be classified into the two broad categories *filtering-based* and *discounting-based*. The difference between filtering and weighting is that the filtering process reduces the information amount while it is enriched by weight factors in the second case. Filtering can, therefore, be seen as *hard selection* while weighting is more like a *soft selection*. Finally, the reputation values are aggregated to calculate one or several reputation scores. Depending on the algorithm, the whole computation process or single process steps can be run through for multiple times.

**Storage and Communication.** After reputation scores are calculated, they are either stored locally, in a public storage or both depending on the structure (central/decentralized/hybrid) of the reputation system. Common reputation systems not only provide the reputation scores but also offer extra information to help the end-users understand the meaning of a score-value. They should furthermore reveal the computation process to accomplish transparency.

In this work, we focus on the computation phase, since the first phase (collection & preparation) and the last phase (storage & communication) strongly depend on the structure of the reputation system (central or decentralized). The computation phase, however, is independent of the structure and can look alike for systems implemented in both central and decentralized environments. It, therefore, works well for design with reuse.

## 3.2   Hierarchical Component Taxonomy

In this section, the computation process is examined in detail. We will introduce a novel hierarchical component taxonomy that is based on the functional blocks of common reputation systems identified in this work. Thereto, we clarify the objectives of the identified classes (functions) and name common examples. Our analysis and selection of reputation systems is based on different surveys [8,13,6,2,1]. Figure 2 gives an overview of the primary and secondary classes identified.

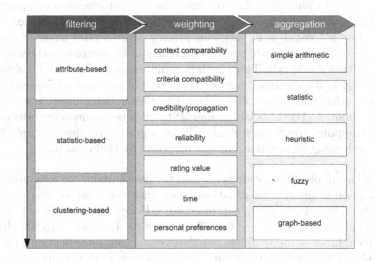

**Fig. 2.** Classes of filtering-, weighting- and aggregation-techniques

Beginning with the filtering phase, the three broad classes *attribute-based*, *statistic-based* and *clustering-based* filtering could be identified:

1. **Attribute-Based Filtering:** In several trust models, input data is filtered based on a constraint-factor defined for the value of single attributes. Attribute-based filters mostly implement a very simple logic, in which an attribute is usually compared to a reference value. Due to their lightweight, they are proper for reducing huge amounts of input data to the part necessary for the reputation calculation. Besides the initial filtering of input data, it is often applied after the weighting phase in order to filter referrals that have been strongly discounted. An example of an attribute often constrained,

is time, since it is desirable to disregard very old ratings. eBay's reputation system, for instance, only considers transactions having occurred in the last 12 months for their overview of positive, neutral and negative ratings. Other models such as Sporas [14] ignore every referral but the latest, if one party rated another party more than once. In this way, simple ballot stuffing attacks can be prevented. In ballot stuffing attacks, parties improve their reputation by means of positive ratings after fake transactions.

2. **Statistic-Based Filtering:** Further techniques that are used to enhance the robustness of trust models against the spread of false rumors apply statistical patterns. Whitby et al. [15], for example, proposed a statistical filter technique to filter out unfair ratings in Bayesian reputation systems applying the majority rule. The majority rule considers feedback that is far away from the majority's referrals as dishonest. In this way, dishonest or false feedback can easily be detected and filtered.

3. **Clustering-Based Filtering:** Clustering-based filter use cluster analysis approaches to identify unfair ratings. These approaches are comparatively expensive and therefore rarely used as filtering techniques. An exemplary procedure is to analyze an advisors' history. Since a rater never lies to himself, an obvious way to detect false ratings is to compare own experience with advisors' referrals. Thus, both fair and unfair ratings can be identified. iCLUB [16], for example, calculates clusters of advisors whose evaluations against other parties are alike. Then, the cluster being most similar to the own opinion is chosen as fair ratings. If there is no common experience (e.g. bootstrapping) the majority rule will be applied. Another example for an approach using cluster filtering was proposed by Dellorcas [17].

Once all available information is reduced to those suitable for measuring trust and reputation in the current situation, it becomes clear that various data differ in their characteristics (e.g. context, reliability). Hence, the referrals are weighted in the second process-step based on different factors. In contrast to the filtering, applied techniques strongly differ. For that reason, our classification of weighting techniques is based on the properties of referrals that are analyzed for the discounting. We identified the following classes:

1. **Context Comparability:** Reputation data are always bound to the specific context in which it was created. Ratings that were generated in one application area might not be automatically applicable in another application area. In eCommerce, for instance, transactions are accomplished involving different prices, product types, payment methods, quality or time. The non-consideration of this context leads to the value imbalance problem where a malicious seller can build a high reputation by selling cheap products while cheating on expensive ones. To increase comparability and avoid such situations, context has become a crucial attribute for many current approaches like [18] or [9].

2. **Criteria Comparability:** Besides the context in which feedback was created, the criteria that underlie the evaluation are important. Particularly, if

referrals from different application areas or communities are integrated, criteria comparability can be crucial. In file-sharing networks, for instance, a positive rating is often granted with a successful transaction independent of the quality of service. On eCommerce platforms, in contrast, quality may be a critical factor for customer satisfaction. Other distinctions could be the costs of reviews, the level of anonymity or the number of peers in different communities or application areas. Weighting based on criteria comparability can compensate these differences.

3. **Credibility/Propagation:** In network structures such as in the web-of-trust, trust can be established along a recommendation or trust chain. Obviously, referrals that have first-hand information about the trustworthiness of an agent are more credible than referrals received at second-hand (with propagation degree of two) or higher. Several models, therefore, apply a propagation (transitivity) rate to discount referrals based on their distance. The biometric identity trust model [19], for instance, derives the reputation-factor from the distance of nodes in a web-of-trust.

4. **Reliability:** Reliability or honesty of referrals can strongly affect the weight of reviews. The concept of feedback reputation that measures the agents' reliability in terms of providing honest feedback is often applied. As a consequence, referrals created by agents having a low feedback reputation will have a low impact on the aggregated reputation. The bases for this calculation can be various. Google's PageRank [20], for instance, involves the position of every website connected to the trustee in the web graph in their recursive algorithm. Epinions[2], on the other hand, allows users to directly rate reviews and reviewers. In this way, the effects of unfair ratings are diminished.

5. **Rating Value:** Trust is event sensitive. For stronger punishment of bad behavior, the weight of positive ratings compared to negative ratings can be calculated asymmetrically. An example for a model using an "adaptive forgetting scheme" was proposed by Sun et al. [21], in which good reputation can be built slowly through good behavior but easily be ruined through bad behavior.

6. **Time:** Due to the dynamic nature of trust, it has been widely recognized that time is one important factor for the weighting of referrals. Old feedback might not be relevant for reputation scoring as new referrals. An example measure for time-based weighting is the "forgetting factor" proposed by Jøsang [22].

7. **Personal Preferences:** Reputation systems are used by various end-users (e.g. human decision makers, services). A reputation system must, therefore, allow the adaptation of its techniques to subjective personal preferences. Different actors might, for example, have different perceptions regarding the importance of direct experience and referrals, the significance of distinct information sources or the rating of newcomers.

The tuple of reputation data and weight-factor(s) serve as input for the third step of the computation process - the aggregation. In this phase, one or several

---

[2] http://www.epinions.com/

trust/reputation values are calculated by composing the available information. In some cases, the weighting and the aggregation process are run through repetitively in an iterative manner. However, the single steps can still be logically separated. The list of proposed algorithms to aggregate trust and reputation values has become very long during the last decade. Here, we summarize the most common aggregation techniques and classify them into the five blocks *simple arithmetic, statistic, heuristic, fuzzy and graph-based models:*

1. **Simple Arithmetic:** The first class includes simple aggregation techniques like ranking, summation or average. Ranking is a very basic way to measure trustworthiness. In ranking algorithms, ratings are counted and organized in a descending order based on that value. This measure has no exact reputation score, however, it is frequently used as a proxy for the relative importance/trustworthiness. Examples for systems using ranking algorithms are message boards like Slashdot[3] or citation counts used to calculate the impact factor in academic literature. Other aggregation techniques that are well known due to the implementation on eBay or Amazon[4] are the summation (adding up positive and negative ratings) or the average of ratings. Summation, though, can easily be misleading, since a value of 90 does not reveal the composition of positive and negative ratings (e.g. +100,-10 or +90,0). The average, on the other hand, is a very intuitive and easy to understand algorithm.

2. **Statistic:** Many of the prominent trust models proposed in the last years use a statistical approach to provide a solid mathematical basis for trust management. Applied techniques range from *Bayesian probability* over *belief models* to *Hidden Markov Models.* All models based on the beta probability density function (beta PDF) are examples for models simply using Bayesian probability. The beta PDF represents the probability distributions of binary events. The *a priori* reputation score is thereby gradually updated by new ratings. Result is a reputation score that is described in a beta PDF function parameter tuple $(\alpha, \beta)$, where $\alpha$ represents positive and $\beta$ represents negative ratings. A well known model using the beta PDF is the the Beta Reputation system [22]. A weakness of Bayesian probabilistic models, however, is that they cannot handle uncertainty. Therefore, belief models extend the probabilistic approach by DempsterShafer theory (DST) or subjective logic to include the notion of uncertainty. Trust and reputation models involving a belief model have been proposed by Jøsang [23] or Yu and Singh [24]. More complex solutions that are based on machine learning, use the Hidden Markov Model, a generalization of the beta model, to better cope with the dynamic behavior. An example was introduced by Malik et al. [25].

3. **Heuristic:** Since statistical approaches are very complex, a shift towards heuristic-based trust modeling has become visible in scientific literature. Heuristic approaches try to provide custom-designed practical and easy to understand and implement solutions. Thereby, the filtering and weighting

---

[3] http://www.slashdot.org/
[4] http://www.amazon.com/

phases are of high importance as the aggregation is mostly based on a combination of rating and weights. Exemplary models were proposed by Xiong and Liu [26] or Zhang and Wang [18].

4. **Fuzzy:** Aggregation techniques classified as fuzzy models use fuzzy logic to calculate a reputation value. In contrast to classical logic, fuzzy logic allows to model truth or falsity within an interval of [0,1]. Thus, it can describe the degree to what an agent/resource is trustworthy or not trustworthy. Fuzzy logic has been proven to deal well with uncertainty and mimic the human decision-making process [27]. Thereby, a linguistic approach is often applied. REGRET [28] is one prominent example of a trust model making use of fuzzy logic.

5. **Graph-Based:** A variety of trust models employ a graph-based approach. They rely on different measures describing the position of nodes in a network involving the flow of transitive trust along trust chains in network structures. As online social networks have become popular as a medium for disseminating information and connecting people, many models regarding trust in social networks have lately been proposed. Graph-based approaches use measures from the field of graph theory such as centrality (e.g. Eigenvector, betweenness), distance or node-degree. Reputation values, for instance, grow with the number of incoming edges (in-degree) and in- or decrease with the number of outgoing edges (out-degree). The impact of one edge on the overall reputation can depend on several factors like the reputation of the node an edge comes from or the distance of two nodes. Popular algorithms using graph-based flow model are Google's PageRank [20] as well as the Eigentrust Algorithm [29]. Other examples are the web-of-trust or trust models particularly designed for social networks as described in [6]. As mentioned above, due to the incremental nature of these algorithms, the weighting and aggregation phases are incrementally run through for several times.

The classification of the computation engine's components used in different trust models in this taxonomy is not limited to one component of each primary class. Depending on the computation process, several filtering, weighting and aggregation techniques can be combined and run through more than once. Malik et al. [25], for instance, introduced a hybrid model combining heuristic and statistical approaches. However, our taxonomy can reveal the single logical components, a computation engine is built on. It, moreover, serves as an overview of existing approaches. Since every currently known reputation system can find its position, to the best of our knowledge, this taxonomy can be seen as complete. Though, an extension by new classes driven by novel models and ideas is possible. Our hierarchical component taxonomy currently contains 3 primary component classes, 15 secondary component classes, 26 component terms and 36 subsets. Table 1 shows an excerpt of the hierarchical component taxonomy with building blocks of the primary class "weighting".

Table 1. Excerpt of the hierarchical component taxonomy

| Primary component class | Secondary component class | Component term | Subset | Description |
|---|---|---|---|---|
| weighting | credibility/ propagation | propagation discount | | Discount referrals along trust chains |
| | reliability | subjective reliability | property similarity | Discount based on similarity of personal properties |
| | | | rating similarity | Discount referrals based on similarity of ratings toward other agents |
| | | objective reliability | Explicit | Discount based on explicit reputation information like referrals or certificates |
| | | | Implicit | Discount based on implicit reputation information like profile age, number of referrals or position |
| ... | ... | ... | ... | ... |

## 4 The Component Taxonomy as a Framework for Design with Reuse

The hierarchical component taxonomy introduced in the former section, serves as a natural framework for the design of reputation systems with reuse. To support this process, we set up a component repository combining a knowledge and a service repository. Thus, it does not only contain information about software components on implementation level but also provides extensive descriptions of the ideas applied on a conceptual level. This comprehensive set of fundamental component concepts and ideas combined with the related implementation allows the reuse of both ideas and already implemented components.

In this section, we first describe the conceptual design of our component repository in detail. Then, we show how we implemented a web application using our thorough repository to provide design knowledge for reuse on a conceptual and an implementation level.

### 4.1 Conceptual Design of the Component Repository

Reuse-based software engineering can be implemented on different levels of abstraction, ranging from the reuse of ideas to the reuse of already implemented software components for a very specific application area. In this work, we want to apply our taxonomy for reuse on two levels - a conceptual level and an implementation level. The developed repository, therefore, provides design knowledge for reuse on two logical layers, as depicted in Figure 3.

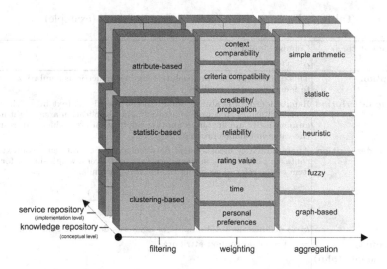

**Fig. 3.** Logical layers of the component repository for design with reuse

**Reuse on Conceptual Level.** When reusing an implemented component one is unavoidably constrained by design decisions that have been made by the developer. A way to prevent this, is to conceive more abstract designs that do not specify the implementation. Thus, we provide an abstract solution to a problem by means of design pattern-like concepts. Design patterns are descriptions of commonly occurring problems and a generic solution to the problems that can be used in different settings [30]. Our design pattern-like concepts consist of essential elements that are exemplary depicted on Table 2.

**Reuse on Implementation Level.** On implementation level we provide fully implemented reusable components by means of web-services in a service-orientated architecture. These services encapsulate the concepts' logic and functionality in independent and interchangeable modules to achieve the separation of concerns. The web-services are incorporated via well-defined interfaces. All service provided are registered as artifacts in the service repository. An artifact contains essential information about one live reachable service such as ID, type (REST or ws), URL, description, parameters, example calls, example output and the design pattern that is implemented by the service.

## 4.2   Implementation of the Repository

We prototypically implemented our repository as a web-based application in a three-tier client-server-architecture[5]. On client-side (presentation layer) we employed the current web standards HTML5, JavaScript and CSS (Bootstrap). On server-side the logic was implemented in PHP on an Apache server (logic layer)

---

[5] http://trust.bayforsec.de

**Table 2.** Design pattern on the conceptual level (example)

| Component term | Context similarity |
|---|---|
| Subset | Absolute congruence |
| Description | This component uses an absolute congruence metric as similarity measure to identify context similarity. |
| Problem description | Reputation data is always bound to the specific context in which it was created. Ratings that were generated in one application area might not be automatically applicable in another application area which can result in the value imbalance problem. |
| Solution description | Apply similarity measurement between context $c_i$ (reference context) and context $c_j$ of referrals in the referral set to deliver a weight-factor for each item of the referral set using the following formula: $$w(c_1, c_2) := \frac{k(c_i) \cap k(c_j)}{k(c_i) \cup k(c_j)}$$ $k(c_i)$ denotes the total number of keywords describing context $c_i$. |
| Applicability | Set of nominal context attributes. |
| Code example (php) | ``` function calculate_values($reference, $context_sets) {     $reference_context = $reference['context_attributes'];     $return_values = array();     while(!empty($context_sets)) {         ...shortened...     }     return $return_values; } ``` |
| Implementation | Context similarity-based weighting service (absolute congruence) |
| Literature | – Mohammad Gias Uddin, Mohammad Zulkernine, and Sheikh Iqbal Ahamed. 2008. CAT: a context-aware trust model for open and dynamic systems. In Proceedings of the 2008 ACM symposium on Applied computing (SAC '08). ACM, New York, NY, USA, 2024-2029. |
| Tags | weighting, context, similarity, congruence |

connecting to a MySQL-Database (persistent layer). All webservices were created in PHP an registered as artifacts in our service repository. This web-application is planned to become a platform for researchers to make their concepts and implementations publicly available.

## 5    Contribution and Future Work

Many surveys of trust and reputation systems give an overview of existing trust and reputation systems by means of a classification of existing models and approaches. In contrast to that, we provide a collection of ideas and concepts classified by their functions. Furthermore, these ideas are not only named but also clearly described in well-structured design pattern-like artifacts which can easily be adapted to a specific situation. Therewith, we reorganized the design knowledge for computation techniques in reputation systems and translated the most common ideas to a uniform format. To directly make use of novel components, the webservices created on implementation level can instantly be reused and integrated in existing reputation systems to extend their capabilities. This approach, to publicly provide implemented computation components as webservices may help to better spread innovative ideas in trust and reputation systems and to give system builders a better choice allowing to experiment with different computation techniques. We, moreover, encourage researchers to focus on the design of single components by providing a platform, where concepts and their prototypical implementation can be made publicly available.

However, there are still many unexplored areas regarding the design with reuse in trust and reputation systems. The following list gives an overview of those issues that will be topic for our future research:

1. Reusability in collection & preparation and storage & communication: The work in hand considers the design of computation techniques with reuse. Reusability could also play a role in other process steps run through in a reputation system. To clarify the opportunities, further research is necessary in this area.
2. Additional views on the component repository: Currently, our hierarchical taxonomy provides a functional view on the identified components. However, a developer could also benefit from additional views, like an attack view, in which the components are classified as possible solutions in a taxonomy of attacks on reputation systems.
3. Generic testbed and evaluation criteria: To measure the quality of a component, a testbed for comparison and a set of sound evaluation criteria such as robustness, efficiency or complexity is needed.
4. Software-supported selection of components: The selection and interpretation of adequate components for new reputation systems in a specific application area requires time, effort and to some extend knowledge of this research area. To increase usability and simplicity, a software application is needed to support a user in this development process.
5. Advanced meta information and machine readability: To take one step further, the most qualified composition could be automatically found and assembled by a software program based on the reputation data (input) provided. The research involves the development of sound principles for automated component composition.

# 6   Conclusion

The research in trust and reputation systems is still growing. In this paper, we presented concepts to foster reuse of existing approaches. We provided a hierarchical taxonomy of computation components from a functional view and described the implementation of a component repository that serves as both a knowledge base and a service repository. In this way, we communicate design knowledge for reuse, support the development of new reputation systems and encourage researchers to focus on the development of single components that can be integrated in various reputation systems to easily extend their capabilities by new features.

**Acknowledgments.** The research leading to these results was supported by the "Bavarian State Ministry of Education, Science and the Arts" as part of the FORSEC research association.

# References

1. Yao, Y., Ruohomaa, S., Xu, F.: Addressing Common Vulnerabilities of Reputation Systems for Electronic Commerce. Journal of Theoretical and Applied Electronic Commerce Research 7(1), 1–20 (2012)
2. Tavakolifard, M., Almeroth, K.C.: A Taxonomy to Express Open Challenges in Trust and Reputation Systems. Journal of Communications 7(7), 538–551 (2012)
3. Hevner, A.R., March, S.T., Park, J., Ram, S.: Design Science in Information Systems Research. MIS Quarterly 28(1), 75–105 (2004)
4. McKnight, D.H., Chervany, N.L.: The meanings of trust. Technical Report MISRC Working Paper Series 96-04, University of Minnesota, Management Information Systems Reseach Center (1996)
5. Gambetta, D.: Can We Trust Trust? In: Gambetta, D. (ed.) Trust: Making and Breaking Cooperative Relations, pp. 213–237. Basil Blackwell, Oxford (1988)
6. Sherchan, W., Nepal, S., Paris, C.: A survey of trust in social networks. ACM Computing Surveys 45(4), 1–33 (2013)
7. Artz, D., Gil, Y.: A survey of trust in computer science and the Semantic Web. Web Semantics 5(2), 58–71 (2007)
8. Jøsang, A., Ismail, R., Boyd, C.: A survey of trust and reputation systems for online service provision. Decision Support Systems 43(2), 618–644 (2007)
9. Rehak, M., Gregor, M., Pechoucek, M., Bradshaw, J.: Representing Context for Multiagent Trust Modeling. In: Proceedings of the IEEE/WIC/ACM International Conference on Intelligent Agent Technology, IAT 2006, Hongkong, China, pp. 737–746 (2006)
10. Swamynathan, G., Almeroth, K.C., Zhao, B.Y.: The design of a reliable reputation system. Electronic Commerce Research 10(3-4), 239–270 (2010)
11. Resnick, P., Kuwabara, K., Zeckhauser, R., Friedman, E.: Reputation systems. Communications of the ACM 43(12), 45–48 (2000)
12. Zhang, L., Jiang, S., Zhang, J., Ng, W.K.: Robustness of Trust Models and Combinations for Handling Unfair Ratings. In: Dimitrakos, T., Moona, R., Patel, D., McKnight, D.H. (eds.) IFIPTM 2012. IFIP AICT, vol. 374, pp. 36–51. Springer, Heidelberg (2012)
13. Noorian, Z., Ulieru, M.: The State of the Art in Trust and Reputation Systems: A Framework for Comparison. Journal of Theoretical and Applied Electronic Commerce Research 5(2), 97–117 (2010)
14. Zacharia, G., Moukas, A., Maes, P.: Collaborative reputation mechanisms for electronic marketplaces. Decision Support Systems 29(4), 371–388 (2000)
15. Whitby, A., Jøsang, A., Indulska, J.: Filtering out unfair ratings in bayesian reputation systems. In: Falcone, R., Barber, S., Sabater, J., Singh, M. (eds.) Proceedings of the 7th International Workshop on Trust in Agent Societies, Rome, Italy, pp. 106–117 (2004)
16. Liu, S., Zhang, J., Miao, C., Theng, Y.L., Kot, A.C.: iCLUB: An Integrated Clustering-based Approach to Improve the Robustness of Reputation Systems. In: The 10th International Conference on Autonomous Agents and Multiagent Systems, AAMAS 2011, Taipei, Taiwan, vol. 3, pp. 1151–1152 (2011)

17. Dellarocas, C.: Immunizing online reputation reporting systems against unfair ratings and discriminatory behavior. In: Proceedings of the 2nd ACM Conference on Electronic Commerce, pp. 150–157. ACM, New York (2000)

18. Zhang, H., Wang, Y., Zhang, X.: A trust vector approach to transaction context-aware trust evaluation in e-commerce and e-service environments. In: Proceedings of the 5th IEEE International Conference on Service-Oriented Computing and Applications, SOCA, Taipei, Taiwan, pp. 1–8 (2012)

19. Obergrusberger, F., Baloglu, B., Sänger, J., Senk, C.: Biometric Identity Trust: Toward Secure Biometric Enrollment in Web Environments. In: Yousif, M., Schubert, L. (eds.) CloudComp 2012. LNICST, vol. 112, pp. 124–133. Springer, Heidelberg (2013)

20. Brin, S., Page, L.: The Anatomy of a Large-Scale Hypertextual Web Search Engine. In: Proceedings of the 7th International Conference on World Wide Web, Brisbane, Australia, vol. 1-7, pp. 107–117

21. Sun, Y., Han, Z., Yu, W., Ray Liu, K.: Attacks on Trust Evaluation in Distributed Networks. In: Proceedings of th 40th Annual Conference on Information Sciences and Systems, CISS, Princeton, USA, pp. 1461–1466 (2006)

22. Jøsang, A., Ismail, R.: The Beta Reputation System. In: Proceedings of the 15th Bled Electronic Commerce Conference, Bled, Slovenia (2002)

23. Jøsang, A.: A logic for uncertain probabilities. International Journal of Uncertainty, Fuzziness and Knowledge-Based Systems 09(03), 279–311 (2001)

24. Yu, B., Singh, M.P.: An evidential model of distributed reputation management. In: Proceedings of the 1st International Joint Conference on Autonomous Agents and Multiagent Systems, AAMAS, Bologna, Italy, pp. 294–301 (2002)

25. Malik, Z., Akbar, I., Bouguettaya, A.: Web Services Reputation Assessment Using a Hidden Markov Model. In: Baresi, L., Chi, C.-H., Suzuki, J. (eds.) ICSOC-ServiceWave 2009. LNCS, vol. 5900, pp. 576–591. Springer, Heidelberg (2009)

26. Li, X., Liu, L.: A reputation-based trust model for peer-to-peer e-commerce communities. In: Proceedings of the IEEE International Conference on E-Commerce, CEC 2003, Newport Beach, USA, pp. 275–284 (2003)

27. Song, S., Hwang, K., Zhou, R., Kwok, Y.-K.: Trusted P2P Transactions with Fuzzy Reputation Aggregation. In: IEEE Internet Computing, vol. 9, pp. 24–34. IEEE Educational Activities Department, Piscataway (2005)

28. Sabater, J., Sierra, C.: Reputation and social network analysis in multi-agent systems. In: Proceedings of the First International Joint Conference on Autonomous Agents and Multiagent Systems, AAMAS 2002, Bologna, Italy, pp. 475–482 (2002)

29. Kamvar, S.D., Schlosser, M.T., Garcia-Molina, H.: The Eigentrust algorithm for reputation management in P2P networks. In: Proceedings of the 12th International Conference on World Wide Web, WWW 2003, Budapest, Hungary, pp. 640–651 (2003)

30. Gamma, E.: Design patterns: Elements of reusable object-oriented software. Addison-Wesley professional computing series. Addison-Wesley, Reading (1995)

# On Robustness of Trust Systems

Tim Muller[1], Yang Liu[1], Sjouke Mauw[2], and Jie Zhang[1]

[1] Nanyang Technological University
{tmuller,yangliu,zhangj}@ntu.edu.sg
[2] University of Luxembourg
sjouke.mauw@uni.lu

**Abstract.** Trust systems assist in dealing with users who may betray one another. Cunning users (attackers) may attempt to hide the fact that they betray others, deceiving the system. Trust systems that are difficult to deceive are considered more robust. To formally reason about robustness, we formally model the abilities of an attacker. We prove that the attacker model is maximal, i.e. 1) the attacker can perform any feasible attack and 2) if a single attacker cannot perform an attack, then a group of attackers cannot perform that attack. Therefore, we can formulate robustness analogous to security.

## 1 Introduction

Robustness refers to the ability of a trust system to function properly under all circumstances. Users may purposely perform actions to attempt to prevent the trust system from functioning properly.

For example, a famous food critic travels around the country visiting restaurants. The critic tastes the food and enjoys the service. A restaurant with good food and good service gets positive reviews. Potential customers read the reviews, knowing that the food critic has a keen eye and are eager to try the restaurants he recommends. Some restaurants recognise the famous food critic, and go above and beyond to provide the critic better food and service than usual. The positive impression sketched by the critic in his review does not translate well to the regular customer, who gets substandard food and service. The restaurant got an unfair advantage over its neighbour, who provides equal quality food and service to all customers. The restaurant exploited the mechanism of the procedure which provides restaurant reviews, and the system malfunctioned.

In trust systems, the intrinsic interactions have the property that one party can betray another party. Such behaviour is unfair and dishonest on the interpersonal level. However, on the level of the trust system, this is expected behaviour. The trust system can deal with users betraying other users; if trusted users would never betray, then trust systems can trivially trust anyone. However, as in the aforementioned example regarding the food critic, there are behaviours that are more than merely unfair and dishonest on the interpersonal level, rather, they deceive the entire system. We study such deceptions of the system, and refer to them as *attacks* - examples are listed in Section 2.1.

J. Zhou et al. (Eds.): IFIPTM 2014, IFIP AICT 430, pp. 44–60, 2014.

Trust systems that are less vulnerable to attacks are deemed more *robust*. A general and formal definition of robustness of trust systems helps in detecting and fixing vulnerabilities, and possibly to verify exploit-freeness. In this paper, we precisely establish the notion of robustness of trust systems, and its aspects.

Robustness of trust systems is related to robustness of (other) software systems, and related to security of software systems. Robustness of a software system typically refers to the capability of the system to deal with or recover from unexpected input. Given two similar algorithms performing a division, the algorithm that checks for and deals with divide-by-zero issues is more robust than the algorithm which does not. Robustness correlates, in software systems, with the number of different input that leads to faulty states.

Security of a software system typically refers to the impossibility of reaching a particular class of faulty states, regardless of input. Secrecy of a message, as a classical example, holds when there are no actions that the attacker can perform that lead to a state where the attacker knows the message. Security is the absence of input that leads to a faulty state.

The notion of robustness of trust systems, as many currently hold (e.g. [24,13]), is somewhere in between these two notions. Lack of robustness in software systems is bad, primarily because a legitimate user may experience problems if he accidentally inputs the wrong data. Lack of security is bad, primarily because an attacker may seek to input the wrong data. Robust trust systems seek to prevent the latter, as we do not want attackers to exploit the workings of the trust system. However, in security, legitimate users are assumed to always input data that does not lead to faulty states (they are assumed to follow protocol). In robust trust systems, we cannot make such assumptions about legitimate users' input - any user could fail at any time. In other words, in robust trust systems we must assume that there are attackers that purposely enter bad input (like security), but we may not assume that non-attackers will not enter bad input (like standard robustness). Our proposal is based on this key notion; the notion that an attackers' devious choice of input should be no more likely to lead to a faulty state than a normal users' randomly selected (and potentially bad) input.

In computer security - be it symbolic security [3] or provable security [15] - the notions surrounding the attacker model and security properties are well established. Deviations from the default attacker model are subject to extra scrutiny. We can learn from computer security that we should not formulate an ad-hoc notion of robustness. Our main contribution is exactly that - an attacker model and notions of robustness properties that are independent of the trust system at hand. Moreover, we learn from computer security that the strategy of the attackers in the attacker model should not be limited by our own ideas regarding attacks on a system. We prove that our attacker model indeed captures all possible strategies of an attacker. Furthermore, again akin to security, we prove that it suffices to verify a robustness property under one attacker, and that robustness against multiple attackers follows automatically.

In Section 2, we introduce the notions and formalisms that we use throughout the paper. Notably, we define types of users and accounts, their states, actions and behaviours and how they synthesise abstract trust systems. In Section 2.1, we list attacks on trust systems found in the literature to establish archetypical attacks that we want to capture with our notions. In Section 3, we define the possible actions of an attacker, called malicious behaviour, in the attacker model. We show that the attacker model matches our intuition, and that it has maximal strength. In Section 4, we define notions related to robustness of trust systems. We define robustness properties, analogous to security properties. We show that if a robustness property holds for one attacker, it holds for several attackers.

## 2   Formalisation of Trust Systems

Trust systems revolve around interactions with an asymmetric power balance, and trust is employed to deal with this imbalance in the form of *trust opinions* ($\mathcal{O}$ is the set of trust opinions). Trust opinions are the building blocks of trust systems, and indicate the likelihood that the target allows the interactions to *succeed* or *fail*. A *subject* constructs a trust opinion about a *target*, before allowing the target to control the interaction. The trust opinion determines whether the subject *accepts* an interaction with a target, possibly together with the *payoff of success* and *payoff of failure* ($\alpha$ and $\beta$ are the sets of payoff of success and failure, respectively). Before a subject can accept an interaction, the target needs to *offer* the interaction. The offer (implicitly or explicitly) sets the pay-off of success and of failure.

Since we study the robustness, we want to reason about behaviour that the designer did not anticipate. We refer to behaviour anticipated by the designer as *ideal behaviour*. Formal *correctness* is a property of a trust system which holds when the trust system provides mathematically correct probabilities in trust opinions, provided all users are ideal. The Beta model [18,11] is an example of a system where formal correctness holds. The Beta model produces mathematically correct results in an ideal trust system [20]. Robustness, as defined more precisely later, is roughly the ability of the system to deal with behaviour that is not ideal. Robustness is sometimes viewed as an extension of correctness, but we argue that it should be seen as a trade-off against correctness, in Section 4.

As motivated in Section 3, even the non-ideal behaviour that concerns robustness is, in some way, restricted. We refer to these non-ideal behaviours as *malicious behaviour*, and a user with malicious behaviour as an *attacker*. There are goals (e.g. obtain a large profit) that attackers should not be more likely to achieve than ideal users. Since, if the malicious users are more likely to achieve these goals, then they have an unfair advantage. We refer to the negation of these goals as *robustness properties* - after their similarity to security properties. A malicious behaviour that breaks a robustness property is an *attack*.

Before we can reason formally about such behaviours, we need to formalise a system in which these behaviours are expressed. We adopt a semantic view of the trust system, philosophically related to transition system spaces [1]. A trust system space (Definition 1) encompasses all trust systems that arise when actual users are instantiated in the trust system space. Figure 1 contains an example of a part of a trust system space.

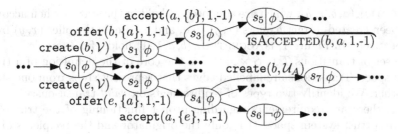

**Fig. 1.** Fraction of an example of a trust system space

A trust system space consists of a set of users, a set of actions, a set of states and a set of transitions. There are conditions on each of these sets (e.g. an account must be created before it can make an offer), and we call such sets *valid* when the conditions are satisfied. First we identify which sets of users, actions, states and transitions are valid, then we define trust system spaces.

Every trust system has a set of users, which in turn control accounts of given types. We say that a set of users $\mathcal{U}$ is *valid* when there is a set of accounts $\mathcal{V}$, such that every account belongs to exactly one user. Formally, there is a function OWNER : $\mathcal{V} \to \mathcal{U}$, if OWNER$(a) = u$ then $u$ *owns* $a$. The set of subjects and the set of targets are subsets of the set of accounts, $\mathcal{V}_S \subseteq \mathcal{V}$ and $\mathcal{V}_T \subseteq \mathcal{V}$, respectively.

Every trust system space has a collection of actions, and every step of the system is an action, as depicted in Figure 1. Each action has an *executor* and *listeners* - denoted by its first and second parameter, respectively. The owner of the executor is the *originator* and the owners of the listeners are the *recipients*. We identify a collection of parameterised actions that are sufficiently ubiquitous in trust systems that we elevate them to a special status:

- create : $\mathcal{V} \times \mathcal{P}(\mathcal{V})$; create$(a, B)$ denotes creation of account $a$, with accounts in $B$ being notified.
- offer : $\mathcal{V}_T \times \mathcal{P}(\mathcal{V}_S) \times \alpha \times \beta$; offer$(a, B, x, y)$ denotes that target $a$ makes an offer to subjects in $B$, with payoff of success $x$ and payoff of failure $y$.
- accept : $\mathcal{V}_S \times \{\{b\}|b \in \mathcal{V}_T\} \times \alpha \times \beta$; accept$(a, B, x, y)$ denotes that subject $a$ accepts the offer made by $b$ (with $B = \{b\}$) with outcome $(x, y)$.
- succeed : $\mathcal{V}_T \times \{\{b\}|b \in \mathcal{V}_S\} \times \alpha \times \beta$ and fail : $\mathcal{V}_T \times \{\{b\}|b \in \mathcal{V}_S\} \times \alpha \times \beta$; succeed$(a, B, x, y)$ and fail$(a, B, x, y)$ denote that target $a$ succeeds or fails the offer accepted by $b$ (with $B = \{b\}$) with outcome $x$ and $y$, respectively.
- recommend : $\mathcal{V}_S \times \mathcal{P}(\mathcal{V}_S) \times \mathcal{V}_T \times \mathcal{O}$; recommend$(a, B, c, t)$ denotes that subject $a$ claims to $B$ that his trust opinion about $c$ equals $t$.

The set of actions $\mathcal{A}$ is valid, if it contains at least these six groups of actions.

A trust system space has a set of states $\mathcal{S}$, which determines which actions are possible and which predicates hold, as depicted in Figure 1. For a state space $S$ of a trust system space to be *valid*, there must exist a projection function $\pi$, which projects the system state onto the state of a single user. In other words, $\pi : \mathcal{U} \times \mathcal{S} \to \mathcal{S}_U$, where $\mathcal{S}_U$ is the state space of a single user. We shorthand $\pi(u, s)$ to $\pi_u(s)$. If $\pi_u(s) = \pi_u(t)$, then we say that $s$ and $t$ are *indistinguishable* to user $u$. We identify three state predicates EXISTS$_s(a)$, ISOFFERED$_s(a, b, x, y)$ and

ISACCEPTED$_s$$(a, b, x, y)$, which are supposed to hold in the state $s$ when account $a$ has been created, target $b$ offers $(x, y)$ to $a$, and $a$ accepts the offer $(x, y)$ from $b$, respectively. In Figure 1, ISACCEPTED$_{s_5}$$(b, a, 1, -1)$ holds, for example.

The set of transitions $\mathcal{T} \subseteq \mathcal{S} \times \mathcal{A} \times \mathcal{S}$ is the core of the definition of a trust system space. Transitions are labelled edges that represent steps from one state to another. We identify two types of requirements on *valid* transitions:

First, there are requirements regarding proper functioning of the trust systems. In a trust system space, (L1) only the originator and the recipients of an action are aware of it, (L2) the result of performing an action in a given state is deterministic, (L3) if two states are indistinguishable to a user, then the effects of an action are identical to that user, (L4) if two states are indistinguishable to a user, that user can perform the same actions (L5) accounts that are created remain existent (to avoid impersonation after deletion) and (L6) offers and acceptances by given users remain unchanged when these users are unaware that an action happened.

L1. For all transitions $(s, \mathsf{a}, t) \in \mathcal{T}$, for all $u \in \mathcal{U}$ that are neither the originator nor a recipient of action $\mathsf{a}$, $\pi_u(s) = \pi_u(t)$.

L2. For all transitions $(s, \mathsf{a}, t) \in \mathcal{T}$ and $(s, \mathsf{a}, t') \in \mathcal{T}$, $t = t'$.

L3. For all transitions $(s, \mathsf{a}, t) \in \mathcal{T}$ and $(s', \mathsf{a}, t') \in \mathcal{T}$, if $\pi_u(s) = \pi_u(s')$ then $\pi_u(t) = \pi_u(t')$.

L4. For all transitions $(s, \mathsf{a}, t) \in \mathcal{T}$, where $u \in \mathcal{U}$ is the originator of $\mathsf{a}$, for all states $s' \in \mathcal{S}$ where $\pi_u(s) = \pi_u(s')$, there is a state $t' \in \mathcal{S}$, such that $(s', \mathsf{a}, t')$.

L5. For all transitions $(s, \mathsf{a}, t)$, if EXISTS$_s$$(b)$ then EXISTS$_t$$(b)$.

L6. For all transitions $(s, \mathsf{a}, t)$, if $b \in \mathcal{V}$ and $c \in \mathcal{V}$ are neither executors nor listeners, then ISOFFERED$_s$$(b, c, x, y)$ iff ISOFFERED$_t$$(b, c, x, y)$, and ISACCEPTED$_s$$(b, c, x, y)$ iff ISACCEPTED$_t$$(b, c, x, y)$, for all $x \in \alpha$, $y \in \beta$.

Second, there are requirements regarding the actions that users can perform. It is (R1) always possible to create new subject or target accounts, (R2) always possible for targets to make any offer, (R3) always possible for subjects to accept existing offers, (R4) always possible for targets to succeed or fail accepted offers and (R5) always possible for subjects to make any recommendations.

R1. For some $\mathcal{C} \subseteq \mathcal{P}(\mathcal{V})$, $\mathcal{C} \neq \emptyset$, for every user $u \in \mathcal{U}$, state $s \in \mathcal{S}$ and set of accounts $C \in \mathcal{C}$, for some $a \in \mathcal{V}_S$ (with $\neg$EXISTS$_s$$(a)$ and OWNER$(a) = u$), $b \in \mathcal{V}_T$ (with $\neg$EXISTS$_s$$(b)$ and OWNER$(b) = u$) and $t, t' \in \mathcal{S}$, we have $(s, \mathtt{create}(a, C), t) \in \mathcal{T}$ and $(s, \mathtt{create}(b, C), t') \in \mathcal{T}$.

R2. For every state $s \in \mathcal{S}$, target $a \in \mathcal{V}_T$ with EXISTS$_s$$(a)$, set of accounts $C \in \mathcal{P}(\mathcal{V})$, payoff of success $x \in \alpha$ and payoff of failure $y \in \beta$, for some states $t \in \mathcal{S}$, we have $(s, \mathtt{offer}(a, C, x, y), t) \in \mathcal{T}$.

R3. For every state $s \in \mathcal{S}$, subject $a \in \mathcal{V}_S$, target $b \in \mathcal{V}_T$, payoff of success $x \in \alpha$ and payoff of failure $y \in \beta$ with ISOFFERED$_s$$(a, b, x, y)$, for some $t \in \mathcal{S}$, we have $(s, \mathtt{accept}(a, \{b\}, x, y), t) \in \mathcal{T}$.

R4. For every state $s \in \mathcal{S}$, target $a \in \mathcal{V}_T$, subject $b \in \mathcal{V}_S$, payoff of success $x \in \alpha$ and payoff of failure $y \in \beta$, with ISACCEPTED$_s$$(a, b, x, y)$, for some $t \in \mathcal{S}$ (or $t' \in \mathcal{S}$), we have $(s, \mathtt{succeed}(a, \{b\}, x, y), t) \in \mathcal{T}$ (or $(s, \mathtt{fail}(a, \{b\}, x, y), t') \in \mathcal{T}$).

R5. For every state $s \in \mathcal{S}$, subject $a \in \mathcal{V}_S$ with $\mathrm{EXISTS}_s(a)$, target $c \in \mathcal{V}_T$ with $\mathrm{EXISTS}_s(c)$, trust opinion $o \in \mathcal{O}$ for some $B \in \mathcal{P}(\mathcal{V})$ and $t \in \mathcal{S}$, we have $(s, \mathtt{recommend}(a, B, c, o), t) \in \mathcal{T}$.

*Remark 1.* We introduce one additional requirement for purely technical reasons, namely that the trust system space is finitely branching; that there are finitely many outgoing transitions in every state. See the technical report [19].

A trust system space is like a chess rule book; a chess rule book defines the users (white and black), the actions ("move pawn C4-C5", etc.), the states (placement of pieces on the board) and the transitions ("move pawn C4-C5" is only possible if it is white turn, if there is a pawn on C4, if C5 is free, and if the resulting state does not put white's king in check).

**Definition 1 (Trust System Space).** *A trust system space is a 4-tuple* $(\mathcal{U}, \mathcal{S}, \mathcal{A}, \mathcal{T})$, *where* $\mathcal{U}$, $\mathcal{S}$, $\mathcal{A}$ *and* $\mathcal{T}$ *are valid sets of users, states, actions and transitions.*

A trust system space is not an actual trust system - similar to how a chess rule book is not a game of chess, To obtain a trust system, users need to be instantiated with a strategy - similar to how a game of chess needs two players with a strategy. We first introduce the notion of a strategy, then we define how a strategy can be applied to a trust system space to obtain an actual trust system.

The users' strategies determine the relative probability of their available actions, as well as the expected time they spend in a certain state. The expected time is also known as a rate (in rated transition systems [14] and continuous-time Markov chains [22]). Rates are an effective way to model the behaviour of independent entities without a global scheduler. Intuitively, each user can increase the probability of performing an action, (only) by increasing the rate of that action.

We define strategies and behaviour based on rates as follows:

**Definition 2 (Strategy and Behaviour).** *A strategy is a function* $f \in \mathcal{F} = \mathcal{S}_U \to (\mathcal{A} \nrightarrow \mathbb{R}_{\geq 0})$, *which assigns a rate to every action available in a state to the user. A combined strategy is a function* $\gamma \in \Gamma = \mathcal{U} \to \mathcal{F}$.
*A behaviour is a distribution over strategies. A discrete behaviour has probability mass function* $B \in \mathcal{B} = \mathcal{F} \to [0,1]$. *If* $B$ *is a discrete behaviour, then its support,* $\mathrm{supp}(B)$, *is the set of strategies where* $B(f) > 0$. *A combined behaviour is a distribution over combined strategies. A discrete combined behaviour has probability mass function* $\theta \in \Theta = \Gamma \to [0,1]$.

In chess, a strategy is, e.g., Kasparov's strategy, and combined strategy is Kasparov versus Fischer[1]. A behaviour is, e.g., "some grandmaster's strategy", and a combined behaviour is "some grandmaster versus an unknown player".

---

[1] Kasparov and Fischer are famous chess players.

The strategy provides rates, rather than probabilities. Given a combined strategy, we can *normalise* the rates to probabilities by dividing the rate of a transition from state $s$ by the sum of the rates of the other transitions $s$. The normalisation of $\gamma$ is $\overline{\gamma}(u, s, a) = \frac{\gamma(u)(\pi_u(s))(a)}{\sum_{u' \in \mathcal{U} \wedge a' \in \mathcal{A} } \gamma(u')(\pi_{u'}(s))(a')}$, where $\gamma(u)(s)(a)$ is taken as 0 when undefined. An *assignment of behaviour* is a shorthand way of defining a combined behaviour. The assignment of behaviour $\overline{\theta} : \mathcal{U} \to \mathcal{B}$, is shorthand for $\theta$, with $\theta(\gamma) = \prod_{u \in \mathcal{U}} \overline{\theta}(u)(\gamma(u))$.

The result of applying behaviour to a trust system space is a rated transition system (with an initial state), as defined in [14]:

**Definition 3 (Rated Trust System).** *A* rated trust system *is a rated transition system* $(S, A, \mathbf{s}_0, W)$, *where* $S$ *is a set of states,* $A$ *is a set of actions,* $\mathbf{s}_0$ *an initial state and* $W : S \times A \times S \to \mathbb{R}_{\geq 0}$ *is a rate function.*
*Let* $M = (\mathcal{U}, \mathcal{S}, \mathcal{A}, \mathcal{T})$ *be a trust system space,* $\overline{\theta}$ *be an assignment of behaviour and* $s_0 \in \mathcal{S}$ *a state. Then* $[\![M, \overline{\theta}, s_0]\!]$ *is a rated transition system* $(S, A, \mathbf{s}_0, W)$ *where: 1)* $S \subseteq \mathcal{S} \times \Theta$, *2)* $A = \mathcal{A}$, *3)* $\mathbf{s}_0 = (s_0, \theta)$, *and 4) when* $(s, \mathsf{a}, t) \notin \mathcal{T}$, $W$ *satisfies* $W((s, f), \mathsf{a}, (t, g)) = 0$ *for all* $f, g : \Theta$, *and when* $(s, \mathsf{a}, t) \in \mathcal{T}$ *where* $u$ *originates* $\mathsf{a}$, $W$ *satisfies* $W((s, f), \mathsf{a}, (t, g)) = E_{\mathsf{a}}(f)$ *for* $f, g : \Theta$, *where 4a) the expected rate* $E_{\mathsf{a}}(f) = \sum_{\gamma \in \mathrm{supp}(f)} f(\gamma) \cdot \gamma(u)(\pi_u(s))(\mathsf{a})$ *and 4b)*
$g(\gamma) = \frac{\overline{\gamma}(u,s,\mathsf{a}) \cdot f(\gamma)}{\sum_{\delta \in \Gamma} \overline{\delta}(u,s,\mathsf{a}) \cdot f(\delta)}.$

The rated trust system is the natural result of applying combined behaviour to a trust system space in an initial state. The state of a rated trust system is determined by both the state in the trust system space and the combined behaviour. The rated transitions can be interpreted as a labelling on the trust system space, where transitions that do not occur in the trust system receive rate 0, and rates of other transitions are determined by the combined behaviour in a straightforward manner, via (4a). Note that after a transition, a combined strategy that assigns low normalised probability to that transition is less likely to be the actual combined strategy, via Bayes' theorem (4b). This is similar to concluding that an opponent that sacrifices his queen without apparent benefit, is unlikely to have Kasparov's strategy.

In this section, we have defined trust system spaces, which define the possible input and the relation between input and output. We define strategies (and distributions thereof) to model how users choose the input they provide. We further define rated trust systems, which model a running trust system with users with strategies.

## 2.1  Known Attacks

We are setting out to provide a general, formal definition of robustness. In order to ensure the applicability and relevance of such a definition, we must keep real attacks in mind. We identify the following attacks:

- The on/off attack, in which the attacker builds his trust value, then fails in one or more interactions and depletes his trust value, and slowly rebuild his trust value with time on his side [23]. This attack is particularly powerful on systems where subjects forget behaviour of targets over time.

- The value imbalance attack, in which an attacker builds his trust value in low stake interactions, and depletes his trust value in high stake interactions [13,10]. This works on systems where the stakes of interactions vary. On some game-theoretical systems, this is expected behaviour and not an attack.
- The reputation lag attack, in which an attacker builds his trust value, then fails interactions in quick succession, before his lowered trust value propagates through the system [13,10].
- The discrimination attack, which is essentially our food critic example from the introduction [10]. It is also known as the conflicting behaviour attack [23].
- The re-entry attack, which is akin to the on/off attack, except depleted accounts are replaced by newly created accounts [13,10].
- The distraction attack, in which the attacker creates many superfluous offers, requests or recommendations in order to prevent its victim to perform relevant actions. It is a special case of the denial-of-service attack in [8].
- The proliferation attack, in which the attacker creates many target accounts and thus represents a large portion of all target accounts, meaning that he may receive a large portion of all interactions too.
- The composite trust attack, which asserts that there are composite interactions [20] where multiple targets are involved. In some cases, the action of the attacker does not influence the outcome of the interaction. The attacker to abuses the action to manipulate his trust value.
- The unfair ratings attack, in which the attacker manipulates the reputation of some targets by providing unfair ratings [10,8,23]. This attack has many subdivisions, some of which are studied in great detail. [25,9].
- The shilling attack, in which the attacker matches the profiles of (groups of) users, to ensure his unfair ratings carry more weight [17]. This attack works for recommender systems.
- The Sybil attack is an extremely powerful attack, in which the attacker creates multiple accounts to perform combinations of the aforementioned attacks [6].

## 3   Malicious Behaviour

As mentioned in the introduction, our notion of robustness hinges on notions of ideal behaviour and malicious behaviour. Each user, ideal or malicious, performs certain actions with a certain probability, at certain times, depending on its state. A function that assigns probability to actions given a state is called a strategy (see Definition 2). Which strategies are ideal depends on the trust system at hand. Typically, trust systems make assumptions about the behaviours of users, denoted in the form of an ideal behaviour. At a formal level, we simply assert that we are given an ideal behaviour $I$ together with the trust system space $M$.

Ideally, a trust system can compute the probabilities of future actions of ideal users. That is, some trust systems (such as [11,18]) provide formally correct answers, provided that users adhere to the assumptions of the system. We refer to the ability of a trust system to provide formally correct answers for ideal users as *correctness*. However, we are interested in users who do not exhibit ideal behaviour. Robustness is the inability of non-ideal behaviour to achieve something that the ideal users cannot. It is clear that these non-ideal behaviours have limitations. As in computer security, we need to construct a model of which non-ideal behaviours an attacker can exhibit. In formal computer security, the default attacker model is called the Dolev-Yao model [5]. The Dolev-Yao model defines what strategies an attacker (in the security domain) may perform - and by elimination, which he may not perform. We define a default attacker - inspired by the Dolev-Yao model - in the trust domain, by providing the set of strategies that the attacker may perform.

The Dolev-Yao attacker is maximally powerful in that he can accomplish anything that a group of attackers can accomplish. This is in fact a key property of the Dolev-Yao attacker, as we do not need to model groups of attackers communicating and coordinating. Modelling one attacker is, provably, enough. Our attacker exhibits the same property, as proven in Theorem 2.

First, we define the attacker model informally, but precisely. An *attacker* is a user with a malicious behaviour. At any time in a *malicious behaviour*:

C1. The attacker has a complete understanding of the system. The attacker (only) has access to all private information of his accounts. The attacker can reason with this information.
C2. The attacker can create accounts.
C3. The attacker can offer any interactions with any of his target accounts.
C4. The attacker can decide to succeed or fail at any interaction with any of his target accounts.
C5. The attacker can make arbitrary recommendations with any of his subject accounts.
C6. The attacker can perform any auxiliary actions (including accepting offers) for subject or targets, with his subject or target accounts, respectively.

The first ability, C1, ensures that our attacker model captures the attacker that uses the available information to optimize his decisions. Effectively, C1 disallows security through obscurity - a well-known anti-pattern in computer security. The other abilities, C2-C5 match at least some of the actions in the attacks from Section 2.1. Account creation, C2, is required for Sybil attacks. Offering interactions, C3, is required for proliferation attacks. The ability to succeed or fail at will,f C4, is required for on/off attacks. The ability to make arbitrary recommendations, C5, is required for unfair ratings attacks. Hence, we see that any reasonable attacker model capturing the attacks from Section 2.1 has at least these capabilities. Finally, the capability to perform any of the auxiliary actions, C6, is included mostly for completeness' sake. It is clear that a real attacker would abuse auxiliary actions, if this would help him achieve his goal. Hence our model should include this capability.

Before introducing the attacker, we need to formalise what it means for a user (i.e. the attacker) to have volition. A user with volition can pick its own strategy in the trust system. We model this by letting a volitional trust system be a set of rated trust systems, each generated by a malicious strategy. A choice of strategy equates to a choice of a rated trust system from a volitional trust system.

**Definition 4 (Volitional Trust System).** *Let $M$ be a trust system space, $I$ be an ideal behaviour, $s_0$ be the initial state, and $e$ be a user. A volitional trust system is a set of rated trust systems denoted $\Upsilon_{(M,I,s_0)}^{e \triangleleft F}$, for some $F \subseteq \mathcal{F}$. Let $[\![M, \theta', s_0]\!] \in \Upsilon_{(M,I,s_0)}^{e \triangleleft F}$ iff $\overline{\theta'}(u \neq e) = I$ and $\overline{\theta'}(e)(f \in F) = 1$.*

The volitional trust system $\Upsilon_{(M,I,s_0)}^{e \triangleleft F}$ only contains rated trust systems based on the trust system space $M$ and initial state $s_0$, where all users except $e$ have behaviour $I$. The only difference between the elements in $\Upsilon_{(M,I,s_0)}^{e \triangleleft F}$ is the strategy of $e$, which can be any strategy in $F$.

We define the maximal attacker model as follows:

**Definition 5 (Maximal Attacker Model).** *The* maximal attacker model *is $\Upsilon_{(M,I,s_0)}^{e \triangleleft \mathcal{F}}$, for trust system space $M$, ideal behaviour $I$, initial state $s_0$ and attacker $e$.*

We may refer to a volitional trust system with an attacker as a *subverted trust system*. If an attacker behaviour $f$ can be imagined within the restraints of our action alphabet $\mathcal{A}$ and the attacker's state space $\mathcal{S}_U$, then there is an subverted trust system $v \in \Upsilon_{(M,I,s_0)}^{e \triangleleft \mathcal{F}}$ where the attacker uses strategy $f$.

We define the intuitive attacker model as follows:

**Definition 6 (Intuitive Attacker Model).** *The* intuitive attacker model *is a volitional trust system $\Upsilon_{(M,I,s_0)}^{e \triangleleft X}$, where: First, for all $(S, A, \mathbf{s}_0, W) \in \Upsilon_{(M,I,s_0)}^{e \triangleleft X}$, $\mathbf{s}, \mathbf{s}' \in S$ and $\mathbf{a} \in A$, if $\pi_u(\mathbf{s}) = \pi_u(\mathbf{s}')$ then $W(\mathbf{s}, \mathbf{a}, \mathbf{t}) = W(\mathbf{s}', \mathbf{a}, \mathbf{t}')$ - for those $\mathbf{t}, \mathbf{t}' \in S$ with $W(\mathbf{s}, \mathbf{a}, \mathbf{t}) \neq 0$ and $W(\mathbf{s}', \mathbf{a}, \mathbf{t}') \neq 0$. Second, for all collections of transitions $(s_0, \mathbf{a}_0, t_0), \ldots, (s_n, \mathbf{a}_n, t_n) \in \mathcal{T}$ where $e$ is the originator of all $\mathbf{a}_i$ and there is no pair of transitions $(s_i, \mathbf{a}_i, t_i), (s_j, \mathbf{a}_j, t_j)$ with both $\pi_e(s_i) = \pi_e(s_j)$ and $\mathbf{a}_i = \mathbf{a}_j$, there is a volitional trust system $(S, A, \mathbf{s}_0, W) \in \Upsilon_{(M,I,s_0)}^{e \triangleleft X}$ such that every $W((s_i, f_i), \mathbf{a}_i, (t_i, g_i))$ is equal to any predetermined value $r_i$.*

The first rule limits the attacker's behaviour in indistinguishable states, i.e., his private information, according to C1. The second rule captures C2-C6, as the set of strategies contains any combination of rates for all actions (including create - C2, offer- C3, succeed and fail - C4, recommend - C5 - and others - C6) that respect rule C1. Since the rate of each action can have an arbitrarily large value, the attacker can perform the action with arbitrary probability smaller than one.

*Remark 2.* The rate is the inverse of time, in an exponential distribution (see, e. g. [2]) - this forms the theoretical basis of rated transitions systems [14] and continuous-time Markov chains [22]. If we accept that the attacker acts according to an exponential distribution, then any positive time corresponds to a rate (as the inverse of time). In this case our notion that the attacker can perform any of his actions (C2-C6) with any probability is trivially satisfied.

Arguably we may reject the notion that the attacker acts according to an exponential distribution. If an attack exists for this attacker, but not for an attacker that acts according to an exponential distribution, then the attack is purely based on exact timing (but not on expected timing). However, we should compare the attacker with an ideal user that also does not act according to an exponential distribution. Thus, the attack cannot purely be based on exact timing. If we, nevertheless, reject the notion that the attacker acts according to an exponential distribution, we must generalise the notion of subverted trust models to hybrid automata [7] or probabilistic timed automata [16] - both automata with both time and probability.

Our intuitive notion of an attacker (Definition 6) corresponds with the attacker that is strongest by definition (Definition 5):

**Theorem 1.** *The maximal and intuitive attacker models are equal.*

*Proof.* See [19].

Malicious behaviour can only be performed by attackers and, by definition, not by ideal users. However, not all malicious behaviour is an attack. Consider a user that only creates an additional account, but never uses that account to make offers, interactions and recommendations, nor uses the private information of that account. Such a user is an attacker on a system where additional account creation is not ideal behaviour, but the behaviour does not accomplish anything, and thus is not an attack. In Section 4, we define additional notions to define attacks and robustness. For now, it suffices to realise that C1-C6 (Definition 5/6) do not define attacks, but rather the toolset of an attacker.

In computer security, security is relative to so-called security properties. A typical example of a security property is secrecy of a certain message $m$. The system is secure, when there is no reachable state in which the security property is violated. In the next section, we define robustness in a similar way, differing from security only where necessary.

## 4   Robustness

We have motivated why we need a formal generic definition of robustness of trust systems. So far, we have introduced the formal machinery and the attacker model, similar to (symbolic) formal security [3] - a methodology that has proven itself in practice. Our definition of robustness properties are also similar to formal computer security. However, there is an alternative way to reason about robustness in a formal and general way, e.g. in [12]. We refer to the alternative approach as the game-theoretical approach, because it gives attackers a utility function and it assumes rationality.

The game-theoretical approach is elegant and powerful, however, our approach has two advantages over the game-theoretical approach: First, we do not have a utility function, but robustness properties. That means that, e.g., distorting trust opinions is bad in itself, rather than because the utility function increases, due to an increased probability that the user interacts with the attacker, due to the distorted trust opinion. In the game-theoretical model, therefore, the notion that distorting trust opinions is an attack, relies on assumptions about the system and the users, whereas intuitively, distorting trust opinions is an attack regardless of the attacker's gains. Second, the game-theoretical notion of robustness is an extension of the notion of correctness - game-theoretic robustness fails trivially in incorrect systems. There are three drawbacks of having robustness as an extension of correctness, rather than a trade-off: Firstly, in many existing systems, correctness cannot be proven, hence robustness cannot be compared. Secondly, a trust system may have goals other than correctness and robustness, thus having users make suboptimal choices by design, and trivially having superior strategies for an attacker. Thirdly, viewing robustness and correctness as a trade-off more naturally represents design decisions in creating trust systems. For example, not incorporating recommendations in trust opinions makes the system robust against unfair rating attacks at the expense of correctness of trust opinions [21].

A robustness property is a predicate that holds in a collection of system states. A robustness property is a predicate, for which it is undesirable that attackers are more likely to satisfy it than ideal users; e.g., "gain 1000\$ in failed interactions". Typically, the probability of breaking the robustness property is non-zero, however, the probability of an ideal user breaking such a property is also non-zero. A trust system is robust when an attacker is no more likely to break the property than an ideal user. The rationale is that the designer modelled the system with ideal users in mind, hence whatever probability the ideal user has to break a property, that probability is acceptable.

In formal computer security, there are tools (e.g. ProVerif [4]) that can determine whether a security property holds, given a specification of the protocol. The algorithms used by the tools are of intractable complexity, but solve the problem at hand sufficiently often to be of practical value. Such tools would be a valuable asset in determining the robustness of a system. The first step towards automated verification, is a standardised formalisation of the problem. We shall use the notion of volitional trust systems and the notion of robustness properties to define robustness. This is fully analogous to how, in formal computer security, the notions of protocols and security properties define security.

We define the notion of a robustness property in a trust system space:

**Definition 7 (Robustness Property).** *A robustness property $\phi$ is a state predicate over the trust system space. If $\phi$ holds in a state $s$ in a trust system space, then $\phi$ also holds in any state $(s, g)$ in a rated trust system.*

Observe that the assignment of probabilities has no impact on which properties hold after a given sequence of actions.

We define the notion of probability of reaching $\phi$:

**Definition 8 (Probability of Reaching $\phi$).** *Given a rated trust system $(S, A, \mathbf{s}_0, W)$, the probability of reaching $\phi$ is recursively defined as $p_\phi(\mathbf{s}_0)$, where for $\mathbf{s} \in S$: $p_\phi(\mathbf{s}) = 1$ if $\phi(\mathbf{s})$, and $p_\phi(\mathbf{s}) = \frac{\sum_{t \in S, a \in A} W(\mathbf{s},\mathbf{a},\mathbf{t}) \cdot p_\phi(\mathbf{t})}{\sum_{t \in S, a \in A} W(\mathbf{s},\mathbf{a},\mathbf{t})}$ if $\neg\phi(\mathbf{s})$.*

The equation defining the probability of reaching $\phi$ does not necessarily terminate. Nevertheless, the value of $p_\phi(s_0)$ is well-defined[2], even if computation is

---

[2] Assuming absence of cycles in the trust system space, which follows from perfect recall.

infeasible. For predicates $\phi$ that only hold in a finite number of states, $p_\phi(s_0)$ can always be computed.

Now, we are interested in two volitional trust systems in particular, one where the user with volition is ideal, and one where the user with volition is malicious. In Section 3, we have defined what volitional trust systems result from malicious behaviours - equivalently in Definitions 5 and 6. A volitional trust system on based on a volitional ideal user is defined as:

**Definition 9 (Ideal Trust System).** *An ideal trust system based on trust system space $M$, ideal behaviour $I$, initial state $s_0$ and user $e$ is the volitional trust system $\Upsilon_{(M,I,s_0)}^{e \triangleleft \mathrm{supp}(I)}$.*

Based on these two types of volitional trust systems, we can verify whether a robustness property holds in a trust system:

**Definition 10 (Robustness of $\phi$).** *In a trust system space $M$ with ideal behaviour $I$ and initial state $s_0$, robustness of $\phi$ holds when the maximal probability of reaching $\neg\phi$ in a subverted trust system $\upsilon \in \Upsilon_{(M,I,s_0)}^{e \triangleleft \mathcal{F}}$ is no greater than the maximal probability of reaching $\neg\phi$ in an ideal trust system $\upsilon' \in \Upsilon_{(M,I,s_0)}^{e \triangleleft \mathrm{supp}(I)}$.*

Observe that robustness of $\phi$ only holds regardless of trust system space $(M)$ and initial state $(s_0)$ when the support of the ideal behaviour is equal to the set of all strategies. In other words, robustness of $\phi$ trivially holds, when all possible strategies are ideal $(\mathrm{supp}(I) = \mathcal{F})$. However, correctness is more difficult to achieve for larger sets of ideal strategies. Thus, as remarked before, robustness and correctness are a trade-off.

The Dolev-Yao attacker, in security, is sufficiently powerful, that any attack that can be performed by a group of attackers, can be performed by a single attacker. Our attacker has the same property, albeit under the assumption that users do not discriminate between users a priori. (Non-discrimination implies that substituting a user for another user with identical behaviour does not essentially change anything.)

**Theorem 2.** *For any robustness property $\phi$ and trust system space, that do not discriminate users, the probability of reaching $\phi$ under two cooperating attackers is equal to the probability of reaching $\phi$ under one attacker.*

*Proof.* See [19].

There are two ways to interpret the implications of Theorem 2. The first is the straightforward interpretation, that our attacker model is sufficiently strong to capture attacks with multiple attackers. It is obvious that this result follows from the capability of creating accounts arbitrarily. The alternative interpretation is relevant when the capability to create accounts at liberty is rejected. Our result shows that if an attack exists for colluding attackers, this attack exists for our maximal attacker. Thus, if robustness of $\phi$ holds in a system where accounts can be created freely, then $\phi$ holds in an otherwise identical system where several attackers, each with a single account, collude.

*Example 1 (Verifying Robustness).* In order to verify robustness of a system, we need to specify a trust system space, specify ideal behaviour and specify robustness properties. In practice, these may come in another specification language than assumed in this paper, in which case translation is necessary. We let the trust system space contain the fraction depicted in Figure 1. After applying the ideal strategies of the owners of $a$, $b$ and $e$, we obtain a rated transition system. The rated transition system can be represented, simply by labelling the edges in the graph with rates. The property $\phi$ in Figure 1 corresponds to "the attacker's (OWNER($e$)'s) offer is not accepted before the ideal target's (OWNER($b$)'s)". Both the subverted trust system and the ideal trust system are sets of rated trust systems, thus collections of different labellings of edges. For every labelling, we can compute the probability that we end up in a state where $\neg\phi$ holds. Now, we can compute the maximal probability that we end up in a state where $\neg\phi$ holds in a set of labellings. We can compare the maximal probability in the subverted trust system with the maximal probability in the ideal trust system. If they are equal, robustness holds, if they differ, robustness does not hold.

The robustness property is a qualitative property, not a quantitative property. There is a straightforward way to introduce a quantitative aspect to robustness properties:

**Definition 11 (Quantitative Robustness Properties).** *In a trust system space $M$ with ideal behaviour $I$ and initial state $s_0$, the* amount of robustness *of $\phi$ is defined as the difference between the maximal probability of reaching $\phi$ in a subverted trust system $\upsilon \in \Upsilon_{(M,I,s_0)}^{e \vartriangleleft \mathcal{F}}$, and the maximal probability of reaching $\phi$ in an ideal trust system $\upsilon' \in \Upsilon_{(M,I,s_0)}^{e \vartriangleleft \mathrm{supp}(I)}$.*

The advantage of the quantitative robustness properties, is that it allows reasoning about robustness of systems where qualitative robustness does not hold. Our quantitative robustness property is more useful than a quantification based on the number/set of strategies that can break the security property. Even if there is only one attack available for the attacker, the attacker can select this strategy. Thus if that strategy exceeds the maximal ideal strategy by 0.5, then the attacker has an unfair advantage of 0.5. When there are multiple attacks available, the attacker can only select one strategy - presumably the most effective one.

## 5   Conclusion

We have introduced formal machinery that allows us to express the notion of trust systems semantically, in the form of trust system spaces. We argue that robustness refers to the distance between a system operating under the designers' assumptions and a real system. The designers' assumptions come in the form of ideal behaviour. When applying (ideal) behaviour to users, non-determinism is replaced by probability, transforming trust system spaces into rated trust systems. The attacker is a special user, whose behaviour is not ideal, but malicious.

Not all non-ideal behaviour can be performed by an attacker. Hence, we provide a model of malicious behaviour, in the form of two equivalent attacker models. Both models define a toolset of strategies of the attacker, in the form of a volitional trust system. One attacker model is based on an intuitive understanding of what an attacker should be able to do. The other attacker model contains, by definition, all strategies that can be performed within a trust system space. They mutually support each other's validity via their equivalence. The definition of the attacker model is one of the main contributions of the paper.

Behaviour being malicious is not sufficient for it to be an attack. An attack is a malicious behaviour that breaks a property with a probability exceeding that of an ideal behaviour. A robustness property is a state predicate that attackers want to break. We introduce probabilistic notions of reachability of a property. We define robustness with respect to a certain robustness property based on the probabilistic reachability of the negation of the state predicate. The definition of robustness with respect to a robustness property (Definition 10) is another of the main contributions of the paper. We further extend the robustness property to a quantified variant, that allows comparison between two systems that both fail to uphold a certain robustness property.

We prove that a multitude of attackers is no more powerful than a single attacker (Theorem 2). This notion is crucial to our initial choice to model all users except the attacker as ideal users, which is, therefore, validated by Theorem 2. The choice to restrict ourselves to one attacker severely simplifies the analysis of robustness properties - both for manual analysis and for possible future automated verification tools.

We identify four different, albeit intertwined, directions of future work. First, to analyse the robustness of real trust systems - to link theory to practice, e.g. in cloud computing, e-commerce or vehicular networks. Second, to research theoretical implications of our approach, e.g. complexity, expressivity, extensions or simplifications. Third, to implement our ideas to allow automated verification (based on tools as PRISM[3] or PAT[4]). Fourth, to find (or at least characterise) trust systems that satisfy given robustness properties.

**Acknowledgements.** This work is supported by "Formal Verification on Cloud" project under Grant No: M4081155.020. This work is partially supported by the A*Star SERC grant (1224104047) awarded to Dr. Jie Zhang.

# References

1. Baeten, J.C.M., Basten, T., Reniers, M.A.: Process algebra: equational theories of communicating processes, vol. 50. Cambridge University Press (2010)
2. Billingsley, P.: Probability and measure, 3rd edn. Wiley (1995)

---

[3] http://www.prismmodelchecker.org
[4] http://www.patroot.com

3. Blanchet, B.: Security protocol verification: Symbolic and computational models. In: Degano, P., Guttman, J.D. (eds.) Principles of Security and Trust. LNCS, vol. 7215, pp. 3–29. Springer, Heidelberg (2012)
4. Blanchet, B., Abadi, M., Fournet, C.: Automated verification of selected equivalences for security protocols. In: Logic in Computer Science, pp. 331–340. IEEE (2005)
5. Dolev, D., Yao, A.C.: On the security of public key protocols. IEEE Transactions on Information Theory 29(2), 198–208 (1983)
6. Douceur, J.R.: The sybil attack. In: Druschel, P., Kaashoek, M.F., Rowstron, A. (eds.) IPTPS 2002. LNCS, vol. 2429, pp. 251–260. Springer, Heidelberg (2002)
7. Henzinger, T.A.: The theory of hybrid automata. Springer (2000)
8. Hoffman, K., Zage, D., Nita-Rotaru, C.: A survey of attack and defense techniques for reputation systems. ACM Comput. Surv. 42(1), 1–31 (2009)
9. Jiang, S., Zhang, J., Ong, Y.-S.: An evolutionary model for constructing robust trust networks. In: Autonomous Agents and Multi-Agent Systems, pp. 813–820. IFAAMAS (2013)
10. Jøsang, A., Golbeck, J.: Challenges for robust trust and reputation systems. In: Security and Trust Management, Saint Malo, France (2009)
11. Jøsang, A., Ismail, R.: The beta reputation system. In: Bled Electronic Commerce Conference, pp. 41–55 (2002)
12. Kerr, R., Cohen, R.: Towards provably secure trust and reputation systems in e-marketplaces. In: Proceedings of the 6th International Joint Conference on Autonomous Agents and Multiagent Systems, p. 172. ACM (2007)
13. Kerr, R., Cohen, R.: Smart cheaters do prosper: defeating trust and reputation systems. In: Autonomous Agents and Multiagent Systems, vol. 2, pp. 993–1000. International Foundation for Autonomous Agents and Multiagent Systems (2009)
14. Klin, B., Sassone, V.: Structural operational semantics for stochastic process calculi. In: Amadio, R.M. (ed.) FOSSACS 2008. LNCS, vol. 4962, pp. 428–442. Springer, Heidelberg (2008)
15. Koblitz, N., Menezes, A.: Another look at "provable security". Cryptology ePrint Archive, Report 2004/152 (2004)
16. Kwiatkowska, M., Norman, G., Sproston, J., Wang, F.: Symbolic model checking for probabilistic timed automata. In: Lakhnech, Y., Yovine, S. (eds.) FORMATS 2004 and FTRTFT 2004. LNCS, vol. 3253, pp. 293–308. Springer, Heidelberg (2004)
17. Lam, S.K., Riedl, J.: Shilling recommender systems for fun and profit. In: International Conference on World Wide Web, pp. 393–402. ACM (2004)
18. Mui, L., Mohtashemi, M., Halberstadt, A.: A computational model of trust and reputation. In: System Sciences, HICSS, pp. 2431–2439. IEEE (2002)
19. Muller, T., Liu, Y., Mauw, S., Zhang, J.: On robustness of trust systems. Technical report, Nanyang Technological University (2014), http://pat.sce.ntu.edu.sg/tim/papers/robustnesstechreport.pdf
20. Muller, T., Schweitzer, P.: A formal derivation of composite trust. In: Garcia-Alfaro, J., Cuppens, F., Cuppens-Boulahia, N., Miri, A., Tawbi, N. (eds.) FPS 2012. LNCS, vol. 7743, pp. 132–148. Springer, Heidelberg (2013)
21. Muller, T., Schweitzer, P.: On beta models with trust chains. In: Fernández-Gago, C., Martinelli, F., Pearson, S., Agudo, I. (eds.) IFIPTM 2013. IFIP, vol. 401, pp. 49–65. Springer, Heidelberg (2013)
22. Stewart, W.J.: Introduction to the numerical solution of Markov chains, vol. 41. Princeton University Press, Princeton (1994)

23. Sun, Y.L., Han, Z., Yu, W., Liu, K.J.R.: Attacks on trust evaluation in distributed networks. In: Information Sciences and Systems, pp. 1461–1466. IEEE (2006)
24. Zhang, J., Cohen, R.: Evaluating the trustworthiness of advice about seller agents in e-marketplaces: A personalized approach. Electronic Commerce Research and Applications 7(3), 330–340 (2008)
25. Zhang, L., Jiang, S., Zhang, J., Ng, W.K.: Robustness of trust models and combinations for handling unfair ratings. In: Dimitrakos, T., Moona, R., Patel, D., McKnight, D.H. (eds.) IFIPTM 2012. IFIP AICT, vol. 374, pp. 36–51. Springer, Heidelberg (2012)

# Design of Intrusion Sensitivity-Based Trust Management Model for Collaborative Intrusion Detection Networks

Wenjuan Li, Weizhi Meng*, and Lam-For Kwok

Department of Computer Science, City University of Hong Kong, Hong Kong, China
{wenjuan.li,yuxin.meng}@cityu.edu.hk

**Abstract.** Network intrusions are becoming more and more sophisticated to detect. To mitigate this issue, intrusion detection systems (IDSs) have been widely deployed in identifying a variety of attacks and collaborative intrusion detection networks (CIDNs) have been proposed which enables an IDS to collect information and learn experience from other IDSs with the purpose of improving detection accuracy. A CIDN is expected to have more power in detecting attacks such as denial-of-service (DoS) than a single IDS. In real deployment, we notice that each IDS has different levels of sensitivity in detecting different types of intrusions (i.e., based on their own signatures and settings). In this paper, we propose a machine learning-based approach to assign intrusion sensitivity based on expert knowledge and design a trust management model that allows each IDS to evaluate the trustworthiness of others by considering their detection sensitivities. In the evaluation, we explore the performance of our proposed approach under different attack scenarios. The experimental results indicate that by considering the intrusion sensitivity, our trust model can enhance the detection accuracy of malicious nodes as compared to existing similar models.

**Keywords:** Network Security, Intrusion Detection, Trust Management, Intrusion Sensitivity, Collaborative Intrusion Detection Network.

## 1 Introduction

Network intrusions (e.g., worms, spamware, Trojans, virus, etc.) have become more and more sophisticated and harmful [25]. To mitigate this problem, intrusion detection systems (IDSs) have been widely deployed in current computers and networks aiming to defend against a variety of attacks, and these detection systems have already become an essential component for current defense mechanism [21].

Traditionally, these intrusion detection systems can be classified into two general types based on their protected environments[1] [21]: *host-based IDS (HIDS)* and *network-based IDS (NIDS)*. The HIDS detects abnormal executions by

---

* Corresponding author and is previously known as Yuxin Meng.
[1] Based on the detection approaches, these intrusion detection systems can be roughly classified as signature-based IDS [27] and anomaly-based IDS [7].

J. Zhou et al. (Eds.): IFIPTM 2014, IFIP AICT 430, pp. 61–76, 2014.
© IFIP International Federation for Information Processing 2014

logging and analyzing system events within a single host while the NIDS is mainly monitoring and analyzing network traffic for identifying suspicious activities. But in a large-scale network environment, a single IDS cannot detect some certain attacks such as denial-of-service (DoS) and distributed DoS (DDoS). The potential damage of these attacks can be significant if failed detected (i.e., causing paralysis of the entire network). In addition, an isolated IDS would be easily bypassed by unknown or novel exploits.

To resolve this issue, IDS collaboration is an effective way to enhance the detection capability of a single IDS. Thus, intrusion detection network (IDN) has been developed, which is a collaborative IDS network, with the purpose of strengthening a single IDS by collecting knowledge and learning experience from other IDS nodes. This collaborative IDN (CIDN) [28] is expected to enhance the overall detection accuracy of intrusion assessment and improve the possibility of identifying novel attacks. However, attackers can compromise some peers (or *some IDS nodes*) in the CIDN and utilize these compromised peers to invade or against the collaborative network. These malicious peers can make use of some attacks including Sybil attacks, newcomer attacks, betrayal attacks to lower the effectiveness and efficiency of a CIDN by sending false information and compromising other honest IDS nodes within the network. In these cases, designing a robust CIDN (i.e., effectively evaluating the trustworthiness of each IDS in the network) becomes very crucial and essential to improve its detection capability and protect this network against insider attacks.

*Contributions.* In our previous work [12], we have identified that each IDS has different levels of sensitivity in detecting particular intrusions and proposed a notion of *intrusion sensitivity*. Our goal of this paper is thus designing a trust management model based on *intrusion sensitivity* to improve the robustness of CIDNs. In particular, we begin by reviewing recent works of building trust models regarding intrusion detection. We then detail the notion of *intrusion sensitivity* and build an *intrusion sensitivity-based trust management model* for a CIDN. Our contributions of this work can be summarized as below:

- We review some related works about establishing trust models in the field of intrusion detection and introduce the tuned CIDN's framework to adapt to our model, which consists of several major components including IDS nodes, trust management component, collaboration component, communication component and query component.
- Our previous work [12] proposed a notion of *intrusion sensitivity* that measures the detection sensitivity of an IDS in detecting different kinds of intrusions. This work we thus aim to develop an *intrusion sensitivity-based trust management model* for CIDNs. To automatically realize the assessment of *intrusion sensitivity*, we further develop a *query component* and an expert knowledge-based KNN classifier to allocate the sensitivity level.
- In the evaluation, we simulated a collaborative intrusion detection network and certain attacks to investigate the performance of our proposed trust management model under different attack scenarios. The experimental

results indicate that our proposed model by considering the *intrusion sensitivity* is more efficient and sensitive in detecting malicious nodes as compared to other similar trust models.

The remaining parts of this paper are organized as follows. In Section 2, we review some related works about trust models in collaborative intrusion detection networks; Section 3 describes our proposed trust model in detail including CIDN framework, intrusion sensitivity and trust evaluation, and analyzes the robustness of the trust model against several common attacks. Section 4 presents experimental settings and describes experimental results and Section 5 analyzes some limitations and challenges. Finally, we conclude our work with future directions in Section 6.

## 2  Related Work

Intuitively, an isolated (or single) intrusion detection system has no information about the whole protected environment and thus is more likely to be bypassed by novel intrusions. To resolve this issue, collaborative intrusion detection networks (CIDNs) [28] have been proposed and implemented which enable an IDS node to achieve more accurate detection by collecting and learning useful information from other IDS nodes.

A number of trust models have been proposed for CIDNs. For instance, Janakiraman and Zhang [9] proposed *Indra*, a distributed scheme based on sharing information between trusted peers in a network to guard a peer-to-peer network as a whole against intrusion attempts. Li *et al.* [11] identified that most distributed intrusion detection systems (DIDS) relied on centralized fusion, or distributed fusion with unscalable communication mechanisms, and then proposed a DIDS based on the emerging decentralized location and routing infrastructure. The experimental results showed that their methods could greatly outperform the traditional hierarchical approach when facing large amounts of diverse intrusion alerts. However, these approaches assume that all peers are trusted which is vulnerable to insider attacks (i.e., some nodes become malicious). Several distributed intrusion detection systems can be classified as:

- *Centralized/Hierarchical systems*: Emerald [16] and DIDS [22];
- *Publish/subscribe systems*: COSSACK [15] and DOMINO [29];
- *P2P Querying based systems*: Netbait [2] and PIER [8].

To identify insider attacks, Duma *et al.* [3] proposed a P2P-based overlay for intrusion detection (Overlay IDS) that mitigated the insider threat by using a trust-aware engine for correlating alerts and an adaptive scheme for managing trust. The trust-aware correlation engine is capable of filtering out warnings sent by untrusted or low quality peers, while the adaptive trust management scheme uses past experiences of peers to predict their trustworthiness. But a major issue is that the past experience of a peer has the same impact regardless of the age of its experience. To resolve this problem, Fung *et al.* [4] proposed a HIDS collaboration framework that enables each HIDS to evaluate the trustworthiness of others based on its own experience by means of a forgetting factor. The forgetting factor can give more emphasis on the recent experience of the peer. Later, Fung *et al.* [5] improved their proposed trust management model by using a Dirichlet-based model to measure the level of trustworthiness among IDS nodes according to their mutual experience. This model had strong scalability properties and was robust against common insider threats and the experimental results demonstrated that the new model could improve robustness and efficiency. As the mechanism of feedback aggregation is a key component in the above trust model, Fung *et al.* [6] further applied a Bayesian approach to feedback aggregation to minimize the combined costs of missed detection and false alarm. Their experiments indicated that the Bayesian approach could make an improvement in the true positive detection rate and a reduction in the average cost.

In addition, Quercia *et al.* [18] proposed a distributed trust framework that satisfied a broader range of properties, which evolved an expressive and tractable trust calculation based on Bayesian formalization, protected user anonymity and integrated a risk-aware decision module. Then, Li *et al.* [10] proposed an objective trust management framework (*OTMF*) using a modified Bayesian approach where the trust in the provider of second-hand information is considered when evaluating trust. They further conducted a performance evaluation and security analysis on *OTMF*, and the results showed that the *OTMF* was more effective and robust as compared to similar frameworks.

Many theories have also been investigated to evaluate the trustworthiness of communication entities such as Information Theory, Game theory and Grey Theory. For example, Sun *et al.* [24] presented an information theoretic framework to quantitatively measure trust and model trust propagation in Ad Hoc networks. In their framework, trust is a measure of uncertainty with its value represented by entropy. They developed four Axioms that addressed the basic understanding of trust and the rules for trust propagation. The simulations showed that their approach could significantly improve the network throughput as well as effectively detect malicious behaviors in Ad Hoc networks. Tuan [26] used the game theory to model and analyze the processes of reporting and exclusion in a P2P network. They found that if a reputation system was not incentive compatible, the more numbers of peers in the system, the less likely that anyone will report about a malicious peer. Later, Cai *et al.* [1] proposed a novel risk assessment method based on grey theory to identify the malicious recommendations. They further showed that grey theory was suitable for P2P networks.

In our previous work [12], we identified that different IDSs may have different levels of sensitivity in detecting different types of intrusions and proposed a notion of *intrusion sensitivity*, which helps detect intrusions and correlate IDS alerts through emphasizing the impact of an *expert IDS*.[2] Based on the notion, in this work, we aim to design an *intrusion sensitivity-based trust management*

---

[2] Note that these IDS nodes are assumed to have more powerful capability and sensitivity in identifying some certain malicious activities.

*model* for CIDNs and compare our model with some similar models in the evaluation. The experimental results under several attack scenarios indicate that our approach can improve the accuracy of identifying insider attacks as compared to the existing trust models.

## 3    CIDN Framework and Intrusion Sensitivity-Based Trust Management Model

A CIDN can enable single IDS nodes to connect, communicate and cooperate with others. In this work, we design a *query component* to allocate its values and consequently establish a trust management model. In this section, we modify a CIDN framework (without a centralized server) based on our previous work [12], introduce how to assign the value of *intrusion sensitivity* and how to evaluate the trustworthiness of an IDS node.

### 3.1    CIDN Design

In Fig. 1, we describe the key components of the adopted CIDN framework: *IDS nodes, trust management component, query component, collaboration component* and *communication component*. This trust model allows an IDS node to evaluate the trustworthiness of others based on its own and others' experience.

***IDS Nodes.*** In the framework, each IDS node (based on either a HIDS or a NIDS) can choose its collaborators according to its own experience. These nodes are associated if they have a collaborative and cooperative relationship. Each node can maintain a list of their collaborated nodes. In this paper, we call this list as *partner list*. The *partner list* is customizable and contains public keys of other nodes and their current trust values.

If a node requests to join this collaborative network, it needs to register to a trusted certificate authority (*CA*) and get its unique proof of identity (including a public key and a private key). For example as shown in Fig. 1, if node $D$ wants to join the CIDN, then it can send a request to a network node, say node $A$. After receiving the request, node $A$ can send back the decision (either accept or decline). If node $D$ is accepted to join the network, it can then receive an initial *partner list* from node $A$.

***Trust Management Component.*** This component is responsible for evaluating the trustworthiness of other nodes. In this work, we mainly consider two types of trust: *feedback-based trust* and *packet-based trust*, aiming to provide a comprehensive trust evaluation in this component:

- *Feedback-based trust* is established based on the feedbacks from partner nodes (which appear in the *partner list*). The feedback will be sent and received by a collaboration component.
- *Packet-based trust* is computed based on the received benign packets and total packets from the target node. This type of trust is objective and is helpful for determining a trusted route and identify malicious nodes.

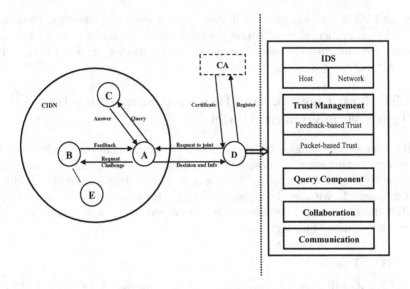

**Fig. 1.** The framework of our designed collaborative intrusion detection network integrating with a query component (aiming to request *intrusion sensitivity*)

***Query Component.*** This is a key component in our designed framework, which can send a set of *queries* to a target node in which a *query* mainly contains a series of alarms (e.g., 5 to 10) while *answers* are alarm rankings sent back from the target node. Basically, these *answers* are decided by the experience, configuration and settings of each IDS node. For example, Snort [23] has classified its rules to three different priorities, thus, the corresponding triggered alarms can be ranked according to the matched rules. On the contrary, certain alarms cannot be correctly classified if lacking of some rules. In this case, the specific *intrusion sensitivity* of an IDS node can be determined according to the *answers*.

As shown in Fig. 1, if node $A$ sends a *query* to node $C$, then node $C$ will send back an *answer* to node $A$. Intuitively, different IDS nods may have different levels of *intrusion sensitivity* with regard to each individual type of intrusions. For example, if an IDS node has more powerful rules in detecting a certain attack like denial of service attack ($DoS$), then it can send back a more accurate alarm ranking for this attack and can be allocated a higher sensitivity level for this particular attack. Based on the different levels of *intrusion sensitivity*, we can emphasize the impact of *expert nodes* in detecting malicious nodes and attacks. In this work, the levels of *intrusion sensitivity* can be automatically assigned by means of a machine learning classifier (e.g., KNN) after receiving the *answers*. The details will be discussed later.

***Collaboration Component.*** This component is mainly responsible for assisting a node to evaluate the trustworthiness (namely *feedback-based trust*) of others by sending out *requests* and *challenges* (in a period of time), and collecting the corresponding *feedback*.

- *Requests* can be sent by an IDS node for alert consultation. For example, an IDS node may request other nodes to help determine the ranking of several alerts. A *request* is mainly used for alert aggregation and is beyond the scope of this paper.
- *Challenges* are sent by an IDS node for evaluating the trustworthiness of another node in the *partner list*. In particular, this node knows the desirable feedback for the challenges so that it can evaluate the trustworthiness of other nodes by analyzing the received feedback (answers).
- *Feedback* will be sent back from other IDS nodes for the corresponding *requests* and *challenges*. If an IDS node receives a request or challenge, this component will send back its feedback as the answers. As shown in Fig. 1, if node $A$ sends a *request/challenge* to node $B$, then node $B$ will send back relevant feedback.

**Communication Component.** This component is responsible for connecting with other IDS nodes and providing network organization and communication between IDS nodes. For instance, for a HIDS-based CIDN, this component can use P2P. In addition, this component can assist a node to evaluate the trustworthiness (namely *packet-based trust*) of other nodes by recording the number of transmitted packets and the state of packets (e.g., benign) based on IDS's rules or normal profiles. The details of trust computation will be discussed next.

### 3.2 Trust Evaluation

To evaluate the trustworthiness of a target node, an IDS node can sent a *challenge* to this target periodically using a random generation process. When receiving the feedback from the target node, the IDS node can give a score to reflect its satisfaction level. As we define two types of trust including *feedback-based trust* $(T_{fd})$ and *packet-based trust* $(T_{pt})$, we develop a single metric called *overall trust* $(T_{total})$ to facilitate the trust evaluation as follows:

$$T_{total} = W_1 \times T_{fd} + W_2 \times T_{pt} \tag{1}$$

where $W_1$ and $W_2$ are weight values and $W_1 + W_2 = 1$. For the feedback-based trust $T_{fd}^{i,j}$ of node $i$ according to node $j$, we can compute it by using the equation described as below:

$$T_{fd}^{i,j} = w_s \frac{\sum_{k=0}^{n} F_k^j \lambda^{tk}}{\sum_{k=0}^{n} \lambda^{tk}} \tag{2}$$

where $F_k^j \in [0,1]$ is the score of the received feedback $k$ and $n$ is the total number of feedback. $\lambda$ is a *forgetting factor* that assigns less weight to older feedback response. $w_s$ is a *significant weight* depends on the total number of received feedback, if there is only a few feedback under a certain minimum $m$, then $w_s = \frac{\sum_{k=0}^{n} \lambda^{tk}}{m}$, and otherwise $w_s = 1$.

On the other hand, in this work, the *packet-based trust* of node $i$ according to node $j$ can be computed based on our another work [14] as below:

$$T_{pt}^{i,j} = \frac{k+1}{N+2} \tag{3}$$

where $k$ is the number of received benign packets and $N$ is the total number of received packets. The detailed derivation and computation can refer to [14].

**Assignment of Intrusion Sensitivity.** As described above, each IDS node can consult alert ranking from other nodes by sending out *queries*. After receiving the *answers*, a node thus can evaluate the *intrusion sensitivity* of other nodes accordingly. However, to automatically assign the levels of *intrusion sensitivity* is a big challenge [12].

To address this issue, we identify that a machine learning classifier based on expert knowledge can be utilized. In this work, we thus use a k-nearest neighbors algorithm (KNN) to automatically allocate the values of *intrusion sensitivity*. The reasons of selecting this classifier are shown as below:

- The KNN classifier aims to classify objects based on the closest training examples in the feature space. That is, an object is classified in terms of its distances to the nearest cluster. In [13], this classifier has proven to be effective in intrusion detection with a high detection accuracy.
- In addition, this classifier can achieve a faster speed with lower computational burden as compared to other classifiers like neural networks in the phases of both training and classification. These properties are desirable when deployed in a resource-limited platform like an *IDS node*.

To evaluate and assign the *intrusion sensitivity* of other nodes using the KNN classifier, there are generally two steps shown as follows:

- We first obtain several scores for the feedback based on expert knowledge and build a classifier model. In this work, we employ three experts from recognized organization regarding intrusion detection and Honeypot[3] to give scores for different sets of queries and answers. We then use a KNN classifier to establish a model.
- When evaluating the intrusion sensitivity of a target node $i$, a node $j$ can send a *query* to node $i$ and obtain the answers. We then use the KNN classifier to assign a value to node $i$ as $I_s^i$ by means of the established model.

In Fig. 2, we give an example to illustrate the assignment of intrusion sensitivity of a node using the KNN classifier. The white point is the incoming feedback waiting for assignment, while based on expert knowledge, we have obtained a set of clusters that are composed of black points (i.e., cluster of *Rate 0.5*). Then, the KNN classifier calculates the Euclidean distance (e.g., ED1, ED2, ED3) between the white-point and the other three clusters respectively. The shorter the

---

[3] www.honeybird.hk/

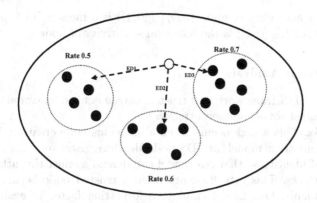

**Fig. 2.** A case to illustrate the assignment of intrusion sensitivity to a node using the KNN classifier

distance, the more similar they are. The Euclidean distance between two points can be computed as below:

$$[Distance\ (P1,\ P2)]^2 = \sum_{0}^{N}(P1_i - P2_i)^2 \tag{4}$$

where $P1_i$ and $P2_i$ are the values of the *ith* attribute of points $P1$ and $P2$ respectively. In real scenarios, each point can be treated as an *answer* to a *query*, and each alarm (and its ranking) in the *answer* can be regarded as an attribute. In this case, we can compute the Euclidean distance between the *current answer* and the *desirable answer*. In Fig. 2, the Euclidean distance between the write point and a cluster (e.g., ED1) can be calculated as below:

$$ED_{cluster}^j = \frac{\sum_{1}^{N_{tn}^j} ED_j^i}{N_{tn}^j} \quad (i = 1, 2...;\ j = 1, 2...) \tag{5}$$

where $ED_{cluster}^j$ means the Euclidean distance between a target node and a cluster $j$, $ED_j^i$ means the Euclidean distance between a target node and a node $i$ of cluster $j$, and $N_{tn}^j$ means the total number of nodes in the cluster $j$.

Finally, the classifier will find the shortest Euclidean distance and assign the level of *intrusion sensitivity*. For example, if a received answer is classified into one cluster, then the corresponding IDS node will be given the sensitivity level the same as that cluster.

**Trust Evaluation of a Node.** To evaluate the trustworthiness of a node $j$, we can use a weighted majority method as follows:

$$T_j = \frac{\sum_{T \geq r} T_{total}^{i,j} D_i^j I_s^i}{\sum_{T \geq r} T_{total}^{i,j} D_i^j} \tag{6}$$

where $r$ is a threshold that node $j$ requests alert ranking to those nodes whose trust values are higher than this threshold. $T_{total}^{i,j}(\in [0,1])$ is the *overall trust value* of node $i$ according to node $j$. $D_i^j(\in [0,1])$ is a measure of *hops* between these two nodes. $I_s^i(\in [0,1])$ is the intrusion sensitivity of node $i$.

### 3.3   Robustness Analysis

The designed CIDN framework and trust management model can achieve good robustness against some common attacks.

*Sybil attacks.* This attack occurs when a malicious node creates a lot of fake identities. In our trust model, an IDS node should register to a *CA* and obtain a unique proof identity so that our model can defend against this attack.

*Betrayal attacks.* This attack occurs when a trusted node becomes a malicious one suddenly. Our model employs a forgetting factor in evaluating the trustworthiness so that we can mitigate this attack.

*Newcomer (re-entry) attacks.* This attack occurs when a malicious node registers as a new user attempting to erase its bad history [20]. But due to our model begins by giving low initial trust values to all newcomers, our model can handle and mitigate this attack.

## 4   Evaluation

In this section, we present a case study to evaluate the effectiveness of our proposed trust model. The collaborative network, which consists of 30 nodes equipped with Snort, is randomly distributed in a $s \times s$ grid region.

To test the trustworthiness of other nodes in the *partner list*, each node sends out *challenges* and *queries* with an arrival rate $\mu$. Each *challenge* contains 5 alarms for ranking while each *query* contains 10 alarms for ranking. We also have two assumptions. 1) For *challenges*, we assume that an honest node always generates feedback truthfully, while a dishonest node always sends feedback opposite to its truthful judgment. 2) For *queries*, we assume that all nodes will rank the alarms truthfully. Some simulation parameters are shown in Table. 1.

$D_i^j$ is anti-proportional to the hops between the nodes in the number of grid steps. The feedback satisfaction is classified as: very satisfied (1.0), satisfied (0.5),

**Table 1.** Simulation parameters in the experiment

| Parameters | Value | Description |
|:---:|:---:|:---:|
| $\mu$ | 15/day | arrival rate |
| $\lambda$ | 0.9 | forgetting factor |
| $r$ | 0.8 | trust threshold |
| $T_{dir,initial}$ | 0.5 | trust value for new comers |
| $m$ | 10 | lower limit of received feedback |
| $s$ | 5 | size of grid region |
| $k1$ | 5 | satisfaction levels |
| $k2$ | 10 | intrusion sensitivity levels |
| $(W_1, W_2)$ | (0.7, 0.3) | weight values for $T_{total}$ |

neutral (0.3), unsatisfied (0.1), and very unsatisfied (0). The *intrusion sensitivity* $(I_s^i)$ are classified into ten levels such as expert (1.0), excellent (0.9), very high (0.8), high (0.7), good (0.6), neural (0.5), not good (0.4), low (0.3), very low (0.2), and lowest (0.1).

## 4.1  The Effect of Intrusion Sensitivity: A Case Study

We first evaluate the performance of *intrusion sensitivity* using a metric of *survival rate*, which is defined as the number of nodes which resist the malicious attack divided by the number of all nodes in the network. In this evaluation, we conduct a worm attack to the above network based on [3].

In particular, IDS nodes were running RedHat Linux 7.3 and Apache 1.3.23 web server with OpenSSL encryption enabled. Note that this configuration is vulnerable to the Slapper worm. Later, we launch worm attacks and investigate the survival rate under the situations with and without the *intrusion sensitivity* respectively. We experimented with 1, 3, 5, and 10 protected peers, whereas all other IDS nodes were vulnerable to the worm attack. If this attack hits a protected node, then this node can warn the other nodes for this attack.

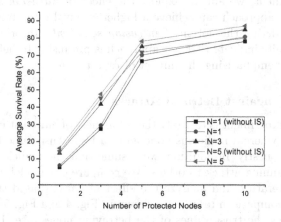

**Fig. 3.** The results of survival rate

For each case, we repeated the experiment 10 times during the experiments. In Fig. 3, we illustrate the average survival rates for different configurations, where $N$ means the number of expert nodes that correlates alerts by considering the *intrusion sensitivity*. There are two observations in the experiment:

 – This figure shows that the average survival rate increases with the number of protected nodes since more protected nodes can increase the probability of detecting this attack as early as possible. That is, the attack may hit first protected node earlier and this node can warn other nodes more quickly.

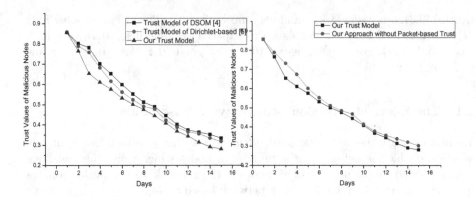

**Fig. 4.** The trust value of malicious peers

**Fig. 5.** The effect of packet-based trust on our approach

- In addition, the average survival rate increases with the number of expert nodes ($N$) which consider the *intrusion sensitivity*. Taking $N = 5$ for an example, our approach can achieve an average survival rate of nearly 87% while the rate decreases to 80.2% without considering the *intrusion sensitivity*.

In this experiment, we aim to explore the effect of *intrusion sensitivity*. It is found that our approach can achieve a higher survival rate under the attack scenario by considering the notion of *intrusion sensitivity*. In other words, the experimental results indicate that our approach is promising to help detect malicious attacks by emphasizing the impact of *expert nodes*.

### 4.2   Defending against Betrayal Attacks

The goal of this experiment is to study the robustness of our trust model against betrayal attacks, where a malicious node gains a high trust value but suddenly starts to act dishonestly. In addition, we assume that the malicious nodes will launch a port scanning attack to others. We compare our model with two similar models in literature and analyze the effect of packet-based trust on trust evaluation. The comparison results are shown in Fig. 4 and Fig. 5 respectively.

Fig. 4 evaluates the trust values of the betraying nodes after launching the betrayal attacks by means of our model and the trust models of [4] and [5] respectively. The observations are described as below:

- By comparing trust models of [4] and [5], it is found that the Dirichlet-based model [5] can achieve a slight improvement than the model of DSOM [4], since the Dirichlet-based model adopts a dynamic test message rate and can react more swiftly.
- By comparing our model with the other two models, it is visible that our model can make the trust values of malicious nodes drop more quickly. The main reason is that our trust model integrates the *intrusion sensitivity* and depends on two trust types (feedback-based and packet-based trust). Therefore, our model can be more sensitive to react to malicious behavior.

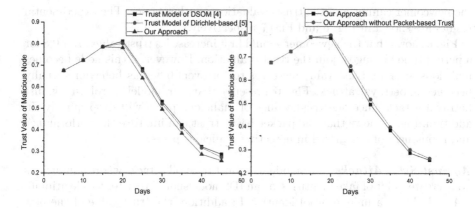

**Fig. 6.** The trust value of malicious peer

**Fig. 7.** The effect of packet-based trust on our approach

On the other hand, Fig. 5 computes the trust values of malicious nodes under two conditions with and without *packet-based trust* respectively. The observations are described as follows:

- It is noticeable that by considering the packet-based trust, our model can perform better, since the packet-based trust can evaluate the trustworthiness of a node in packet level. When a node becomes malicious, it will launch port scanning attack so that these malicious packets can be detected by Snort. In this case, it can improve the detection accuracy of malicious peers and make our model react to malicious behaviors faster by considering the packet-based trust.
- In addition, Fig. 4 shows that our approach can achieve a similar performance without the packet-based trust, as compared to the Dirichlet-based model [5]. However, our approach can still outperform the model of [5] a bit, since our model integrates the notion of *intrusion sensitivity*. This makes our trust model be more sensitive to malicious behaviors.

In this work, once the trust values of malicious nodes drop below the trust threshold of 0.8, these nodes can be ignored and their impact is completely eliminated. The experimental results above demonstrate that our proposed trust model is promising and effective in improving the detection accuracy of malicious nodes as compared to similar models.

### 4.3 Defending against Newcomer and Sybil Attacks

*Against Newcomer Attacks.* For the newcomer (re-entry) attacks in which a malicious node registers as a new user to erase its bad history, we also conduct an experiment to simulate this situation. It is found that our model is robust against this type of attacks as only a lower initial trust value like 0.5 will be assigned to a newcomer. Due to the initial trust value is lower than 0.8, the newcomer cannot join the trust evaluation of other nodes. The experimental results are shown in Fig. 6 and Fig. 7 respectively.

Fig. 6 shows that the newcomer should first increase its trust values over 0.8 for a period time aiming to join the trust evaluation. However, if this node becomes malicious after its trust value increases to (or over) 0.8, this behavior actually becomes a betrayal attack. Fig. 6 presents that our model is robust against betrayal attack since the trust values of malicious peers will drop quickly. In addition, Fig. 7 shows that the packet-based trust can improve the performance and robustness of our model in detecting malicious peers.

***Against Sybil Attacks.*** Our model is robust to Sybil attacks where a malicious node creates a lot of fake identities, as an IDS node should register to a legitimate *CA* and obtain a unique proof identity. In addition, the trust value of the new joined node is only 0.5 in which the new node cannot make any negative effect on the performance of the network.

## 5   Challenges and Limitations

We have demonstrated the performance of our model in a simulated environment. In this section, we discuss the challenges and limitations of our current work.

– We acknowledge that the current framework may increase some burden for a node, since it needs to send many messages with other nodes. However, the workload can be predicted as these messages are sent in a period of time. To investigate this issue, we have two directions in our future work: 1) studying the performance of our model with different message arrival rate; and 2) exploring the real burden of communication under our framework.
– We also acknowledge that it is a big challenge to objectively and correctly assign the values of *intrusion sensitivity* based on expert knowledge, as experts may have different views regarding the settings of IDS nodes. Therefore, different levels of intrusion sensitivity may be assigned by different experts. To address this issue, we consider one of the potential solutions is to further specify the criterion for evaluating the *intrusion sensitivity*.
– In this work, we have simulated a CIDN environment during the evaluation. Although it is convenient for us to evaluate the effect of different parameters (e.g., arrival rate) in this simulated environment, it is still a big challenge to test our model in a real environment to investigate its practical performance. We thus consider this as one of our future work.

## 6   Conclusion and Future Work

A collaborative intrusion detection network (CIDN) is expected to have more power in detecting attacks in which an IDS can collect information and learn experience from other nodes. In this paper, we advocate that each IDS node may have different levels of sensitivity in detecting different types of intrusions.

We therefore design a trust management model for CIDNs based on the notion of *intrusion sensitivity* aiming to emphasize the impact of an expert node in identifying malicious nodes. In particular, as a study, we develop an expert knowledge-based KNN classifier that can automatically assign the value of *intrusion sensitivity* to an IDS node. The experimental results under different attack scenarios show that our approach is more effective and sensitive in detecting malicious peers as compared to other similar trust models.

There are many possible topics in further work. Following work could include discussing the calculation of other trust types such as recommendation trust in the trust management model and verifying the impact of the intrusion sensitivity with even larger experiments. Future work could also include evaluating other classifiers in assigning the levels of intrusion sensitivity and investigating the performance of our model in alert aggregation.

**Acknowledgments.** We thank all anonymous reviewers for their valuable comments in improving this paper.

# References

1. Cai, F., Fugui, T., Yongquan, C., Ming, L., Bing, P.: Grey Theory Based Nodes Risk Assessment in P2P Networks. In: ISPA, pp. 479–483 (2009)
2. Chun, B., Lee, J., Weatherspoon, H., Chun, B.N.: Netbait: A Distributed Worm Detection Service. Technical Report IRB-TR-03-033, Intel Research Berkeley (2003)
3. Duma, C., Karresand, M., Shahmehri, N., Caronni, G.: A Trust-Aware, P2P-Based Overlay for Intrusion Detection. In: DEXA Workshop, pp. 692–697 (2006)
4. Fung, C.J., Baysal, O., Zhang, J., Aib, I., Boutaba, R.: Trust Management for Host-Based Collaborative Intrusion Detection. In: De Turck, F., Kellerer, W., Kormentzas, G. (eds.) DSOM 2008. LNCS, vol. 5273, pp. 109–122. Springer, Heidelberg (2008)
5. Fung, C.J., Zhang, J., Aib, I., Boutaba, R.: Robust and scalable trust management for collaborative intrusion detection. In: Proceedings of the 11th IFIP/IEEE International Conference on Symposium on Integrated Network Management (IM), pp. 33–40 (2009)
6. Fung, C.J., Zhu, Q., Boutaba, R., Basar, T.: Bayesian Decision Aggregation in Collaborative Intrusion Detection Networks. In: NOMS, pp. 349–356 (2010)
7. Ghosh, A.K., Wanken, J., Charron, F.: Detecting Anomalous and Unknown Intrusions Against Programs. In: Proceedings of the 1998 Annual Computer Security Applications Conference (ACSAC), pp. 259–267 (1998)
8. Huebsch, R., Chun, B.N., Hellerstein, J.M., Loo, B.T., Maniatis, P., Roscoe, T., Shenker, S., Stoica, I., Yumerefendi, A.R.: The Architecture of PIER: an Internet-Scale Query Processor. In: Proceedings of the 2005 Conference on Innovative Data Systems Research (CIDR), pp. 28–43 (2005)
9. Janakiraman, R., Zhang, M.: Indra: a peer-to-peer approach to network intrusion detection and prevention. In: WETICE, pp. 226–231 (2003)
10. Li, J., Li, R., Kato, J.: Future Trust Management Framework for Mobile Ad Hoc Networks. IEEE Communications Magazine 46(2), 108–114 (2008)
11. L.Z.,, C.Y.,, B.A.: Towards Scalable and Robust Distributed Intrusion Alert Fusion with Good Load Balancing. In: Proceedings of the 2006 SIGCOMM Workshop on Large-Scale Attack Defense (LSAD), pp. 115–122 (2006)

12. Li, W., Meng, Y., Kwok, L.-F.: Enhancing Trust Evaluation Using Intrusion Sensitivity in Collaborative Intrusion Detection Networks: Feasibility and Challenges. In: Proceedings of the 9th International Conference on Computational Intelligence and Security (CIS), pp. 518–522. IEEE (2013)

13. Meng, Y., Kwok, L.F.: Adaptive False Alarm Filter Using Machine Learning in Intrusion Detection. In: Proceddings of the 6th International Conference on Intelligent Systems and Knowledge Engineering (ISKE), pp. 573–584 (2011)

14. Meng, Y., Kwok, L.-F., Li, W.: Towards Designing Packet Filter with a Trust-Based Approach Using Bayesian Inference in Network Intrusion Detection. In: Keromytis, A.D., Di Pietro, R. (eds.) SecureComm 2012. LNICST, vol. 106, pp. 203–221. Springer, Heidelberg (2013)

15. Papadopoulos, C., Lindell, R., Mehringer, J., Hussain, A., Govindan, R.: COSSACK: Coordinated Suppression of Simultaneous Attacks. In: Proceedings of the 2003 DARPA Information Survivability Conference and Exposition (DISCEX), pp. 94–96 (2003)

16. Porras, P.A., Neumann, P.G.: Emerald: Event Monitoring Enabling Responses to Anomalous Live Disturbances. In: Proceedings of the 20th National Information Systems Security Conference, pp. 353–365 (1997)

17. Qin, Z., Jia, Z., Chen, X.: Fuzzy Dynamic Programming based Trusted Routing Decision in Mobile Ad Hoc Networks. In: Proceedings of the 5th IEEE International Symposium on Embedded Computing (SEC), pp. 180–185 (2008)

18. Quercia, D., Hailes, S., Capra, L.: B-Trust: Bayesian Trust Framework for Pervasive Computing. In: Stølen, K., Winsborough, W.H., Martinelli, F., Massacci, F. (eds.) iTrust 2006. LNCS, vol. 3986, pp. 298–312. Springer, Heidelberg (2006)

19. Roesch, M.: Snort: Lightweight Intrusion Detection for Networks. In: Proceedings of the 13th USENIX Conference on System Administration (LISA), pp. 229–238 (1999)

20. Resnick, P., Kuwabara, K., Zeckhauser, R., Friedman, E.: Reputation systems. Communications of the ACM 43(12), 45–48 (2000)

21. Scarfone, K., Mell, P.: Guide to Intrusion Detection and Prevention Systems (IDPS), pp. 800–894. NIST Special Publication (2007)

22. Snapp, S.R., et al.: DIDS (Distributed Intrusion Detection System) - Motivation, Architecture, and An Early Prototype. In: Proceedings of the 14th National Computer Security Conference, pp. 167–176 (1991)

23. Snort. Homepage (May 2012), http://www.snort.org/

24. Sun, Y.L., Yu, W., Han, Z., Liu, K.: Information Theoretic Framework of Trust Modelling and Evaluation for Ad Hoc Networks. IEEE Journal of Selected Areas in Communications 24(2), 305–317 (2006)

25. Symantec Corp., Internet Security Threat Report, vol. 16 (July 2012), http://www.symantec.com/business/threatreport/index.jsp

26. Tuan, T.A.: A Game-Theoretic Analysis of Trust Management in P2P Systems. In: ICCE, pp. 130–134 (2006)

27. Vigna, G., Kemmerer, R.A.: NetSTAT: a Network-based Intrusion Detection Approach. In: ACSAC, pp. 25–34 (1998)

28. Wu, Y.-S., Foo, B., Mei, Y., Bagchi, S.: Collaborative Intrusion Detection System (CIDS): A Framework for Accurate and Efficient IDS. In: Proceedings of the 2003 Annual Computer Security Applications Conference (ACSAC), pp. 234–244 (2003)

29. Yegneswaran, V., Barford, P., Jha, S.: Global Intrusion Detection in the DOMINO Overlay System. In: Proceedings of the 2004 Network and Distributed System Security Symposium (NDSS), pp. 1–17 (2004)

# Exploiting Trust and Distrust Information to Combat Sybil Attack in Online Social Networks

Huanhuan Zhang, Chang Xu, and Jie Zhang

School of Computer Engineering
Nanyang Technological University, Singapore
zhan0376@e.ntu.edu.sg

**Abstract.** Due to open and anonymous nature, online social networks are particularly vulnerable to the Sybil attack, in which a malicious user can fabricate many dummy identities to attack the systems. Recently, there is a flurry of interests to leverage social network structure for Sybil defense. However, most of graph-based approaches pay little attention to the distrust information, which is an important factor for uncovering more Sybils. In this paper, we propose an unified ranking mechanism by leveraging trust and distrust in social networks against such kind of attacks based on a variant of the PageRank-like model. Specifically, we first use existing topological anti-Sybil algorithms as a subroutine to produce reliable Sybil seeds. To enhance the robustness of these approaches against target attacks, we then also introduce an effective similarity-based graph pruning technique utilizing local structure similarity. Experiments show that our approach outperforms existing competitive methods for Sybil detection in social networks.

**Keywords:** Sybil Attack, Social Networks, Sybil Defense, Trust and Distrust, Transitivity.

## 1 Introduction

Online social networks (e.g. Facebook) have gained great popularity and become an indispensable part of people's life. However, due to their open and anonymous attributes, these systems are particularly vulnerable to the Sybil attack, where adversary can create an unlimited number of fake identities with the intention to subvert the targeted system. According to a report on Facebook in August 2012, there are more than 83 million illegitimate accounts in the social network out of its 955 million active accounts.[1] These undesirable accounts are fabricated for various purposes such as spreading spam or gathering more 'likes' from users to promote products. Similarly, a lot of fake Twitter followers are sold rampantly on e-markets and bought by people to increase popularity or launch underground illegal activities.[2] Besides, malicious users can manipulate Sybils to pollute a

---

[1] http://www.bbc.co.uk/news/technology-19093078
[2] http://www.digitaltrends.com/social-media/
guess-what-twitter-is-still-teeming-with-fake-accounts/

J. Zhou et al. (Eds.): IFIPTM 2014, IFIP AICT 430, pp. 77–92, 2014.

voting mechanism for some reputation systems (e.g. YouTube, Yelp) and thereby outvote honest users [4].

Recently, there is a flurry of interests to leverage social network structure for Sybil defense. Many proposals have been developed that attempt to detect Sybil nodes by utilizing topological features of social networks [2–4, 9, 10]. The basic rationale behind is based on two assumptions: (1) strong trust relationship among nodes, which makes it difficult for Sybil nodes to establish many social connections with honest nodes, even if they can easily fabricate substantial Sybil identities and build arbitrary topology networks among themselves. As a result, Sybil region connects to the main network via relatively few links, which results in *quotient cut* between non-Sybil and Sybil regions. (2) honest region is *fast mixing*, in which random walks from a non-Sybil node can quickly reach a stationary distribution after $O(log(n))$ steps compared to Sybil nodes.

However, most of the existing graph-based anti-Sybil mechanisms are vulnerable to *target attack* [10], in which an adversary has prior knowledge about the location of *honest seeds*, which are utilized for identity authentication, and launches Sybil attack by substantially compromising these honest entities as well as their nearby nodes. As a result, many dummy nodes seem to be honest due to direct connection with honest seeds, rendering the structure-based schemes ineffective. In addition, for existing Sybil defense mechanisms to work effectively, it is required that non-Sybil nodes in real social networks are well mixed to avoid sparse internal cuts. Nevertheless, this assumption does not conform to reality, since mixing time is substantially larger than anticipated [7]. As a result, these graph-based solutions cannot produce desirable detection accuracy by only relying on the inherent trust underlying social networks and limited topological features.

To address these problems, we propose an unified ranking mechanism by leveraging trust and distrust information in social networks to combat the Sybil attack. Specifically, we propose a simple but effective method to produce reliable Sybil seeds combining with current social network-based anti-Sybil schemes. Moreover, in order to enhance those topological designs against *target attacks*, an effective graph pruning strategy is introduced by exploiting local structure similarity between neighboring nodes. Finally, a ranking mechanism based on a variant of the PageRank-like algorithm is presented to combine trust and distrust together to output trustworthiness of nodes in the social network. Nodes with less trustworthiness scores are more likely to be Sybils. Experiments on three real data sets are conducted to verify the effectiveness of our methods. The results indicate that our mechanism can outperform existing state-of-the-art anti-Sybil approaches. Our method thus shades light on exploiting trust and distrust information for building an effective Sybil defense mechanism.

## 2   Related Work

The Sybil attack has attracted more and more attention in the community since it was introduced in 2002 [1]. Traditional solutions to combat the Sybil attack rely on trusted identities provided by a certify authority. However, such centralized mechanisms suffer from the challenge of finding trusted identities due to the open membership in distributed systems.

In recent years, there is a surge of interests to leverage social network structures for Sybil defense. SybilGuard [2] and SybilLimit [3] are the first two decentralized protocols to exploit topological features to detect Sybil nodes. In SybilGuard, each node performs random route of the length $\Theta(\sqrt{n}logn)$, and a suspect is accepted if its random route intersects with a verifier's. When the number of attack edges is bounded to $O(\sqrt{n}/logn)$, SybilGuard accepts at most $\Theta(\sqrt{n}logn)$ Sybil nodes per attack edge with a high probability. SybilLimit improves upon SybilGuard's bound by using multiple walks, which allows it to accept at most $O(logn)$ Sybil nodes per attack edge. However, both of them suffer from high false rate. SybilInfer [12] adopts the Bayesian inference technique that assigns to each node its probability of being Sybil, but suffers from high computational cost. Viswanath et al. [6] explain the rationale behind graph-based anti-Sybil schemes from the perspective of *graph partitioning*. They state that existing community detection algorithms can be utilized to detect Sybils. However, it is not easy to choose a reasonable metric to achieve better detection accuracy. And such community-based algorithms are vulnerable to targeted Sybil attacks. In addition, Mohaisen et al. point out that mixing time is much larger than what is anticipated in Sybil defense schemes, implying that social networks are generally not fast mixing [7]. Such a finding renders ineffective all defense schemes that are based on the mixing property. Cao et al. [10] develop a Sybil ranking mechanism which distinguishes Sybil from non-Sybil nodes based on their relative trustworthiness. SybilRank is validated in a real social graph-Tuenti to be effective and efficient against the Sybil attack. Since it depends on the *honest seeds* to propagate trust among network, this approach also suffers from target attacks.

In addition, some proposals are developed to incorporate distrust information in social graphs to mitigate the Sybil attack. SumUp [4] is an anti-Sybil approach designed for a distributed voting system. It leverages the social network among users to limit the number of fake votes collected from Sybil identities to $O(1)$ per attack edge. This design utilizes negative feedback to further diminish the voting capability of attackers and accumulates less fake votes. SybilDefender [9] proposes a Sybil community detection algorithm to detect the Sybil group surrounding a Sybil seed. However, no theoretical or empirical analysis is provided to guarantee that such a seed is actually a Sybil node, which is one of the main concerns of our work. Another recent work using the distrust factor is presented by Chao et al. [11]. They take the insight into the topological structure of criminal accounts' social relationship on Twitter and provide an inference algorithm to detect criminal accounts by propagating malicious scores from seeds (i.e., a set of known fake accounts). But their work is unable to incorporate known honest seeds and cannot differentiate non-Sybil from Sybil nodes. The purpose of our work is to leverage trust and distrust information in social networks against the Sybil attack.

## 3   Problem Formulation

### 3.1   System and Threat Model

A social network is modeled as a graph $G = (V, E)$, where each node in $V$ represents a user in the network and each edge in $E$ represents trust relationship between users. We use $n = |V|$ to denote the total number of users and $m = |E|$ to denote the total number of trust edges. The degree of a node $v_i \in V$ is $deg(v_i)$.

In the attacking scenario, there may be one or more attackers in a social network. All of these participants are controlled by an adversary. To launch the Sybil attack, an adversary fabricates multiple fake identities, which disguise as real users in the system to participate in illegal activities. However, they can only establish few *attack edges* with honest nodes. We divide the whole graph into *non-Sybil* and *Sybil* regions illustrated in Fig. 1. The trusted identity and Sybil seed will be used in the unified ranking mechanism.

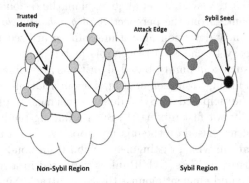

**Fig. 1.** Illustration of online social network under Sybil attack

### 3.2   Assumptions

Our design is based on previous graph-based Sybil defense mechanisms that satisfy the following basic assumptions:

- There exist one or more known honest nodes. These nodes are utilized to break the symmetry and considered as *honest seeds* to implement identity verification.
- Honest region is *fast mixing*, in which random walks from a benign node can quickly reach a stationary distribution after $O(log(n))$ steps, compared to random walks from Sybil nodes. Although this characteristic is not so strictly satisfied in the real world, we assume nodes in non-Sybil regions are more tightly connected compared with Sybil nodes.
- There is a limited number of attack edges. For the inherent trust relationship among nodes, an adversary can create an arbitrary size of Sybil group but establish a limited number of connections with honest nodes. Thus, it results in disproportionately *small cut* between non-Sybil and Sybil regions, which is an obvious sign for detecting Sybils.

# 4    Similarity-Based Graph Pruning

Most of the topological Sybil defense mechanisms rely on a basic assumption that one or more honest nodes are known in advance. These nodes (also known as *honest seeds*) are utilized for identity verification and partitioning the entire network into the non-Sybil and Sybil regions. However, once honest seeds are compromised by a set of disruptive nodes, these topological systems would under-perform [10]. Indeed, such attacks may be easily accomplished by an adversary through establishing as many social connections as possible with high degree honest nodes. This type of attacks is called target seeding attack or simply *target attack*. To the best of our knowledge, no work has been proposed in the literature to solve this problem.

In this paper, we present a group pruning technique that effectively reduces the impact from target attacks by enforcing that the number of attack edges around honest seeds is few. This avoids the situation where a large number of Sybil nodes are accepted due to nearby honest seeds, hence evades Sybil detection. This strategy leverages local structural similarity underlying social networks. Intuitively, corresponding to the fast mixing and inherent trust assumptions, we speculate that the similarity between benign nodes and honest seeds is much higher compared to the similarity between benign nodes and Sybil nodes. Thus, by eliminating edges with low-similarity value ($w_{ij} \leq T_s$), where $w_{ij}$ is the similarity of nodes $i$ and $j$ and $T_s$ is the threshold to determine whether one edge should be trimmed, the number of attack edges is likely to be lower than that of the original network. Different structural similarity metrics in social networks have been proposed for measuring the strength of social links and predicting future interactions, such as cosine similarity, Jaccard similarity, and etc. [8]. In a social network, it is difficult for an adversary to simultaneously trick an honest node and its neighbors into trusting it. Hence, we choose the *number of common friends* as a metric to measure the structure similarity in the eliminating process.

In our method, pruning is firstly performed in local regions around honest seeds. Its goal is to prevent honest seeds and their nearby nodes in the network from being tricked by a set of disruptive nodes. On the other hand, pruning should not have much impact on honest users. This is partially determined by the size of the pruned region, which is denoted by $T_p$, the maximum diameter between honest seeds and the pruned nodes. The pruned network shall satisfy the following two requirements: (1) It should minimize attack edges nearby *honest seeds*. (2) It shall also maximize the number of honest nodes because some benevolent nodes may be disconnected from the entire graph. We can balance the trade-off by adjusting two parameters-pruning diameter $T_p$ and similarity threshold $T_s$. Specific parameter choices will be examined in the experiments. For those disconnected identities during pruning process, we initially mark them as Sybil accounts. These nodes will be re-visited in the following ranking phase. The detailed pruning process is described in Algorithm 1.

---

**Algorithm 1.** Graph Pruning()

---

**Input:** $G$ : Graph $G = (V, E)$; $H_0$ : Set of honest seeds;
         $T_s$ : Similarity threshold; $T_p$ : Pruned diameter

**Output:** $G_{prune}$: Pruned graph

1   Consider all the edge weight in graph $G$ to be 1 ;
2   $V_{ST_p}$ is the set of nodes within the distance from honest seeds less than $(T_p + 1)$;
3   Initially, $V_{ST_p} = \{H_0\}$ ;
4   **for** *all vertex* $v \in V$ **do**
5      |   **if** $Distance(v, H_0) < (T_p + 1)$ **then**
6      |    |   Add $v$ to the $V_{ST_p}$ ;

7   $E_{ST_p} = \{(u, v) \mid u \in V_{ST_p}$ or $v \in V_{ST_p}\}$, set of edges connecting nodes in $V_{ST_p}$ ;
8   Let $G_{ST_p} = (V_{ST_p}, E_{ST_p})$;
9   $G_{static} = G - G_{ST_p}$, the undesired pruned graph;
10   $G_{static} = (V_{static}, E_{static})$, where $V_{static} = V - V_{ST_p}$ and $E_{static} = E - E_{ST_p}$;
11   Define $W$ as the new weight matrix of graph $G_{ST_p}$;
12   **for** *each pair vertice* $(u', v') \in G_{ST_p}$ **do**
13      |   Count their number of common friends $numf$ and set $W_{u',v'} = numf$ ;

14   Let $G'' = G_{ST_p}$ and $V_{disconnet} = \emptyset$ ;
15   **for** *each pair vertice* $(u', v') \in G_{ST_p}$ **do**
16      |   **if** $W_{u',v'} \leq T_s$ **then**
17      |    |   Delete edge $(u', v')$ from $G''$ ;
18      |    |   **if** $u'$ *or* $v'$ *is isolated* **then**
19      |    |    |   Delete the node from $G''$ ;
20      |    |    |   Add the node to $V_{disconnet}$ ;

21   Finally, $G_{prune} = G_{static} \cup G''$ ;
22   return $G_{prune}$.

---

# 5   Unified Ranking Mechanism

Our unified ranking mechanism attempts to detect Sybil nodes by taking the following three steps: (1) producing a set of well-connected Sybil seeds by the Sybil seed selection algorithm; (2) propagating trust and distrust scores from a set of known honest and Sybil seeds among the entire social network according to the closeness of *social relationships*. (3) integrating the trust and distrust scores into an unified trustworthiness for each node, ranking nodes according to their trustworthiness and filtering out Sybil nodes based on the ranked list. The detailed and formal description as well as the insight of the unified ranking mechanism are given in the subsequent sections.

## 5.1   Sybil Seed Selection Algorithm

Most of graph-based Sybil defense mechanisms are developed only relying on the inherent trust underlying social networks, while ignore the distrust information.

Studies conducted on Twitter reveal that criminal accounts, even those hidden deeply within complicated structure, can be detected by propagating malicious scores from a set of known criminal accounts, indicating that distrust plays an important role in unveiling malicious nodes [11]. However, few work is provided to leverage trust and distrust information to combat Sybil attacks. SybilDefender [9] introduces a Sybil community detection algorithm to identify Sybil groups from the perspective of a given Sybil seed. Such seed is randomly selected from those nodes marked as Sybils in their identification algorithm. However, this selection strategy suffers from some drawbacks. First, no theoretical or empirical analysis is provided to guarantee that each identified Sybil node is actually Sybil. Second, if the Sybil seed connects with honest users via *attack edges*, the Sybil community detection algorithm will mistakenly classify many benign nodes as Sybils. In this paper, we present a Sybil seed selection algorithm to produce reliable Sybil seeds, which can be utilized in our ranking mechanism to effectively distinguish non-Sybil from Sybil nodes.

Our method focuses on looking for connected Sybil nodes by exploiting the link dependency property among social networks. Such property indicates linked or neighboring nodes tend to have the same class labels and can be used to improve the detection accuracy. Intuitively, corresponding to the basic assumptions-*fast mixing* and *small cut*, we observe that honest users are more likely to connect with honest nodes rather than Sybils. Similarly, most Sybil nodes mainly establish social connections with their colluding entities. For well-performed Sybil detectors, most of nodes can be accurately marked despite those ambiguous nodes either located on the border between non-Sybil and Sybil regions or sparsely connected to the main network. Thus, there exists different size of clusters in which each node has the same label. Based on this insight, we can start from a Sybil seed and expand it by adding its neighboring nodes which are also identified as Sybils.

Additionally, SybilRank [10] is validated to be an effective and efficient algorithm for detecting Sybil nodes among existing anti-Sybil schemes. In this paper, we treat this algorithm as a subroutine to seek for Sybil seeds. Algorithm 2 illustrates the detailed selection procedure for SybilRank. Let $Ir$ denote the trust vector returned by the SybilRank scheme. $N(v_i)$ is the set of neighbors for node $v_i$ in the network. Sybil seed selection is performed as follows: first, all the nodes in the network are classified into two categories: non-Sybil ( labelled as 1) and Sybil ( labelled as 0) by setting a cut-off threshold $\eta$. $I(.)$ is the indicator function that takes value 1 if the trust score of node $v_i$ is larger than $\eta$ and 0 otherwise. For each Sybil node, we calculate its spamicity value according to its neighbors' class labels. The *spamicity* metric is defined as follows:

$$SP(v_i) = \frac{\Sigma_{j \in N(v_i)} |I(j, \eta)|}{|N(v_i)|} \tag{1}$$

Then, we search for the nodes whose $SP$ is 1. Besides, the human evaluation procedure is introduced to further filter out those misclassified honest nodes. For normalization, the human evaluation can be formalized as a binary Oracle function defined in Equation 2. Subsequently, from the *Suspend* set, we seek for tightly connected Sybil groups as Sybil seed candidates.

$$O(v_i) = \begin{cases} 0 & \text{if } v_i \text{ is Sybil} \\ 1 & \text{if } v_i \text{ is Honest} \end{cases} \tag{2}$$

This selection process repeats until $SeedCandidate \neq \phi$. Finally, the sets *SeedCandidate* are returned, which can be treated as Sybil seeds.

---

**Algorithm 2.** Sybil Seed Selection()

---

**Input**: **G**: Social Network; Ir: Trust Vector outputted by SybilRank.
**Output**: *SeedCandidate*: set of Sybil Seeds
1  $[\mathbf{r}_\nabla, Index] = SORT(Ir)$;
2  $\theta = 0.01 * k, \quad k = 1$ ;
3  $\eta = \mathbf{r}_\nabla(n * \theta)$ ;
4  $I(v_i, \eta) = \begin{cases} 1 & \text{if } \mathbf{r}_\nabla(v_i) > \eta \\ 0 & \text{if } \mathbf{r}_\nabla(v_i) \leq \eta \end{cases}$ ;
5  $m = \Sigma_{v_i}\{v_i | I(v_i, \eta) == 0\}$;
6  **for** $i \leftarrow 1$ **to** $m$ **do**
7  $\quad$ Source=Index(i);
8  $\quad$ Calculate $SP$ for each node using Equation 1;
9  $Suspend^* = |\{v_i | SP(v_i) == 1\}|$;
10 $Suspend = \{v_i | O(v_i) == 0, v_i \in Suspend^*\}$;
11 $s = |Suspend|$;
12 $SeedCandidate = \phi$;
13 **for** $k \leftarrow 1$ **to** $s$ **do**
14 $\quad$ add $Suspend(k)$ to $SeedCandidate$ ;
15 $\quad$ **for** $p \leftarrow 1$ **to** $s$ **do**
16 $\quad\quad$ **if** $Suspend(p) \in N(SeedCandidate)$;
17 $\quad\quad$ add $Suspend(p)$ to $SeedCandidate$;
18 **if** $SeedCandidate == \phi$ **then**
19 $\quad$ $k = k + 1$ ;
20 $\quad$ $\theta = 0.01 * k$ ;
21 $\quad$ repeat step 3-17;
22 Return $SeedCandidate$.

---

## 5.2 Unified Ranking Algorithm

To leverage trust and distrust in social networks, we present our unified ranking mechanism based on a variant of the PageRank-like model–*Personalized PageRank* algorithm, which is an essential technique for ranking and prediction [14]. Our ranking algorithm consists of two main components. The first component is to respectively propagate benign and malicious scores from a seed set of known honest and Sybil seeds among the entire network and the second component is to integrate the trust and distrust values into an unified trustworthiness for each node, which can be used to effectively discriminate non-Sybil from Sybil nodes.

**Propagation Phase.** Given the topological structure of the social network and a set of labeled nodes, we can propagate trust/distrust scores from these seeds to their neighboring nodes according to their closeness of social relationships. The propagation process can be modelled in the following formula:

$$r(v_i) = \alpha * \frac{\Sigma_{j \in N(v_i)} r(j)}{|N(j)|} + (1 - \alpha) * d(v_i) \tag{3}$$

where $r(v_i)$ denotes the score value of node $v_i$. $\alpha$ is the jump probability. Generally, $\alpha = 0.85$ [14]. $d$ is the normalized score vector for the seed set. After trust and distrust propagation, two opposite scores are obtained for each node. In order to distinguish them, we *negatively* bias the initial scores towards the Sybil seeds. Thus, each node is assigned a negative value after distrust propagation. And the corresponding initial vector $d$ is defined in Equation 4, where $SS$ denotes the set of Sybil seeds.

$$d(v_i) = \begin{cases} \dfrac{-1}{|SS|} & \text{if } v_i \in SS \\ 0 & \text{otherwise} \end{cases} \tag{4}$$

**Integration Phase.** In propagation phase, each node is assigned two scores, namely trust value and distrust value. The following questions are: can they solely be used to differentiate non-Sybil from Sybil nodes? If not, how can we combine them together such that the integrated value can identify Sybil nodes with lower false rate? In this paper, we utilize a simple but effective weighted scheme to obtain the final trustworthiness shown in Equation 5. Empirical analysis in the following section demonstrates that such combination model can greatly filter out most of Sybil nodes from rankings.

$$Total(v_i) = a * TR(v_i) + (1 - a) * DTR(v_i) \tag{5}$$

where $TR(v_i)$ and $DTR(v_i)$ respectively denote trust and distrust scores for node $v_i$. The parameter $a$ is used to measure the weights of trust and distrust values for the overall trustworthiness.

# 6   Experimental Analysis

## 6.1   Experimental Design

**Datasets and Attack Model.** We use three data sets from popular online social networks to stimulate the honest region. Table 1 summarizes the properties of these datasets. These social graphs have been commonly utilized to evaluate existing anti-Sybil schemes[3].

In addition, two kinds of topological structures, *random graph* (ER model) and *scale-free* (PA model), are used to simulate attack regions. For each type

---

[3] http://snap.stanford.edu/data/

of attack, we first generate $m$ nodes to be *Sybil supporters*, which serve for compromising honest region by establishing social connections with them. Then these dummy supporters introduce $\psi$ additional Sybil nodes to form *ER* or *scale-free* topology among themselves with average degree of 10. The number of attack edges connecting non-Sybil and Sybil regions is $g$. In our simulations, we have $m = 100$, $g = 200$. The experiment is repeated 100 times with different attack scenarios. In addition, 50 honest nodes are picked from the top 500 non-Sybil nodes that have the highest degree to perform as verifiers or trust sources.

**Table 1.** Dataset of social graph used in experiments

| OSN | Node | Edge | Average Degree | CC |
|---|---|---|---|---|
| Facebook | 4,039 | 88,234 | 19.88 | 0.221 |
| AstroPh | 18,772 | 396,160 | 22 | 0.3158 |
| HepTh | 9,877 | 51,971 | 5.67 | 0.2734 |

**Evaluation Metrics.** Three metrics are used to exhibit the effectiveness of our proposed techniques: number of accepted Sybil nodes (*false negative*), number of rejected benign nodes (*false positive*) and AUC curve. AUC represents the area under the Receive Operating Characteristic (ROC) curve and is a widely used metric for evaluating the quality of ranking within networks [10]. The AUC ranges between 0 and 1, with larger numbers indicating that a randomly selected honest node is ranked higher than a random Sybil node.

**Comparative Sybil Defense Methods.** Two most recent and effective graph-based Sybil detection mechanisms are evaluated, namely SybilRank and ACL. SybilRank [10] is a ranking mechanism that sorts nodes in a network according to their trustworthiness. Nodes with low trust values are likely to be Sybils. ACL [14] is originally proposed to detect a local community in a social graph and it is based on the normalized version of Personalized PageRank algorithm. Alvisi *et al.* proved that such an approach can be utilized to detect Sybil nodes. Both SybilRank and ACL employ the power iteration technique, but SybilRank terminates the iteration process after only $O(log(n))$ steps. In addition, we choose the SybilRank algorithm to seek for Sybil seeds due to its better performance.

## 6.2 Performance of Similarity-Based Graph Pruning Technique

Based on the three real-world datasets including Facebook, AstroPh and HepTh described in Table 1, we conduct experiments to investigate the performance of our graph pruning strategy against target attacks. To infiltrate into the entire graph, we let Sybil supporters intentionally connect to the 1000 benign nodes which are the closest to the honest seeds. The number of additional Sybil nodes $\psi$ varies from 100 to 1000. Then, SybilRank and ACL are implemented separately for Sybil classification on original graph and pruned graphs. Fig. 2 depicts

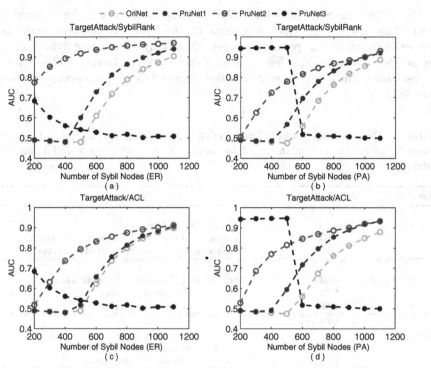

**Fig. 2.** The performance comparison of SybilRank and ACL methods when graph pruning technique is applied with respect to the size of Sybil region under target attacks. OriNet denotes the original network, PrunNet1, PrunNet2, PrunNet3 correspond to pruned graphs by setting $T_p = 1$, $T_p = 2$, $T_p = 3$ respectively.

the improved results on Facebook graph. The performance of pruning strategy implemented on other social graphs yield similar results. Fig. 2(a) and (b) show the detection results of SybilRank for ER and PA attack models, and (c) and (d) correspond evaluation result returned by ACL. Specifically, we have $T_s = 1$ for our experiments. This appears to be reasonable since it is hard for an adversary to fool a real user and his/her friends together.

As illustrated, both SybilRank and ACL schemes can be enhanced through graph pruning against target attacks, especially when the threshold $T_p = 2$. As we expected, no benign node is disconnected from the network in this case. However, when increasing $T_p$ to 3, the AUC curve for Sybil defense exhibits instability and becomes even worse than the original graph. By checking the false positive metric, we find that for both attack scenarios at least 800 benign nodes are isolated from the social graph. Furthermore, as the size of ER Sybil region increases, the AUC curves of both detection schemes monotonous decrease. We speculate the reason behind this is that although attack capacity is reduced due to elimination, many Sybil nodes can take priority to be accepted over disconnected honest nodes. But for PA Sybil region the curve keeps higher and falls sharply when number of Sybil nodes is 600. This phenomenon is attributed to the underlying Sybil structure. Since a large fraction of nodes in scale-free model have low degree which constitute the *heavy-tail* in the power-law node degree distribution, the pruning process will heavily affect these Sybil nodes to be isolated for larger $T_p$. Hence, despite those isolated benign nodes, most of honest nodes can be accurately classified. In the following experiments, we set threshold $T_p = 2$.

**Table 2.** The Sybil seeds selected in Algorithm 2 for different compromised network, where $\theta$ denotes the cut-off threshold to classify all the nodes to non-Sybil and Sybil categories

| Num.Sybil | Threshold $\theta$ | Sybil Seed Sets |
|---|---|---|
| | 0.02 | 0 |
| $No.Sybil = 200$ | 0.03 | 2 two-seeds |
| | 0.04 | 3 two-seeds, 2 three-seeds, 4-seeds cluster |
| | 0.05 | 2 two-seeds, 3 three-seeds, 40-seeds cluster |
| | 0.02 | 0 |
| $No.Sybil = 300$ | 0.03 | 2 two-seeds, 1 three-seeds, 7-seeds cluster |
| | 0.04 | 78-seeds cluster |
| | 0.05 | 97-seeds cluster |
| | 0.02 | 2 two-seeds |
| $No.Sybil = 400$ | 0.03 | 2 two-seeds |
| | 0.04 | 1 two-seeds, 102-seeds cluster |
| | 0.05 | 209-seeds cluster |
| | 0.02 | 0 |
| $No.Sybil = 500$ | 0.03 | 0 |
| | 0.04 | 4 two-seeds, 2 three-seeds, 10-seeds cluster,16-seeds cluster |
| | 0.05 | 1 two-seeds, 210-seeds cluster |
| | 0.02 | 0 |
| $No.Sybil = 600$ | 0.03 | 0 |
| | 0.04 | 5 two-seeds |
| | 0.05 | 230-seeds cluster |

## 6.3   Performance of Sybil Selection Algorithm

The experimental results illustrated in Fig. 2 have validated the effectiveness of our pruning strategies against target attacks. In this experiment, we combine the SybilRank algorithm with graph pruning technique to seek for reliable Sybil seeds. We treat the trust vector output by SybilRank as an input value for Sybil seed selection algorithm. By adjusting the threshold $\theta$ to be used in partitioning the whole graph into non-Sybil and Sybil regions, we obtain the following Sybil seed selection results for different attack scenarios shown in Table 2. From all these results, we can see that our method can catch tightly connected Sybil seed, whereas the size is very small by setting the cut-off threshold $\theta$ to be a lower value. With the increment of $\theta$, it is more likely to catch relatively large Sybil clusters which occupy large coverage of Sybil community. However, larger $\theta$ implies more nodes should be manually inspected which is not applicable in real case. Since we are attempting to cope with the Sybil attack problem, the performance of using these Sybil seeds to detect Sybils is our major concern. In the following experiment, we verify that the factor of Sybil seeds' size has a smaller impact on the defense performance.

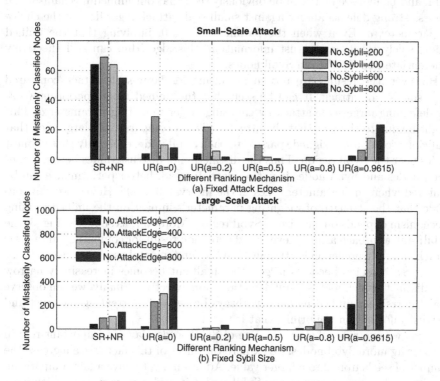

**Fig. 3.** The performance of unified ranking mechanism by varying weighting parameter $a$. $SR + NR$ means the SybilRank scheme without pruning step and $UR$ is the unified ranking scheme.

## 6.4 Evaluation of Unified Ranking Mechanism

In this section, we investigate the effects of two components in our unified ranking mechanism, namely weighting parameter $a$ and the size of Sybil seeds. In addition, to have a fair comparison, we simulate another type of attack scenarios. To simulate the Sybil region, we let Sybil supporters connect to non-Sybil region starting from 200 attack edges. Meanwhile, Sybil supporters introduce 5000 additional Sybil nodes and establish an ER topology amongst themselves. Then we gradually increase the number of attack edges to a larger number 800. This attack type is called *large-scale attack*. Correspondingly, the attack type utilized in Sections 6.2 and 6.3 refers to *small-scale attack*.

We first check the effectiveness of our unified ranking mechanism by varying the weighting parameter $a$. By performing the Sybil seed selection algorithm, we obtain two Sybil seeds for each attack scenario. The detection results are illustrated in Fig. 3, where the value 0.9615 denotes the ratio between size of Sybil and benign seeds. It can be obviously seen that our unified mechanism can possess strong defense ability against small-scale attack regardless of the choice of parameter $a$. Even when the parameter $a = 0$, implying that the unified model solely relies on distrust information, this algorithm can still effectively differentiate non-Sybil from Sybil nodes.

However, the results are not so promising for large-scale attack compared with small-scale attack. It can be seen that the unified model performs worse for defending large-scale attack by choosing larger weighting parameter $a$. This might be due to the fact that the attack region is comparatively large such that malicious scores are assigned sparsely to each Sybil node, especially those honest nodes near the Sybil region. Thus the distinction of distrust values between non-Sybil nodes and Sybil nodes is not so clear. Instead, better performance can be achieved when the parameter $a$ lies in the interval $[0.2, 0.8]$. Hence, we can conclude that the strength of weighting parameter's impact on the unified ranking mechanism depends on the size of Sybil region. Moreover, as shown in Fig. 3, the SybilRank approach also achieves good detection result for combating large-scale attack. This phenomenon is attributed to the fundamental assumption-*small cut*. As the Sybil region becomes larger, the small cut becomes increasingly narrow and distinct, which makes Sybil detection more effective. Finally, we can observe that the resilient unified model can always be derived by treating the trust and distrust information uniformly, that is to set $a = 0.5$.

Next, we examine whether the size of Sybil seeds plays an important role in uncovering more Sybil nodes. To explore the effect of this factor, we increase the number of seeds from 2 to a larger value. Additionally, to have a fair comparison, we randomly select another two Sybil nodes in order to verify the usefulness of our selected Sybil seeds. By setting the parameter $a = 0.5$, we obtain the following detection results using the unified mechanism shown in Fig. 4.

First, we observe that the unified mechanism can achieve higher detection accuracy by incorporating large Sybil seed cluster. Despite this case, the detection accuracy does not appear to heavily fluctuate with the increment of number of Sybil seeds. We speculate the reason is also due to the *small cut* assumption, which is the basis for designing anti-Sybil mechanisms. That is, due to the limited number of *attack edges* connecting non-Sybil and Sybil regions, the Sybil community surrounding Sybil seeds will accumulate a large fraction of malicious scores regardless how many malicious nodes propagate distrust value initially. During the distrust propagation process, most of Sybil nodes can be penalized and assigned more malicious scores than honest users. It indicates that the performance of the unified model is not so sensitive to the size of Sybil seeds. Second, the model performs worse when incorporating randomly chosen Sybil nodes, which demonstrates that the Sybil seeds selected in Algorithm 2 are much reliable and useful in uncovering more Sybil nodes.

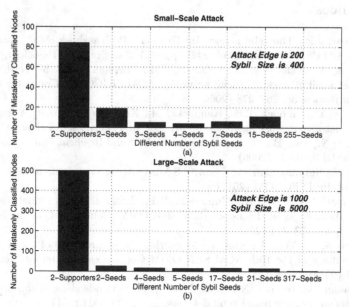

**Fig. 4.** The performance of unified ranking mechanism by varying the size of Sybil seeds. 2-Supporters are the randomly selected Sybil seeds. k-Seeds represents a Sybil cluster consisting of k connected Sybil nodes.

# 7   Conclusion

In this paper, we focus on leveraging both trust and distrust information to defend against Sybil attacks in social networks. First, a graph pruning strategy is introduced to diminish the attack ability near honest seeds by utilizing local structure similarity, leading to the improved robustness of Sybil defense mechanisms against target attacks. Moreover, we provide a Sybil seed selection algorithm to produce reliable Sybil seeds combining with current anti-Sybil schemes. Then, an unified ranking mechanism based on a variant of PageRank-like algorithm is proposed to combine trust and distrust information together to output integrated trustworthiness for nodes in a network. These trustworthiness values can be utilized to effectively distinguish Sybil from non-Sybil nodes. Experimental results demonstrate that our unified ranking mechanism can achieve better performance and outperform state-of-the-art Sybil defense approaches.

**Acknowledgement.** This work is supported by the MoE AcRF Tier 2 Grant M4020110.020 and the ACI Seed Funding M4080962.C90 awarded to Dr. Jie Zhang.

# References

1. Douceur, J.R.: The sybil attack. In: Druschel, P., Kaashoek, M.F., Rowstron, A. (eds.) IPTPS 2002. LNCS, vol. 2429, pp. 251–260. Springer, Heidelberg (2002)
2. Haifeng, Y., Kaminsky, M., Gibbons, P.B., Flaxman, A.: Sybilguard: defending against sybil attacks via social networks. ACM SIGCOMM Computer Communication Review 36, 267–278 (2006)
3. Haifeng, Y., Gibbons, P.B., Kaminsky, M., Xiao, F.: Sybillimit: A near-optimal social network defense against sybil attacks. In: Security and Privacy (2008)
4. Tran, D.N., Min, B., Li, J., Subramanian, L.: Sybil-Resilient Online Content Voting. NSDI 9, 15–28 (2009)
5. Tran, N., Subramanian, L., Chow, S.S.M.: Optimal sybil-resilient node admission control. In: INFOCOM (2011)
6. Viswanath, B., Post, A., Gummadi, K.P., Mislove, A.: An analysis of social network-based sybil defenses. ACM SIGCOMM Computer Communication Review 41(4), 363–374 (2011)
7. Mohaisen, A., Yun, A., Kim, Y.: Measuring the mixing time of social graphs. In: Proceedings of the 10th ACM SIGCOMM Conference on Internet Measurement. ACM (2010)
8. Mohaisen, A., Hopper, N., Kim, Y.: Keep your friends close: Incorporating trust into social network-based sybil defenses. In: INFOCOM (2011)
9. Wei, W., Xu, F., Tan, C.C., Li, Q.: Sybildefender: Defend against sybil attacks in large social networks. In: INFOCOM (2012)
10. Qiang, C., Sirivianos, M., Yang, X., Pregueiro, T.: Aiding the detection of fake accounts in large scale social online services. In: NSDI (2012)
11. Chao, Y., Harkreader, R., Zhang, J., Shin, S., Gu, G.: Analyzing spammers' social networks for fun and profit: a case study of cyber criminal ecosystem on twitter. In: Proceedings of the 21st International Conference on World Wide Web, pp. 71–80. ACM (2012)
12. Danezis, G., Mittal, P.: SybilInfer: Detecting Sybil Nodes using Social Networks. In: NDSS (2009)
13. Ghosh, S., Viswanath, B., Kooti, F., Sharma, N.K., Korlam, G., Benevenuto, F., Ganguly, N., Gummadi, K.P.: Understanding and combating link farming in the twitter social network. In: Proceedings of the 21st International Conference on World Wide Web. ACM (2012)
14. Berkhin, P.: A survey on pagerank computing. Internet Mathematics 2(1), 73–120 (2005)

# Anomaly Detection for Mobile Device Comfort

Mehmet Vefa Bicakci[1], Babak Esfandiari[1], and Stephen Marsh[2]

[1] Department of Systems and Computer Engineering,
Carleton University, Ottawa, Ontario, Canada
mehmetvefabicakci@cmail.carleton.ca,
babak@sce.carleton.ca
[2] Faculty of Business and Information Technology,
University of Ontario Institute of Technology,
Oshawa, Ontario, Canada
stephen.marsh@uoit.ca

**Abstract.** As part of the Device Comfort paradigm, we envision a mobile device which, armed with the information made available by its sensors, is able to recognize whether it is being used by its owner or whether its owner is using the mobile device in an "unusual" manner. To this end, we conjecture that the use of a mobile device follows diurnal patterns and introduce a method for the detection of such anomalies in the use of a mobile device. We evaluate the accuracy of our method with two publicly available data sets and show its feasibility on two mobile devices.

**Keywords:** Anomaly Detection, Device Comfort, Mobile Device, Soft Security.

## 1 Introduction

Mobile devices (such as smartphones and tablets) have become popular convergent platforms that can be used for many tasks from banking to photography to e-mail. Modern mobile devices also come with a large number of sensors including accelerometers, gyroscopes, magnetometers, proximity and ambient light sensors, Global Positioning System (GPS) sensors, and Bluetooth, WiFi and cellular connectivity.

The data that can be garnered from the aforementioned sensors and the nature of the task that the user is carrying out on the mobile device can be used by the mobile device to have a pretty accurate picture of the contextual and behavioural patterns of the mobile device user.

We envision a mobile device that can get to know its owner. Such a mobile device would be able to detect if it is being used by a user other than its owner or whether the owner is behaving in an "unusual" manner based on the behavioural and contextual patterns that the owner established with the mobile device. We believe that the detection of such "anomalies" in the context and user behaviour are valuable for protecting the mobile device, the data on the mobile device, and last but not least, the owner of the mobile device.

J. Zhou et al. (Eds.): IFIPTM 2014, IFIP AICT 430, pp. 93–108, 2014.

Device Comfort [1] is an application of computational trust to (*soft*) mobile device security aiming to provide the aforementioned protection and more by making use of behavioural biometrics, contextual information and policy to let the mobile device reason about its owner's behaviour and the context. Via its contextually determined security posture, or "comfort level," and the policy elements, the mobile device can warn its owner against performing potentially dangerous tasks and, if necessary according to the policy, prevent such tasks from being performed. As a result, Device Comfort aims to help the user understand and reflect upon the potentially harmful consequences of the (possibly unusual) behaviours he/she performs with a comfort-enabled computing device.

As the last two paragraphs hint, the *threat model* considered by Device Comfort (and hence this paper) is related to soft security and human aspects of computing. As part of its threat model, Device Comfort aims to defend a personal computing device (and its user) against "unusual" and/or "inappropriate" use of the device, the definition of which is an area of research. User behaviour resulting from distractions or inattention, which has the potential to compromise security, is also considered as a possible threat. Last but not least, the Device Comfort threat model also considers physical intrusions and theft.

We believe anomaly detection is one of the building blocks of Device Comfort, where an "anomaly score" can be one of the sources of information that are used to determine the comfort level of a mobile device. As such, in this work we focus on performing anomaly detection using the behavioural and contextual patterns that a mobile device user establishes with his/her mobile device for the enablement of Device Comfort.[1]

We conjecture that there exists a 24-hour cycle in the behavioural and contextual information that can be sensed via the sensors and the operating system of a mobile device, and we propose to exploit such diurnal patterns for anomaly detection purposes. Our approach consists of partitioning each day's data into *time slices* that have fixed and equal length and comparing the time slices of "today" to those of the past days.

We evaluated the accuracy of our approach using two data sets containing mobile device usage data, and to show the feasibility of our approach on actual mobile devices, we deployed our software on two mobile devices.

We find that with the first data set cellular location, phone call, and Bluetooth discovery features contribute more to the accuracy of our method compared to text message contacts and the names of the applications started by the user. With the second data set, we find that the called phone numbers and Bluetooth discovery results make a greater contribution to overall accuracy compared to WiFi discovery results and text message contacts.

As part of investigating the feasibility of deployment, we find that performing anomaly detection on actual mobile devices is feasible even with relatively aggressive anomaly detection parameters, where the computational performance is not affected from the user's point of view, whereas the battery life is affected negatively.

---

[1] In particular, the policy elements which determine *what* happens when an anomaly is detected are left for future work.

The rest of this paper is organized as follows: In the next section, we review work related to anomaly detection on (mobile and non-mobile) personal computing devices, the section following which introduces and describes our methodology. Afterwards, we describe our evaluation strategy and present our results. The paper ends with a concluding section which includes a number of future work items as well.

## 2    Related Work

Anomaly detection for mobile (and non-mobile) personal computing devices is an area in which numerous proposals have been made. We summarize our review of related work in four subsections, the first of which briefly discusses the algorithms and features used by the authors, followed by a subsection noting the data sets used by the authors. The third subsection reports on the deployment of the related proposals. In the fourth subsection, we briefly compare our approach to those of the related proposals.

### 2.1    Methodologies and Used Features

Shi et al. [2] utilize a mobile phone user's behavioural patterns in the form of GPS-based location, phone call, text message exchange and web browsing history. The user's location is spatio-temporally clustered using the Gaussian Mixture Model clustering algorithm. For each feature other than the location, probabilistic models conditioned on the time of day are built, where, given the time of day and the number of hours since the last "good" (i.e., "observed before") event and the number of "bad" events in the past 24 hours, an authentication score is computed. The feature values specific to certain times of the day are not taken advantage of. For example, the approach does not consider whether the *specific* phone number being called is usually called in the morning or the afternoon, but only considers that it is a "good" phone number that had been called before.

Li [3] uses the names of started applications, location (as inferred from cellular towers), and phone call and text messaging histories for anomaly detection, which is performed by considering how prevalent feature values fused with the cellular location are in the training data. Li does not consider the time of day as a feature, noting in [3] that it contributes negatively to the overall performance.

Yazji et al. in [4,5] propose to detect anomalies in the spatio-temporal patterns of a mobile phone user via two methods. The first method involves the summarization of the distribution of user's presence to produce a spatio-temporal matrix, whereas the second method exploits the Markov properties of trajectories. Both methods are very specific to spatio-temporal analysis.

Branscomb [6] investigates whether the number of seconds of a mobile phone user's time spent in each application category can be used to verify the identity of the user. Temporal patterns are modelled via a binary feature reflecting whether the applications are being used on a weekday or during a weekend.

Crawford [7] verifies the identity of the mobile phone user with keystroke and voice dynamics, the feature vectors describing which are classified using Naive Bayes, Decision Tree and k-Nearest Neighbours classifiers. Zhu et al. [8] propose to classify the motions of the mobile phone user (as measured with accelerometers and gyroscopes of a mobile phone) using k-Means clustering and an $n$-gram language model. Crawford and Zhu et al. do not consider the time of day as a feature, and it may not be sensible to do so as the used features may not vary according to the time of the day.

In [9], Yazji et al. target laptops and perform anomaly detection via the use of k-Means clustering, where the timestamped file-system and network accesses made by the user in every five-minute-long time quanta are classified as normal or anomalous.

In contrast, in [10] Salem et al. propose to detect "masquerader" attackers by focussing on their search-related file-system access patterns on desktop computers, where accesses made at every two-minute-long time quanta are summarized and input to the one-class SVM algorithm for classification. The authors do not use the time of day as a feature.

## 2.2  Data Sets

We observe that only Li [3] and Yazji et al. (in [4,5]) use data sets available to the research community. Li uses the Reality Mining data set [11], and Yazji et al. use the Reality Mining and GeoLife [12] data sets.

To the best of our knowledge, the *RUU* (*Are You You?*) data set collected by Salem et al. for the evaluation of their proposal in [10] had been published in the past, but is no longer available as of this writing.

## 2.3  Deployment

Mobile devices have limited computational power and battery life. As a result, we believe that it is important to verify the deployment feasibility of an anomaly detection method targeted for mobile devices.

In the three proposals by Yazji et al., a server works hand-in-hand with the mobile device to perform computation- and energy-intensive tasks. This is in contrast to the other proposals we have reviewed, which perform anomaly detection locally on the mobile device.

We notice that only Zhu et al. and Branscomb have fully deployable solutions which implement data collection and anomaly detection functionalities.[2] Crawford, Salem et al., Shi et al., and Yazji et al. (in [9]) only deploy the data collection logic, whereas Li and Yazji et al. (in [4,5]) do not have a deployable implementation.

---

[2] We should note that Zhu et al. evaluate their approach in a deployed setting indicating the completeness of their implementation. According to [6, p. 30], Branscomb has a "proof-of-concept app."

## 2.4    Discussion

Our approach, as will be introduced in the next section, makes use of a time-quantum-based summarization method similar to some of the related proposals, and we use the time of day as a feature while taking into account the feature values that are specific to certain times of the day.

In contrast to most related proposals, we evaluate our method using *two* data sets that are available to the research community – the Reality Mining [11] and the Social Evolution [13] data sets.

Finally, we deploy our approach on two mobile devices to determine the feasibility of performing anomaly detection on an actual mobile platform.

## 3    Methodology

We envision that a comfort-enabled mobile device would retrain itself every midnight based on the past $N$ days' behavioural and contextual data, and classify the data encountered on the day following the midnight as anomalous or normal based on the training data.

According to Chandola et al. [14], this scheme corresponds to a semi-supervised anomaly detection approach, where a one-class machine learning algorithm builds a model based on only the normal data instances and is tested against normal and anomalous data instances.

### 3.1    Data Model

To model data, we use a "summarization" method, where we divide each day into equal- and fixed-length *time slices* of configurable size. For example, if we choose four-hour-long time slices, then we will have six time slices per day of mobile device usage, each of which summarizes the behavioural and contextual patterns in the use of a mobile device.

Our summarization method consists of instantiating per time slice a data structure, each of which contains the following pieces of information: (1) Time of day at which the time slice begins, (2) time of day at which the time slice ends, and (3) a set of hash tables, one per feature type that is being summarized.

Each of the aforementioned hash tables is populated as follows: the hash table is keyed with the feature value, and the keys of the hash table point to values indicating how many times the feature value in question had been observed in the time slice to which the hash table belongs.[3]

For example, for a hash table for the text message exchange feature, the hash table would be keyed with tuples in the following form "$(phoneNumber, direction)$", and the hash table values corresponding to the keys would be the *number of times* for which text messages had been exchanged with the phone number in the given direction – incoming or outgoing.

---

[3] For the cellular location (cellular area and cell identifier) feature, we record the number of minutes spent in the particular location instead.

Using such a data model, we aim to find diurnal patterns in a mobile device user's behaviour, where if the time slice $ts$ belonging to "today" does not match any time slices belonging to the past $N$ days with room for some temporal error, then we can consider today's time slice $ts$ to be anomalous – the mobile phone may have been compromised physically, or the user may have been behaving "unusually."

## 3.2   Anomaly Detection Method

To detect anomalies, we use a variant of the k-Nearest Neighbours algorithm adapted to anomaly detection. The use of a distance-based anomaly detection algorithm allows us to use custom distance functions with complex data structures.

The overall strategy of the k-Nearest Neighbours-based anomaly detection algorithm we use was introduced by Eskin et al. in [15]. The algorithm consists of finding in the training data set the $k$ nearest neighbours of each test data instance $d_{test}$, and for each $d_{test}$, summing the distances of $d_{test}$ to its nearest neighbours to obtain an anomaly score. The anomaly score of each test data instance $d_{test}$ is then compared to an operator-set threshold value to make a prediction: if a distance sum is greater than the threshold value, then anomalous, otherwise, normal. Using this logic, only data points with very far neighbours or not a lot of near neighbours are predicted as anomalous by the algorithm.

**Distance Function.** To compute the distance between two time slices we use the distance function in the following equation:

$$distance_{timeSlice}(ts_1, ts_2) =$$

$$\begin{cases} MAX\_DISTANCE & \text{if } |t^{ts_1} - t^{ts_2}| > DELTA \\[2em] \dfrac{\sum\limits_{i \in FNE} distance_f(f_i^{ts_1}, f_i^{ts_2})}{|FNE|} & \text{otherwise} \end{cases}$$

$$(1)$$

where $t^{ts_x}$ represents the time of day at which time slice $ts_x$ begins, and $f_i^{ts_x}$ represents the $i$th feature of time slice $ts_x$, and $FNE$ represents the set of feature types which are non-empty in both time slices.

The constant $DELTA$ allows us to configure the "leniency" in the finding of diurnal patterns with respect to the time of day. As can be seen in Equation 1, if the two time slices $ts_1$ and $ts_2$ start at times of the day that are more than $DELTA$ hours apart, we assign $MAX\_DISTANCE$ as the distance between the two time slices in order to never consider these two time slices as near neighbours.

If $ts_1$ and $ts_2$ start at relatively similar times of the day according to the $DELTA$ constant, then we use the $distance_f$ function to compute the pairwise distance of each feature (hash table) in the two time slices, with the restriction that we only consider the feature types which are not empty in both time slices. The average of the computed distances is assigned as the distance between the two time slices in question, which corresponds to equally weighting each feature type.[4]

**Distances between Features.** The distances between the values of each feature type are obtained using the Jaccard distance metric, which is implemented in the function named *distance_f* referenced in Equation 1.

To compute the Jaccard distance, we "convert" the feature hash tables into sets by considering only the keys in the hash tables, which correspond to, for example, the phone numbers which had been called in the time slice to which the feature belongs. Afterwards, the Jaccard distance is computed as follows: $1 - \frac{|A \cap B|}{|A \cup B|}$, where $A$ and $B$ correspond to the sets obtained by hash table conversion process.

With the Jaccard distance we ignore the values in the feature hash tables which indicate the number of times each feature value had been observed in a time slice. We have also experimented with the Binary Weighted Cosine (BWC) distance [16] which takes into account the number of observations by making use of the cosine similarity. In our experiments, the BWC distance produced results that are slightly worse than those obtained with the Jaccard distance. This phenomenon can be explained with the fact that the BWC distance makes use of cosine similarity in addition to Jaccard similarity, the former of which considers two feature vectors (i.e. the features in two time slices) similar based on their relative orientations in Euclidean space.[5] We conjecture that in our experiments the number of times where taking into account frequencies of feature values improves the classification results is less than the number of times where taking frequencies into account degrades the results. As a result of the above reasoning we use the Jaccard distance in this paper.

**Empty Feature Values and Empty Time Slices.** One open problem is the handling of features for which values are not available in both time slices, which we call "empty feature values." While one can consider two empty hash tables as "equal" with a distance of zero, we choose to ignore feature types corresponding to empty hash tables in both time slices based on the empirical observation that doing so enables us to obtain more accurate results.

Another open problem is the handling of "empty time slices," which occur when the mobile device is switched on but no behavioural/contextual data is available – i.e. no phone calls are made, no location updates are observed, and no Bluetooth or WiFi discovery results are available.

While the existence of an empty time slice at a time of the day which is usually very "busy" in terms of the collected features may indicate an anomaly,

---

[4] We should note that a custom weighted sum scheme is certainly possible, but is left for future work.

[5] For example, two time slices in which two phone numbers are called with the same *ratio* of frequencies would be parallel in Euclidean space, and therefore very similar according to cosine similarity.

we choose to ignore empty time slices because we cannot reliably verify the identity of a mobile device user if there is no data available.[6]

# 4    Evaluation

## 4.1    Data Sets

We evaluate our approach using the Reality Mining and the Social Evolution data sets.

The Reality Mining data set [11] is the result of a study carried out in the 2004–2005 academic year, and includes data belonging to roughly 100 participants – faculty, staff and students of MIT, where for each participant the names of started applications, Bluetooth discovery results, location (as inferred from cellular towers), and phone call and text message exchange histories were recorded along with timestamps.

The Social Evolution data set [13] was collected during the 2008–2009 academic year and includes the features collected from the mobile phones of roughly 80 participants in a dormitory in MIT: Bluetooth and WiFi discovery results, and phone call and text message histories.

The Reality Mining data set was used by Li [3] and Yazji et al. [4,5] for evaluation purposes as well.

## 4.2    Feature Extraction

From the Reality Mining data set, we extract the following features: timestamps, names of applications started, the results of Bluetooth discoveries, from which we extract the name and Bluetooth address of the discovered devices, cellular tower information (cellular tower area and cell identifiers), and the numbers with which phone calls and text messages were exchanged. For text messaging, we extract the direction (incoming vs. outgoing) of text messages as well.

From the Social Evolution data set, we extract the following features: timestamps, the results of Bluetooth discoveries, where we use the identifier of the detected study participant as the "fake" Bluetooth address and name of a detected device,[7] the results of WiFi discoveries, and phone call and text message exchange histories.

## 4.3    Evaluation Method

The data sets that we use for evaluation lack anomalous mobile device usage data. As a result of this limitation, we use a "1-versus-rest" evaluation scheme,

---

[6] Furthermore, the existence of empty time slices may indicate the need for more features in order to discriminate the empty time slices from others.

[7] We use fake Bluetooth addresses and names, because only the identifiers of the *participants* of the study were detected and recorded in Bluetooth discovery results in the Social Evolution data set.

where for each data set, one at a time, we consider each participant of the data set as the user/owner of a mobile device, and consider all other participants as "attackers" or, in other words, sources of anomalous usage data. While this evaluation scheme may not be realistic in the simulation of anomalous usage, it has been used in a large number of related proposals: [2,3,4,5,6,7].

To evaluate our method, we use the following strategy: We instantiate time slices from the data of all of the data set participants, and we consider the data belonging to the current mobile device "owner" data set participant $User_A$ as a stream of days composed of *normal* time slices. We start by training an anomaly detection model on the first $D$ days' time slices belonging to $User_A$. Afterwards, we use the time slices on $(D+1)$th day of $User_A$'s data as *normal* testing data, via which we obtain true negatives and false positives. Finally, as *anomalous* testing data, we take a sample of the time slices belonging to the *other* participants of the data set $User_x$, where $x \in \{B, C, D, E, ...\}$. These anomalous time slices let us obtain true positives and false negatives.[8]

Once the testing for this evaluation "iteration" is complete, we shift the training period to the right by one day so that the training period is composed of the time slices from the days 2 to $(D + 1)$ belonging to $User_A$. The time slices on day $(D + 2)$ are considered as *normal* time slices for testing, and another sample of time slices belonging to the other participants is taken and considered as *anomalous* testing data.

This procedure is continued until we reach the end of $User_A$ data "stream," after which we repeat the same procedure where we consider $User_B$ as the mobile device owner, and all other users (including $User_A$) as attackers/sources of anomalous usage.

### 4.4 Evaluation Metric

Because of the class imbalance inherent in our evaluation method, where anomalous time slices are more numerous than normal time slices, we use the Area Under Curve (AUC) summary metric as the performance evaluation metric. AUC is a measure of the correctness of the machine learning algorithm under evaluation, where an AUC value of 0.5 indicates an algorithm that cannot make predictions better than random guessing, whereas an AUC value of 1.0 corresponds to perfect prediction performance. As a result, the higher the AUC value, the better the performance of an algorithm. Unlike accuracy, the AUC metric is not affected by class imbalance.

In order to obtain an AUC value for one evaluation "iteration," we vary the anomaly score threshold to obtain all possible combinations of false positive and true positive rates corresponding to the performance of the anomaly detection algorithm's performance. After plotting the true positive rate against the false positive rate, we compute the area under the resulting Receiver Operating Characteristic curve to obtain an AUC value for one evaluation "iteration."

---

[8] We have verified that the manner in which we sample anomalous time slices does not introduce more than ±2.5 AUC percentage points.

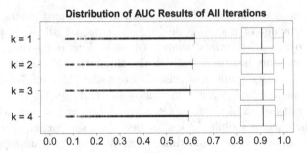

**Fig. 1.** Performance of k-NN with the Reality Mining Data Set (Each boxplot summarizes 12431 iterations)

### 4.5  Classification Performance

We present our results in the form of boxplots, which depict the variation of AUC values across all evaluation "iterations," each of which correspond to the performance of an anomaly detection model on a particular test day for a particular data set participant.

**Parameter Selection with k-NN.** With the aim of selecting the most appropriate value of $k$, we experiment with the k-Nearest Neighbours algorithm on the Reality Mining data.

In these experiments, we use all of the features extracted from the Reality Mining data set, and set the time slice length and leniency equal to 4 hours and set the training period length equal to 21 days.

Our results can be seen in Figure 1, from which one can see that varying $k$ does not appear to affect the performance of k-NN. Based on these observations, we continue our experiments with $k$ set to 1.

**Results with Individual Features.** In this set of experiments, we enable each feature in each data set one by one to determine how much each feature contributes to the overall performance of our approach. We use k-NN with $k$ set to 1, and we set the time slice length and leniency equal to 4 hours and set the training period length equal to 21 days.

We present our results in Figures 2a and 2b, from which we observe that with the Reality Mining data set the cellular location, phone call history and Bluetooth discovery features perform better than the other features, and with the Social Evolution data set the phone call history and Bluetooth discovery perform better than the text messaging history and WiFi discovery features.

As can be seen in Figures 2a and 2b, when we make use of all of the features in each data set, the performance is not better than the performance obtained with the best feature on its own.

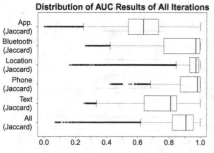
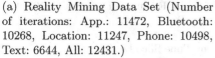
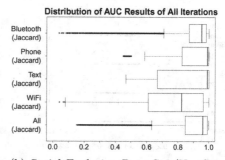

(a) Reality Mining Data Set (Number of iterations: App.: 11472, Bluetooth: 10268, Location: 11247, Phone: 10498, Text: 6644, All: 12431.)

(b) Social Evolution Data Set (Number of iterations: Bluetooth: 7630, Phone: 8878, Text: 3144, WiFi: 4286, All: 12197.)

**Fig. 2.** Performance of Individual Features

This observation motivated us to experiment with "match score level fusion," [17] where we trained one anomaly detection model per feature type and combined the anomaly scores of individual features of each test time slice to obtain one anomaly score per test time slice. We do not report our results with match score level fusion because this fusion method does not bring improvements over the method we have described in this paper.

**Results with Different Time Slice Lengths.** In the above-mentioned experiments, we used a time slice length of 4 hours, which means that the anomaly detection delay of a mobile device can be up to 4 hours. We would like to reduce the time slice length in order to reduce the anomaly detection delay, but while doing so we also risk an increase in the time complexity of our method because shorter time slices translate to more time slices. The experiments in this section quantify the effects of reducing the time slice length from 4 hours to one half of an hour.

In these experiments, we use k-NN with $k$ set to 1. We use all of the features, and we set the time slice leniency equal to 4 hours and set the training period length equal to 21 days.[9]

We present our results in Figures 3a and 3b, where we can observe that reducing the time slice length from 4 hours to one half of an hour reduces the median *and* the spread of the AUC values resulting from the experiments with the Reality Mining data set, whereas with the Social Evolution data set the AUC value spread increases, and the median decreases. Despite these observations, we cannot conclusively state whether the reduction in the time slice length affects the performance of our method.

---

[9] We should also note that we use aggressive sampling with these experiments in order to keep the experiment run-times reasonable, which reduces the significance of the conclusions we can draw from the results of these experiments.

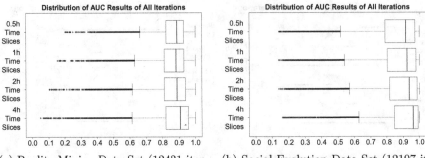

(a) Reality Mining Data Set (12431 iterations).

(b) Social Evolution Data Set (12197 iterations).

**Fig. 3.** Performance of Different Time Slice Lengths

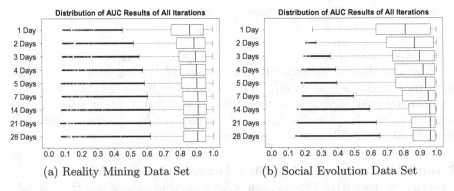

(a) Reality Mining Data Set

(b) Social Evolution Data Set

**Fig. 4.** Performance of Different Training Period Lengths (Each boxplot summarizes approximately 12000 iterations)

**Results with Different Training Period Lengths.** Finally, we vary the training period length between 1 day and 28 days to observe the effect of the training period length on the accuracy of our approach. We would like to reduce the training period length as much as possible to reduce the time complexity of our approach, whereas reducing the training period length too much may degrade the accuracy of our method.

In these experiments, we use k-NN with $k$ set to 1. We use all of the features, and we set the time slice length and leniency equal to 4 hours.

We present the results with the Reality Mining data set in Figure 4a, and those with the Social Evolution data set in Figure 4b. As can be seen in both figures, decreasing the training period length reduces the overall accuracy of our method, where the AUC value median decreases, and the AUC value spread increases. We can also observe that with the Social Evolution data set, the reduction in the overall accuracy is more visually apparent.

**Variance in Classification Performance.** As can be seen in Figures 2a, 2b, 3a, 3b, 4a and 4b, the boxplots have relatively large spreads and long whiskers indicating high variances in our results. After plotting for each data set partici- pant a scatter plot of the AUC values corresponding to each iteration/test day, we observe the following: (1) A number of data set participants' identity cannot reliably be verified via their mobile device usage patterns. These participants suffer from a large number of false positives (i.e. normal time slices predicted as anomalous) which highly vary the results across evaluation iterations. (2) Other data set participants whose mobile device usage patterns can be more reliably used for verification also suffer from occasional false positives.

### 4.6   Mobile Device Feasibility Study

To show the feasibility of our method on mobile devices, we deploy our imple- mentation on two actual smartphones. We should note that our intention with this deployment experiment is not the testing of our method's accuracy in a deployed setting.

**Deployment Overview.** As the target deployment platforms, we choose Nokia N900, a smartphone from the year 2009, which has modest specifications in comparison to modern smartphones, and Samsung Galaxy Nexus, a more recent and more powerful smartphone from the year 2011.

We use Python programming language to implement and deploy our method.[10] Because Python is an interpreted programming language, we believe we incur a performance hit in the form of higher CPU utilization for computation-intensive tasks.

**Experimental Set-Up.** For this experiment, our software collects Bluetooth and WiFi discovery results every 25 and 30 seconds, respectively. We set the time slice length equal to one minute, and as a result perform a k-Nearest Neighbours- based anomaly detection run every minute against the training data, which is chosen to be the data from the past five days.

Note that the parameters of the aforementioned experimental set-up involve a departure from the parameters we use for the evaluation of our method's accuracy. We choose aggressive settings (such as frequent wireless discoveries and frequent anomaly detection iterations) to obtain a worst-case scenario in terms of the user experience and resource utilization.

We evaluate the deployment qualitatively via a user experience study and quantitatively via resource utilization measurements. For the former, we report our findings resulting from the primary author's use of each of the target mobile

---

[10] The N900's Linux-based operating system, Maemo, natively supports Python, whereas we resort to the Scripting Layer for Android (SL4A) to run our software on the Galaxy Nexus, which ships with Google's Linux-based Android operating system for mobile devices.

devices for at least one week, during which the mobile device in question was used as a personal music player and to make occasional phone calls. For the latter, we report CPU, Random Access Memory (RAM) and persistent (Flash) memory utilization and the battery life.

**Results.** Throughout the qualitative user experience study, from a computational performance point of view, we could not notice that our software had been running in the background. For example, we did not experience any interruptions in phone calls or music playback on either deployment platform, even though we could observe the CPU (via a "desktop" applet on the N900) utilization peak as anomaly detection runs were being performed every minute.

From an overall performance point of view, however, our software did have negative effects: On both deployed platforms, the battery life was affected negatively, and we needed to recharge the battery more frequently compared to what was needed without our anomaly detection software.

In quantitative terms, each anomaly detection run causes a maximum CPU utilization period lasting 6 to 7 seconds on the N900 and 2 to 3 seconds on the Galaxy Nexus. Memory usage, on both platforms, is between 75 and 80 MegaBytes with five days of training data loaded in memory. SQLite3 databases containing approximately 40 days of data use approximately 95 MegaBytes of persistent (Flash) memory.

Finally, battery life on the N900 is approximately 15–16 hours, whereas with the Galaxy Nexus the battery life is approximately 23–24 hours.

## 5   Conclusion

To conclude, in this work we use a time slice model to summarize contextual and behavioural information that can be obtained from some of the sensors found on modern smartphones and perform anomaly detection using a variant of the k-Nearest Neighbours algorithm.

We evaluate the accuracy of our method with the Reality Mining and the Social Evolution data sets. We find that location, phone call and Bluetooth discovery features to perform better than the other features of the Reality Mining data set, and that with the Social Evolution data set, phone call and Bluetooth discovery features to perform better than the other features.

We cannot conclusively state that the reduction of the time slice length from 4 hours to half an hour affects the accuracy of our method, and we verify that the length of the training period is positively correlated with accuracy.

Finally, we find that the impact of our method to a mobile device user's experience is acceptable in terms of computational performance, while we believe that the battery life can be improved by increasing the time slice length and the feature collection periods at the cost of increased anomaly detection latency and possibly decreased accuracy.

As part of future work, we would like to evaluate the *accuracy* of our method on actual mobile devices, possibly with different time slice lengths. One of the preconditions to the evaluation of accuracy in deployed settings is the automatic calculation of the anomaly score threshold at run-time, for example by fixing the false positive rate to a certain percentage using the training data, as Yazji et al. do so in [4,5,9].

Personalized feature weighting when the mobile device retrains itself (which we envision would be performed while the device is being charged) is another future work direction.

Dissimilarity vector-based classification would allow us to adapt conventional machine learning algorithms – such as one-class SVMs or k-Means clustering – to our method and could potentially provide better accuracy.

Other data sets containing mobile device usage data, such as the Nodobo data set [18], can be used to further evaluate our method.

Last but not least, we would like to integrate our method with an implementation of the Device Comfort framework, where the anomaly scores produced by our method could be used, in part, to produce a trust (or comfort) level for the mobile device. Based on its comfort level, the user interface of a computing device may change its behaviour, for which there have been a number of proposals, which include but are not limited to those made by Storer et al. [19] and Murayama et al. [20].

**Acknowledgements.** This work was funded by the Communications Research Centre, Canada.

# References

1. Marsh, S., Briggs, P., El-Khatib, K., Esfandiari, B., Stewart, J.A.: Defining and Investigating Device Comfort. Journal of Information Processing 19, 231–252 (2011)
2. Shi, E., Niu, Y., Jakobsson, M., Chow, R.: Implicit authentication through learning user behavior. In: Burmester, M., Tsudik, G., Magliveras, S., Ilić, I. (eds.) ISC 2010. LNCS, vol. 6531, pp. 99–113. Springer, Heidelberg (2011)
3. Li, F.: Behaviour Profiling for Mobile Devices. PhD thesis, University of Plymouth, Plymouth, Devon, Great Britain, United Kingdom (2012)
4. Yazji, S., Dick, R.P., Scheuermann, P., Trajcevski, G.: Protecting private data on mobile systems based on spatio-temporal analysis. In: Benavente-Peces, C., Filipe, J. (eds.) PECCS, pp. 114–123. SciTePress (2011)
5. Yazji, S., Scheuermann, P., Dick, R., Trajcevski, G., Jin, R.: Efficient location aware intrusion detection to protect mobile devices. Personal and Ubiquitous Computing 18(1), 143–162 (2014)
6. Branscomb, A.S.: Behaviorally identifying smartphone users. Master's thesis, North Carolina State University, Raleigh, NC (2013)
7. Crawford, H.A.: A framework for continuous, transparent authentication on mobile devices. PhD thesis, University of Glasgow, Glasgow, Scotland, United Kingdom (2012)
8. Zhu, J., Wu, P., Wang, X., Zhang, J.: Sensec: Mobile security through passive sensing. In: 2013 International Conference on Computing, Networking and Communications (ICNC), pp. 1128–1133 (January 2013)

9. Yazji, S., Chen, X., Dick, R., Scheuermann, P.: Implicit user re-authentication for mobile devices. In: Zhang, D., Portmann, M., Tan, A.-H., Indulska, J. (eds.) UIC 2009. LNCS, vol. 5585, pp. 325–339. Springer, Heidelberg (2009)
10. Salem, M., Stolfo, S.: Modeling user search behavior for masquerade detection. In: Sommer, R., Balzarotti, D., Maier, G. (eds.) RAID 2011. LNCS, vol. 6961, pp. 181–200. Springer, Heidelberg (2011)
11. Eagle, N., Pentland, A.S., Lazer, D.: Inferring friendship network structure by using mobile phone data. Proceedings of the National Academy of Sciences (2009)
12. Zheng, Y., Xie, X., Ma, W.Y.: Geolife: A collaborative social networking service among user, location and trajectory. IEEE Data Engineering Bulletin 33(2), 32–40 (2010)
13. Madan, A., Cebrian, M., Moturu, S., Farrahi, K., Pentland, A.: Sensing the 'health state' of a community. IEEE Pervasive Computing 11(4), 36–45 (2012)
14. Chandola, V., Banerjee, A., Kumar, V.: Anomaly detection: A survey. ACM Comput. Surv. 41(3), 15:1–15:58 (2009)
15. Eskin, E., Arnold, A., Prerau, M., Portnoy, L., Stolfo, S.: A geometric framework for unsupervised anomaly detection. In: Barbar, D., Jajodia, S. (eds.) Applications of Data Mining in Computer Security. Advances in Information Security, vol. 6, pp. 77–101. Springer US (2002)
16. Rawat, S.: Efficient Data Mining Algorithms for Intrusion Detection. PhD thesis, University of Hyderabad, Hyderabad, India (2005)
17. Ross, A., Jain, A.: Information fusion in biometrics. Pattern Recognition Letters 24(13), 2115–2125 (2003); In: Bigun, J., Smeraldi, F. (eds.) AVBPA 2001. LNCS, vol. 2091, pp. 354–359. Springer, Heidelberg (2001)
18. McDiarmid, A., Bell, S., Irvine, J., Banford, J.: Nodobo: Detailed mobile phone usage dataset (2011) (unpublished), http://www.nodobo.com
19. Storer, T., Marsh, S., Noel, S., Esfandiari, B., El-Khatib, K., Briggs, P., Renaud, K., Bicakci, M.V.: Encouraging second thoughts: Obstructive user interfaces for raising security awareness. In: 2013 Eleventh Annual International Conference on Privacy, Security and Trust (PST), pp. 366–368 (July 2013)
20. Murayama, Y., Fujihara, Y., Saito, Y., Nishioka, D.: Usability issues in security. In: Christianson, B., Malcolm, J., Stajano, F., Anderson, J. (eds.) Security Protocols 2012. LNCS, vol. 7622, pp. 161–171. Springer, Heidelberg (2012)

# Improving the Exchange of Lessons Learned in Security Incident Reports: Case Studies in the Privacy of Electronic Patient Records

Ying He, Chris Johnson, Yu Lyu, and Arniyati Ahmad

School of Computing Science, University of Glasgow, UK
yingh@dcs.gla.ac.uk, christopher.johnson@glasgow.ac.uk,
{y.luy.1,a.ahmad.1}@research.gla.ac.uk

**Abstract.** The increasing use of Electronic Health Records has been mirrored by a similar rise in the number of security incidents where confidential information has inadvertently been disclosed to third parties. These problems have been compounded by an apparent inability to learn from previous violations; similar security incidents have been observed across Europe, North America and Asia. This paper presents the results of an empirical study that evaluates the utility and usability of conventional text-based security incident reports with a graphical formalism based on the Goal Structuring Notation. The two methods were compared in term of the users' ability to identify a number of lessons learned from investigations into previous incidents involving the disclosure of healthcare records. These lessons included both the causes of the incident but also the participants' ability to understand the reasons why particular recommendations were proposed as ways of avoiding future violations. Even using a relatively small sample, we were able to obtain statistically significant differences between the two approaches. The study showed that the graphical approach resulted in higher accuracy in terms of number of correct answers generated by participants. However, subjective feedback raised further questions about the usability of both approaches as the readers of security incident reports try to interpret the lessons that can increase the security of patient data.

**Keywords:** Lessons Learned, Security Incident, Electronic Patient Record, Generic Security Template, Empirical Study.

## 1 Introduction

According to Symantec, the healthcare accounted for 42% in the total number of attacks on electronic information systems in 2012 [1]. At 36% in 2013, healthcare continues to be the sector responsible for the largest percentage of disclosed data breaches by industry [2]. Almost identical breaches have occurred across Europe, North America and Asia [3]. Learning from the incident enables the organisation to extract meaningful information from incidents, and use this information to improve security management systems [4]. Effective communication mechanism

J. Zhou et al. (Eds.): IFIPTM 2014, IFIP AICT 430, pp. 109–124, 2014.

is needed to synthesis the information from the incident into the security incident management system so as to prevent a similar incident.

Popular communication mechanisms include formal reports, less formal meetings, newsletters, emails, as well as presentations to management [4]. However, the detailed incident reports that are produced in the post-incident activity [5] have not been given enough attention. Those reports contain comprehensive information, which is typically classified into two types, business impact and remediation information [5]. Business impact information involves how the incident is affecting the organisation in terms of mission impact, financial impact, etc. For example, "The missing external hard drive is believed to contain numerous research-related files containing personally identifiable information and/or individually identifiable health information for over 250,000 veterans, and information obtained from the Centres for Medicare & Medicaid Services (CMS), Department of Health and Human Services (HHS), on over 1.3 million medical providers"[6], Remediation information information mainly refers to the suggested remediation actions, plans, procedures, and lessons learned. For example, "We recommend that the Assistant Secretary for Information and Technology revise VA Directive 6601 to require the use of encryption, or an otherwise effective tool, to properly protect personally identifiable information and other sensitive data stored on removable storage devices when used within VA."[6].

As for a purpose of sharing, it is suggested to avoid sharing business impact information with outside organisations unless there is a clear value proposition or formal reporting requirements. When sharing information with peers and partner organisations, incident response teams should focus on exchanging remediation information [5]. The remediation information information reported describes (1) the security issues, e.g. "The position sensitivity level for the IT Specialist was inaccurately designated as moderate risk, which was inconsistent with his programmer privileges and resulted in a less extensive background investigation", (2) the security objectives violated during this process, e.g. "Position Sensitivity Level Assessments were Not Adequately Performed", and (3) the recommendations, e.g. "We recommend that the Under Secretary for Health direct the Medical Centre Director to re-evaluate and correct position sensitivity levels and associated background investigations for positions at the Birmingham VAMC" [6]. Those granular information are inter-related, however, they are scattered documented in a pure textual based report that makes it difficult for the readers to identify the relationships among them. This issue has been compounded by the lengthy security incident report, which is usually around hundred of pages [6]. The stakeholders responsible for protecting patient data lack the time and the motivation to spend the many hours needed to read and digest existing reports. This creates significant problems within the wider scope of security management systems; it can be difficult to accurately assess the likelihood or consequences of future attacks when managers are unaware of previous incidents.

Graphical techniques can address some of these limitations. The Generic Security Template (G.S.T.) has been developed [3, 7] to help readers understand the lessons learned from previous security incidents. In particular, it extends the

Goal Structuring Notations (GSN) [8] to provide an overview of previous data breaches. The intention is to map out the security objectives, security issues and recommendations that are embedded in the many pages of text that are used in conventional reports. More information on the GSN and the G.S.T. is provided in section III. Fig. 1 provides an excerpt from one of these diagrams. It is based on a report into the disclosure of personal information about 250,000 veterans and over 1.3 million medical providers by the US Veterans Affairs Administration (VA) [6]. This incident report provides the case study that is used throughout this paper. The leaf nodes in this diagram are used to gather together the recommendations that were intended to avoid future incidents. The internal nodes are used to show how each of these findings supports higher level goals and sub-goals intended to ensure that systems meet an acceptable level of security, defined in terms of the US Government's Federal Information System Controls Audit Manual (FISCAM) [9]. Further information about the graphical technique is provided in [3, 7, 10]. The use of graphical overviews is intended to make it easier to identify recommendations that can be transferred from a previous incident to prevent similar breaches from occurring in other organisations.

Previous work has shown that GSN can be used to map common lessons from data breaches in healthcare organisations in healthcare organisations in both the United States and in China [3]. Although these incidents occurred in very different contexts, the security concerns and the consequences for patient confidentiality show remarkable similarities. This previous work provided initial case studies but did not, present empirical support for the benefits of using graphical representations compared to text-based reports of security incidents. This paper, therefore, presents a controlled experiment to investigate whether graphical approaches can be used to augment conventional, text-based documents. The remainder of the paper is structured as the following, section 2 reviews the related work, section 3 briefly introduces the G.S.T., section 4 outlines the experiment design, section 5 presents the experiment procedure, section 6 prepares data to analyse the results, section 7 analyses the results, and section 8 summarises the paper.

## 2   Related Work

There is a natural reluctance to share details of previous security breaches - reports may inspire new attacks or publicize vulnerabilities. However, a growing number of regulatory agencies now provide detailed reports that are intended to help avoid any recurrence of previous failures. Security management systems have also been introduced into many healthcare organisations to ensure previous security incidents inform threat and risk assessments [11]. Improving situation awareness, in particular about security breaches, help persuade end users of the importance of existing policies and procedures. There are further benefits from the wider dissemination of incident reports. Security engineers can learn important lessons about the analysis, containment, eradication, and recovery from previous attacks.

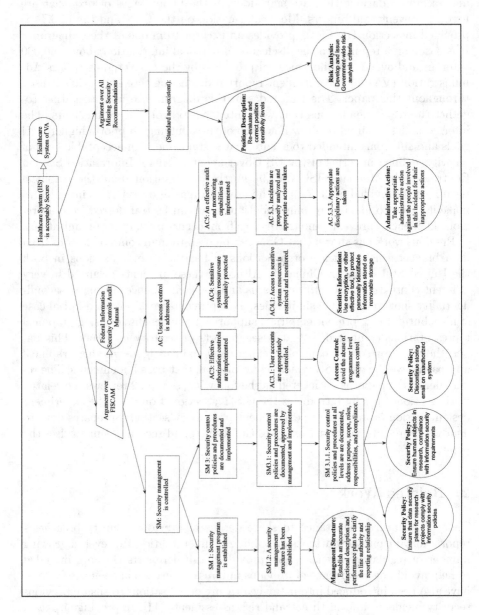

**Fig. 1.** Generic Security Template - VA dataloss 2007

The introduction has argued that existing, text-based reports can be supported through the use of graphical notations that provide an overview of many dozens of pages of detailed prose. Fig.1 uses the Goal Structuring Notations to summarize key findings from an enquiry into a loss of confidential patient data from the US Veterans Affairs Administration [6]. The aim is to present the security objectives in a structured and coherent manner. It is also hoped that this use of a semi-formal notation will encourage greater consistency and correctness [12, 13]. However, the notation introduces unfamiliar syntax and semantics. There is a danger that our use of these techniques can prevent stakeholders from understanding the arguments in security incident reports [14–16]. This paper, therefore, presents a controlled experiment to evaluate the utility of graphical representations for security incident reports.

## 3   The Generic Security Template

As mentioned, the G.S.T. extends the Goal Structuring Notations (GSN) [8] to provide an overview of previous security breaches. GSN is the dominant approach in the UK defence sector, increasingly being used in safety-critical industries to improve the structure, rigor, and clarity of design requirements. A particular strength is that it also links the evidence to show that particular requirements have been met. The same approach has more recently been extended to document security requirements [3, 7]. There are four principal notations used in the GSN, A *Goal* is a claim, the statements that the goal structure is designed to support. *Evidence* exists to support the truth of the claimed goal, which can be documented by providing a solution in GSN. *Strategy* is inserted between goals at two levels of abstraction, to explain how the top-level goal is addressed by the aggregation of the goals presented at the lower level. *Context* is used to declare supplementary information and provide adequate understanding of the context surrounding the claim (or strategy). Usually it presents concepts clarification introduced in the claim (or strategy) [8].

The G.S.T. has customised the GSN. Instead of collecting evidence to support design and development requirements, it collects lessons (i.e. security causes and recommendations) from previous security incidents. These lessons are defined to be the knowledge or understanding gained by experience [17]. In the G.S.T., it refers to the security issues that cause a security breach, and the security recommendations intended to avoid any recurrence. The evidence of compliance with the security objectives is presented in the form of a specific security standard or guideline applied to the organisation where the security incident happened. This has reflected the granular information described in section 1. Generic, is defined as "characteristic of or relating to a class or group of things; not specific". In other words, the intention is to create a GSN diagram that conveys the lessons learned from specific previous security breaches at a level of abstraction that helps others to use them to improve the security of other systems. Fig.2 presents the notations used in the Generic Security Template.

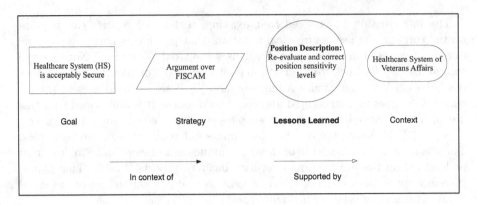

**Fig. 2.** Customised GSN Notations

Fig.2 presents the notations used in the Generic Security Template. In particular, rather than using the evidence derived from validation and verification to support safety arguments. The G.S.T. uses the findings from previous data breach incidents (i.e. leaf nodes of Fig. 1) to support security arguments in terms of the compliance with the security guideline (i.e. internal nodes of Fig. 1). The other concepts remain the same between both application areas.

## 4    Experiment Design

### 4.1    Experiment Objective and Scope

A controlled experiment was conducted to evaluate whether the use of graphical techniques helps improve the comprehension of the lessons from previous security incident reports compared to conventional text-based approaches. The aim was not to show that graphical techniques could replace conventional reports; in contrast the focus was in the use of our extended GSN approach to provide a map or overview of complex text-based reports. Accuracy, efficiency and task load are compared quantitatively in this experiment and the following hypotheses are proposed for the comparison.

*H1: Participants will be better able to identify the Lessons learned (security issues, security recommendations) in security incident report with the help of the G.S.T. than using Text-based Document alone;*

*H2: Participants will be better able to identify the compliance with the security objectives in security incident report with the help of the G.S.T. than using Text-based Document alone;*

*H3: The time taken to complete the designed task will be less using the G.S.T. than that using the text-based Document alone;*

*H4: The task load will be lower using the G.S.T. than using the text-based Document alone.*

Ease of use is compared qualitatively based on the feedback obtained from participants.

## 4.2   Experiment Variables

**Dependent Variables.** We evaluate the usability [18] in terms of the accuracy, efficiency, ease-of-use and task load compared to the conventional, text-based approach. *Accuracy*, is measured by assessing the quality of the security causes, recommendations and the compliance with the security objectives from the security incident. *Efficiency*, is measured by the time it takes to complete the experiment task. *Ease of use*, is evaluated by the feedback obtained from the post-experiment questionnaire. *Task load*, is measured by the application of NASA's Task Load Index to assess workload [19].

**Independent Variables.** *Generic Security Template (G.S.T.)*, we used the same G.S.T. across all participants. This presents findings from the US Veteran's Affairs administration 2007 Dataloss Incident [6]. *Text-based approach*, we developed an executive summary (reduced to four pages) and a simplified security guidelines (reduced to three pages) from the FISCAM. More details on the experiment material preparation are provided in 4.3.

**Controlled Variables.** *Participants*, the participants were post-graduate and undergraduate students with different education background. *Tasks*, the experiment itself lasted for maximum one hour. Participants had to identify causes, recommendations and the relationships with security objectives using either a conventional text-based document or using the graphical overview plus the existing report.

**Extraneous Variable.** *Experience with GSN*, is defined as an extraneous variable in this experiment. People who have experience with GSN will have an obvious advantage in comprehending the security incident with the help of the G.S.T. People who have experience with GSN were excluded from this experiment.

## 4.3   Experiment Materials

**Security Incident Report.** Security Incident Report. The technical context of the task focused on a data loss incident involving the Veterans Affairs' Administration [6]. The original report was around 80 pages long and hence we could not use it directly within the time available for the experiment. We also felt that our more focused approach was more appropriate for an initial study that could, in turn, inform future empirical work over a longer period of time and with a larger number of participants. We, therefore, provided both groups with the executive summary from the VA report reduced to four pages. As is mentioned, the evidence of compliance with the security objectives is presented in the form of a specific security standard or guideline applied to the organisation where the security incident happened. Therefore, a simplified version of security guidelines (reduced to three pages) cited from the FISCAM that are relevant to this incident are also provided as a part of the security incident report.

**The G.S.T.** The G.S.T. used in this experiment is created from the above mentioned security incident report only. It is an abstraction and extraction of the desirable information and did not bring any other information that can bias the results of the experiment.

**The Questionnaire.** We developed separate tasks description for the two groups and a post-experiment questionnaire, to provide subjective insights into perceived workload. A slightly different version of this post-experiment questionnaire was developed for the group using the graphical overview of the security incident. They were asked to provide information about the usability of the approach by completing subjective questionnaire.

### 4.4    The Pilot Study

Two security experts reviewed the design of the experiment pilot studies then helped to identify issues that had not been identified during the preparation of the materials. In the first pilot study, participants had to identify security issues, recommendations and compliance with the security objectives; writing them down using freestyle text. This was to simulate how security incident reports are analysed in practice, where people normally have no tools assisting them throughout this process. The feedback from the participants showed that the task was very mentally demanding and they were not able to complete it within one hour. We corrected this problem by introducing a table that provided guidance on the security issues and recommendations. The participants are required to fill in the blanks cells in the table. For the measurement of compliance with the security objectives, we have used multi-choice questions as the measurement mainly focuses on the relationships between the security objectives and the recommendations for prevention. Two more participants conducted a pilot test of the new experiment design. They were able to finish the tasks and stated that the level of mental effort was acceptable.

### 4.5    Experiment Task Design

In Group A, the experiment materials included the textual incident report (reduced executive summary and reduced security guidelines from FISCAM), the graphical G.S.T. and a task description. The pilot study had confirmed the arguments presented in the opening sections of this paper; that it can be difficult for readers to identify the causes, recommendation and the compliance with the security objectives of previous security incidents from existing textual reports. We, therefore, created tasks that guided the participants' analysis:

Task 1: Identify security issues and recommendations from the security incident report with the help of the G.S.T. They had to complete missing information from a table that provided partial information about the causes and recommendations. Table 1 is an exempt of the table. Issue Category and Description are provided. The participants need to fill in the blank about the recommendation description.

**Table 1.** An exempt of the security issue and recommendation table

| Issue Category | Issue description | Recommendations description |
|---|---|---|
| Access Control Related | The IT Specialist was improperly given access to multiple data sources. | |

Task 2: Answer multiple-choice questions on compliance of the security objectives. This removed the additional contextual support of the tabular format used in task one and provided a stepping stone towards the open ended analysis of security incident reports that proved problematic in the pilot studies.

In Group B, the experiment materials included the textual incident report without the G.S.T. but participants had the same task descriptions as the first group.

## 5    Experiment Procedures

### 5.1    Experiment Treatment

There was only one treatment in the experiment using a between groups (Group A and B) design. The empirical comparisons are between one group using a conventional text-based document and another using the graphical overview as well as the existing report.

### 5.2    Participants

Twenty-four subjects were assigned to either of the two experimental conditions using the textual report only or using both the textual report and the graphical overview. Group A consists of one undergraduate student and eleven postgraduate students, within which three of them have information security experience; Group B has one undergraduate student and eleven postgraduate students, within which three of them have information security experience. Each of the group have three females and nine males.

### 5.3    Training of the Participants

A pre-scripted familiarisation tutorial was provided before the experiment. Participants from both Group A and B attended the same tutorial session. This was to ensure that they received equal knowledge related to the handling of security incidents. The participants were introduced to the Goal Structuring Notations and G.S.T.

### 5.4    Experiment Execution

The experiment was conducted on a one-to-one mode to provide any support needed during the whole process including the familiarization tutorial session, the experiment session and the post-experiment questionnaire session. During the familiarization tutorial session, the participant had unlimited time to study the material and to have any question clarified. The participants were allowed to refer to the tutorial document or notes. The participants were instructed to inform the experiment conductor if they had any trouble in understanding the questions. During the post-experiment questionnaire session, an informal interview was conducted to make sure their attitudes were consistent with the answers they have provided. They are also requested to write down their subjective feedback on the G.S.T.

## 6    Results - Prepare the Data

### 6.1    Scoring Scheme for the Experiment Tasks

Sample answers for the experimental tasks were agreed on by two independent security experts.

### 6.2    Preparation for Task 1 - Open-Ended Questions

For Task 1, the answers expected were qualitative. The marking was based on the description of security issues and recommendations expected from the sample answers. The answers for each task were marked by two further independent experts (Rater A and B) using an agreed scoring scheme. The participants' answers were classified into four categories, which are "Correct", "Incomplete", "Wrong" and "Blank". A correct answer completely described the recommendation to support the given issue; incomplete answers show that the participant had a partial understanding of the recommendation, but lacked comprehension of an important aspect of it. Wrong answers showed that the participant did not understand a particular recommendation. Blank, no answer was provided at all. The following paragraph provides an example from task one:

The report identifies the security concern: "The IT Specialist was improperly given access to multiple data sources". An answer is marked as, *Correct,* if the participant states that the recommendation associated with this issue was to "Consider the conditions under which programmer level access may be granted for research project". A correct answer completely describes the recommendation to support the given issue; *Incomplete,* if the answer is stated as "Ensure the access control is appropriately granted". Incomplete answers show that the participant had a partial understanding of the recommendation, but lacked comprehension of an important aspect of it; *Wrong,* if the answer provided is not relevant to a particular recommendation. *Blank,* if no answer was provided at all.

Each participant was free to use his or her own words to describe the recommendations in this part of the study. The group identifiers were removed so that Rater A and B marked the answers without knowing whether or not the participants had access to the G.S.T. diagram.

## 6.3   Preparation for Task 2 - Multi-choice Questions

Task 2 used multi-choice questions to examine the participant's ability in understanding the compliance with the security objectives. Less subjectivity was involved in interpreting the answers. There can be more than one correct choice for each question and participants were asked to select all of the responses they believe were relevant to the questions. Below is an example.

*What are the security recommendations for addressing the security objective "User Access Control"?*

*a. Develop and implement policies describing the conditions under which programmer level access may be granted for research purposes.*

*b. Effective procedures are implemented to determine compliance with authentication policies.*

*c. Attempts to log on with invalid passwords are limited. Use of easily guessed passwords (such as names or words) is prohibited.*

*d. None of the above*

Correct answer: a, b

The sample answers were prepared by the independent security expert A. Each answer was classified as, *Correct, Correct but broad, Incomplete, Incomplete and broad, Wrong*, and *Blank*. A *correct* answer contained and only contained all the acceptable choices (e.g. a, b); *Correct but broad* contained all the acceptable choices, but also incorrect choices (e.g. a, b, c); *Incomplete* answers contained only some of the acceptable choices but not all (e.g. a). *Incomplete and broad* answers contained some of the acceptable choices and also other choices. (e.g. a, c); *Wrong* answers contained none of the acceptable choices (e.g. c).There was only one blank answer out of 144 responses; therefore we ignore this in the subsequent analysis.

# 7   Results - Analysis

## 7.1   Results for Accuracy (Task 1)

Out of a total number of 168 answers to the seven questions by 24 participants, three were left blank with one in Group A and two in Group B. During the debrief, the participants stated that, for the blank response, they could understand the questions but could not find the answer in the given materials. We ignore these blank answers in the subsequent analysis. Inter-rater reliability was checked for each question in Task 1, recall that these open ended questions were assessed by two independent raters. The results are listed in Table 2. Questions 1, 2 have achieved "almost perfect agreement"; Questions 3, 4, 5, and 6 have achieved "substantial agreement"; Question 7 has achieved "Fair agreement"[20].

A third independent security expert was invited to decide whether he agreed with Rater A or Rater B. The third security expert came to a 65.3% agreement with the Rater A and a 34.7% agreement with Rater B. Their interpretation was definitive for our analysis; in other words where there was disagreement between the first two assessments, the third rater decided which score was correct.

**Table 2.** Inter-rater reliability for each question (Rater A and B)

| | Inter-rater reliability check for each question | | | | | | |
|---|---|---|---|---|---|---|---|
| Question No. | *1* | *2* | *3* | *4* | *5* | *6* | *7* |
| Kappa Value | 0.85 | 0.80 | 0.75 | 0.57 | 0.72 | 0.78 | 0.50 |

## 7.2  Comparing the Performance of Task 1

Since the results are categorical data, we use cross-tabulation analysis to analyse the results. As is shown in Table 3, the results from the Cross-tabulation analysis (Table 3) show that 62.7% of the responses from Group A were correct, which is 17.6% higher than Group B. This might seem a relatively low level of accuracy. However, it is important to recall that our marking scheme was careful to distinguish between complete, perfect responses and partially correct or incomplete answers. The total percentage of Incomplete and Correct answer is 81.9% in Group A, which is 13.8% higher than Group B. As is shown in Table 4, the Chi-Square Test ($P = 0.048 < 0.05$) shows that these results are statistically significant. Therefore, hypothesis H1 "Participants will be better able to identify the recommendations and causes in security reports with the help of a graphical method than using text alone" is supported.

This result again shows that Group A has demonstrated a slightly higher level of comprehension than Group B. Therefore, hypothesis H1 "Participants will be

**Table 3.** The performance of Task 1 using Cross-tabulation

| | | Task | | | Total |
|---|---|---|---|---|---|
| | | *Wrong* | *Incomplete* | *Correct* | |
| Group A | Count | 15 | 16 | 52 | 83 |
| | % within Group | 18.1% | 19.3% | 62.7% | 100.0% |
| Group B | Count | 27 | 18 | 37 | 82 |
| | % within Group | 32.9% | 22.0% | 45.1% | 100.0% |
| Total | Count | 42 | 34 | 89 | 165 |
| | % within Group | | | | 100.0% |

**Table 4.** Chi-Square Tests performance of Task 1 using Cross-tabulation

| | Chi-Square Tests | | |
|---|---|---|---|
| | *Value* | *df* | *Asymp. Sig. (2-sided)* |
| Pearson Chi-Square | 6.068a | 2 | .048 |
| Likelihood Ratio | 6.129 | 2 | .047 |
| Linear-by-Linear Association | 6.032 | 1 | .014 |
| N of Valid Cases | 165 | | |

better able to identify the recommendations and causes in security reports with the help of a graphical method than using text alone"is supported.

## 7.3   The Results for Accuracy (Task 2)

The results from the cross-tabulation analysis show that the participants from Group A achieved a 33.3% accuracy rate, which is 9.7% higher than Group B. The total percentage of Correct, Broad, Incomplete, and Incomplete but broad answer is 87.5%, which is 18.1% higher than Group B. As is shown in Table 5, the Chi-Square Test ($P = 0.038 < 0.05$) shows that these results are statistically significant. This multi-choice results were not due to coincidence. Therefore, hypothesis H2 "H2: Participants will be better able to identify the compliance with the security objectives in security incident report with the help of the G.S.T. than using Text-based Document alone"  is supported in Task 2.

**Table 5.** Chi-Square Tests performance of Task 2 using Cross-tabulation

|  | Chi-Square Tests | | |
|---|---|---|---|
|  | *Value* | *df* | *Asymp. Sig. (2-sided)* |
| Pearson Chi-Square | 10.140a | 4 | .038 |
| Likelihood Ratio | 10.449 | 4 | .034 |
| Linear-by-Linear Association | 2.995 | 1 | .084 |
| N of Valid Cases | 144 | | |

## 7.4   The Results for Efficiency (Time)

The mean total time used by Group A was almost equal that in Group B; 47.3 versus 47.8 minutes. The total time taken across all tasks is not statistically significant ($P = 0.932 > 0.05$). Therefore, we can accept the null hypothesis that "the mean time taken to complete our experimental tasks using a textual security incident report and a textual report with a graphical overview are not significantly different."Hypothesis H3 is not supported. One interpretation of these results is that significant time is required to understand security incidents, irrespective of whether they are presented in graphical or textual format. However, this would require further empirical support to determine whether or not other graphical notations might lead to significant differences in the time taken to understand security incident reports. It is also important for further work to consider the learning effects that might be expected through repeated use of the graphical maps.

## 7.5   The Results for Task Load Index (TLX)

We used NASA's Task Load Index [19] to assess workload using a post-evaluation questionnaire. The t-test results show a significant difference ($P = 0.047 < 0.05$)

in the first dimension of the task load index regarding "how mentally demanding was the whole task". With a mean value of task load, 12.75 versus 15.50, participants expressed a lower subjective level of workload in terms of "mentally demand"when using the G.S.T. The results for the other four dimensions of the Task Load Index are not significantly different. However, a more sustained analysis is required to replicate these findings across a wider range of workload measures and with a larger sample of potential users.

### 7.6    Subjective Feedback

In Group A, approximately half of the participants expressed some difficulty in understanding the text based Security Incident Report. Half of the participants reported that they have no difficulty in completing task 1 of Group A: identifying security elements from the security incident report with the help of the G.S.T. Group B reported a slightly higher level of understanding of the Security Incident Report. However, less than half of the participants suggested that they have no difficulty in completing task 1 of Group B: identifying lessons learned from the security incident report, and the rate is much lower than that of Group A. These subjective findings are consistent with the quantitative results in section 6.3.

The participants' answers to the open questions regarding the overall experience of using the graphical overviews suggested that a longer training session might have helped them to better prepare for the tasks. Several participants mentioned that they had experienced learning effects; their confidence in answering the questions increased as they worked their way through the questions. This finding from Group A reveals generally positive feedback for the G.S.T. Group B did not use the G.S.T. during the experiment. They were asked to review the G.S.T. after the experiment and provide the feedback by completing Questionnaire Section 6 designed for Group B. Almost all of them suggested that they would have no difficulty in understanding the G.S.T. and agreed that the G.S.T. can help them better comprehend existing security incident reports. Two thirds of the participants reported their willingness to use the G.S.T. if they are requested to do a similar task in future. "It will help to understand terminologies security elements easily, less confusing, very structured and don't have to waste time, most importantly very easy to understand with less information". In summary, the participants overall experience with the G.S.T. is positive, however, questions remain about the ability of participants to apply the lessons from the report within their own organisation rather than answering directed questions about the contents of a security report.

## 8    Conclusions and Future Work

There have been numerous empirical studies to evaluate the utility and usability of graphical notations, including Entity-Relationship diagrams [21], UML[22] [23] etc. However, as far as we are aware, there have been no previous studies to assess the strengths and weaknesses of graphical notations to help transfer the lessons learned from previous security incidents. These studies are urgently needed as both the Obama administration and the European Commission have recently published proposals to support the mandatory reporting of security incidents across national critical infrastructures, including healthcare. In this paper, we have presented the results derived from an initial study into the use of Goal Structuring Notation (GSN) to represent and reason about the recommendations made in a report of a data confidentiality breach involving the US Veterans' Affairs Administration. We were able to show significant benefits from the use of a graphical technique in answering a number of comprehension questions when compared to the more conventional use of text-based incident reports. However, we could not demonstrate any significant benefits in terms of the time taken to complete our experimental tasks, nor could we demonstrate significant benefits when participants were asked to identify the compliance with the security objectives provided by multiple-choice questions.

It is important to stress that this was a preliminary study. The sample size was relatively small due to practical reasons: (1) the approach is new and people have little experience with security incident analysis; (2) the tasks were mentally demanding; (3) participation was voluntary. However, our work did yield important insights into the difficulties that engineers face when trying to understand the implications that previous security incident reports have for their own organisations.

**Acknowledgment.** The first author would like to thank the China Scholarship Council (CSC) for funding this research work.

# References

1. Symantec: Internal security threat report 2011 trends, vol. 17 (2012)
2. Symantec: Internet security threat report 2013, vol. 18. (2013)
3. He, Y., Johnson, C.: Generic security cases for information system security in healthcare systems. In: Proceedings of the 7th IET International Conference on System Safety, Incorporating the Cyber Security Conference, pp. 1–6. IET (2012)
4. Hadgkiss, J.: Computer security incident response teams: Exploring the incident learning capability (2004)
5. Hadgkiss, J.: Computer security incident handling, step-by-step (1997)
6. Administration, U.V.A.: Administrative investigation loss of va information va medical center birmingham, al. Volume Report No. 07-01083-157 (2007)
7. He, Y., Johnson, C., Renaud, K., Lu, Y., Jebriel, S.: An empirical study on the use of the generic security template for structuring the lessons from information security incidents. In: Proceedings of the 6th International Conference on Computer Science and Information Technology, pp. 178–188. IEEE Press (2014)
8. Kelly, T.P.: Arguing safety-a systematic approach to safety case management (1998)
9. Dacey, R.F.: Federal Information System Controls Audit Manual (FISCAM). DIANE Publishing (2010)

10. He, Y., Johnson, C., Lu, Y., Lin, Y.: Improving the information security management: An industrial study in the privacy of electronic patient records. In: Proceedings of the 27th IEEE International Symposium on Computer-Based Medical Systems (CBMS 2014). IEEE Press (2014)

11. Commissioner, E.: Directive 2009/140/ec of the european parliament and of the council of 25 november 2009 (2009)

12. Craigen, D.: Formal methods technology transfer: Impediments and innovation. In: Lee, I., Smolka, S.A. (eds.) CONCUR 1995. LNCS, vol. 962, pp. 328–332. Springer, Heidelberg (1995)

13. Hinchey, M.G.: Confessions of a formal methodist. In: SCS, 17–20 (2002)

14. Finney, K., Fedorec, A.: An empirical study of specification readability. In: Teaching and Learning Formal Methods. Academic Press, New York (1996)

15. Finney, K.: Mathematical notation in formal specification: Too difficult for the masses? IEEE Transactions on Software Engineering 22(2), 158–159 (1996)

16. Carew, D., Exton, C., Buckley, J.: An empirical investigation of the comprehensibility of requirements specifications. In: International Symposium on Empirical Software Engineering, p. 10. IEEE (2005)

17. Weber, R., Aha, D.W., Becerra-Fernandez, I.: Intelligent lessons learned systems. Expert Systems with Applications 20(1), 17–34 (2001)

18. Folmer, E., Bosch, J.: Architecting for usability: a survey. Journal of Systems and Software 70(1), 61–78 (2004)

19. Hart, S.G., Staveland, L.E.: Development of nasa-tlx (task load index): Results of empirical and theoretical research. Human Mental Workload 1(3), 139–183 (1988)

20. Landis, J.R., Koch, G.G.: The measurement of observer agreement for categorical data. Biometrics, 159–174 (1977)

21. Shoval, P., Shiran, S.: Entity-relationship and object-oriented data modeling—an experimental comparison of design quality, vol. 21, pp. 297–315. Elsevier (1997)

22. Glezer, C., Last, M., Nachmany, E., Shoval, P.: Quality and comprehension of uml interaction diagrams-an experimental comparison, vol. 47, pp.675–692 (2005)

23. Razali, R., Snook, C., Poppleton, M., Garratt, P., Walters, R.: Usability assessment of a uml-based formal modelling method. In: 19th Annual Psychology of Programming Workshop (PPIG 2007), pp. 56–71. Citeseer (2007)

# A Privacy Risk Model for Trajectory Data

Anirban Basu[1], Anna Monreale[2], Juan Camilo Corena[1], Fosca Giannotti[3],
Dino Pedreschi[2], Shinsaku Kiyomoto[1], Yutaka Miyake[1], Tadashi Yanagihara[4],
and Roberto Trasarti[3]

[1] KDDI R&D Laboratories, Japan
{basu,corena,kiyomoto,miyake}@kddilabs.jp
[2] University of Pisa, Italy
{annam,dino}@di.unipi.it
[3] ISTI-CNR, Italy
{fosca.giannotti,roberto.trasarti}@isti.cnr.it
[4] Toyota ITC, Japan
ta-yanagihara@jp.toyota-itc.com

**Abstract.** Time sequence data relating to users, such as medical histories and mobility data, are good candidates for data mining, but often contain highly sensitive information. Different methods in privacy-preserving data publishing are utilised to release such private data so that individual records in the released data cannot be re-linked to specific users with a high degree of certainty. These methods provide theoretical worst-case privacy risks as measures of the privacy protection that they offer. However, often with many real-world data the worst-case scenario is too pessimistic and does not provide a realistic view of the privacy risks: the real probability of re-identification is often much lower than the theoretical worst-case risk. In this paper we propose a novel empirical risk model for privacy which, in relation to the cost of privacy attacks, demonstrates better the practical risks associated with a privacy preserving data release. We show detailed evaluation of the proposed risk model by using $k$-anonymised real-world mobility data.

**Keywords:** privacy, risk, utility, model, anonymisation, sequential data.

## 1 Introduction

The big data originating from the digital breadcrumbs of human activities, sensed as a by-product of the ICT systems, record different dimensions of human social life. These data describing human activities are valuable assets for data mining and big data analytics and their availability enables a new generation of personalised intelligent services. Most of these data are of sequential nature, such as time-stamped transactions, users' medical histories and trajectories. They describe sequences of events or users' actions where the timestamps make the temporal sequentiality of the events powerful sources of information. Unfortunately, such information often contain sensitive information that are protected under the legal frameworks for user data protection. Thus, when such data has to be released to any third party for analysis, privacy-preserving mechanisms are utilised

J. Zhou et al. (Eds.): IFIPTM 2014, IFIP AICT 430, pp. 125–140, 2014.

to de-link individual records from their associated users. Privacy-preserving data publishing (PPDP) aims at preserving statistical properties of the data while removing the details that can help the re-identification of users. Any PPDP method provides a worst-case probabilistic risk of user re-identification as a measure for how safe the anonymised data is.

One such well-known anonymisation model typically used for PPDP is the $k$-anonymity model [1, 2]. It states that in the worst case, there are at least $k$ (and no less) users that can be re-identified given a $k$-anonymised dataset. Thus, the re-identification probability for any single user, in the worst case, is equal to $1/k$. The higher the value of $k$, the lower the probability of any attack succeeding. However, at the same time the higher the value of $k$, the lower the utility of the data where the utility relates how well the anonymised data represents the original one. This worst case scenario hardly gives us the view of the realistic re-identification probabilities, which are often much lower than $1/k$. We envisage that the worst case guarantee, by itself, is not sufficient to help the user understand the risks; and it is also not enough to communicate in a legal language the risks associated with any of these anonymisation methods.

In this paper, we propose an empirical risk model for privacy based on $k$-anonymous data release. We also discuss the relation of risk to the cost of any attack on privacy as well as the utility of the data. We validate our model against experimental car trajectory data gathered in the Italian cities of Pisa and Florence.

The rest of the paper is organised as follows. In §2, §3 and §4, we propose our empirical risk model with a running example based on $k$-anonymous sequence data the inadequacy of worst-case risk evaluation. We validate our empirical model by tests on real world trajectory data in §5 followed by the state-of-the-art related to the information privacy and its measurements in §6 before concluding the paper in §7.

## 2   From Theoretical Guarantees to an Empirical Risk Model

### 2.1   Preliminaries: Trajectory Data

A trajectory dataset is a collection of trajectories $\mathcal{D}_T = \{t_1, t_2, \ldots, t_m\}$. A trajectory $t = \langle x_1, y_1, ts_1 \rangle, \ldots, \langle x_n, y_n, ts_n \rangle$, is a sequence of spatio-temporal points, i.e., triples $\langle x_i, y_i, ts_i \rangle$, where $(x_i, y_i)$ are points in $\mathbf{R}^2$, i.e., spatial coordinates, and $ts_i$ ($i = 1 \ldots n$) denotes a timestamp such that $\forall 1 < i < n \ ts_i < ts_{i+1}$. Intuitively, each triple $\langle x_i, y_i, ts_i \rangle$ indicates that the object is in the position $(x_i, y_i)$ at time $ts_i$. A trajectory $t' = \langle x'_1, y'_1, ts'_1 \rangle, \ldots, \langle x'_m, y'_m, ts'_m \rangle$ is a sub-trajectory of $t$ ($t' \preceq t$) if there exist integers $1 < i_1 < \ldots < i_m \leq n$ such that $\forall 1 \leq j \leq m \ \langle x'_j, y'_j, ts'_j \rangle = \langle x_{i_j}, y_{i_j}, ts_{i_j} \rangle$. We refer to the number of trajectories in $\mathcal{D}_T$ containing a sub-trajectory $t'$ as $support$ $of$ $t'$ and denote it by $N_{\mathcal{D}_T}(t') = |\{t \in \mathcal{D}_T | t' \preceq t\}|$.

## 2.2   The $k$-anonymity Framework for Trajectory Data

A well known method for anonymisation of data before release is $k$-anonymity [2]. The $k$-anonymity model was also studied in the context of trajectory data [3–5]. Given an input dataset $\mathcal{D}_T \subseteq T$ of trajectories, the objective of the data release is to transform $\mathcal{D}_T$ into some $k$-anonymised form $\mathcal{D}'_T$. Without this transformation, the publication of the original data can put at risk the privacy of individuals represented in the data. Indeed, an intruder who gains access to the anonymous dataset may possess some background knowledge allowing him/her to conduct attacks that may enable inferences on the dataset. We refer to any such intruders as an attacker. An attacker may know a sub-trajectory of the trajectory of some specific person and could use this information to infer the complete trajectory of the same person from the released dataset. Given the attacker's background knowledge of partial trajectories, a $k$-anonymous version has to guarantee that the re-identification probability of the whole trajectory within the released dataset has to be at most $\frac{1}{k}$. If we denote the probability of re-identification of the trajectories as $\Pr(re\_id|t')$ based on the trajectory $t'$ known to the attacker then the theoretical $k$-anonymity framework implies that $\forall t' \in T, \Pr(re\_id|t') \leq \frac{1}{k}$. The parameter $k$ is a given threshold that reflects the expected level of privacy.

Note that, given a trajectory dataset $\mathcal{D}_T$ and an anonymity threshold $k > 1$ we can have trajectories with a support lower than $k$ ($N_{\mathcal{D}_T}(t') < k$) and trajectories that are frequent at least $k$ times ($N_{\mathcal{D}_T}(t') \geq k$). The first type of trajectories are called $k$-harmful because their probabilities of re-identification are greater than $\frac{1}{k}$. In [5], the authors show that if a $k$-anonymisation method returns a dataset $\mathcal{D}'_T$ by guaranteeing that for each $k$-harmful trajectory $t'$ in the original dataset, $t' \in \mathcal{D}_T$, either $N_{\mathcal{D}'_T}(t') = 0$ or $N_{\mathcal{D}'_T}(t') \geq k$, then we have the property that for any trajectory $t$ known by an attacker (harmful or not), $\Pr(re\_id|t') \leq \frac{1}{k}$.

This fact is easy to verify. Indeed, given a $k$-anonymous version $\mathcal{D}'_T$ of a trajectory dataset $\mathcal{D}_T$ that satisfies the above condition, and a trajectory $t$ known by the attacker two cases can arise:

- $t$ **is $k$-harmful in** $\mathcal{D}_T$: In this case we can have either, $N_{\mathcal{D}'_T}(t) = 0$, which implies $\Pr(re\_id|t) = 0$, or $N_{\mathcal{D}'_T}(t') \geq k$, which implies $\Pr(re\_id|t) = \frac{1}{N_{\mathcal{D}'_T}(t)} \leq \frac{1}{k}$.

- $t$ **is not $k$-harmful in** $\mathcal{D}_T$: In this case we have $N_{\mathcal{D}_T}(t) = F \geq k$ and $t$ can have an arbitrary support in $\mathcal{D}'_T$. If $N_{\mathcal{D}'_T}(t) = 0$ or $N_{\mathcal{D}'_T}(t) \geq F$, then the same reasoning as in the previous case applies. If $0 < N_{\mathcal{D}'_T}(t) < F$ then the probability to re-identify a user to the trajectory $t$ is the probability that that user is present in $\mathcal{D}'_T$ times the probability of picking that user in $\mathcal{D}'_T$, i.e., $\frac{N_{\mathcal{D}'_T}(t)}{F} \times \frac{1}{N_{\mathcal{D}'_T}(t)} = \frac{1}{F} \leq \frac{1}{k}$.

The aforementioned mathematical condition that any $k$-anonymous dataset has to satisfy, is explained as follows. Given the attacker's knowledge of partial trajectories that are $k$-harmful, i.e., occurring only a few times in the dataset, they can enable a few specific complete trajectories to be selected, and thus the probability that the sequence linking attack succeeds is very high. Therefore, there must be at least $k$ trajectories in the anonymised dataset matching the attacker's knowledge. Alternatively, there can be no trajectories in the anonymised dataset matching the attacker's knowledge. If the attacker knows a sub-trajectory occurring many times (at least $k$ times) then this means that it is compatible with too many subjects and this reduces the probability of a successful attack. If the partially observed trajectories lead to no match then it is equivalent to saying that the partially observed trajectories could be in any other dataset except from the one under attack, thus leading to an infinitely large search space. This is, somewhat, equivalent to $k \to \infty$. Thus, in this case, $\lim_{k \to \infty} \Pr(re\_id|t') = 0$.

This is the theoretical worst-case guarantee of the probability of re-identification of a $k$-anonymised dataset. However, we shall see in the following sub-section that this does not give us a complete picture of the probabilities of re-identification.

### 2.3   Why Is the Theoretical Worst-Case Guarantee Inadequate?

In order to explain the inadequacies of the theoretical worst-case guarantee, let us consider a toy example of trajectories. Let $\mathcal{D}_T$ be the example dataset. We can choose, as an example, a value of $k = 3$ and obtain the 3-anonymous dataset $\mathcal{D}'_T$, for which the theoretical worst-case guarantee is that $\forall t'$, $\Pr(re\_id|t') \leq \frac{1}{3}$.

$$
\mathcal{D}_T = \begin{cases}
t_1 & : A \to B \to C \to D \to E \to F \\
t_2 & : A \to B \to C \to D \to E \to F \\
t_3 & : A \to B \to C \to D \to E \to F \\
t_4 & : A \to D \to E \to F \\
t_5 & : A \to D \to E \to F \\
t_6 & : A \to D \to E \\
t_7 & : B \to K \to S \\
t_8 & : B \to K \\
t_9 & : B \to K \\
t_{10} & : D \to E \to J \to F
\end{cases}
\qquad
\mathcal{D}'_T = \begin{cases}
t'_1 & : A \to B \\
t'_2 & : A \to B \\
t'_3 & : A \to B \\
t'_4 & : A \to D \\
t'_5 & : A \to D \\
t'_6 & : A \to D \\
t'_7 & : A \to D \\
t'_8 & : B \to K \\
t'_9 & : B \to K \\
t'_{10} & : B \to K
\end{cases}
$$

(a) Original                     (b) 3-anonymised

**Fig. 1.** Converting $\mathcal{D}_T$ to $k$-anonymised $\mathcal{D}'_T$ with $k = 3$

However, we observe from figure 2 that the actual probability of re-identification is often much lower than the theoretical worst-case scenario, but this fact is not demonstrated by the theoretical guarantee.

### 2.4   Empirical Risk Model for Anonymised Trajectory Data

In the last sub-section, we demonstrated that the theoretical worst-case guarantee does not demonstrate the distribution of attack probabilities. The worst-case

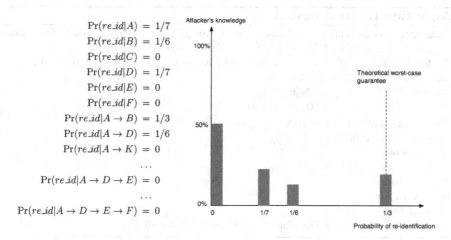

(a) Re-identification probabilities          (b) Probability density distribution

**Fig. 2.** Probability distribution of re-identification

scenario also does not illustrate the fact that a large majority of the attacks have far lower probabilities of success than the worst-case guarantee. Thus, we propose an empirical risk model for anonymised sequence data. If $t'$ represents attacker's knowledge; $h = |t'|$ denotes the number of observations in the attacker's knowledge then the intent is to approximate a probability density and a cumulative distribution of $\Pr(re\_id|t')$ for each value of $h$. This can be achieved by iterating over every value of $h = 1, \ldots, M$ where $M$ is the length of the longest trajectory in $\mathcal{D}_T$. For each value of $h$, we consider all the sub-trajectories $t' \in \mathcal{D}_T$ of length $h$ and compute the probability of re-identification $\Pr(re\_id|t')$ as described in Algorithm 1. In particular, for each value of $h$ a further iteration can be run over each value of $t'$ of length $h$, in which we compute $N_{\mathcal{D}'_T}(t')$, $N_{\mathcal{D}_T}(t')$ and the probability of re-identification by following the reasoning described in Section 2.2 for the computation of this probability. Algorithm 1 presents the pseudocode of the attack simulation.

The advantages of this approach is that this model supports arguments such as: (a) "98% of the attacks have at most $10^{-5}$ probability of success"; and (b) "only 0.001% of the attacks have a probability close to $\frac{1}{k}$". The disadvantages of this model are: (a) a separate distribution plot is necessary for each value of $h$; and (b) the probability of re-identification increases with the increase in $h$. The illustration in Figure 3 demonstrates the aforementioned advantages and disadvantages of the risk model.

For the simulation of the attack we need to select a set of trajectories $BK_T$ from the original dataset of trajectories. The optimal solution would be to take the all possible sub-trajectories in the original dataset and compute the probability of re-identification. Since the set of attack trajectories can be quite large, in order to avoid a combinatorial explosion, two strategies can be adopted.

**Algorithm 1.** Attack Simulation

**Require:** The $k$-anonymised dataset $\mathcal{D}'_T$, the original dataset $\mathcal{D}_T$, the set of trajectories for the attacks $BK_T$ and anonymity threshold $k$.

1: **for** $h = 1, \ldots, M$ where $M$ is the length of the longest trajectory in $\mathcal{D}_T$ **do**
2:    **for** $t'$ of length $h$ in $BK_T$ **do**
3:       $N(t')_{\mathcal{D}_T} \leftarrow |\{t \in \mathcal{D}_T | t' \preceq t\}|$.
4:       $N(t')_{\mathcal{D}'_T} \leftarrow |\{t \in \mathcal{D}'_T | t' \preceq t\}|$.
5:       **if** $N(t')_{\mathcal{D}_T} \geq k$ and $N(t')_{\mathcal{D}'_T} \leq N(t')_{\mathcal{D}_T}$ **then**
6:         $\Pr(re\_id|t') \leftarrow 1/N(t')_{\mathcal{D}_T}$.
7:       **else**
8:         $\Pr(re\_id|t') \leftarrow 1/N(t')_{\mathcal{D}'_T}$.
9:       **end if**
10:   **end for**
11: **end for**
12: **return** Cumulative Distribution of $\Pr(re\_id|t')$ for all $h$.

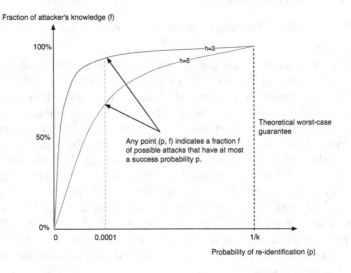

**Fig. 3.** Representative cumulative density distribution for attacks in the toy example

First, we can extract from the original dataset of trajectories a random subset of trajectories that we can use as background knowledge for the attacks to estimate the distributions. Secondly, we can use a prefix tree to represent in a compact way the original dataset and then, by incrementally visiting the tree we can enumerate all the distinct sequences for using them as an adversary's background knowledge.

**Risk versus Cost.** One of the most important open problems that makes the communication between the experts in law and in computer science hard is how to evaluate whether an individual is identifiable or not, i.e., the evaluation of privacy risks for an individual. Usually, the main legal references to this problem suggests to measure the difficulty in re-identifying the data subject in terms of "time and manpower". This definition is surely suitable for traditional computer security problems. As an example, we can measure the difficulty to decrypt a message without the proper key in terms of how much time we need to try all possible keys i.e., the time and resources required by the so-called *brute force* attack. In the field of privacy the computer science literature shows that the key factor affecting the difficulty to re-identify an anonymous data is the *background knowledge* available to the adversary. Thus, we should consider the difficulty to acquire the knowledge that enables the attack to infer some sensitive information. If we are able to measure the *cost* of the acquisition of the background knowledge then we can provide a single risk indicator that takes into consideration both the probability of success of an attack and its cost. Combining the two factors and providing one single value could help the communication of a specific privacy risk in the legal language.

We propose three methods for measuring the cost of an attack and a way to combine it with the probability of re-identification. We also propose to normalise the probability of re-identification $\Pr(re\_id|t')$ with the cost of gaining the knowledge of $t'$ by the attacker. The longer the $t'$, the higher the cost to acquire such knowledge. Thus, $\Pr(t') = \Pr(re\_id|t')/C(t')$ where $C(t')$ is the cost function proportional to the length of $t'$. We can then estimate the distribution of $\Pr(t')$ over all $t'$ to obtain a unique combined measurement of risk over all possible attacks.

The cost function $C(t')$ can be derived from various alternatives. (1) One option would be to use a sub-linear cost function akin to that incurred in machine-operated sensing. The initial costs of setting up the sensing equipment are high but subsequent observations are cheaper and cheaper. Thus, $C(t') = 1 + log(|t'|)$ is a good approximation. (2) Another option is a linear cost where a spying service is paid a fixed fee per observation, leading to $C(t') = \alpha|t'|$. (3) A third alternative is a super-linear cost where the attacker directly invests time and resources to sensing, thus making the cost function $C(t') = e^{-\beta|t'|}$.

## 3   Data Utility Measures: Coverage and Precision

Alongside the risk versus cost estimations, it is also important to identify the usability of the anonymised data and show the relation between usability and privacy risk. In this context, we introduce two usability measures: *coverage* and *precision*. While a trajectory can consist of multiple hops, it can also be seen as a chain of smaller trajectories, each of which just contain the start point (the origin) and the end point (the destination). We call these smaller trajectories as *ODpairs* (or, origin-destination pairs). Given a $k$-anonymisation function that maps $\mathcal{D}_T$ into $\mathcal{D}'_T$, we define *coverage*:

$$coverage = |ODpairs(\mathcal{D}_T) \cap ODpairs(\mathcal{D}'_T)|/|\mathcal{D}_T| \qquad (1)$$

and *precision* as:

$$precision = |ODpairs(\mathcal{D}_T) \cap ODpairs(\mathcal{D}'_T)|/|ODpairs(\mathcal{D}'_T)| \qquad (2)$$

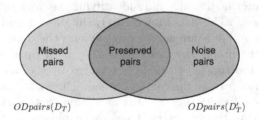

$ODpairs(D_T)$ $ODpairs(D'_T)$

**Fig. 4.** Diagrammatic representation of coverage and precision

The coverage versus risk for a given risk threshold can be estimated as follows. Given an anonymised dataset $\mathcal{D}'_T$ and a specified probability threshold $p$ where $0 \leq p \leq \frac{1}{k}$, all trips $t$ containing attack based on $t'$ with $\Pr(re\_id|t') > p$ can be retrieved as:

$$RiskyTrips(p) = \{t \in \mathcal{D}'_T | \exists\, t' : \Pr(re\_id|t') > p \text{ and } t' < t\} \qquad (3)$$

Thus, the coverage of the dataset $\mathcal{D}_T$ with respect to the risk threshold $p$ is defined as follows

$$coverage = |ODpairs(\mathcal{D}'_T) \setminus ODpairs(RiskyTrips(p))|/|\mathcal{D}'_T| \qquad (4)$$

The characteristics of the mobility data that are preserved with high fidelity if we measure a high coverage rate are: (a) presence (of users in locations), (b) flows (i.e., the number of trips between any origin-destination pair), and (c) overall distance travelled in *all* trips.

The characteristics that are not necessarily preserved include the properties of sequences of individual trips, e.g., distribution of trip length and routine trips.

## 4    Privacy-by-Design for Data-Driven Services

The *privacy-by-design* model for privacy and data protection has been recognised in legislation in the last few years years. Privacy-by-design is an approach to protect privacy by inscribing it into the design specifications of information technologies, accountable business practices, and networked infrastructures, from the very start. It was developed by Ontario's Information and Privacy Commissioner, Dr. Ann Cavoukian, in the 1990s.

Privacy officials in Europe and the United States are embracing this paradigm as never before. In Europe, in the comprehensive reform of the data protection rules, proposed on January 25, 2012 by the EC, the new data protection legal framework introduces, with respect to the Directive 95/46/EC, the reference to data protection by design and by default (Article 23 of the Proposal for a Regulation and Article 19 of the Proposal for a Directive). These articles compel the controller to *"implement appropriate technical and organizational measures and procedures in such a way that the processing will meet the requirements of this Regulation and ensure the protection of the rights of the data subject."* and to *"implement mechanisms for ensuring that, by default, only those personal data are processed which are necessary for each specific purpose of the processing ..."*.

In [6] Monreale at al. define a methodology for applying the *privacy-by-design* principle in the context of data analytics. This work states that one of the most important points to take into consideration for releasing technological frameworks that offer *by-design* the privacy protection is the trade-off between privacy guarantees and the data quality.

The model presented in above sections provides a methodology for the evaluation of this trade-off. Indeed, the availability of this model allows us to define a methodology of risk evaluation of datasets that have to be used for specific services; and this methodology allows us to establish a well-defined relation between the risks of re-identification of any individual represented in the data and the usability of the anonymous data for the specified services.

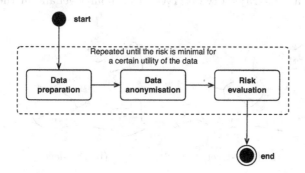

**Fig. 5.** Refining privacy and risk until the risk is minimal for a certain utility of the data

In Figure 5 we depict this methodology that is composed of three phases: (a) data preparation, (b) data anonymisation, and (c) risk evaluation.

The cycle, illustrated in figure 5 needs to be repeated with respect to the different dimensions (e.g., spatial and temporal granularity, refresh window) obtaining a collection of anonymised datasets $\mathcal{D}_T^{ti}$ with associated risks $R^i$. Given a class of services that are to be facilitated by the published data, the anonymised dataset $\mathcal{D}_T^{ti}$ will be chosen for which the associated risk $R^i$ is *minimal* with acceptable utility of the published data.

## 5    Experimental Validation

In this section we present a detailed evaluation of the proposed risk model by using real-world mobility data. We used a large dataset of real GPS traces from vehicles, collected during the period between May 1 and May 31, 2011, donated by an Italian company called *OctoTelematics*. The dataset contains the GPS traces collected in the geographical areas around Pisa and Florence, in central Italy, for around 18,800 vehicles making up around 46,000 trips. For our simulations, we extracted from the whole dataset the data on May 10, 2011 that contained 8,330 participating users and 15,345 trajectories.

To begin with, the privacy-sensitive locations captured through GPS readings were obfuscated using Voronoi tessellation [7]. The trajectory data containing tessellated locations (signifying vertices in a trajectory graph) was further subjected to $k$-anonymisation for $k = 3$, $k = 5$, and $k = 10$ by using the method proposed in [5]. Before applying this anonymisation, we subjected the sequence data to two further steps: generalisation of temporal information and transformation of trajectories. The first step – generalisation of the temporal information associated with each location visited by the user – consisted of two levels of generalisations: one that contains sequences of Voronoi areas where the time associated with each location is generalized at an hour-level (*hour-level data*) and another one where the time is at a day-level (*day-level data*). Figure 6 illustrates an example of a user trajectory observed at an hour-level and at the day-level.

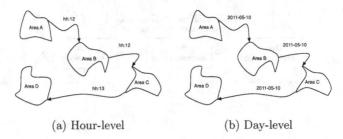

(a) Hour-level                (b) Day-level

**Fig. 6.** An example of user trajectory through the different tessellated areas observed at an hour-level and at a day-level

The second step consisted of the transformation of the generalised trajectories into sequences of *ODpairs*; in particular, we divided the whole user sequence into smaller sequences and for each small sequence we extracted its origin and its destination.

In our evaluation we performed two different analyses. First, we applied our risk model showing the evaluation of the privacy risks obtained from the two anonymised datasets described above, and then, we measured the data utility in terms of *precision* and *coverage* described in §3.

## 5.1   Risk Analysis

In order to evaluate the privacy risks on the two anonymised sequence datasets we applied the methodology described in §2.4. Therefore, we estimated the cumulative distribution of the probability of re-identification for each value of $h = |t'|$, which

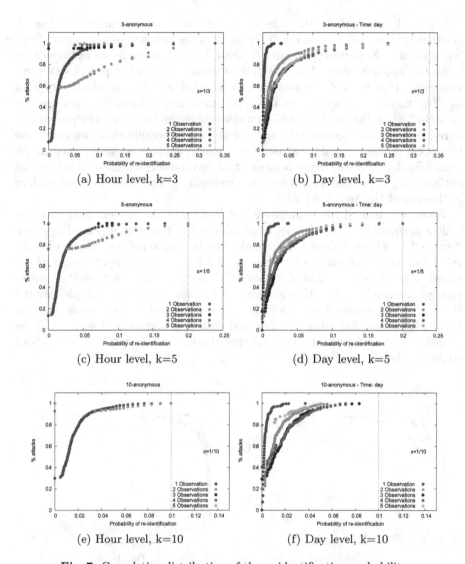

**Fig. 7.** Cumulative distribution of the re-identification probability

denotes the number of observations in the attacker's knowledge. We simulated a set of attacks by randomly selecting from the original database a subset of trajectories and using them as background knowledge. In particular, in our experiment for each $h$, we drew from the original database, $10,000$ sub-sequences with length $h$. We considered $h = 1, \ldots, 5$ because the longest sequence in the original data has length 5. Figure 7 shows the results obtained with this attack simulation. The first column of images contains the plots related to the cumulative distributions related to the *hour-level dataset* while the second column contains the results obtained from the *day-level dataset*.

Our analyses highlight that the empirical protection guaranteed by the algorithm of anonymisation is much higher than the theoretical protection. Only few attacks have a protection very close to $\frac{1}{k}$. We observe as an example that when the *day-level dataset* is anonymised with $k = 5$ our empirical risk analysis shows that 90% of the attacks have at most a risk of re-identification of $\frac{1}{10}$. The findings are similar in the other anonymised datasets. Moreover, we note that when the number of observations increases too much the probability of re-identification becomes very low and often zero because these sequences are infrequent in the original database. These long sequences no longer exist in the published database since the process of anonymisation tends to eliminate the outliers (i.e., sequences with a very low frequency). This effect is more evident in the case of the *hour-level data*.

We also estimated the cumulative distribution of the re-identification probability normalised with the cost of obtaining the background knowledge (see Section 2.4). Figure 8 depics the cumulative distribution of our single risk indicator obtained considering a sub-linear cost for the acquisition of the attacker's knowledge. We observe that if we assign a cost to the attack then the protection guaranteed is higher; thus allowing us to express in a very simple way the risk to the individuals if the whole dataset is published. Indeed, as an example figure 8(b) shows that when the *day-level dataset* is anonymised with $k = 5$ the probability of re-identification considering also the attack cost is at most about $0.025$ ($\frac{1}{20}$) for 90% of the attacks.

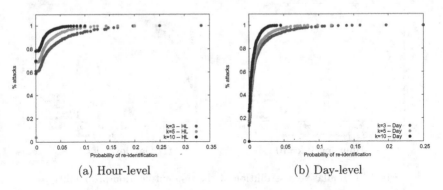

(a) Hour-level                    (b) Day-level

**Fig. 8.** Risk analysis with Background Knowledge Cost

## 5.2   Data Quality Evaluation

In our experiment we also evaluated the data quality by measuring the *precision* and the *coverage* defined above. Table 1(a) shows these two measures for the $k$-anonymous versions of the *hour-level dataset* while table 1(b) shows the same information for the *day-level dataset*.

**Table 1.** Precision versus coverage of the $k$-anonymised experimental data

|  (a) Time: hour-level |  |  | (b) Time: day-level |  |  |
| --- | --- | --- | --- | --- | --- |
| k | Precision | Coverage | k | Precision | Coverage |
| 3 | 1.00 | 0.27 | 3 | 0.98 | 0.87 |
| 5 | 1.00 | 0.15 | 5 | 0.97 | 0.83 |
| 10 | 1.00 | 0.04 | 10 | 0.96 | 0.72 |

As expected the anonymisation preserves very well the precision of the *ODpairs*; this means that the data transformation does not introduce noise, while it tends to suppress some *ODpairs* and this affects the data coverage. This behaviour is more evident in the *hour-level dataset*. Lastly, we also analysed how the *coverage* changes by varying the risk in the dataset. Figure 9 outlines the results. In line with our expectations, the *coverage* increases with the privacy risk. However, we observe that with a risk of re-identification of 0.1 we can have a *coverage* of about 90% in the *hour-level dataset* anonymized with $k = 5$. The situation improves a lot in the *day-level dataset*. Thus, this is a good tool for managing the trade-off between privacy and data utility.

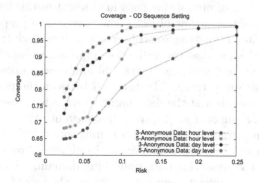

**Fig. 9.** Coverage with respect to privacy risk

# 6   The State-of-the-Art

Research in information privacy consists of a vast corpus of multi-disciplinary work combining results from the fields of psychology, law, computer science amongst others. Privacy in information systems has been often governed by a set of fair practices that help organisations manage users' information in responsible manners [8]. There often exists a disconnection between the interpretation of privacy needs from the perspective of the user and the prescribed privacy preserving mechanisms offered by devices and systems. Hong et al. [9] presented privacy risk models for ubiquitous systems in order to convert privacy from an abstract concept into specific issues relating to concrete applications. Kosa et al. [10], in an attempt to represent and measure privacy, presented an interesting finite state machine based representation of at most nine privacy states for any individual in a computer system. A recent work by Kiyomoto et al. [11] proposes a privacy policy management mechanism whereby a match is made between user's personal privacy requirements and organisational privacy policies. PrivAware [12] was presented as a tool to detect and report unintended loss of privacy in a social network. Krishnamurthy et al. [13] measured the loss of privacy and the impact of privacy protection in web browsing both at a browser level as well as a HTTP proxy level. Tao et al. [14] put forward a model for quality of service (QoS) for web services that quantified users' privacy risks in order to make the service selection process manageable. Banescu et al. [15] came up with a privacy compliance technique for detecting and measuring the severity of privacy infringements.

With richer user data available for data mining, work in privacy preserving data mining and privacy preserving data publishing have gained momentum in the recent years. Techniques such as adding random noise and perturbing outputs while preserving certain statistical aggregates are often used [16–19]. Some notable work data anonymisation work include $k$-anonymity [2], $l$-diversity [20], $t$-closeness [21], $p$-sensitive $k$-anonymity [22], $(\alpha, k)$-anonymity [23] and $\epsilon$-differential privacy [24]. The $k$-anonymity model has been also studied and adapted in the context of movements data in different works: [3] exploits the inherent uncertainty of the moving object's whereabouts; [4] proposes a technique based on *suppression* of the dangerous observations from each trajectory; and [5] proposes a data-driven spatial generalization approach to achieve $k$-anonymity. A critique by Domingo-Ferrer and Torra [25] analyses the drawbacks of some of those anonymisation methods. The trade-off between the privacy guarantees of anonymisation models and the data mining utility have been considered by authors in [26, 27]. Sramka et al. [28] compared data utility versus privacy based on two well known privacy models – $k$-anonymity and $\epsilon$-differential privacy.

Our proposed empirical risk model draws inspirations from the existing research in the privacy preserving data publishing domain. We envision that our model provides a clear understanding of privacy (or the lack of it) in released but anonymised data with relation to risk, privacy, cost of attacks and data utility.

## 7    Conclusions

In this paper we have proposed an empirical risk model that provides a complete and realistic view on the privacy risks, which can be derived from the release of trajectory data. Our model is able to empirically evaluate the real risks of re-identification taking into account also the cost of any attack on privacy as well as the relation between the risk and the utility of the data. With legislature becoming increasingly detailed about data protection, it is essential to be able to communicate well how privacy, risk and cost of attacks are associated when applying mathematical models for privacy preserving data release. We have presented promising evaluations of our model for the well-known $k$-anonymisation applied to real trajectory data from the Italian cities of Pisa and Florence. In the future, we plan to evaluate our model with different types of real data of sequential nature. Furthermore, we intend to investigate risk models suitable for other types of data.

# References

1. Samarati, P.: Protecting respondents identities in microdata release. IEEE Transactions on Knowledge and Data Engineering 13(6), 1010–1027 (2001)
2. Sweeney, L.: k-anonymity: A model for protecting privacy. International Journal of Uncertainty, Fuzziness and Knowledge-Based Systems 10(05), 557–570 (2002)
3. Abul, O., Bonchi, F., Nanni, M.: Never walk alone: Uncertainty for anonymity in moving objects databases. In: The 24th IEEE International Conference on Data Engineering (ICDE), pp. 376–385 (2008)
4. Terrovitis, M., Mamoulis, N.: Privacy preservation in the publication of trajectories. In: MDM, pp. 65–72 (2008)
5. Monreale, A., Andrienko, G.L., Andrienko, N.V., Giannotti, F., Pedreschi, D., Rinzivillo, S., Wrobel, S.: Movement data anonymity through generalization. TDP 3(2), 91–121 (2010)
6. Monreale, A., Pedreschi, D., Pensa, R., Pinelli, F.: Anonymity preserving sequential pattern mining. Artificial Intelligence and Law (to appear, 2014)
7. Voronoï, G.: Nouvelles applications des paramètres continus à la théorie des formes quadratiques. deuxième mémoire. recherches sur les parallélloèdres primitifs. Journal für die Reine und Angewandte Mathematik 134, 198–287 (1908)
8. Westin, A.F.: Privacy and freedom. Washington and Lee Law Review 25(1), 166 (1968)
9. Hong, J.I., Ng, J.D., Lederer, S., Landay, J.A.: Privacy risk models for designing privacy-sensitive ubiquitous computing systems. In: The 5th Conference on Designing Interactive Systems: Processes, Practices, Methods, and Techniques, pp. 91–100. ACM (2004)
10. Kosa, T.A., El-Khatib, K., Marsh, S.: Measuring privacy. Journal of Internet Services and Information Security (JISIS) 1(4), 60–73 (2011)
11. Kiyomoto, S., Nakamura, T., Takasaki, H., Watanabe, R., Miyake, Y.: PPM: Privacy policy manager for personalized services. In: Cuzzocrea, A., Kittl, C., Simos, D.E., Weippl, E., Xu, L. (eds.) CD-ARES Workshops 2013. LNCS, vol. 8128, pp. 377–392. Springer, Heidelberg (2013)
12. Becker, J.L., Chen, H.: Measuring privacy risk in online social networks (2009)
13. Krishnamurthy, B., Malandrino, D., Wills, C.E.: Measuring privacy loss and the impact of privacy protection in web browsing. In: The 3rd Symposium on Usable Privacy and Security, pp. 52–63. ACM (2007)
14. Yu, T., Zhang, Y., Lin, K.-J.: Modeling and measuring privacy risks in qos web services. In: The 3rd IEEE Conference on E-Commerce Technology and the 8th IEEE International Conference on and Enterprise Computing, E-Commerce, and E-Services, p. 4. IEEE (2006)
15. Banescu, S., Petković, M., Zannone, N.: Measuring privacy compliance using fitness metrics. In: Barros, A., Gal, A., Kindler, E. (eds.) BPM 2012. LNCS, vol. 7481, pp. 114–119. Springer, Heidelberg (2012)
16. Agrawal, R., Srikant, R.: Privacy-preserving data mining. ACM SIGMOD Record 29(2), 439–450 (2000)

17. Dinur, I., Nissim, K.: Revealing information while preserving privacy. In: The 22nd ACM SIGMOD-SIGACT-SIGART Symposium on Principles of Database Systems, pp. 202–210 (2003)
18. Evfimievski, A., Gehrke, J., Srikant, R.: Limiting privacy breaches in privacy preserving data mining. In: The 22nd ACM SIGMOD-SIGACT-SIGART Symposium on Principles of Database Systems, pp. 211–222 (2003)
19. Blum, A., Dwork, C., McSherry, F., Nissim, K.: Practical privacy: the sulq framework. In: The 24th ACM SIGMOD-SIGACT-SIGART Symposium on Principles of Database Systems, pp. 128–138 (2005)
20. Machanavajjhala, A., Kifer, D., Gehrke, J., Venkitasubramaniam, M.: l-diversity: Privacy beyond k-anonymity. ACM Transactions on Knowledge Discovery from Data (TKDD) 1(1), 3 (2007)
21. Li, N., Li, T., Venkatasubramanian, S.: t-closeness: Privacy beyond k-anonymity and l-diversity. In: The 23rd IEEE International Conference on Data Engineering (ICDE), pp. 106–115 (2007)
22. Truta, T.M., Vinay, B.: Privacy protection: p-sensitive k-anonymity property. In: The 22nd International Conference on Data Engineering Workshops, p. 94. IEEE (2006)
23. Wong, R.C.-W., Li, J., Fu, A.W.-C., Wang, K. ($\alpha$, k)-anonymity: an enhanced k-anonymity model for privacy preserving data publishing. In: The 12th ACM SIGKDD international Conference on Knowledge Discovery and Data Mining, pp. 754–759 (2006)
24. Dwork, C.: Differential privacy. In: Bugliesi, M., Preneel, B., Sassone, V., Wegener, I. (eds.) ICALP 2006. LNCS, vol. 4052, pp. 1–12. Springer, Heidelberg (2006)
25. Domingo-Ferrer, J., Torra, V.: A critique of k-anonymity and some of its enhancements. In: The 3rd International Conference on Availability, Reliability and Security (ARES), pp. 990–993. IEEE (2008)
26. Rastogi, V., Suciu, D., Hong, S.: The boundary between privacy and utility in data publishing. In: The 33rd International Conference on Very Large Databases, pp. 531–542. VLDB Endowment (2007)
27. Brickell, J., Shmatikov, V.: The cost of privacy: destruction of data-mining utility in anonymized data publishing. In: The 14th ACM SIGKDD International Conference on Knowledge Discovery and Data Mining, pp. 70–78 (2008)
28. Sramka, M., Safavi-Naini, R., Denzinger, J., Askari, M.: A practice-oriented framework for measuring privacy and utility in data sanitization systems. In: EDBT/ICDT Workshops, p. 27. ACM (2010)

# Providing Trustworthy Advice Online

## An Exploratory Study on the Potential of Discursive Psychology in Trust Research

Sarah Talboom and Jo Pierson

iMinds – SMIT – VUB, Brussels, Belgium
{sarah.talboom,jo.pierson}@vub.ac.be

**Abstract.** The Internet serves as an important source for people who are looking for information and advice from peers. Within search behavior a central role is reserved for trust; it will guide the decision to participate online, to share experiences or to pick up information. This paper explores insights from discursive psychology as a potentially interesting approach for trust research in online peer environments. This allows for a certain shift of focus. Instead of looking at the information seeker, we focus on the information provider: How does he try to present himself – and the information sources he refers to in his arguments – as trustworthy and authoritative? Within this theoretical perspective trust is being studied as something that is highly negotiable depending on context and the effect the information provider tries to achieve. Throughout the paper conversation fragments - collected from an online forum on home-improvement - are incorporated to clarify and illustrate some central concepts of discursive psychology.

**Keywords:** trust, footing, cognitive authority, experiential knowledge, factual versions, category entitlements, discursive psychology.

## 1 Introduction

The Internet is an important source for people looking for information, advice or the opinion of peers. This paper is part of a broader research project where we try to understand how trust emerges in online environments where people – who do not know each other outside the platform – come together to share experiences and exchange advice or information. Think of online forums and review sites - such as for example TripAdvisor[1] or Epinions[2] - but also consumer reviews displayed on retail websites like Amazon[3]. Trust plays an important role in the decision whether or not to participate and to share and pick up information [1][2][3]. However, the focus of this specific paper is not so much on how trust occurs between individual people online or which factors will ensure the creation of trustworthy feelings towards the online contribution of a specific person. Rather, we explore a discursive psychology approach as

---

[1] www.tripadvisor.com
[2] www.epinions.com
[3] www.amazon.com

J. Zhou et al. (Eds.): IFIPTM 2014, IFIP AICT 430, pp. 141–156, 2014.
© IFIP International Federation for Information Processing 2014

a means to understand how participants in these online environments try to present themselves and the sources they refer to in their arguments as being trustworthy and authoritative. In addition we also investigate how their messages provide insight into what people consider to be trustworthy sources and how this is being discussed online. When it comes to research related to this topic, studies often emphasize the information seeker's side [4]. Far fewer studies focus on those individuals who provide such online environments with advice. The empirical part is also often directed to questioning the information seeker instead of analyzing naturalistic records. This while online discussions – where the "truth" of a message is being settled – can provide an alternative view on trust in information sources [5]. The work of authors like McKenzie [6], Neal and McKenzie [7] and Tuominen and Savolainen [8] offer such an alternative approach. They concentrate on online conversations in order to comprehend information use, and to understand how the value of sources is being negotiated online. The work of these authors departs from social constructionism and discursive psychology. In this study we look at how insights from this theoretical perspective can offer a potentially useful approach to perform trust research.

A discursive approach allows us to understand the way forum members seek to present their advice as being trustworthy and correct. It permits to focus on how members try to justify their own opinions, advice or information, and which claims other members use to reject the opinions, advice or information from others. By identifying the claims and practices people use to substantiate their own opinion or to undermine the advice of others, we gain insights into how members of a community collectively construct the reliability and authority of certain information sources. People seek to substantiate their advice, using external sources as well as peer / own experience as a source of knowledge. The choice of a particular source possibly represents what kind of resources these people find viable and useful within a certain context. Forum members will refer to a particular source in their arguments when they believe this source can back up their own opinion. So either they believe this source is trustworthy and/or they believe other people consider this source to be trustworthy.

## 2     Structure and Approach

This paper is structured as follows: During the first section we briefly discuss some problems and insights we encountered while starting up an exploratory qualitative analysis of forum threads. It is within this specific context that discursive psychology will be introduced as a potentially interesting and alternative approach to studying authority and trust. We briefly explain the main principles of a discursive approach in social psychology and continue with the work of Potter [9] on the construction of factual accounts. Here, the emphasis is on how people try to strengthen their statements via those strategies that either aim to manage the nature of the author of an argument, or construct a description that seems to be created independent of the forum member himself. The paper ends with a conclusion and a clear link to further research – which will be a thorough discursive analysis of forum threads and interview transcripts. In order to elucidate the structure, we will spend a short paragraph explaining our approach and case study. Throughout this paper we will frequently use some online conversation fragments in order to clarify and illustrate certain theoretical concepts, and also to immediately apply these concepts to our own case study.

The excerpts that are being used are part of a larger data set containing 380 forum threads collected from an online Belgian/Flemish home-improvement forum in the winter of 2012/2013. Some ethical considerations on the use of online and publicly available data can be read in the appendix of this paper.

## 3    Case Study of an Online Home-Improvement Forum

Home-improvement is a popular topic in Belgium/Flanders, where almost three-quarter of families own their own home [10]. The choice for a platform on home-improvement was motivated by the fact that people in the process of home-construction or - improvement are often forced to take decisions on subjects they do not fully know and understand. According to the Belgian employers' organization active in the construction sector – *Confederatie Bouw* – the sector is evolving rapidly. Everything needs to be greener, more sustainable, quicker and cheaper. At the same time everything is also becoming more technical and complex as new products, materials and construction processes enter the market. This makes it much more difficult for homeowners to make a decision, and staying informed becomes ever so important [11]. The online forum *"Bouwinfo"* – with 400 000 unique visitors per month and around 3 000 active members – seems to offer a way for people to get information on home-improvement tasks. On this discussion platform, people gather to exchange information and advice, or to swap experiences. 80% of the forum contributions are made by private individuals: people who are not active in the construction sector [12]. This implies that information being shared on Bouwinfo is often strongly related to personal experience or experiential knowledge [13], instead of professional knowledge. But what can the conversations on Bouwinfo tell us about the way people select and discuss information sources?

## 4    Who Is Entitled to Make Knowledge Claims Online?

If we were to ask forum members – in our case people occupied with home-improvement tasks – the kind of information sources they prefer when it comes to renovation and construction work, we would never get an unequivocal answer. Setting aside the fact that their feedback would strongly depend on individual preferences – some people count more on the advice of a professional than others – the answer would also depend on the context they have in mind when we question them, and on what these people already know about the subject matter. While analyzing the selection of forum threads, we noticed the same type of variation in how people on the discussion board would construct, accept or reject certain claims, opinions or advice. For example, the experiences Bouwinfo members often referred to can be divided into two different categories, each linked to a different type of source. Experiences in the first category are linked to the construction professional – or a person working in the construction sector. Experiences in the second category are linked to the experienced homeowner – or a person occupied with or experienced in performing a home-improvement task. In some occasions one of two categories was used to support or boost a message, while in other occasions the same category was given as a reason for skepticism.

In the following fragment (figure 1) a forum member, who – as we could see in his user ID – is a professional landscaper, presents forum members with information based on his own experience. In the first part of this fragment [A], the emphasis is on experience as an argument to eliminate the possible idea that the information table has an official character. In this way our member reduces the potential risk of liability: *"it is not something official, it is just based on my own experience as a landscaper"*. Throughout the second part [B], he presents his professional experience as justification of his claim to possess trustworthy knowledge. In order to do that, he questions the value of studies carried out by an official research centre. Within just two lines, he uses his own experience as a landscape professional to hedge (*"certainly not official"*), to claim knowledge (*"100% experience"*), and to undermine the authority of another source (*" without some kind of WTCB hassle"*).

*"[A] Below you find a table with indications on moss growth, certainly not official! [B] 100% experience without any study or some kind of WTCB[4] hassle"*

Thomas[5] (member since 2007 – over 3000 messages)

**Fig. 1.** Professional experience as a claim of knowledge – Discussion about keeping paving tiles moss-free

In a next example, instead of using the experience of a construction professional to boost a message, the authority of the construction professional is being questioned. In the first fragment (figure 2 – different discussion) a member rejects the advice of a construction contractor as a suitable source of information within the specific context of soil stability.

*"It is perfectly possible **that your construction contractor has years of experience … But even then I would not trust him when it comes to advice on foundations**. In this case you just order a stability study with a structural engineer whose study will be based on your plan and soil investigation"* [6]

Iris (member since 2009 – over 500 messages)

**Fig. 2.** Questioning the authority of a construction professional – Discussion about piled foundations

---

[4] WTCB is the Scientific and Technical Centre for the Construction Industry. It is a Belgian private research institution whose main task is 1) to perform scientific and technical research, 2) to provide technical information, assistance and advice to its members and 3) to contribute to the overall development and innovation in the construction sector [14].

[5] All quotations are translated from Dutch and provided with a pseudonym. Only year of membership and an approximate number of messages are recorded. Other features about membership were retained. A motivation for this decision can be found in the appendix; where we discuss some ethical considerations.

[6] All of the original fragments were displayed in a regular font. We use a bold font in order to emphasize certain components in the text.

In the third fragment (figure 3 – different discussion) the member goes one step further. She states that *"they say a lot"*, using "they" to refer to people in the garden-ing/construction sector. The forum member tries to undermine the authority of con-struction professionals by implicitly suggesting that they do not know what they are talking about. She even goes so far as to state that the only people entitled to provide guidance are the ones with personal experience.

*"[Brand X] is in my opinion the best brand. Why don't you go with [brand Y]?  I have had a [brand Y] lawn mower for years and it has a very strong engine. **"They" say a lot but per-sonal experience is the only true measure. I may be a woman but I know what works and what doesn't."***

Tessa (member since 2012 – over 100 messages)

**Fig. 3.** Questioning the authority of a construction professional – Discussion about lawn mowers

The way one constructs or downgrades the authority of either construction profession-als or homeowners clearly varies based on the context of a conversation and the goal one wants to achieve – for example persuading versus rejecting. It is therefore not possible to state that the advice of a construction professional will prevail over the opinion of peers with experience or visa versa. There is no generally accepted attitude or opinion regard-ing the authority of a particular source. Whether a person has the right to speak with knowledge, can be seen as situational and variable; something that is negotiated within a particular context and constructed to fulfill a specific function. This is exactly where the perspective of discursive psychology / social constructionism / discourse in social psy-chology can offer an important approach! It illustrates what Potter and Wetherell [15] mean when they mention that an empirical claim can also emphasize the need for an analysis of discourse. According to the aforementioned authors, studying variation in utterances and accounts from a realistic approach would cause some difficulties in dis-playing this variation. Instead of eliminating variation, variation itself becomes the topic of research within discourse research in social psychology [15].

## 5    An Introduction to the Discursive Psychology Approach

Trying to find your way through discursive psychology literature can at best be confus-ing. This is partly so because the name only came up during the 90's, while the approach itself emerged much earlier. Initially – during the late 80's – authors referred to "dis-course [analysis] in social psychology"; such as for example in the pioneering work of Potter and Wetherell [15]. It isn't until a few years later – when the field has already expanded and deepened – that the name discursive psychology pops up [16]. Discursive psychology or discourse in social psychology (DP) is seen as one of the main but less mainstream approaches and positions in social psychology [17]. At the same time it is also more than just an approach: *"it is an alternative metatheory or a different philoso-phy of science* [17]. It implies a specific approach to social and psychological phenome-na; and is sometimes considered both a method and a theoretical perspective [18]. Potter however recently emphasized DP as being more an approach than a method whose *"basic methodological and analytic principles follow from its meta-theoretical, theoreti-cal and conceptual arguments [...]."* [16]. Discursive psychologists believe that many of the phenomena – studied as internal mental processes within traditional psychology – are actually created within discourse. Based on this premise, DP therefore implies both a theoretical and methodological shift of focus [19]. Within DP, a researcher examines *"how psychological issues and objects are constructed, understood and displayed as people interact in both everyday and institutional situations."* [16]. From this respect, the decision on who can be considered an authority in the field of construction work will not be made in the individual minds of people. The right to speak with authority will be discussed, negotiated, settled and questioned again within everyday conversations on the discussion platform of Bouwinfo. The emphasis is on social practices and not on the individual cognitive process. The most obvious – but not the only – way to study such issues is by working with naturalistic data [15] [16]. Texts – in the broadest sense of the word – that are not developed or designed to serve the needs of a researcher. Forum conversations can therefore be seen as natural texts.

An important starting point in many studies and handbooks on DP explains the focus within DP as a focus on discourse[7] itself – discourse as the primary object of study or *"as a topic in its own right"* [15]. This is directly opposed to the vision of cognitive and traditional social psychological approaches in which language is often regarded as a window through which the world reveals itself, or as a mirror that exposes the inner state of the speaker/writer [8]. DP does not explain discourse as a result of or a medium for an inner mental state [15][20][21]. It puts the referential function of language – or language as a means to bring about the social reality – and the expressive function of language – or language as conduit for the feelings and attitudes of the speaker/writer – between brackets [18]. The central focus of discourse analysis within social psychology can be illustrated by referring to the concepts of variation, function and construction [8][15][22]. Language allows for the creation of a particular version of social reality. Forum members describe their own experiences with certain home-improvement activities and give their version of events. The concept of variation becomes clear when we realize that different versions of an event can be constructed. Discourse is constructive in the sense that through language people – members – construct their version of the world, it is not a perfect reflection of reality. In order to do so, members rely on what Potter and Wetherell call *pre-existing linguistic resources*, which makes discourse not only constructive but also something that is constructed [15]. This highlights the influencing role of culture, history and context. Language is also oriented towards action: for example, through discourse people can try to justify their accounts, or they can question the accounts of others. So there exist both a variety of versions, as well as a variety of functions, purposes and goals.

## 6    The Creation of Factual Versions

DP shares a similar interest with rhetorical psychology: they both emphasize the way people use arguments in their talk. Within DP this translates into studying fact construction in everyday conversations [21]. Within this study we have been guided by the work of Potter on the construction of factual accounts. By managing either the nature of the producer of a description, or by constructing a description that seems to

---

[7] Potter and Wetherell [15] define discourse – based on the work of Gilbert and Mulkay (1984) – as including all forms of spoken interaction and written texts, both formally and informally.

be created independently from the producer of the message, people seek to construct their messages as factual [9]. In the next section concepts such as factuality, cognitive authority, category entitlements and footing are discussed based on both theory and examples from our data set.

Conversations on the forum of Bouwinfo tend to be shaped around the exchange of advice, opinions and information. What stood out while analyzing the conversations was that members try to substantiate their claims based on different strategies and different types of evidence. One way to justify a claim was to try and present their advice as being a fact. On other occasions members also tried to undermine the advice of others. This was done by inter alia asking about the source of a member's argument or by questioning a member's interest in formulating advice. This was for example demonstrated in section 4 of this paper.

In the fragment below (figure 4) forum member Jonas provides his advice with a sense of factuality by adding a reference to an important Belgian research institute on construction. Isaac and Freddy however question the integrity of Jonas and suspect him to be a construction professional in disguise. They base their suspicion on the fact that Jonas has made two extremely positive contributions about one specific brand.

*"That is correct. But I don't know the products of [brand X]. I do know that the products of [brand Y]* **have a WTCB certificate** *– I believe [Brand X] has no certificate – and that they are* **a lot cheaper.***"*

Jonas (member since 2012 – less than 10 messages)

*"Nice first message! You probably have no interests in this company?* 😊 *"*

Isaac (member since 2010 – over 100 messages)

*"Exactly the same holds for his second message: [url towards specific thread]. Apparently his shares are on the decline* 😊 *"*

Freddy (member since 2009 – over 2000 messages)

**Fig. 4.** Questioning the integrity of a member – Discussion about solutions against humidity

This finding strongly aligns with what Potter describes in his work *"Representing Reality: Discourse, Rhetoric and Social Construction"* [9]. In chapters 5 and 6 he focuses on the way people seek to equip their claims with a touch of factuality and on the strategies people use in order to avoid the accusation of a conflict of interest. This contrasts highly with those studies who try to grasp the nature and the correctness of arguments or who try to link arguments to the interests of people. The author addresses the notions of *stake*, *entitlement* and *footing* as important concepts when constructing or undermining factual versions [9].[8] What these concepts have in common, is that all three of them refer to the identity of the producer and how this identity

---

[8] Besides stake, footing and entitlement – which emphasize how the identity of the producer can be managed – Potter also formulates some techniques aimed at creating – what he calls – *"out-there-ness"*. Techniques such as *empiricist discourse, active voicing* and *detail and focalization* all share that *"[...] they construct the description as independent of the agent doing the production"*[9].

can contribute to the creation of factual versions or arguments [9]. The conversation mentioned above shows a clear link with the concept of *stake* or *interest* and involves a very explicit accusation addressed to Jonas. In the work of Potter, these kinds of accusations are not discussed. He does not look at how people assign certain interests to the utterances of others. Instead his focus is on how people seek to construct versions that are resistant to accusations such as a conflict of interest [9].

## 6.1    Stake Inoculation

A specific rhetorical strategy people can use is what Potter [9] calls *stake inoculation*. Potter [23] mentions a nice comparison in order to clarify this concept: *"Just as flu inoculation is intended to prevent flu, a stake inoculation is intended to prevent a claim being undermined as a product of stake."*. Looking back at the text fragment and the contribution of Jonas, Jonas indicates implicitly that the products of brand Y are better than the products of brand X. Recommending a specific brand without any kind of motivation or argument makes a recommendation vulnerable; it might give rise to the idea that there is a certain degree of self-interest involved. Think for example of the contributions of Isaac and Freddy where they accuse Jonas of trying to sell his own products. Jonas seeks to substantiate his preference for a certain brand by making reference to a "neutral" – in this case scientific – source. However, based on this fragment it becomes clear that stake inoculation does not always make a success story.

## 6.2    Category Entitlements

Another way in which an argument can be injected with some "truth" or credibility, is when the speaker (or author) is assigned to a certain category of people who can claim certain knowledge – or what Potter calls *category entitlement*: *"people in particular categories – official and unofficial – are expected to know certain things or to have certain epistemological skills."* [24]. In this case you do not need to ask how it is that someone knows something. The mere fact that this person belongs to a certain category is sufficient; it qualifies this person as being knowledgeable or as having expertise. Who is considered knowledgeable also depends on the specific context and the specific category [9]. Potter further emphasizes that entitlements are not inherent to a certain category. (Knowledge) entitlements are worked up, constructed and built up [9]. This ties in with the work of Horton-Salway. Based on the work from inter alia Hester and Eglin (1997) she emphasizes the ethnomethodological notion of *"culture-in-action"* or the fact that one should have attention for *"the situated nature of knowledge claims and the local recognition of cultural categories and members' related entitlements."* [25]. She cites Hester and Eglin (1997) who state that categories are learned and get meaning within the context in which they are used. According to Horton-Salway [25] it is therefore important that an analyst is aware that membership within a certain category and its related knowledge entitlements are established within a local context. It is not something a priori or fixed. This vision on knowledge claims, categories and member's related entitlements is in line with the view of discursive psychology.

### 6.3    Cognitive Authority

A clear link can be found between category entitlements and the concept of cognitive authority. In the following paragraph cognitive authority is first discussed as a notion derived from cognitive psychology. Afterwards, based on the work of McKenzie [6], the concept is being explained as something that is constructed within conversations and connects more with discursive psychology and the notion of category entitlements. In *"Second-hand knowledge: An inquiry into cognitive authority"* Patrick Wilson [26] makes a distinction between cognitive or epistemic knowledge and administrative or performatory knowledge. In a later journal article for Library Trends he clearly summarizes these two distinct types of knowledge. Administrative authority relates to the position someone has. This position allows a person to give orders and hand out punishments if necessary: *"Administrative or performatory authorities [...] are authorized to do or command or forbid something [...]."*. Within this article the focus is on cognitive authority or authority based upon claims relating to a specific type of knowledge: *"Cognitive authorities are authorities on something [...]."* [27]. Yet you cannot assign yourself the label of a cognitive authority. According to Wilson it is important that others recognize you as an authority. He links this to social perception and recognition: *"It is not what you "really know" but what others think you know that gives you authority; you get cognitive authority by getting others to think you know things."* [27]. You can be recognized by one, by some or by all as someone who knows things within a certain domain. For example, in the fragment below a forum member of Bouwinfo (Sil-figure 5) refers to the opinion of a construction professional in order to back up his own point of view. This suggests that our member considers this professional to be someone who has cognitive authority on the level of insulation materials.

*"I would reject the use of [product X] because it is a foil. My [insulation brand] **installer said** that I should preferably use hard insulation plates. This would prevent the material to be blown against the roof tiles"*

Sil (member since 2007 – over 500 messages)

**Fig. 5.** Referring to a cognitive authority in argument – Discussion about roof insulation

*"Oh my, **I don't know whether your installer knows** how to place a foil. The foil should be firmly fixed so that it becomes impossible to flit against the roof tiles. **Did this constructor accidentally happen to sell [brand] ecological insulation plates** instead of a dirty chemical PE [polyethylene] or PU [polyurethane] foil? In my own house I will blow insulation flocks against a (correctly positioned) foil. **The contractors that have been down here** didn't mention that there was anything wrong with this approach."*

Mark (member since 2011 – over 1500 messages)

**Fig. 6.** Questioning authority and integrity – Discussion about roof insulation

Yet we can see in the remainder of the conversation that not every member shares the same vision on who can or cannot be considered an authority on the level of roof insulation. Mark (figure 6) questions the authority and the independence of the construction professional mentioned by Sil (figure 5): *"I don't know whether your installer knows* [what he is doing]". He also tries to undermine the credibility of this advice by referring to the possible interests this contractor may have: *"Did this constructor accidentally happen to sell [...]?"*. When people mention that someone is an authority on a certain subject, this can either mean that everyone agrees that this person is an authority on [insulation material] or this can mean that one sees this person as an authority and that one believes that others should feel the same way [26]. This makes for an interesting approach: Whom do people – occupied with construction work and home-improvement tasks – see as authoritative sources? And how is this label of authority being negotiated in online conversations?

We also need to have attention to what Wilson [27] calls the "scope" of authority. Let us continue with the example of the discussion about roof insulation. Our installer in fragment 1 (figure 5) can be considered someone who is knowledgeable on the level of construction work, on insulation materials, or as someone who is only knowledgeable when it comes to roof insulation. The area in which someone has knowledge varies from a very broad range – construction work – to a very small part – roof insulation. The "degree" of authority can – besides having a scope from narrow to broad – vary from little to a lot. According to the forum member, his installer has plenty of authority since – implicitly – our member is willing to adjust his entire approach to the opinion of his insulation installer. A final question Wilson [27] asks is *"What leads us to recognize a person as having authority?"*. He makes a distinction between people who are somewhat knowledgeable themselves – who can test the person both formally and informally – and people who are not knowledgeable – and who will have to rely on reputation or performance. Previous research also indicated reputation and performance as key elements for trust [4].

**Cognitive Authority, Credibility and Trust.** Within our wider research on the emergence of trust in online textual environments, trust is being operationalized as *"the degree to which someone is willing or considering to follow up the advice of (a) forum member(s)."*. Based on a literature review on trust we found that this willingness to trust someone is influenced by identity, reputation, expertise and experience [4]. A link between trust, credibility and cognitive authority can also be found in the words of Wilson [26]: *"The person whom I recognize as having cognitive authority is the one whom I think should be allowed to have influence on my thinking, for I suppose he has a good basis for saying what he does. [...] The authority's influence on us is thought proper because he is thought credible, worthy of belief."*. When you consider a person as an authority within a certain domain, you will be more willing to trust them. The extent to which someone is recognized as someone with cognitive authority, will be closely related to reputation, expertise and experience. Yet with regard to our own research context, we could question what type of people are being acknowledged as an authority. Who is sufficiently competent so that we are willing to follow up this person's advice concerning a construction or renovation project? Which knowledge claims – professional versus experiential – are important and how are they being negotiated online?

**Cognitive Authority Online.** The work of McKenzie [6] and Neal and McKenzie [7] is interesting related to the concept of cognitive authority. These authors use the concept as a framework to understand how an individual makes a decision on the authority of an information source. The first study looks at how pregnant women search for information and describes the context-specific discursive techniques these women use to either augment or undermine the authority of a source. The second study tries to understand how bloggers with a chronic disease present certain information sources as (not) being authoritative and how these bloggers use these versions of authority to substantiate their own claims. Both studies argue that traditional ideas on cognitive authority should be revised when you study the concept in an online environment. Instead of focusing on the cognitive process of an individual and how this person tries to determine whether or not a certain source is important, both authors consider authority – or an authoritative source of information – as something that is negotiated collaboratively on a community level. McKenzie [6] therefore prefers the concept of "cognitive knowledge" from Jordan (1977) since this notion acknowledges the role of the community in defining which information sources can be seen as appropriate and allows for authoritative knowledge to be defined according to the context. This view on the construction of authority is in line with the vision of social constructionism and discursive psychology.

## 6.4    (Change of) Footing

The notion of footing originates from the work of Goffman and is mentioned in his work *"Forms of Talk"*. In this book – which is a compilation of different essays – a full chapter is devoted to the concept. Goffman [28] defines a change in footing as *"[...] a change in the alignment we take up to ourselves and the others present as expressed in the way we manage the production or reception of an utterance."*. A clearer description of footing can be found in the work of Howitt and Cramer [29] where they state that *"Footing refers to whether the speaker talks as if they are the author of what is being said, the subject of the words that are being said, or whether they are presenting or animating the words of someone else."*. This description links back to the different participant roles – or different production formats [28] – a person can take on or use when he or she is acting as a speaker or writer. The author – or the person who composed the words, the principal – or the person whose viewpoint is expressed in the message and who believes what is being said, and the animator – or the person who brings the words to the listener(s). Howitt and Cramer claim that these three types of footing do not exclude each other and thus all three of them can – but need not – be present in a text.

A shift in footing closely connects with the idea of creating a factual version; mentioned earlier. By changing your footing – for example from being both author, principal and animator of a story to being only the messenger – a person can try to create a version that seems more credible [8] [20]. A clear example of such a change in footing can be found in the following fragment (figure 7) where a forum member – after giving his own opinion in his own words – acts as an animator by transferring the words of a person whom he believes has some cognitive authority.

> *"I would reject the use of [product] because it is a foil. My [insulation brand] installer said that I should preferably use hard insulation plates. This would prevent the material to be blown against the roof tiles"*
>
> Sil (member since 2007 – over 500 messages)

**Fig. 7.** Change of footing in argument – Discussion about roof insulation

Here it is quite clear that the animator/writer is quoting the author of the words. Clearly the forum member is not formulating this quotation in exactly the same manner with exactly the same words. What is more important is that this member brings this message as if the construction professional has formulated this exact sentence. In this way the quoted opinion of the person with so-called cognitive authority backs up the statement from the forum member. The author links his message to a certain category of people – construction professionals – because he believes this category has a certain level of necessary knowledge. By substantiating his own opinion with the opinion of a construction professional he tries to augment the credibility of his version. However, in order to understand this change of footing, we should look at the full context of the conversation. People will try to maintain their level of accountability by producing factual versions or by shifting their footing. According to Tuominen and Savolainen [8] a change in footing will certainly become important when people try to defend a certain version which is not generally accepted – in this case for example when all previous messages would claim the use of insulation flocks instead of hard insulation plates.

## 7     Reflection and Conclusion

Within this paper we tried to consider our broader research project – on the emergence of trust in online textual environments – from a discursive perspective. The inspiration to explore this approach came from some issues that occurred while starting up a qualitative content analysis of online forum discussions. Initially we thought it would be rather easy to identify which information sources forum members referred to as being valuable and trustworthy. However, throughout this initial analysis we were faced with a variety of ways in which forum members would construct, accept or reject certain claims, opinions or advice based on a variety of sources – from so called expert sources to scientific sources, not to mention using own experience as an authoritative source. We tried to frame these issues by looking at what a discursive psychology perspective could teach us. Instead of trying to eliminate variation in accounts, variation in the discourse of people is seized as an important topic for research. Questions on forum members' attitudes or thoughts on trust – who do members believe have the authority to say something useful or who do members trust – fade into the background and questions on how people discuss authority, which strategies they use and for what purposes become the focus of research. *"[…] DP does not seek to produce knowledge of things but an understanding of the processes by which they are 'talked into being'."* [30].

The next step is to apply this framework to a discourse analysis of both forum threads and interview transcripts. Our preliminary results from the initial analysis will be re-evaluated based on the theoretical framework mentioned in this paper. Here we will map how forum members seek to strengthen their own advice by – inter alia – referring to what they consider as an authoritative source and how they try to present these sources as being authoritative. The findings from this analysis of forum conversations can than be weighed against the results of in-depth interviews with forum members and forum visitors – people looking for information or advice on Bouwinfo. While both conducting and analyzing these interviews with forum members, we will have to pay sufficient attention to our role as an interviewer. Willig [30] emphasizes that within a semi-structured interview – in contrast to those texts that occur naturally – participants will adapt to the interview setting. According to the author, this would provide more information about the discursive strategies people use in an interview than the ones they apply in everyday life.

This paper used conversation fragments displayed on a specific forum in order to emphasize the difficulty in determining whom people trust. It appears that this strongly depends on context and function or goal. Trust literature widely accepts the idea of trust being something context-specific [31][32][33]. However, the examples that follow such a statement are often a bit obvious. Is it not pretty straightforward that you trust a construction professional with construction work but not with taking care of your car? To our sense, context will be even more important and specific than indicated in literature. Sometimes a person will trust a construction professional and sometimes he will trust his peers.

It should be clear that several – both online and offline – environments may be subject to a DP analysis. For our convenience we stick to the same topic. For example, consider an analysis of home-improvement blogs where homeowners talk about their decisions related to construction work. Or even websites, platforms and product manuals where construction professionals deliver content. There may be a difference in the way homeowners and construction professionals make authority claims and implicitly mention whom they trust.

# References

1. Ridings, C.M., Gefen, D., Arinze, B.: Some antecedents and effects of trust in virtual communities. J. Strateg. Inform. Syst. 11(3), 271–295 (2002)
2. Hertzum, M., Andersen, H.H.K., Andersen, V., Hansen, C.B.: Trust in information sources: seeking information from people, documents, and virtual agents. Interact. Comput. 14(5), 575–599 (2002)
3. Ljung, A., Wahlforss, E.: People, Profiles & Trust: On interpersonal trust in web-mediated social spaces (2008), www.Lulu.com
4. Talboom, S., Pierson, J.: Understanding Trust within Online Discussion Boards: Trust Formation in the Absence of Reputation Systems. In: Fernández-Gago, C., Martinelli, F., Pearson, S., Agudo, I. (eds.) Trust Management VII. IFIP AICT, vol. 401, pp. 83–99. Springer, Heidelberg (2013)

5. Savolainen, R.: Judging the quality and credibility of information in internet discussion forums. J. Amer. Soc. Inform. Sci. Tech. 62(7), 1243–1256 (2011)
6. McKenzie, P.J.: Justifying Cognitive Authority Decisions: Discursive Strategies of Information Seekers. Libr. Quart. 73(3), 261–288 (2003)
7. Neal, D.M., McKenzie, P.J.: Putting the pieces together: Endometriosis blogs, cognitive authority, and collaborative information behavior. J. Med. Libr. Assoc. 99(2), 127–134 (2011)
8. Tuominen, K., Savolainen, R.: A Social Constructionist Approach to the Study of Information Use as Discursive Action. In: Vakkari, P., Savolainen, R., Dervin, B. (eds.) Information Seeking in Context: Proceedings of an International Conference on Research in Information Needs, Seeking and Use in Different Contexts, pp. 81–96. Taylor Graham, London (1997)
9. Potter, J.: Representing reality: Discourse, Rhetoric and Social Construction. SAGE Publications Ltd., London (1996)
10. Heylen, K.: The evolution of the housing situation in Flanders: 2004-2009. Policy Research Center for Spatial Planning and Housing. Ministry of the Flemish Community (2012) (in Dutch) http://economie.fgov.be/nl/modules/digibib/bevolking/1804_de_evolutie_van_de_woonsituatie_in_vlaanderen_silc-gegevens_voor_de_periode_2004-2009.jsp
11. Construction and renovation. Everything you need to know. Edition 2013. Confederatie Bouw (2013) (in Dutch) http://www.confederatiebouw.be/Portals/0/documenten/ikzoekeenvakman/Bouwen%20en%20verbouwen.pdf
12. CIM Metriweb: Report on 'Bouwinfo' (March 2012) (in Dutch)
13. Borkman, T.: Experiental Knowledge: A New Concept for the Analysis of Self-Help Groups. Soc. Sci. Rev. 50(3), 445–456 (1976)
14. Presentation WTCB, http://www.wtcb.be/homepage/index.cfm?cat=bbri&sub=presentation (2014) (in Dutch)
15. Potter, J., Wetherell, M.: Discourse and Social Psychology: Beyond Attitudes and Behaviour. SAGE Publications Ltd., London (1987)
16. Potter, J.: Discourse Analysis and Discursive Psychology. In: Cooper, H., Camic, P.M., Long, D.L., Panter, A.T., Rindskopf, D., Sher, K.J. (eds.) APA Handbook of Research Methods in Psychology, vol. 2, pp. 111–130. American Psychological Association Press, Washington (2012)
17. Foster, D.: Social psychology. In: Nicholas, L. (ed.) Introduction to Psychology, ch. 12, 2nd edn., pp. 254–282. UTC Press, Cape Town (2008)
18. van den Berg, H.: Discourse analysis. KWALON 2 (2004) (in Dutch)
19. Billig, M.: Political Rhetoric. In: Sears, D.O., Huddy, L., Jervis, R. (eds.) Oxford Handbook of Political Psychology, pp. 222–253. Oxford University Press Inc., New York (2003)
20. Potter, J.: Discourse Analysis and Constructionist Approaches: Theoretical Background. In: Richardson, J.T.E. (ed.) Handbook of Qualitative Research Methods for Psychology and the Social Sciences, pp. 125–140. British Psychological Society, Leicester (1996)
21. McKinlay, A., McVittie, C.: Social Psychology and Discourse. John Wiley & Sons, West Sussex (2009)
22. Harre, R., Stearns, P.: Discursive Psychology in Practice. SAGE Publications Ltd., London (1995)

23. Potter, J.: Attitudes, social representations and discursive psychology. In: Wetherell, M. (ed.) Identities, Groups and Social Issues, pp. 119–173. SAGE Publications Ltd., London (1996)
24. Edwards, D., Potter, J.: Discursive Psychology. SAGE Publications Ltd., London (1992)
25. Horton-Salway, M.: The Local Production of Knowledge: Disease Labels, Identities and Category Entitlements in ME Support Group Talk. Health 8(3), 351–371 (2004)
26. Wilson, P.: Second-Hand Knowledge: An Inquiry into Cognitive Authority. Greenwood Press, Westport (CT) (1983)
27. Wilson, P.: Bibliographic Instruction and Cognitive Authority. Libr. Trends. 39(3), 259–270 (1991)
28. Goffman, E.: Forms of Talk. Basil Blackwell, Oxford (1981)
29. Howitt, D., Cramer, D.: Methods and Techniques in Psychology. Pearson Education Benelux, Amsterdam (2007) (in Dutch)
30. Willig, C.: Introducing Qualitative Research In Psychology. McGraw-Hill International, Berkshire (2013)
31. Sherchan, W., Nepal, S., Paris, C.: A Survey of Trust in Social Networks. ACM Comput. Surv. CSUR. 45(4) (2013)
32. Castelfranchi, C., Falcone, R.: Trust Theory: A Socio-Cognitive and Computational Model. John Wiley & Sons Ltd., West Sussex (2010)
33. Alfarez, A.R., Hailes, S.: Supporting trust in virual communities. In: Proceedings of the 33rd Hawaii International Conference on System Sciences, vol. 6 (2000)
34. Ess, C.: Ethical decision-making and Internet research. Recommendations from the aoir ethics working committee. Association of Internet Researchers (2002), http://aoir.org/reports/ethics.pdf
35. Ess, C.: Internet research ethics. In: Joinson, A., McKenna, K., Postmes, T., Reips, U.D. (eds.) The Oxford Handbook of Internet Psychology, pp. 487–502. Oxford University Press, Oxford (2007)
36. Hine, C.: Virtual Ethnography: Modes, Varieties, Affordances. In: Fielding, N., Lee, R.M., Blank, G. (eds.) The Sage Handbook of Online Research Methods, pp. 257–270. SAGE Publications Ltd., London (2008)
37. Pfeil, U., Zaphiris, P.: Applying qualitative content analysis to study online support communities. Univ. Access. Inform. Soc. 9(1), 1–16 (2010)
38. Jensen, C., Potts, C., Jensen, C.: Privacy practices of Internet users: Self-reports versus observed behavior. Int. J. Hum.-Comput. Stud. 63(1-2), 203–227 (2005)

# Appendix: Ethical Considerations in Studying Online Conversations

The selection and collection of threads on Bouwinfo was carried out without asking the formal consent of individual members. This decision was made based on a trade off between the research context itself and guidelines mentioned in leading studies on research ethics such as the work done by the Association of Internet Researchers [34], Ess [35], Hine [36] and Pfeil and Zaphiris [37]. When selecting online conversations, entire threads were recorded – with some discussions going back to 2006. Bouwinfo has a rather high turnover; with a small core of permanent members and a large majority of members who participate less frequently and tend to drop out when construction or home-improvement works are over. Two aspects that would make it difficult to ask for consent. The General Terms and Conditions of the platform mention that conversations can be used for personal purposes and that intellectual property rights are held by the board administrator. Based on this finding, together with the observation that the forum is easily accessible for non-members and that conversations take place between adults on non-sensitive topics[9], we decided to consider Bouwinfo as a public space. Of course we are aware that in reality the Terms and Conditions are often not read [38]. We also do not expect members to constantly consciously consider the public character of the forum whenever they post a message. These two aspects together might establish a feeling with members that they share their questions, frustrations and advice within a limited circle of people. Considering this short reflection, special attention will be paid to safeguard the privacy and anonymity of our members. All quotations are translated from Dutch to English. This makes it rather difficult to trace back a conversation on the discussion platform – even after one would translate it back to Dutch. Real nicknames of forum members are not included – sometimes people attach importance to their online identity and to their forum name [37] – nor the exact title of the tread. Only the broader topic is mentioned so that the reader of this paper can get a limited view on the context of the conversation. The focus in the quotations is on how forum users try to shape their advice as factual versions and not on the actual content of the conversation. Finally, permission to gather and analyze the data was obtained from the forum owner.

---

[9] Most of the time people on Bouwinfo exchange information or tips and tricks related to construction works or home-improvement tasks. Occasionally sensitive content on personal topics (i.a about family life) is being discussed in "off topic" threads. These conversations were not included in this study.

# Extending Trust Management with Cooperation Incentives: Achieving Collaborative Wi-Fi Sharing Using Trust Transfer to Stimulate Cooperative Behaviours

Carlos Ballester Lafuente and Jean-Marc Seigneur

University of Geneva, ISS & Medi@LAB, GSEM & SdS, CUI
7 route de Drize, Carouge CH1227, Switzerland
Carlos.Ballester@unige.ch, Jean-Marc.Seigneur@reputaction.com

**Abstract.** There are still many issues to achieve collaborative Wi-Fi sharing: the legal liability of the sharer; high data access costs in some situations (mobility when going over a monthly subscription quota, roaming...); no appropriate incentives to share. Current trust management could exclude the malicious users, but still could not foster Wi-Fi sharing. We have extended an appropriate trust metric with cooperation incentives to mitigate all the above issues. We have evaluated our proposal with a trust metric and incentive effectiveness through simulations and we have found the bootstrapping time for such a system and the average depletion time for its users linking it with the size of the system's user base, proving the feasibility for such a combination.

**Keywords:** Wi-Fi, collaborative sharing, trust, cooperation incentives, trust points.

## 1 Introduction

According to the International Telecommunication Union (ITU) [1], the number of subscribers using mobile broadband Internet services has raised from 268 million in 2007 to an impressive 2.1 billion users in 2013, accounting for more than the 50% of the world's Internet usage.

This previous fact and the emergence and fast growth of applications such as social networking, user generated content, location services, collaborative tools, augmented human and augmented reality applications etc., has fueled the user's need for permanent connectivity wherever she/he is, and under all circumstances. While in regular day-to-day environments this need can be fulfilled with regular wireless access provided via hotspots (wireless access points) or mobile data transmission technologies such as 2G, 3G, HDSPA, UMTS, etc., situations on which the user is a) roaming (does not have access to his mobile operator because of being in a different country), b) out of the area of network coverage or c) has already consumed her or his monthly data allowance, might deter the user to connect through such previous mentioned mobile technologies, as the cost can be very high. These three previous reasons make connectivity through regular means to be difficult to attain, thus impeding the use of

J. Zhou et al. (Eds.): IFIPTM 2014, IFIP AICT 430, pp. 157–172, 2014.

such smart mobile applications, augmented reality applications, or the mere upload of data and statistics for user tracking or measuring purposes.

In order to solve such a challenge, we have envisioned a collaborative wireless access sharing. Simply put, locals to the environment become mobile hotspots on the fly, sharing their mobile data access, via their personal mobile hotspot in their device, with a foreigner for the (rather short or not) period of time that they might be in range. In this way, all the users that are either roaming or with no access to mobile data are still able to upload fundamental data and statistics and even use applications on places where normally they wouldn't be able to get connectivity through their own means or would be too expensive to do so. All of this, without having to deploy real fixed wireless access points and signal amplifiers, and not limiting the area of coverage, as the access points are carried by the local people, which might be static or on the move.

In such scenarios where several strangers are expected to interact for the sake of data transmission, trust and cooperation incentives are of vital importance to ensure the robustness and reliability of the overall system. Cooperation incentives can be used to complement and collaborate with trust management as users can benefit from them while using the system, thus encouraging user's good behaviour. By providing cooperation incentives, there are economic dynamics involved, encouraging the users to keep using the system in a rightful way as they benefit from it. This in turn, encourages the user to earn a good trust level, as other users are more likely to interact with highly trusted users than less trusted ones, reinforcing the trust system.

In this paper, we present how we integrate trust management and cooperation incentives with our collaborative wireless access sharing service, being the aim of the paper to evaluate the computational trust management and cooperation incentives working together and to obtain results about its feasibility.

The rest of the document is organized as follows. First, section 2 presents the current issues on collaborative Wi-Fi sharing, and following, section 3 describes how the related work has tried to tackle these issues. After, section 4 presents the trust management and cooperation incentives framework. Next, section 5 shows the simulation, and the results obtained from it. Finally, section 6 concludes the paper.

## 2     Current Issues

There are many issues related with Wi-Fi sharing and accessing mobile data that need to be addressed in order for a collaborative Wi-Fi sharing service to be as useful and reliable as possible. Following we detail the most important points to be addressed.

### 2.1     Legal Liability of the Sharer

One of the biggest concerns with Wi-Fi access sharing is that all the data traffic goes out from the same source – the wireless router or access point – rendering the owner of the device liable for any action that any user with whom she or he has shared the access with has performed, illegal content download, malicious actions taken against any entity or any other legally punishable action.

This legal liability might deter many users from sharing their Wi-Fi or other type of data access, thus making it difficult for a service of this kind to succeed. In our collaborative Wi-Fi sharing service, we address this issue protecting the sharer against legal liability by putting into play some protection mechanisms. These mechanisms and their internals are out of the scope of this paper, that focuses on the computational trust management and cooperation incentives used in addition to these legal aspects mechanisms.

## 2.2    High Roaming Costs

As stated before, roaming costs incurred by users when operating their smartphones in another country, and also extra costs derived from going over a certain monthly data allowance for local users might deter those users from using any application or accessing data when on that situations.

High roaming costs make the access of mobile data while abroad very expensive, and thus, impede users to access applications and other online sources normally, as the price they might pay in order to use these services would escalate very quickly. A recent study on international roaming costs [2] carried out by the OECD, sets the average price per MB when roaming in the EU/EEA area at an average of 2.60€. This is likely to change in the future given that the EU is pushing to eliminate the roaming costs (or most of them), even though our assumptions remain valid up to today and the next years, plus roaming would still exist outside the EU.

With our collaborative Wi-Fi sharing service, we want to overcome the problem of high roaming and monthly allowance surpass costs, allowing users who are not in their home country or who have depleted their monthly quota in their home country to still be able to obtain connectivity through collaborative Wi-Fi sharing.

## 2.3    Lack of Cooperation Incentives

Even though all these previous issues were to be solved, one last issue affecting in general peer-to-peer and sharing services still remains. The "Tragedy of the Commons" [3] states that it is unavoidable in the human nature the depletion of a shared resource by individuals, acting independently and rationally according to each one's self-interest, despite their understanding that depleting the common resource is contrary to the group's long-term best interests. Even though the tragedy of the commons was first applied to mainly economic and sociology fields, it can be extrapolated to P2P and other sharing services as can be seen in [4] and [5].

Without a strong incentive being present, there is no real reason for users to share back as much at least as they got available when some other user shared, as it is in the very human nature to be self-interested agents, thus acting exclusively for their own benefit. This lack of incentives will ultimately render the service unusable, as there will be no resources to share, but many users willing to use shared resources. In our service, we solve this problem by integrating cooperation incentives with trust management as explained in following sections.

# 3    Related Work

In this section we present the closest work to ours, both regarding trust and cooperation and similar systems and architectures.

## 3.1    Trust and Cooperation

The need of cooperation incentives to strengthen trust management on cooperative systems has been already the issue of discussion of several papers.

In Fernandes et al. [7] the authors introduce a framework to provide incentives for honest participation in trust management infrastructures. The aim of their system is to improve the quality of information provided by reducing free-riding and fostering honesty. In order to achieve this, they use two strategies: i) to provide rewards for participants that advertise their experiences to others, and ii) to impose the credible threat of stopping the rewards for participants who consistently provide suspicious feedback. In the paper they successfully prove that this two aforementioned measures effectively works as an incentive that strengthens the underlying trust metric, deterring participants from cheating or misbehaving.

In Bogliolo et al. [6] the authors argue that the success of user-centric networks strongly depends on the willingness of the participants to cooperate. Incentives can help in encouraging users to cooperate and reputation-based incentives and remuneration are proposed to increase users' motivation and to discourage selfish behaviors. Quantitative properties of cooperation incentives are defined and analyzed through model checking. Their model considers users providing services, which are called requestees and users receiving services, which are called requesters. The model presents four phases of cooperation: i) discovery and request ii) negotiation iii) transaction and iv) evaluation and feedback. Their reputation system defines cooperative attitude, which depends on dispositional trust and service trust level, which represents the threshold under which the service is not accessible. The authors also introduce a virtual currency system where reputation-based and reward-based incentives are combined by including the trust level of the requestee towards the requester as a parameter affecting the cost of the negotiated service. Finally, they prove through Markov decision process analysis that mixing incentive strategies such as reputation and reward proves effective in inducing pro-social behaviors. Also they prove that cooperation incentives favor both requester and requestee as honest requesters get services at a lower price and reputation and cooperative attitude impact earnings in requestees.

## 3.2    Similar Systems and Architectures

There are other systems that aim to provide connectivity through sharing in order to tackle the same or similar problems. Here we describe them and we present how they address the issues explained in the previous section.

**Open Garden**

The Open Garden application [8] enables users to access the most appropriate connection without configuring their devices or jumping through hoops. It also enables users to access Internet as cheaply as possible. Users can find the fastest connection and most powerful signal without checking every available network, and can move between networks seamlessly. Open Garden provides a way to access more data at faster speeds in more locations. Consumers actually become part of the network, sharing connections when and where they provide the best possible access. The service is still quite new and many features have not been thoroughly reviewed by real users, though it is complicated to assess the veracity of the authors' claims.

*Legal Liability of the Sharer*
Open Garden does not address the problem of the sharer being legally liable over the actions that any user connected to her or his Wi-Fi network might undertake.

*Strong Authentication of the Client*
Open Garden aims for seamlessly connectivity without the intervention of the user. It doesn't authenticate the clients or sharers in any possible means and connections are made automatically without any initial configuration or authentication step.

*Mobile Data Limits*
No possibility to set any limit, thus no control over how much data is shared risking the danger of going over a certain monthly quota.

*High Roaming Costs*
By offering seamless connectivity between devices allowing easily the sharing of a Wi-Fi connection over 3G or 4G data, Open Garden effectively addresses the problem of high roaming costs, as foreign users can connect to other local users through their on the fly mesh network and obtain data access at no cost for them.

*No Incentive*
Open Garden does not yet offer any incentive in the form of credits or rewards. However, it plans to use some form of credits based on what can be seen on their Web site.

**ULOOP**

The ULOOP [9] FP7 European project brings in a fresh approach to user-centricity by exploring user-provided networking aspects in a way that expands the reach of a multi-access backbone. ULOOP addresses the user as a key component of networking services in future Internet architectures. Building upon current (commercial) examples ULOOP explores not only the adequate technical sustainability of user-centric models, but also legislation implications and the potential of community-driven services and how these new aspects may give rise to novel business models both from a user and from an access perspective. The aim of ULOOP if to seamlessly expand the backbone of the network through the end users' devices, extending the area of coverage while offloading the often saturated provider networks.

*Legal Liability of the Sharer*
ULOOP does not address the problem of the sharer being legally liable over the actions that any user connected to her or his Wi-Fi network might undertake.

*Strong Authentication of the Client*
ULOOP assumes worldwide strong authentication of any user: a ULOOP user cannot be given more than one ULOOP digital identity. Also it puts in place a trust metric, but the metric does not need to be as attack-resistant as a unique digital id given per user worldwide is assumed in ULOOP.

*Mobile Data Limits*
No possibility to set any limit, thus no control over how much data is shared risking the danger of going over a certain monthly quota.

*High Roaming Costs*
By seamlessly expanding the backbone of the network through the end users' devices, extending the area of coverage while offloading the often saturated provider networks, ULOOP addresses the issue of high costs while roaming as any ULOOP node can connect to a ULOOP gateway and after some negotiation steps it will have access to the Internet through it.

*No Incentive*
ULOOP provides cooperation incentives in the form of credits, which can be gained while acting as a gateway and providing services to other ULOOP nodes and can be spent while acting as a node when requesting services from a gateway.

**Air Mobs**
Air Mobs [10] is an application that enables users to share their excess data with users who might be running up against their monthly limits. Essentially, one user agrees to let their mobile device act as a tethering hub that will send data from their LTE smartphone over Wi-Fi to any users nearby. In exchange, the central hub user gets a "data credit" that gives them access to other users' data in the future. Put another way, the new app creates a sort of "cap-and-trade" market for mobile data that helps users exceed the hard limits set on their consumption by rationing data with one another based on their needs at given times.

*Legal Liability of the Sharer*
Air Mobs does not address the problem of the sharer being legally liable over the actions that any user connected to her or his Wi-Fi network might undertake.

*Strong Authentication of the Client is Still Difficult*
Air Mobs does not provide any means of authentication.

*Mobile Data Limits*
Air Mobs monitors network connectivity and status in order to give the user the ability to control how much of her data plan she is willing to share, making sure other users cannot use more data than the amount designated by the owner of the hosting device.

*High Roaming Costs*
Air Mobs provides network connectivity when one device has no available Internet connection or roaming costs are too high, thus tackling effectively this problem.

*No Incentive*
Air Mobs creates incentive via a secondary credit market –a user will be willing to share her or his data connection since she or he will get data in return.

### 3.3    Summarizing Table

Following, we summarize all the previous characteristics of Open Garden, ULOOP and Air Mobs in the form of a table, in order to ease the comparison between them. The information on which of the issues each of the services address can be found in Table 2.

**Table 1.** Current issues on Wi-Fi sharing addressed by each system

| Issue | Open Garden | ULOOP | Air Mobs |
|---|---|---|---|
| *Legal liability* | X | X | X |
| *Authentication* | X | √ | X |
| *Mobile data limits* | X | X | √ |
| *Roaming costs* | √ | √ | √ |
| *Incentives* | √ | √ | √ |

## 4    Trust and Cooperation Incentives

The aim of this section is to describe in detail the main components of our model, namely the trust management metric and the cooperation incentives.

### 4.1    Trust Transfer

Trust transfer [17] has been proven to protect against Sybil attacks when pieces of evidence are limited to direct observations and recommendations based on the count of event outcomes. Trust transfer implies that recommendations move some of the trustworthiness of the recommending entity to the trustworthiness of the trustee. This approach is particularly efficient for our system, as besides assessing trust we can use the metric to reward in the form of trust points the agents that share their Wi-Fi connectivity, effectively combining trust management with cooperation incentives as will be explained in following sections.

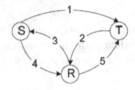

**Fig. 1.** Trust Transfer process

Based on Fig. 1, Trust Transfer works in the following manner:

1. The subject requests an action, requiring a total amount of trustworthiness TA in the subject, in order for the request to be accepted by the trustor.
2. The trustor queries its contacts, in order to find recommenders willing to transfer some of their positive event outcomes count to the subject. Trustworthiness is based on event outcomes count in trust transfer.
3. If the contact has directly interacted with the subject and the contact's RP allows it to permit the trustor to transfer an amount of the recommender's trustworthiness to the subject, the contact agrees to recommend the subject. It queries the subject whether it agrees to lose A of trustworthiness on the recommender side.
4. The subject returns a signed statement, indicating whether it agrees or not.
5. The recommender sends back a signed recommendation to the trustor, indicating the trust value it is prepared to transfer to the subject. This message includes the signed agreement of the subject.

## 4.2    Cooperation Incentives

Trust Transfer can be easily and effectively integrated and turned into cooperation incentives, as the trust points that are transferred can be used as a sort of "virtual currency" in order to exchange them against provided services, in this particular case, Wi-Fi connectivity. In this subsection, we explain both which the cooperation incentives in place are and how to extend them and make them more attractive through friend-of-a-friend (FoaF) chains.

### Basic Incentives

In order to foster interaction amongst users in a collaborative environment such as the one described in this paper, there is a need to offer incentives to the users besides providing them with the appropriate safety features such as a solid trust metric.

Trust Transfer can effectively be used as a cooperation incentive enabler, by using its trust points as the de facto "currency" in order to be able to use the services other users have to offer, in this case Wi-Fi connectivity sharing. By awarding trust points to the service provider proportionally to the duration of the Wi-Fi sharing period, we foster cooperation among users as not only the trust points reflect the good behaviour of the user giving her a good reputation, but also enable her to in turn obtain Wi-Fi connectivity when roaming or being out of data by using those trust points earned previously in order to pay for the service.

The more you share in the system, and the more different users you share with, the easiest will be to in turn find another user which will accept your trust points as payment, be it because of having interacted directly with her or using trust transfer mechanisms to find another user who can lend the service requester those needed points as explained in the previous section.

We reckon that these incentives are limited by your own circle of direct interactions and acquaintances inside the system, and this is why we exploit another capability of trust transfer, which is being able to transfer trust points through chains of trust with multiple hops, as explained in the next subsection.

### Small World Network Subsets

To empower the cooperation incentives provided by Trust Transfer and the trust points, some other mechanism in order to extend the usefulness of those points needs to be introduced, as Trust Transfer contemplates mainly that trust points are to be used "one-to-one", or as most with one degree of indirection. This means that in a scenario where several strangers are supposed to cooperate and to share services, it would be difficult to spend those points as the likeliness of finding in the same environment another user which one has already interacted with, or as most within one degree of separation is highly unlikely.

In order to overcome this limitation, we have explored the probabilities of finding longer "friend-to-friend" chains, applying the principles of small worlds [11] and degrees of separation. For the sake of simplicity, we assume that most of the system's users come from networks which are already highly connected, such as Facebook.

Social Networks like Facebook have been proven to have a degree of separation of around 4.76 to 6 with almost a 100% of probabilities [12, 13]. The problem of finding the probabilities for a subset of a small world network to find a chain of 6 degrees of separation or less can be modelled as random node failures (different from targeted attacks) in the complete network until we are left with the desired amount of nodes, which would be our subset of the small word network. In order to model a social network like Facebook, we need to use a scale-free network which exhibits both short paths and high clustering degree. Such a network can be modeled by using a KE (Klemm and Eguíluz) [14] Network, which is a type of scale-free network which complies with both properties.

While the most used metrics to determine the properties of a network are L (characteristic path length) and C (clustering), those can produce misleading results when used to re-evaluate such properties when eliminating large portions of random nodes, as disconnected or isolated users or small unreachable clusters can skew the results. It is thus a better estimate of the properties of a network, as stated in Crucitti et al. [15], the one produced by the global and local efficiency ($E_{glob}$ and $E_{loc}$). The efficiency of a network is defined as the effectiveness of the network to propagate information both globally and locally, meaning the possibility of finding a path in between two nodes of that network for the information to propagate. Those definitions can be modelled mathematically as seen in Fig. 2.

$$E_{\text{glob}}(\mathbf{G}) = \frac{\sum_{i \neq j \in \mathbf{G}} \epsilon_{ij}}{N(N-1)} = \frac{1}{N(N-1)} \sum_{i \neq j \in \mathbf{G}} \frac{1}{d_{ij}} \qquad E_{\text{loc}}(\mathbf{G}) = \frac{1}{N} \sum_{i \in \mathbf{G}} E(\mathbf{G_i})$$

**Fig. 2.** Global and local efficiency on a network

Taking this formula into account, and applied over a network inducing random failures and targeted attacks, the authors in [15] have come up with the results that can be seen in Fig. 3.

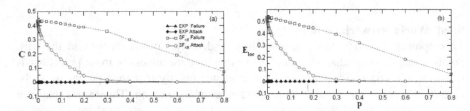

**Fig. 3.** Clustering and efficiency loss for percentages of random failure in nodes and targeted attacks [15]

As we have seen in the previous graphs, until the network is not at least a 20% of the original, the efficiency or clustering size is not big enough to even consider it a functioning network. Nevertheless, there are other aspects that have not been taken into account in the purely mathematical demonstration:

- Facebook is especially high clustered (much more than any of the networks in the previous results), to which one could argue that the removal would not impair the network as badly as that.
- When users decide to adopt a system which is collaborative and based in friendships, most likely it will be adopted in an «epidemic» way, on which friends and friends of friends would install it, leading to an also highly clustered and connected sub-network.
- The interactions between disconnected users while using our system, would in the long run create a small world by itself.

In our simulations, we apply these same principles and we calculate for a given user base population, how quick the full system would bootstrap and which is the minimum amount for such a user base which would enable reasonable probabilities of finding such FoaF chains so the cooperation incentives are more useful and in turn, encourage the users to cooperate and behave properly.

## 5    Evaluation

In this section, we proceed to present the details of the simulation environment, and the results obtained from running those simulations, both in terms of bootstrapping time and user data depletion times.

## 5.1    Simulation Environment

The model has been simulated using AnyLogic [18]. AnyLogic is a simulation tool that supports System Dynamics, Process-centric (Discrete Event), and Agent Based modeling, based on the Eclipse platform. The flexibility of its modeling language provides the opportunity to capture the complexity and heterogeneity of a given system to any desired level of detail, and its object-oriented model design paradigm provides for modular, hierarchical, and incremental construction of large models. The simulation environment corresponds to a real world area, which is the airport of the city of Geneva, Switzerland. The environment has been modeled respecting the real dimensions of the airport, and also the real proportions of both local and foreign travelers and permanent workforce of the airport [16]. The exact details of the simulation are as follows:

- 450 meters long and 150 meters wide, spanning 3 floors of this same size
- Around 13 million passengers in 2012, from which 55% are foreigners and 45% are locals.
- 840 staff and permanent workers (working in shifts).

Taking into account this previous data, each of the simulation runs has been done with 3000 agents which simulate passengers (both local and foreign in the proportions previously mentioned) and 280 workers (assumed always locals) at any time, included in those numbers. To make the scenario as realistic as possible, agent renewal happens with a normal distribution with an average of 2 hours in order to simulate the passengers leaving and new ones arriving. Workers are also renewed in 8 hour shifts. We assume that locals have an average of 15-20 friends (acquaintances or previously interacted users) and foreigners an average of 2. All local workers are known to each other.

## 5.2    Simulation Results

In order to study the feasibility of the system, we have run several simulations each with a different user base for the system. This user base is a key point, as it will determine the threshold from which the system might be usable both from the bootstrapping point of view and from incentives perspective. Note that when we talk about user base (or system users), we are not talking about the amount of agents in the simulation, which are fixed according to the criteria mentioned in the previous section, but to the total amount of users in the world using this system. This user base is what enables the probabilities of finding long FoaF chains in order to enhance the cooperation incentives provided by Trust Transfer. Each simulation runs for a real-world whole day, measured in seconds (86400 seconds).

### Bootstrapping Measurements

For the system to be usable, the bootstrapping time needs to be as low as possible in order for the foreigner passengers to be able to connect to locals while in their short time at the airport. We consider that the system is bootstrapped if half of the agents that can provide connectivity have successfully shared at least once their Wi-Fi with a foreign or a local agent that might have run out of data. For each of the graphs presented below, the Y axis represents amount of agents and the X axis simulation time, measured in seconds. We have run the simulation for different sizes of user base population, ranging from 2 million system users to 200 million system users with an intermediate simulation accounting for a 20 million system user base. The results can be seen in Figs. 4-6.

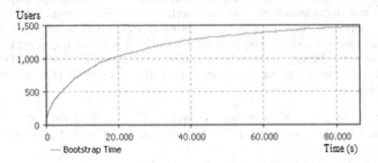

**Fig. 4.** Bootstrap time with 200,000,000 system users worldwide

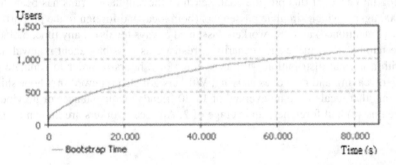

**Fig. 5.** Bootstrap time with 20,000,000 system users worldwide

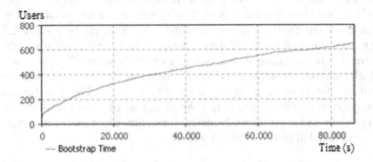

**Fig. 6.** Bootstrap time with 2,000,000 system users worldwide

As can be seen from the results, if we want to achieve the aforementioned objective of half the agents having shared their Wi-Fi with foreigners in a reasonable time, the only configuration achieving this is the one with 200 million system users. This accounts for 750 agents in roughly 7,500 to 8,000 seconds, which is close to the average time for agent renewal in the simulation, making it a feasible time for the system to be bootstrapped.

## Resource Depletion Measurements

Another interesting measurement for us is how quick users run out of data capacity, and which is the average time that it takes for a given user to be depleted of her data capacity.

We have run the simulation for different sizes of user base population, ranging from 2 million system users to 200 million system users with an intermediate simulation accounting for a 20 million system user base. For each of the figures, the left-hand graph represents the amount of data depleted users in a given point of time, being the Y axis the amount of users and the X axis the time in seconds, and the right-hand graph represents the average time that took for those users to be depleted of their data capacity, measured in seconds. The results can be seen in Figs. 7-9.

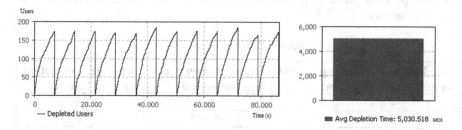

**Fig. 7.** Amount of depleted users and average depletion time with 200,000,000 system users worldwide

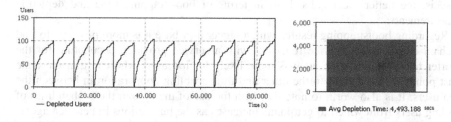

**Fig. 8.** Amount of depleted users and average depletion time with 20,000,000 system users worldwide

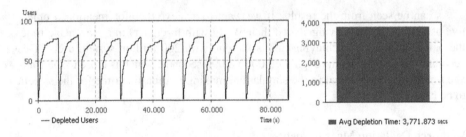

**Fig. 9.** Amount of depleted users and average depletion time with 2,000,000 system users worldwide

As can be seen from the results, with a smaller system user base the amount of depleted users in each renewal period is also smaller, but the average depletion time for each of those agents is lower as well. The implications of this will be discussed in the next subsection.

### 5.3    Discussion

From the previous simulation runs carried out, we can summarize the results in Table 2 as follows:

**Table 2.** Summary of results

| User Base (in millions) | Bootstrap time (in hours) | Depleted users per renewal period | Average depletion time (in hours) |
|---|---|---|---|
| 200 | 2.26 | 175-185 | 1.39 |
| 20 | 7.87 | 95-105 | 1.24 |
| 2 | > 24 | 75-85 | 1.04 |

As can be seen from the summary in Table 2, the bigger the system user base is, the better the results, both in terms of bootstrapping time and depletion measurements.

Regarding bootstrapping results, with a bigger user base it is more probable to find a chain connecting a service requester with a service provider, accounting for the shorter bootstrapping time, as it is more likely to find users who can transfer some trust points from one end to the other and thus enabling cooperation in between the two users. It is also worth to note that with the use of the system the probabilities of finding users from which to get points increases as the interactions in between agents increase. This translates into an increase of the probabilities of finding a chain of agents from which to get points lent from one end to the other by 0.1% per interaction per agent.  Arguably, it could be said that a 20 million user base could be enough to obtain a reasonable bootstrapping time (~7.8 hours), but with a user base closer to 200 million we can achieve times which are closer to the agent renewal time in our scenario, making it closer to the ideal situation.

Regarding data depletion, as true as it is that with smaller system user amounts there are less agents that get depleted from their daily quota allowance, this is due to the fact that also there are less agents being able to connect and to allow connections in order to share Wi-Fi as it is more difficult to find a longer user chain to transfer trust points. In the other hand, it can also be seen that the average time taken to deplete a user from her daily data quota is higher the bigger the user base is, meaning that even though more users are depleted in each agent renewal period, those users take longer to be depleted due to the higher amount of agents being able to share their Wi-Fi connection. It is also worth to note that even being a higher number of depleted users, those account only for ~10% approximately of the total amount of agents being able to share their Wi-Fi connectivity (175-185 out of 1500).

## 6    Conclusion and Future Work

In this paper, we have proposed extending trust management with cooperation incentives for collaborative Wi-Fi sharing and we have identified the most important shortcomings affecting these kinds of services and systems. Through the use of trust management and cooperation incentives we have put in place measures to eradicate or mitigate all of them, and finally, we have shown through simulation the effectiveness of the combination of our trust and cooperation incentives schema in regards of bootstrapping time and data depletion, linking it to the amount of users the system has and finding which is that ideal amount.

It is left for future work to compare our trust metric and incentives schema with other trust metrics such as EigenTrust or Appleseed.

**Acknowledgments.** The research leading to these results has received funding from the EU IST Seventh Framework Programme (FP7) under grant agreement n° 318508, project MUSES (Multiplatform Usable Endpoint Security), grant agreement n° 257418, project ULOOP (User-centric Wireless Local Loop) and grant agreement n° 258142, project TEFIS (TEstbed for Future Internet Services).

## References

1. International Telecommunication Union (ITU) report, The World in 2013: ICT Facts and Figures (2013)
2. Díaz-Pinés, A.: International Mobile Data Roaming. Organization for Economic Co-operation and Development (May 2011)
3. Hardin, G.: The Tragedy of the Commons. Science #13, pp. 1243–1248 (December 1968)
4. Greco, G.M., Floridi, L.: The Tragedy of the Digital Commons. IEG - Research Report (October 2003)
5. Macian, C., Infante, J.: The tragedy of the commons vs. P2P success: An analysis of the conditions for cooperative sustainability in the file-sharing world. In: ITS 2008, Montreal, Canada (June 2008)
6. Aldini, A., Bogliolo, A.: Model Checking of Trust-Based User-Centric Cooperative Networks. In: AFIN 2012, Rome, Italy (2012)

7. Fernandes, A., Kotsovinos, E., Östring, S.A.M., Dragovic, B.: Pinocchio: Incentives for honest participation in distributed trust management. In: Jensen, C., Poslad, S., Dimitrakos, T. (eds.) iTrust 2004. LNCS, vol. 2995, pp. 63–77. Springer, Heidelberg (2004)
8. Open Garden, http://opengarden.com/
9. ULOOP Project, http://www.uloop.eu
10. Air Mobs, http://eeiiaa.com/blog/?p=785
11. Milgram, S.: The small world problem. Psychology Today 2(1), 60–67 (1967)
12. Backstrom, L., et al.: Four degrees of separation. In: Proceedings of the 3rd Annual ACM Web Science Conference. ACM (2012)
13. Ugander, J., et al.: The anatomy of the facebook social graph. arXiv preprint ar-Xiv:1111.4503 (2011)
14. Klemm, K., Eguiluz, V.M.: Highly clustered scale-free networks. Physical Review E 65(3), 036123 (2002)
15. Crucitti, P., et al.: Efficiency of scale-free networks: error and attack tolerance. Physica A: Statistical Mechanics and its Applications 320, 622–642 (2003)
16. Geneva Airport Statistics, http://gva.ch/en/desktopdefault.aspx/tabid-244/
17. Seigneur, J.-M., Gray, A., Jensen, C.D.: Trust transfer: Encouraging self-recommendations without sybil attack. In: Herrmann, P., Issarny, V., Shiu, S.C.K. (eds.) iTrust 2005. LNCS, vol. 3477, pp. 321–337. Springer, Heidelberg (2005)
18. AnyLogic simulation framework, http://www.anylogic.com/

# A Calculus for Trust and Reputation Systems

Alessandro Aldini

Department of Base Science and Fundamentals, University of Urbino, Italy
alessandro.aldini@uniurb.it

**Abstract.** Trust and reputation models provide soft-security mechanisms that can be used to induce cooperative behaviors in user-centric communities in which user-generated services and resources are shared. The effectiveness of such models depends on several, orthogonal aspects that make their analysis a challenging issue. This paper aims to provide support to the design of trust and reputation infrastructures and to verify their adequacy in the setting of software architectures and computer networks underlying online communities. This is done by proposing a formal framework encompassing a calculus of concurrent systems, a temporal logic for trust, and model checking techniques.

## 1 Introduction

Cooperation is a key factor for the success of service- and user-centric networks in which user-generated contents are exchanged, remote resources are shared, and services provided by third parties are executed online. Trust and reputation systems provide extrinsic motivations to favor cooperation in spite of selfishness, malicious behaviors, and mistrust towards unknown users. The metrics provided by these systems help to estimate quantitatively the subjective reliance on the ability, integrity, honesty and disposition of each user, to be shared within the community with the aim of making explicit a collective notion of reputation. Even more important, reputation is defined not only to give a perception of the public trustworthiness of users, but also to provide enabling conditions for participating actively in the community by exchanging services and resources.

The design and implementation of trust and reputation systems is not an easy task as it depends on several, orthogonal aspects. Solutions can be centralized or distributed, can rely (or not) on the presence of a trusted third party, can use first-hand or second-hand reputation systems using (non-)linear adjustment mechanisms, can involve explicit (based, e.g., on voting) or implicit evaluation means, and so on [14]. As a consequence, the analysis of the effectiveness of these systems against the typical obstacles to cooperation (lack of motivation, selfishness, free-riding, ...) and the variety of attacks (slandering, self-promoting, sybil, ...) is a challenging issue.

In this paper, we propose a framework for:

- the formal modeling of the behavior of cooperative, concurrent, and distributed systems;

J. Zhou et al. (Eds.): IFIPTM 2014, IFIP AICT 430, pp. 173–188, 2014.

- the formal specification of trust and reputation infrastructures governing the interactions in these systems;
- the formal verification of the effectiveness of the trust policies adopted by these infrastructures to stimulate cooperation and to contrast attacks.

These objectives are achieved by means of a process algebraic approach to software architecture design, in which functional modeling (through typical process algebraic operators) and specification of the trust model are defined separately at the syntactic level and joined automatically at the semantic level. This separation of concerns facilitates all the design issues and the execution of sensitivity analysis aimed at evaluating the effects of the chosen system architecture and trust model. The formal specification of trust-based properties relies on a temporal logic for trust that extends classical state-based and action-based logics, while the verification of such properties is supported by model checking techniques.

In the rest of the paper, we first introduce a real-world case study, which accompanies the presentation of the formal framework as a running example through which we show how to apply our approach in practice. Afterwards, we present the syntax for a calculus of concurrent processes and the syntax for a specification language of trust systems. We then define a unifying formal semantics, which subsumes the definition of specific labeled state-transition systems, and the temporal logic for specifying trust properties that can be model checked through standard techniques. Conclusions about related work and future directions terminate the paper.

## 1.1  Running Example

As a real-world example, we consider an incentive-based cooperation model for wireless and mobile user-centric environments recently proposed [6]. Basically, cooperative networks involve users providing services, called *requestees*, and recipients of such services, called *requesters*. For the sake of simplicity, we assume that each user behaves either as requester or as requestee. The cooperation model is based on soft-security mechanisms (like trust management and virtual currency) and a process entailing four phases: ($i$) the requester looks for a service in the community and then sends a request to the chosen requestee; ($ii$) the two parties negotiate parameters and cost of the transaction; ($iii$) if an agreement is reached, the requestee provides the negotiated service and the requester pays for it; ($iv$) both parties evaluate the quality of experience and provide feedback. In each phase, trust is used to govern choices and to provide incentives for both parties, e.g., by making offered quality of service and related cost directly dependent on trust. The objective consists of inducing a prosocial attitude to collaboration while isolating selfish and cheating behaviors.

In the following, we abstract away from the details of the specific incentive strategies and we concentrate on showing how to employ our approach in order to model a scenario like the one surveyed above, specify the underlying trust and reputation models, and perform model checking based sensitivity analysis aiming at demonstrating the influence of each policy and configuration parameter chosen by the involved parties.

## 2   Modeling Trust Systems

In this section we show how to define separately functional behavior of the system and trust infrastructure. In both cases, we present formal syntax, semantics, and examples related to our running case study.

By following principles inspired by architectural description languages [3], we distinguish between *process behaviors*, which describe behavioral patterns, and *process instances*, which represent specific entities exhibiting a certain behavioral pattern, as well as we separate the definition of individual entities from the specification of their parallel composition and communication interfaces. This separation of concerns is applied also to distinguish the description of a system of interacting entities from the specification of the reputation infrastructure governing any interaction based on trust. The objective is an improvement of usability concerning the modeling issues of the different aspects that come into play in the specification of trust-based distributed systems.

### 2.1   Modeling Individual Processes

We start by introducing a calculus for the specification of individual process terms, which represent process behaviors modeling behavioral patterns. We denote with *Name* the set of visible action names, ranged over by $a, b, \ldots$. Moreover, we assume a special name $\tau$ to denote invisible, internal actions.

The set of process terms of our calculus is generated through the following syntax:

$$P ::= \underline{0} \mid a \cdot P \mid \tau \cdot P \mid P + Q \mid a.P \mp b.Q \mid B$$

where:

- $\underline{0}$ represents the inactive, terminated process term.
- $a \cdot P$ (resp., $\tau \cdot P$) denotes the process term that executes $a$ (resp., $\tau$) followed by the behavior of $P$.
- $P + Q$ represents a nondeterministic choice between process terms $P$ and $Q$.
- $a.P \mp b.Q$, which is called *trusted choice* operator, denotes an external, guarded choice based on trust.
- $B$ represents a process constant equipped with a defining equation of the form $B \stackrel{\text{def}}{=} P$, which establishes that process constant $B$ behaves as process term $P$, thus enabling the possibility of defining recursive behaviors.

In the following, we restrict ourselves to consider guarded process terms, i.e., all of the (finite) occurrences of process constants are immediately preceded by the action prefix operator. Before detailing the interpretation of these operators, we introduce the underlying semantic model, which is based on classical labeled transition systems.

**Definition 1.** *A labeled transition system (lts) is a tuple $(Q, q_0, L, R)$ where $Q$ is a finite set of states, of which $q_0$ represents the initial one, $L$ is a finite set of labels, and $R \subseteq Q \times L \times Q$ is a finitely-branching transition relation, such that $(p, l, q) \in R$ is denoted by $p \stackrel{l}{\longrightarrow} q$.*

Given $Act = \{\tau\} \cup Name \cup \{a^- \mid a \in Name\}$, which is ranged over by $\alpha, \ldots$, the behavior of a process term $P$ is defined by the smallest lts $[\![P]\!]$ such that the states in $Q$ represent process terms (with $P$ being the initial state $q_0$), the labels in $L$ are given by actions in the set $Act$, and the transitions in $R$ are obtained through the application of the following operational semantic rules:

$$prefix \qquad a\,.\,P \xrightarrow{a} P \qquad \tau\,.\,P \xrightarrow{\tau} P$$

$$choice \qquad \frac{P \xrightarrow{\alpha} P'}{P+Q \xrightarrow{\alpha} P'} \qquad \frac{Q \xrightarrow{\alpha} Q'}{P+Q \xrightarrow{\alpha} Q'}$$

$$trusted\ choice \qquad a.P \mp b.Q \xrightarrow{a} P \qquad a.P \mp b.Q \xrightarrow{b^-} Q$$

$$recursion \qquad B \stackrel{def}{=} P \qquad \frac{P \xrightarrow{\alpha} P'}{B \xrightarrow{\alpha} P'}$$

The rules for prefix, nondeterministic choice, and recursion are standard, while the trusted choice operator establishes that $a.P \mp b.Q$ executes either $a$ followed by $P$ or (a decorated version of) $b$ followed by $Q$. The intuition is that this operator is used to communicate one of two possible actions to another process and that the choice will be guided by the trust towards such a process: if trust is beyond a certain threshold, then the offered action is $a$, otherwise it is $b$. The isolated semantics of this operator offers both actions, as the identity of the interacting process is still unknown, but it uses a decoration to distinguish which action is to be considered in the absence of sufficient trust.

*Example 1.* With respect to our running example, let us model the behavior of a generic (potentially dishonest) requester possibly interacting with $n$ requestees and the behavior of a generic requestee possibly interacting with $m$ requesters.

The process term describing the requester behavioral pattern is:

$$Requester \stackrel{def}{=} send\_req\_1.Wait_1 + \ldots + send\_req\_n.Wait_n$$
$$Wait_i \stackrel{def}{=} rec\_accept\_i.Service_i + rec\_refuse\_i.Requester \qquad 1 \le i \le n$$
$$Service_i \stackrel{def}{=} pay\_i.Requester + not\_pay\_i.Requester \qquad 1 \le i \le n$$

while the requestee counterpart is as follows:

$$Requestee \stackrel{def}{=} rec\_req\_1.Decision_1 + \ldots + rec\_req\_m.Decision_m$$
$$Decision_i \stackrel{def}{=} send\_accept\_i.\tau.\,Payment_i \mp send\_refuse\_i.Requestee \quad 1 \le i \le m$$
$$Payment_i \stackrel{def}{=} rec\_pay\_i.Requestee + not\_rec\_pay\_i.Requestee \qquad 1 \le i \le m$$

□

A process instance, called entity, is an element exhibiting the behavior associated to a process term. The kernel $[\![I]\!]$ of the semantics of an entity $I$ belonging to the behavioral pattern defined by process term $P$ is given by the behavior of $P$, in which every action $\alpha$ is renamed to $I.\alpha$ [3]. With abuse of terminology, we say that $I$ is of type $P$, and we write $I.B$ to specify that the behavior of $I$ in the current state is given by the process term associated to $B$.

*Example 2.* In our running example, we consider a system with a single requester, modeled by the entity $Req_A$ of type *Requester*, and three requestees, which are represented by the entities $Req_1$, $Req_2$, and $Req_3$, each one of type *Requestee*.  □

## 2.2  Modeling Trust and Reputation

The execution of the interactions in which every entity in a system is involved depends strictly on the trust infrastructure regulating the communications within the community. Hence, before introducing the semantics for interaction, we first define formally such an infrastructure with respect to a set $S$ of individual entities, by assuming that each entity name is unique to avoid ambiguity.

Let $IName = \{I.a \mid I \in S \wedge a \in Name\}$ be the set of interacting action names. Moreover, $\mathbb{T}$ represents the domain of trust values. Even if in principle we may adopt any trust domain by adequately defining the semantics of the structures manipulating trust values, for the sake of presentation in the following we assume it to be a totally ordered set, the maximum (resp., minimum) value of which is denoted by $\top$ (resp., $\bot$).

A trust system is a tuple consisting of a set $S$ of interacting processes and of the following structures:

- *Trust table* $tt : S \times S \rightarrow \mathbb{T}$, such that $tt[I; J]$ denotes the direct trust of entity $I$ towards entity $J$ as a result of previous interactions between them. Each row $tt[I; \_]$ is initialized with the dispositional trust of $I$, which is the initial willingness of $I$ to trust unknown users.
- *Recommendation table* $rt : S \times S \rightarrow \mathbb{T}$, such that $rt[I; J]$ contains either the trust value recommended by $I$ about $J$ to other entities, or the special symbol $\delta$ to specify that $I$ does not provide recommendations about $J$.
- *Trust threshold function* $tth : S \rightarrow \mathbb{T}$, such that $tth(I)$ represents the minimum amount of trust (towards other entities) required by $I$ to execute a trusted interaction.
- *Trust variation function* $tv : IName \rightarrow \mathbb{T}$, such that $tv(I.a)$ is the trust feedback that $I$ associates to the execution of interactions through action $a$.
- *Trust function* $tf : S \times S \rightarrow \mathbb{T}$, such that $tf(I, J)$ computes the trust of $I$ towards $J$ according to a trust formula taking into account direct trust (deriving from the trust table) and reputation (deriving from the recommendation table).

We implicitly assume that the trust structures are parameterized with respect to a given type of service, and that several, mutual independent structures are needed if we intend to model a system offering different types of services, each one requiring separate trust information. In this case, every action must be parameterized as well with respect to the service type, in order to guide each interaction among entities according to the related trust information.

As far as the trust function $tf$ is concerned, here we do not define it as its specification strictly depends on the chosen trust model and, as we will see, it does not affect the definition of the semantics for interacting processes. Function *tf* may be based on several different methods [16,24,23], an example of which will be given with respect to our case study. We can argue similarly in the case of the specific relation existing between trust table and recommendation table and, in particular, the way in which an entity provides feedback to other entities on the basis of personal experience. However, some aspects of such a relation (that change depending whether the reputation system is centralized or distributed) deserve discussion here.

In a centralized scenario, we can envision a trusted third party collecting trust information from all the entities. Such a collection contributes to form the reputation of each entity as perceived by the community. Hence, it is reasonable to assume that every entity requiring a recommendation has access to such information in the same way and obtains the same feedback. From a semantics viewpoint, this scenario is captured by formalizing the relation between trust table and recommendation table.

For instance, in a very simple scenario, the recommendation provided by $I$ about $J$ is exactly the trust of $I$ towards $J$, under the assumption that $I$ had some direct experience with $J$ (otherwise the suggested value would be simply the dispositional trust of $I$). Let $ct : \mathcal{S} \times \mathcal{S} \to \{0, 1\}$ be the *contact table*, such that $ct[I; J] = 1$ if and only if entities $I$ and $J$ interacted with each other (initially, $ct[I; J] = 0$ for each pair of entities in the set $\mathcal{S}$). Then, the relation between trust table and recommendation table is described by the following equation:

$$rt[I; J] = \begin{cases} tt[I; J] \; if \; ct[I; J] = 1 \\ \delta \qquad \quad otherwise \end{cases} \tag{1}$$

thus assuming that all the entities recommend exactly the trust values resulting from their own experience, if any. Notice that this would not be the case in the presence, e.g., of entities providing inaccurate feedback or attackers cheating deliberately other entities. In order to model such a case, it is sufficient to alter some rows (or specific entries) of the recommendation table with respect to the trust table.

In a distributed scenario, the absence of a centralized trusted third party has two important effects. Firstly, different entities may have access to different information if they are in contact with different neighbors. Secondly, an entity may provide, for the same recommendation, different values to different entities. These situations are managed by adding a dimension to the recommendation table, such that each recommendation is specified by the identities of the recommender entity, the recommended entity, and the entity receiving the recommendation. Formally, if $ct[I; J] = ct[I; K] = 1$ then $rt[I; J; K]$ denotes the trust value recommended by $I$ about $J$ to $K$. In this case all the formulas depending on the recommendation table are changed accordingly.

*Example 3.* In our running example, let trust be a discrete metric such that $\mathbb{T} = [0..10]$. Initially, the trust table is as follows:

| | $Req_A$ | $Req_1$ | $Req_2$ | $Req_3$ |
|---|---|---|---|---|
| $Req_A$ | | 8 | 8 | 8 |
| $Req_1$ | 2 | | 2 | 2 |
| $Req_2$ | 3 | 3 | | 3 |
| $Req_3$ | 5 | 5 | 5 | |

The recommendation table is calculated by means of Equation 1 (notice that we are not considering self-promoting behaviors, which, however, could be modeled). Even if we assume a distributed scenario, requester and requestees are connected without any restriction and can communicate with each other. The trust threshold function establishes that the requester issues requests without any reputation constraint, $tth(Req_A) = 0$, and that for each requestee the service trust threshold is equal to requestee's dispositional trust: $tth(Req_1) = 2$, $tth(Req_2) = 3$, and $tth(Req_3) = 5$.

The trust variation function establishes that the requester increases (resp., decreases) by one unit the trust towards any requestee accepting (resp., refusing) a request, namely $tv(Req_A.rec\_accept\_i) = 1$ and $tv(Req_A.rec\_refuse\_i) = -1$ for $1 \leq i \leq 3$. Each requestee increases trust towards the requester in case of paid service, $tv(Req_i.rec\_pay\_1) = 1$ for $1 \leq i \leq 3$. The first two requestees decrease trust by the same amount in case of unpaid service, $tv(Req_i.not\_rec\_pay\_1) = -1$ for $1 \leq i \leq 2$, while the third one is more cautious and applies the maximum penalty, $tv(Req_3.not\_rec\_pay\_1) = -10$. All the other actions do not imply any trust variation.

Finally, the trust formula is abstracted as follows. Let:

$$Rec_{I,J} = \mathcal{S} \backslash \{\{I, J\} \cup \{K \mid rt[K; J] = \delta\}\}$$

be the set of entities from which $I$ receives recommendations about $J$. Then:

$$tf(I, J) = \begin{cases} tt[I; J] & \text{if } Rec_{I,J} = \emptyset \\ \rho_I \cdot tt[I; J] + (1 - \rho_I) \cdot \frac{\sum_{K \in Rec_{I,J}} rt[K;J]}{|Rec_{I,J}|} & \text{otherwise} \end{cases}$$

where $\rho_I$ represents the risk factor for $I$, i.e., how much of its trust towards other entities depends on previous direct experience. The factor that is multiplied by $1 - \rho_I$ represents the average trust towards $J$ resulting from recommendations provided by third entities. For the three requestees, in the following we assume that the risk factor is equal to 0.5, 0.8, and 0.8, respectively.

In general, notice that the most risky profile is adopted by the first requestee, while the third requestee is characterized by the most cautious behavior [1]. □

## 2.3   Modeling Interacting Processes

The semantics of interacting entities arises from the parallel composition of a set $\mathcal{S}$ of individual entities following the communication rules established by a synchronization set $SS$, which is a set of names of the form $I.a\_to\_J.b$. In particular, $I.a\_to\_J.b$ denotes a synchronization between $I$ and $J$ in which $I$ offers action $a$ and $J$ responds with action $b$. In other words, $I.a$ is the output part of the communication, $J.b$ represents the input counterpart, and $I.a\_to\_J.b$ is the name of the synchronized action.

*Example 4.* In our running example, the synchronization set for the group of entities $\{Req_A, Req_1, Req_2, Req_3\}$ includes the actions:

$$Req_A.send\_req\_i\_to\_Req_i.rec\_req\_1$$
$$Req_i.send\_accept\_1\_to\_Req_A.rec\_accept\_i$$
$$Req_i.send\_refuse\_1\_to\_Req_A.rec\_refuse\_i$$
$$Req_A.pay\_i\_to\_Req_i.rec\_pay\_1$$
$$Req_A.not\_pay\_i\_to\_Req_i.not\_rec\_pay\_1$$

where $1 \leq i \leq 3$.

The system topology resulting from such a synchronization set reveals that the requester may interact with every requestee, while communications among requestees do not occur, except for the potential exchange of recommendations. Notice that such an exchange is modeled implicitly through the definition of the recommendation policy. According to the trust infrastructure described in the previous section, the system topology has the following effect on the calculation of reputation. Each requestee receives recommendations from any other requestee if such a requestee has interacted with the requester, while the requester does not receive recommendations, meaning that $tf(Req_A, Req_i) = tt[Req_A; Req_i]$ for $1 \leq i \leq 3$ independently of the risk factor chosen by $Req_A$.  □

The interacting semantics of $\mathcal{S}$ is given by the parallel composition of the semantics $[\![I]\!]$ of all the entities $I \in \mathcal{S}$. In the semantic rules for parallel composition, let $P, P', Q, Q', \ldots$ denote process terms representing the local behavior $[\![I]\!]$ of any entity $I \in \mathcal{S}$. Moreover, let $\mathcal{P}$ be a vector of local behaviors with as many elements as the number of entities in $\mathcal{S}$, each one expressing the current local behavior of the related entity. Then, $\mathcal{P}[P'/P]$ denotes the substitution of $P$ with $P'$ in $\mathcal{P}$. The semantic rule for internal actions is as follows:

$$\frac{P \in \mathcal{P} \quad P \xrightarrow{I.\tau} P'}{\mathcal{P} \xrightarrow{I.\tau} \mathcal{P}[P'/P]}$$

The rule establishes that every entity executes its internal actions independently from each other. Then, based on the trust information, interactions among entities occur (or do not occur) and their execution provides feedback. In order to emphasize the separation of concerns between trust modeling and behavior modeling, the rule premises concerned with the trust structures are specified syntactically as external side conditions. Hence, the semantic rules expressing interactions are:

$$\frac{P, Q \in \mathcal{P} \quad I.a\_to\_J.b \in SS \quad P \xrightarrow{I.a} P' \quad Q \xrightarrow{J.b} Q'}{\mathcal{P} \xrightarrow{I.a\_to\_J.b} \mathcal{P}[P'/P, Q'/Q]} \quad \begin{array}{l} tt[I;J]=update(tt[I;J],tv(I.a)) \\ tt[J;I]=update(tt[J;I],tv(J.b)) \\ tf(I,J) \geq tth(I) \end{array}$$

and:

$$\frac{P, Q \in \mathcal{P} \quad I.a\_to\_J.b \in SS \quad P \xrightarrow{I.a^-} P' \quad Q \xrightarrow{J.b} Q'}{\mathcal{P} \xrightarrow{I.a\_to\_J.b} \mathcal{P}[P'/P, Q'/Q]} \quad \begin{array}{l} tt[I;J]=update(tt[I;J],tv(I.a)) \\ tt[J;I]=update(tt[J;I],tv(J.b)) \\ tf(I,J)<tth(I) \end{array}$$

where function *update* formalizes the effect of the interaction upon the trust between the involved parties. For instance, if we assume $\mathbb{T}$ to be a finite set of integers and $tv(I.a)$ to denote the trust gain/loss, then we have:

$$update(v, k) = \begin{cases} max(\bot, v + k) & \text{if } k < 0 \\ min(\top, v + k) & \text{if } k > 0 \end{cases}$$

Intuitively, the first rule states that if entities $I$ and $J$ enable, respectively, the interacting actions $I.a$ and $J.b$, the communication guided by $I$ is allowed, i.e., $I.a\_to\_J.b \in SS$, and $J$ is trusted enough by $I$, i.e., $tf(I, J) \geq tth(I)$, then the interaction is executed and both $I$ and $J$ update their mutual trust accordingly. The second rule behaves essentially the same, except that it models the case in which the communication from $I$ to $J$ occurs if $I$ does not trust $J$ enough, see action $I.a^-$ and the premise $tf(I, J) < tth(I)$, in compliance with the use of the trusted choice operator. Notice that, in order to consider the case in which the contact table is necessary for the trust calculation, the update $ct[I; J] = 1$ must be added to the premises to keep track of the interaction.

The separation of concerns – between functional behavior modeling and trust representation – is realized at the syntax level and favors independent reasoning and control. All the information and policies concerning trust are not involved syntactically in the specification of the process terms modeling the functional behavior of systems. Instead, they are described in a separate infrastructure, thus facilitating modeling and then sensitivity analysis. Functional behavior and trust management are combined at the semantics level in a fully automatic way governed by the operational semantic rules.

As far as the resulting semantic model is concerned, if trust has a finite value domain, then a concrete treatment of semantics is applied, meaning that the actual instantiations of the trust parameters become part of the formal semantics by contributing to label the states of the labeled transition system expressing the system behavior. Such a condition is achieved easily whenever trust is a finite, discrete metric, as usual in several trust-based systems [14]. In order to define the formal semantics of a system of interacting entities, we need to extend the notion of lts in order to take into account in each state the trust information affecting the application of the semantic rules. In particular, it is worth noticing that the variables of the trust infrastructure needed to determine the enabled transitions are represented by the entries of the trust and recommendation tables. In the following, we limit ourselves to consider the case of the trust table, as the extension including both tables is straightforward.

**Definition 2.** *Given a domain $V$ of trust variables and a domain $\mathbb{T}$ of trust values, a trust labeled transition system (tlts) is a tuple $(Q, q_0, L, R, T, P)$ where*

$(Q, q_0, L, R)$ *is a lts, $T$ is a finite set of trust predicates of the form $v = k$, with* *$v \in V$ and $k \in \mathbb{T}$, and $P : Q \to 2^T$ is a labeling function that associates a subset* *of $T$ to each state of the tlts.*

Hence, the semantics of a trust system made of a set $\{I_1, \ldots, I_n\}$ of entities obeying the synchronization set $SS$ and the trust table $tt$ is the smallest tlts such that the following conditions hold. Firstly, each state in $Q$ represents a $n$-length vector of process terms modeling the local behavior of each entity $I_j$, $1 \leq j \leq n$; the initial state $q_0$ is associated to the vector modeling the initial local state of each entity; the trust predicates in $T$ denote all the possible assignments in the trust table $tt$ and the labeling function $P$ associates a configuration of such a table to each state, by assuming that the initial state of the tlts is labeled by the initialization of $tt$ according to the given trust infrastructure. Secondly, the transitions in $R$ are obtained through the application of the semantic rules for parallel composition and, therefore, the set of labels $L$ is given by the set $IAct$, ranged over by $i$, containing internal actions of the form $I_j.\tau$ and interactions in $SS$. Therefore, a transition $(p, i, q) \in R$ determines, depending on the global state $p$ and the action $i$, both the vector of local states and the set of trust predicates labeling $q$.

*Example 5.* The initial state of the tlts related to our running example is associated to the vector of process terms:

$$[Req_A.Requester, Req_1.Requestee, Req_2.Requestee, Req_3.Requestee]$$

and is labeled with the trust predicates given by the trust table depicted in Example 3. The transitions departing from this state are three, labeled with $Req_A.send\_req\_i\_to\_Req_i.rec\_req\_1$, $1 \leq i \leq 3$, respectively.                   □

## 3   Model Checking Trust Properties

The formal semantics of a trust system of interacting processes is based on tlts, which is an instance of doubly labeled transition systems [21], and of Kripke transition systems [8]. Hence, it is possible to employ temporal logics for such systems in order to define a trust logic for specifying both conditions based on the actions labeling the transitions and requirements based on the trust information labeling the states. We call such a language trust temporal logic (TTL). In particular, TTL embodies features of the classical branching-time state-based Computation Tree Logic [11] and of its action-based variant ACTL [12].

TTL includes the definition of state formulas, which are applied to states of a tlts, and path formulas, which are applied to sequences of transitions of a tlts. The syntax of TTL is defined as follows:

$$\Phi ::= true \mid i \mid v \geq k \mid \Phi \wedge \Phi \mid \neg\Phi \mid A\pi \mid E\pi$$
$$\pi ::= \Phi_{\mathcal{A}_1}U\Phi \mid \Phi_{\mathcal{A}_1}U_{\mathcal{A}_2}\Phi$$

where $v = tt[I; J]$, with $I$ and $J$ entity names, $k \in \mathbb{T}$, $i \in IAct$, and $\mathcal{A}_1, \mathcal{A}_2 \subseteq IAct$. Inspired by other logics merging action/state-based predicates [4], atomic propositions are either actions or trust predicates of the form $v \geq k$, where variable $v$ denotes any entry of the trust table and $k$ belongs to the trust domain. State formulas are ranged over by $\Phi$. Intuitively, a state satisfies the atomic proposition $i$ if it enables a transition labeled with $i$, while it satisfies the atomic proposition $v \geq k$ if it is labeled with a trust predicate that assigns to $v$ a value greater than (or equal to) $k$. Composite state formulas are obtained through the classical connectives. The operators $A$ and $E$ denote the universal and existential path quantifiers. A state satisfies $A\pi$ (resp., $E\pi$) if *every* path (resp., *at least one* path) departing from such a state satisfies the path formula $\pi$. Path formulas are ranged over by $\pi$, while $U$ is the indexed until operator. Intuitively, a path satisfies the until formula $\Phi_{\mathcal{A}_1}U\Phi'$ if the path visits a state satisfying $\Phi'$, and visits states satisfying $\Phi$ while performing only actions in $\mathcal{A}_1$ until that point. Similarly, the until formula $\Phi_{\mathcal{A}_1}U_{\mathcal{A}_2}\Phi'$ is satisfied by a path if the path visits a state satisfying $\Phi'$ after performing an action in $\mathcal{A}_2$, and visits states satisfying $\Phi$ while performing only actions in $\mathcal{A}_1$ until that point. We observe that a path satisfying $\Phi_{\mathcal{A}_1}U_{\mathcal{A}_2}\Phi'$ must include a transition to a state satisfying $\Phi'$, while this is not required for $\Phi_{\mathcal{A}_1}U\Phi'$ if the initial state of the path satisfies $\Phi'$.

Similarly as argued in the previous section, if the states of the tlts include reputation-based information deriving from the recommendation table, we can enrich TTL with reputation-based state predicates.

Now, let us define formally some notion about paths with respect to a tlts $(Q, q_0, L, R, T, P)$. A path $\sigma$ is a (possibly infinite) sequence of transitions of the form: $p_0 \xrightarrow{i_0} p_1 \ldots p_{j-1} \xrightarrow{i_{j-1}} p_j \ldots$ where $p_{j-1} \xrightarrow{i_{j-1}} p_j \in R$ for each $j > 0$. Every $p_j$ in the path is denoted by $\sigma(j)$. Moreover, let $p_j \xrightarrow{A} p_{j+1}$ if and only if $i_j \in \mathcal{A} \subseteq L$. We denote with $Path(q)$ the set of paths starting in state $q \in Q$. Then, the formal semantics of TTL is as shown in Table 1.

**Table 1.** Semantics of TTL

$$q \models true \qquad holds\ always$$
$$q \models v \geq k \qquad iff\ (v = k') \in P(q) \wedge k' \geq k$$
$$q \models i \qquad iff\ \exists p: q \xrightarrow{i} p \in R$$
$$q \models \Phi \wedge \Phi' \qquad iff\ q \models \Phi\ and\ q \models \Phi'$$
$$q \models \neg\Phi \qquad iff\ q \not\models \Phi$$
$$q \models A\pi \qquad iff\ \forall \sigma \in Path(q): \sigma \models \pi$$
$$q \models E\pi \qquad iff\ \exists \sigma \in Path(q): \sigma \models \pi$$

$$\sigma \models \Phi_{\mathcal{A}_1}U\Phi' \quad iff\ \exists k \geq 0:$$
$$\sigma(k) \models \Phi' \wedge (for\ all\ 0 \leq i < k: \sigma(i) \models \Phi \wedge \sigma(i) \xrightarrow{\mathcal{A}_1} \sigma(i+1))$$

$$\sigma \models \Phi_{\mathcal{A}_1}U_{\mathcal{A}_2}\Phi' \quad iff\ \exists k > 0:$$
$$\sigma(k) \models \Phi' \wedge (for\ all\ 0 \leq i < k-1: \sigma(i) \models \Phi \wedge$$
$$\sigma(i) \xrightarrow{\mathcal{A}_1} \sigma(i+1)) \wedge \sigma(k-1) \models \Phi \wedge \sigma(k-1) \xrightarrow{\mathcal{A}_2} \sigma(k)$$

TTL can be mapped to the logic UCTL [21], for which an efficient on-the-fly model checking algorithm is implemented. The unique non-trivial difference between the two logics is that TTL allows for action-based atomic propositions, while UCTL does not. The atomic proposition $i$ of TTL can be represented through the UCTL until operator as follows. Denoted with *false* the formula $\neg true$, then $i$ is expressed by the formula $E(false\ _\emptyset U_{\{i\}}\ true)$, which establishes that from the current state a transition labeled with $i$ is enabled that leads to a state satisfying the atomic formula *true*, i.e., given $q$ the current state, it holds that $\exists p : q \xrightarrow{\ i\ } p \in R$.

Finally, we provide two flavors of classical operators like *next* ($X$), *eventually* ($F$), and *always* ($G$), depending on the kind of until operator used. To this end, we introduce the following notations:

$$
\begin{array}{ll}
X\Phi = false\ _\emptyset U_{IAct}\ \Phi & X_{\mathcal{A}_1}\Phi = false\ _\emptyset U_{\mathcal{A}_1}\ \Phi \\
EF\Phi = E(true\ _{IAct}U\ \Phi) & EF_{\mathcal{A}_1}\Phi = E(true\ _{IAct}U_{\mathcal{A}_1}\ \Phi) \\
AF\Phi = A(true\ _{IAct}U\ \Phi) & AF_{\mathcal{A}_1}\Phi = A(true\ _{IAct}U_{\mathcal{A}_1}\ \Phi) \\
EG\Phi = \neg AF\neg\Phi & EG_{\mathcal{A}_1} = \neg AF_{IAct-\mathcal{A}_1}\ true \\
AG\Phi = \neg EF\neg\Phi & AG_{\mathcal{A}_1} = \neg EF_{IAct-\mathcal{A}_1}\ true
\end{array}
$$

For instance, $EG\Phi$ holds in $p$ if there exists a path in $Path(p)$ every state of which (including $p$) satisfies $\Phi$, while $EG_{\mathcal{A}_1}$ holds in $p$ if there exists a path in $Path(p)$ every transition of which is labeled with an action in $\mathcal{A}_1$.

*Example 6.* With respect to our running example, we focus on the comparison between the two limiting profiles, i.e., risky and cautious, which characterize the behavior of the requestees. After adequate translation of the model, the following properties have been recast and checked both in PRISM [17] and in NuSMV [10].

The first parameter under analysis is the risk factor and the related impact upon the capability of being influenced by recommendations. To this aim, we formulate the following condition to check. Can the risky requestee accept a request without sufficient direct trust towards the requester? The related property is stated formally as follows:

$$
EF(tt[Req_1; Req_A] < 2 \wedge Req_1.send\_accept\_1\_to\_Req_A.rec\_accept\_1)
$$

where the state predicate $tt[Req_1; Req_A] < 2$ describes the trust condition and the action predicate $Req_1.send\_accept\_1\_to\_Req_A.rec\_accept\_1$ represents the behavior to observe, while the formula schema expresses the eventuality of reaching a state satisfying both predicates. The property is satisfied, because by virtue of the assumption $\rho = 0.5$, positive recommendations provided to the risky requestee can balance (and overcome the effect of) negative direct experiences. The same property can be recast in the case of the cautious requestee:

$$
EF(tt[Req_3; Req_A] < 5 \wedge Req_3.send\_accept\_1\_to\_Req_A.rec\_accept\_3)
$$

which is not satisfied, thus confirming the prudent behavior of this requestee.

An interesting analysis concerns the consequences of a malicious behavior of the requester. The following property:

$$AG(\ Req_A.not\_pay\_3\_to\_Req_3.not\_rec\_pay\_1 \rightarrow$$
$$AG(\neg Req_3.send\_accept\_1\_to\_Req_A.rec\_accept\_3))$$

is satisfied, thus establishing that after experiencing a cheating behavior of the requester (action $Req_A.not\_pay\_3\_to\_Req_3.not\_rec\_pay\_1$) the cautious requestee does not trust the requester anymore (in every future state it holds that the action $Req_3.send\_accept\_1\_to\_Req_A.rec\_accept\_3$ cannot be enabled). By replacing the cautious requestee with the risky requestee, the corresponding property is violated. Actually, not very surprisingly, even the following property is satisfied:

$$EF(EG_{\mathcal{A}_1})$$

where $\mathcal{A}_1$ is the set of actions:

$$\{\ Req_A.send\_req\_1\_to\_Req_1.rec\_req\_1,$$
$$Req_1.send\_accept\_1\_to\_Req_A.rec\_accept\_1,$$
$$Req_1.\tau,$$
$$Req_A.not\_pay\_1\_to\_Req_1.not\_rec\_pay\_1\ \}.$$

This means that a certain point can be reached starting from which the requester can obtain services from the risky requestee infinitely often without paying for any of them. This situation is an immediate consequence of the first property, which demonstrates that the direct mistrust of the risky requestee towards the requester is not sufficient to exclude the cheating behavior.

On the other hand, let us now consider a completely honest requester. This variant can be obtained either by eliminating from requester's process terms any action $not\_pay\_i$ or, even better, by removing the related actions from the synchronization set $SS$. In this scenario, we verify whether eventually a point is reached starting from which every issued request is accepted:

$$EF(AG_{IAct-\mathcal{A}_1})$$

where $\mathcal{A}_1$ is the set of actions:

$$\{\ Req_1.send\_refuse\_1\_to\_Req_A.rec\_refuse\_1,$$
$$Req_2.send\_refuse\_1\_to\_Req_A.rec\_refuse\_2,$$
$$Req_3.send\_refuse\_1\_to\_Req_A.rec\_refuse\_3\ \}.$$

Such a property holds as expected.

Separating functional behavior modeling and trust management specification allows for a clear verification of the impact of trust policies upon specific properties by simply adjusting the trust parameters of certain entities. For instance, let us replace the cautious requestee with a paranoid requestee characterized by strict trust requirements, and then let us consider the capability of such an entity of accepting services. To this aim, we adjust the trust infrastructure only, by tuning $\rho$, $tth$, and dispositional trust for entity $Req_3$. As an example, with $\rho = 0.8$, $tth(Req_3) = 5$ (as for the cautious requestee), and dispositional trust less than 4, we obtain that the following property is not satisfied:

$$EF(Req_3.send\_accept\_1\_to\_Req_A.rec\_accept\_3)$$

meaning that the paranoid requestee does not serve any request. The property turns out to hold if the dispositional trust is set to 4, in which case we also observe that, given $\mathcal{A}_1 = \{Req_3.send\_accept\_1\_to\_Req_A.rec\_accept\_3\}$, the property:

$$E((tt[Req_1; Req_A] < 10 \wedge tt[Req_2; Req_A] < 10)\ _{IAct}U_{\mathcal{A}_1}\ true)$$

does not hold. More precisely, at least one of the other two requestees must recommend top trust towards the requester in order to allow the paranoid requestee to accept a request.

Finally, let us consider a coalition attack by two requestees against the third one. The condition of interest is formulated as follows. Can malicious requestees provide false feedback to the risky requestee thus avoiding her/him from accepting any request? To this aim, it is sufficient to extend the recommendation table by setting $rt[Req_2; Req_A; Req_1] = rt[Req_3; Req_A; Req_1] = 0$ (while all the other entries are as usual), and then check the TTL formula:

$$\neg EF(Req_1.send\_accept\_1\_to\_Req_A.rec\_accept\_1).$$

This property is satisfied, thus revealing the effectiveness of the attack. By tuning the dispositional trust of the risky requestee, we observe that the attack can be avoided if and only if such a parameter is set to at least 4. On the other hand, if the false feedback is provided by $Req_3$ only, $Req_1$ can accept requests (even without altering her/his dispositional trust), but only after a successful interaction between $Req_2$ and $Req_A$. In this case, we have also verified that extremely positive recommendations by $Req_2$ ($rt[Req_2; Req_A; Req_1] = top$) protect $Req_1$ from coalition attacks of (up to) 4 malicious requestees.

## 4   Related Work and Future Directions

In the literature, formal methods have been used successfully to model trust and trust relationships [20,13,15]. However, usually these techniques represent trust without an integration with formal approaches to the modeling and verification of concurrent/distributed systems. Theoretical analysis of cooperation strategies is proposed in formal frameworks like, e.g., game theory [18], and the theory of semirings [22]. The analysis of trust chains is investigated also in a process algebraic setting, either with a specific focus on access control policies [19], or by employing equivalence checking based analysis [7]. In this paper we have proposed a process algebraic framework in which trust modeling and system specification are combined and model checking techniques are applied to verify the effects of trust models and related parameters upon cooperation in concurrent and distributed systems.

An extension under development concerns the semantics, which is currently based on nondeterministic labeled transition systems. Without altering the syntax of the language, the idea is to employ quantitative information deriving from the trust infrastructure in order to implement nonfunctional trust-based choice policies at the level of the semantics for interacting processes. For instance, trust can be interpreted as a weight guiding the choice among concurrent trust-based interactions, which thus becomes either probabilistic or prioritized. In the former case, the semantics would be based on probabilistic tlts. Further extensions are concerned with the use of reward structures expressing metrics that can be related to trust. This is the case, e.g., of the service cost, as well as any other parameter related to the quality of experience that may be influenced by (or may affect) trust. As an example, every time an interaction modeling a payment from $I$ to $J$ occurs, a certain reward depending on the trust relation between $I$ and $J$ is cumulated to express the amount paid by $I$. Then, similarly as done in the setting of quantitative model checking [5,4,9], we can employ a version of TTL extended with probabilities and rewards to estimate the tradeoff existing between trust and other metrics, which is necessary to evaluate mixed cooperation incentive strategies [1,2].

**Acknowledgment.** This work has been partially supported by the MIUR project CINA (Compositionality, Interaction, Negotiation, Autonomicity for the future ICT society).

# References

1. Aldini, A.: Formal Approach to Design and Automatic Verification of Cooperation-Based Networks. Journal on Advances in Internet Technology 6, 42–56 (2013)
2. Aldini, A., Bogliolo, A.: Modeling and Verification of Cooperation Incentive Mechanisms in User-Centric Wireless Communications. In: Rawat, D., Bista, B., Yan, G. (eds.) Security, Privacy, Trust, and Resource Management in Mobile and Wireless Communications, pp. 432–461. IGI Global (2014)
3. Aldini, A., Bernardo, M., Corradini, F.: A Process Algebraic Approach to Software Architecture Design. Springer (2010)
4. Aldini, A., Bernardo, M., Sproston, J.: Performability Measure Specification: Combining CSRL and MSL. In: Salaün, G., Schätz, B. (eds.) FMICS 2011. LNCS, vol. 6959, pp. 165–179. Springer, Heidelberg (2011)
5. Baier, C., Cloth, L., Haverkort, B., Hermanns, H., Katoen, J.-P.: Performability Assessment by Model Checking of Markov Reward Models. Formal Methods in System Design 36, 1–36 (2010)
6. Bogliolo, A., Polidori, P., Aldini, A., Moreira, W., Mendes, P., Yildiz, M., Ballester, C., Seigneur, J.-M.: Virtual Currency and Reputation-Based Cooperation Incentives in User-Centric Networks. In: Proc. 8th Wireless Communications and Mobile Computing Conf (IWCMC 2012), pp. 895–900. IEEE (2012)
7. Carbone, M., Nielsen, M., Sassone, V.: A Calculus for Trust Management. In: Lodaya, K., Mahajan, M. (eds.) FSTTCS 2004. LNCS, vol. 3328, pp. 161–173. Springer, Heidelberg (2004)

8. Chaki, S., Clarke, E.M., Ouaknine, J., Sharygina, N., Sinha, N.: State/Event-Based Software Model Checking. In: Boiten, E.A., Derrick, J., Smith, G.P. (eds.) IFM 2004. LNCS, vol. 2999, pp. 128–147. Springer, Heidelberg (2004)
9. Chen, T., Forejt, V., Kwiatkowska, M., Parker, D., Simaitis, A.: Automatic Verification of Competitive Stochastic Systems. Formal Methods in System Design 43(1), 61–92 (2013)
10. Cimatti, A., Clarke, E., Giunchiglia, E., Giunchiglia, F., Pistore, M., Roveri, M., Sebastiani, R., Tacchella, A.: NuSMV 2: An OpenSource Tool for Symbolic Model Checking. In: Brinksma, E., Larsen, K.G. (eds.) CAV 2002. LNCS, vol. 2404, pp. 359–364. Springer, Heidelberg (2002)
11. Clarke, E.M., Emerson, E.A., Sistla, A.P.: Automatic Verification of Finite State Concurrent Systems using Temporal Logic Specifications. ACM Transactions on Programming Languages and Systems 8(2), 244–263 (1986)
12. De Nicola, R., Vaandrager, F.W.: Actions versus State based Logics for Transition Systems. In: Guessarian, I. (ed.) LITP 1990. LNCS, vol. 469, pp. 407–419. Springer, Heidelberg (1990)
13. Huang, J., Nicol, D.: A Calculus of Trust and Its Application to PKI and Identity Management. In: Proc. 8th Symposium on Identity and Trust on the Internet (IDtrust 2009), pp. 23–37. ACM (2009)
14. Jøsang, A.: Trust and Reputation Systems. In: Aldini, A., Gorrieri, R. (eds.) FOSAD 2007. LNCS, vol. 4677, pp. 209–245. Springer, Heidelberg (2007)
15. Jøsang, A.: Subjective logic book, draft (2013), http://folk.uio.no/josang/papers/subjective_logic.pdf
16. Kamvar, S.D., Schlosser, M.T., Garcia-Molina, H.: The Eigentrust Algorithm for Reputation Management in P2P Networks. In: Proc. 12th Conf. on World Wide Web (WWW 2003), pp. 640–651. ACM (2003)
17. Kwiatkowska, M., Norman, G., Parker, D.: PRISM 4.0: Verification of Probabilistic Real-Time Systems. In: Gopalakrishnan, G., Qadeer, S. (eds.) CAV 2011. LNCS, vol. 6806, pp. 585–591. Springer, Heidelberg (2011)
18. Li, Z., Shen, H.: Game-Theoretic Analysis of Cooperation Incentives Strategies in Mobile Ad Hoc Networks. IEEE Transactions on Mobile Computing (2012)
19. Martinelli, F.: Towards an Integrated Formal Analysis for Security and Trust. In: Steffen, M., Zavattaro, G. (eds.) FMOODS 2005. LNCS, vol. 3535, pp. 115–130. Springer, Heidelberg (2005)
20. Nielsen, M., Krukow, K.: Towards a formal notion of trust. In: Proc. 5th ACM SIGPLAN Conf. on Principles and Practice of Declaritive Programming (PPDP 2003), pp. 4–7 (2003)
21. ter Beek, M.H., Fantechi, A., Gnesi, S., Mazzanti, F.: An Action/State-Based Model-Checking Approach for the Analysis of Communication Protocols for Service-Oriented Applications. In: Leue, S., Merino, P. (eds.) FMICS 2007. LNCS, vol. 4916, pp. 133–148. Springer, Heidelberg (2008)
22. Theodorakopoulos, G., Baras, J.S.: On Trust Models and Trust Evaluation Metrics for Ad Hoc Networks. IEEE Journal on Selected Areas in Communications 24, 318–328 (2006)
23. Zhang, Y., Lin, L., Huai, J.: Balancing Trust and Incentive in Peer-to-Peer Collaborative Systems. Journal of Network Security 5, 73–81 (2007)
24. Zhou, R., Hwang, K.: PowerTrust: A Robust and Scalable Reputation System for Trusted Peer-to-Peer Computing. IEEE Transactions on Parallel and Distributed Systems 18(4), 460–473 (2007)

# Knots Maintenance for Optimal Management of Trust Relations

Libi Gur[1], Nurit Gal-Oz[2], and Ehud Gudes[1]

[1] Ben-Gurion University, Beer-Sheva, 84105, Israel
{libigu,ehud}@cs.bgu.ac.il
[2] Sapir Academic College, D.N. Hof Ashkelon 79165, Israel
galoz@sapir.ac.il

**Abstract.** The knot model is aimed at obtaining a trust-based reputation in communities of strangers. It identifies groups of trustees, denoted as knots and among whom overall trust is strong, and is thus considered the most capable solution for providing reputation information to other members within the same knot. The problem of identifying knots in a trust network is modeled as a graph clustering problem. When considering dynamic and large-scale communities, the task of keeping the clustering correct over time is a great challenge. This paper introduces a clustering maintenance algorithm based on the properties of knots of trust. A maintenance strategy is defined that addresses violations of knot properties due to changes in trust relations that occur with time in response to the dynamic nature of the community. Based on this strategy, a reputation management procedure is implemented in two phases: the first identifies the essence of change and makes a decision regarding the need to improve knot clustering. The second phase locally modifies the clustering to preserve a stable network structure while keeping the network correctly clustered with respect to the knot utility function. We demonstrate by simulation the efficiency of the maintenance algorithm in preserving knots quality, for cases in which only local changes have occurred, to ensure the reliability of the reputation system.

**Keywords:** trust, reputation, maintenance, model, clustering.

## 1 Introduction

The fast growth of the internet encouraged the creation of user-cooperative applications called virtual communities. In these communities, users may choose to make their identities known or to remain anonymous. Therefore, reputation and trust play major roles in such virtual communities by enabling users to interact with other virtual users (total strangers) and to establish interactions that are based on mutual benefit. Reputation allows members to build trust or a level of confidence in other members within the context of decision making or other objectives. The method of choice for providing the means through which reputation and ultimately trust can be quantified and disseminated is a reputation system. A reputation system computes and publishes reputation scores for a set

J. Zhou et al. (Eds.): IFIPTM 2014, IFIP AICT 430, pp. 189–204, 2014.

of entities (e.g., services or experts) within a community, and those scores are inferred from a collection of ratings supplied by another group of entities (e.g., members of the community). The ratings are typically transferred to a reputation engine that plugs them into a specific reputation algorithm to dynamically compute the reputation scores.

Several trust-based reputation strategies and models were developed to produce reputation metrics for specific communities [1] Most of these strategies treat a community as a single, homogeneous entity and do not explicitly address the issue of community diversity. The knot-aware trust-based reputation model for virtual communities introduced by Gal-Oz et al. [2] refers to a community as a collection of knots (sub-communities). A knot is defined as a group of community members having overall "strong" trust relations between them. As was shown in [2] defining such knots enables reputation to be more accurately computed, which, in turn, results in the derivation of more reliable trust measures. Naturally, it also helps protect members from fraud and manipulation by other virtual members. The knot-aware clustering algorithm presented in [3] partitions the community into knots of members who have strong trust relations between them, while the trust relations of members who are not in the same knot are much weaker. The main goal of the knot-aware management system is to maintain knots attributes and encourage honesty among members by identifying and subsequently excluding members with dishonest or biased recommendations. Whenever reputation changes and trust relations are being modified, the reputation management algorithm must examine the accumulated trust relations of members and exclude members from their knot accordingly. A re-clustering algorithm is then applied to cluster the excluded members to gain maximum utility for the whole community.

Over time, the reputation system evolves and changes occur. These changes incude the participation of community members in new transactions, the creation of new trust relations among members, and the modification of existing trust relations, which together cause the existing knot structure to become sub-optimal. Keeping the knots model consistent is not straightforward. The reputation system must be able to collect the information pertaining to its members' new experiences and, according to some predefined criteria, invoke a maintenance algorithm that is based on this information to maintain knot properties. Successful maintenance may detect users who try to manipulate the reputation system to their own benefit, thereby causing an attack on the system. The detection of such dishonest behavior may result in their removal from their original knot, which will reduce their inuence considerably. A successful reputation system and especially its maintenance strategy should be evaluated by the quality both of its reputation computation and of its defense against attacks.

In this paper we investigate the problem of maintenance strategy in the knots model, in which knots are constructed using a graph clustering algorithm. The maintenance algorithm must consider the existing clusters and make as few changes as possible to restore their quality. Such maintenance algorithm must be compared to the complete re-clustering using all available information, since such re-clustering may be problematic for two reasons: first, for a large community it may be very computationally heavy, and second, it may completely change the structure of the knots, which may cause instability in the computation of some users reputations. A good maintenance algorithm, therefore, which should avoid these two problems, is presented in this paper. Although the algorithm is specic to the knots model, the overall strategy is of a general nature, and as such, it can be applied to other trust-based reputation models.

This paper makes three major contributions. First, we propose a knot-aware reputation management algorithm by which the knot-aware system can maintain its knots properties based on the different viewpoints and opinions of of all of its knots. We evaluate the resulting knots based on objective clustering quality measures, compare them to the results of a complete reclustering algorithm, and analyze and evaluate the possible design choices of the knot management algorithm to determine which ones are optimal. Next, we investigate the problem of when to apply the knot-aware management algorithm since executing such an algorithm is computationally intensive, and therefore, it should probably not be invoked every time there is a minor reputation change or for every new rating performed in the system. Finally, we conduct an evaluation based on a large-scale simulation of a virtual community to demonstrate the effectiveness of our algorithm, including its ability to detect attacks.

The rest of the paper is organized as follows. The next section provides the necessary background on the knots model and knots clustering and presents an overview of related work. Section 3 discusses the strategy of knots maintenance and the main parameters of the algorithm. In section 4 the knot management algorithm is formally defined and all states of reputation and trust modifications are tabulated. Section 5 present the experimental evaluation. It uses a simulation of a large-scale virtual community that is based on an existing knots structure and then simulate thousands of new ratings ratings, causing the trust relations between members to change, thereby necessitating invocation of the maintenance algorithm. This section contains analyses of parameters of the knot-aware management algorithm for different graphs and different frequencies of changes. The results are then used to determine knot qualities. Finally, we simulate some attacks against the reputation system and show knot maintenance algorithm effectiveness in the detection of those attacks. We conclude in section 6 and suggest some directions for future research.

## 2   Related Work and Background

In this section we first review related work on reputation-based clustering algorithms and their maintenance and then review the Knots clustering algorithm of [3] and define its main parameters, which will also be used by the knots maintenance algorithm in the rest of the paper.

## 2.1  Related Work

Two recent papers present cluster computing management based on Scheduling [4,5]. After the clusters are established, the trust relations of the community network may change due to members activities. A perfect clustering is not limited to the initial clustering of network. Rather, It should respond to the natural dynamics of the community network. Cluster initialization, therefore, should only be executed once, while cluster maintenance needs to be performed repeatedly. An example of such application-based scheduling is the P2P scheduling system [4], which includes trust, incentives, fairness, security, and new criteria for evaluating performance. It encompasses the activities involved in the management of network applications. The maintenance of reputation is discussed in [5], where two constraints are emphasized. The rst is that the maintenance operation will not be continuously monitoring and checking the clustering at any given moment, a setup that would require too many resources and cause overhead in the system, which together would result in overall poor maintenance performance efciency. The second constraint is related to the number of ratings needed to perform each update, as the implementation of maintenance and reputation adjustment operations based on only a few ratings at a time will also lead to system inefficiency. Considering these two constraints [5] introduced a scheduling algorithm that decides when, during a certain time interval, the behavior of members should be checked. Such recurrent maintenance based on periodic checks is essential to the proper evaluation of trust and reputation and a major objective of our work.

The vast majority of the papers in the literature handle cluster maintenance using a node-centric approach [6] and work in the presence of node mobility. These cluster maintenance algorithms handle situations of change that include a node moving away from a cluster, a new node joining a cluster, a cluster splitting due to its excessive num- ber of nodes, and the merging of clusters. In contrast to the node-centric approach, Wang et. al [7] presented a cluster-centric maintenance algorithm that is based on a number of interesting properties of diameter-2 graphs. Rather than requiring complete cluster topology information to be maintained at each node, this algorithm depends on a spanning tree maintained at some specic node that functions as a maintenance leader, makes maintenance decisions, and informs all the other nodes in the original cluster. Unlike these algorithms, our knot maintenance algorithm is edge-centric. An edge between two nodes, indicating a trust relationship, belongs to one cluster (intra-knot) or is located between two clusters (inter-knot). Changes in edge values due to newly formed trust relations and the modification of existing trust relations are handled by the knot maintenance algorithm.

Most of protocols handle cluster maintenance by periodic re-clustering [8,9] and re-cluster the nodes from time to time to satisfy specic cluster characteristics, which results in the consumption of excessive network resources. The knot maintenance algorithm separates the clustering into two phases, cluster initialization and cluster maintenance. During the latter phase, initial cluster congurations may be modied, depending on members behavior. Cluster initialization should only be executed once, while cluster maintenance must be performed repeatedly. As such, our algorithm aims to minimize overhead and enhance knots stability.

## 2.2 Review of the Knots Clustering Algorithm

In this section we review the knot clustering algorithm of Gal-Oz et al. [3] and present some basic terms that will be used later. The virtual community is described, without loss of generality, as a community in which experts in specic elds offer their advice and consulting services to community members who seek such services. A community consists of individual members, all of who may participate in community ac- tivities, such as searching for an expert, interacting with an expert, and sharing opinions about experts with other members. Although experts are a subclass of members, they are considered as two disjoint sets for simplicity. The trust that two members have in the same expert (Trust Expert) is used to infer their implicit trust in each other (Trust Member). Gal-Oz et al. [3]] discussed the problem of partitioning the members of the community into knots and introduced a knots clustering algorithm. The problem of partitioning the community into knots is similar to the optimization problem known as Correlation Clustering (CC) [10]. The community is being represented as a graph $G = (V, E)$(called a community graph) in which vertices correspond to members and edge weights describe direct trust relations between the members. The knot clustering problem is very close to the CC optimization problem, since the latter is dened on a graph in which the edge label indicates whether two nodes are similar (+) or different (-) and the task is to cluster the vertices such that similar vertices are grouped together. Unlike other clustering algorithms, the CC algorithm does not require that the number of clusters be specified in advance. The solution of the CC optimization problem is known to be NP-hard. Bansal et al. [10] discussed the NP- completeness proof and also presented both a constant factor approximation algorithm and a polynomial-time approximation scheme to nd the clusters in this setting. Ailon et al. [11] propose a randomized 3-approximation algorithm for the same problem.

The knot clustering solution presented in [3] differs from the classical CC problem in that it attempts to satisfy several major objectives derived from the virtual communities domain and trust knots. First, the algorithm considers weighted edges and not just (+,-) edges. The goal is to create strong knots, having as many high weighted edges indicating strong trust relations and as few low weighted edges within a knot. The weight of an edge is based on the value of the direct trust (based on first-hand interaction) between the pair of vertices at its end-points. The weight of an edge is based on the value of the direct trust (based on rst-hand interaction) between the pair of vertices at its end-points. These values are used to compute the similarity between vertices, which is referred to as the Mutual Trust in Member (MTM) relation and corresponds to the minimum trust either member has for the other [2]. In this way, the edge weight is used as the input for the clustering algorithm, which must decide whether or not its two end-vertices should reside in the same cluster.

Secondly, is the use of the trust indirectness property [12]. Based on a more general trust, indirect trust is derived from the ratings of other members, which are known as transitive trust-chains [13]. The knot clustering uses transitive trust to provide knots with modified level of distributed trust among knot's members. This is done by clustering together two nodes that have a neighbor node(s) with high trust between them even if there is no strong trust relation between these two original nodes. Finally, the algorithm ensures that the indirect trust relations between any pair of members in any knot possess reliability, which depends on limiting the knot diameters [14]. Thus, the knots clustering algorithm requires that the length of the path between each pair of vertices be limited. This limitation, denoted the Trust Chain Length (TCL), denes the length of the longest trust chain connecting any two vertices within any knot in the cluster.

In the knot clustering algorithm, the edge weight is not exactly the MTM. The edge weight must reflect the community perception of how strong a trust relation should be between two members of the same knot. Therefore, the MTM is normalized by a weighting function called the WF, which uses a Trust Threshold Level (TTL) that is dened in the range of [0.5,1] since trust in our model is in the ranges of [0;1], such that 1 represents complete trust and 0 represents complete distrust. WF output that has a positive sign signifies that the two members should be assigned to the same knot; otherwise, they should not. The value of the WF reects the extent to which the decision is believed to be true, i.e., the condence in the decision [3].

The problem of partitioning the community into knots is solved by a heuristic algorithm that uses the hierarchical approach [15]. First the community graph denoted by $CC = <V, E_{cc}>$ is generated by assigning each edge $e_{ij} \in E_{cc}$ a label and a weight $w_{ij}$, based on $MTM(e_{ij})$ and the weighting function. Next, the hierarchical clustering algorithm is applied on the CC graph, calculating the connectivity components of the graph based on the positive edges. In the initial state all vertices form singleton clusters. Then pairs of clusters are iteratively merged based on their merging utility, denoted MCC. In each iteration the two clusters for which the MCC is highest are merged into a single cluster. The result of the clustering is defined by a clustering matrix $M^c = \{x_{ij} | i, j = 1, \ldots, |V|\}$ where $x_{ij} = 1$ if vertices $v_i$ and $v_j$ belong to the same cluster or $x_{ij} = 0$ if they are in different clusters.

The quality of the clustering is measured by two desired properties of knots. First, the **Strength** of the clustering (Strength(C)) is measured by the total strength of its knots where the strength of a knot is computed by the average of its vertices degree. Second, the **Stability** of a knot represents the minimal amount of trust loss that would justify splitting the knot into two sub-knots. More specifically, we search for a minimum cut (MinCut) of the knot, i.e., the cut having the smallest sum of MTM values of edges. Intuitively, if the MinCut value of a knot is high, many changes (e.g., decrease or increase of MTM value on intra-knot or inter-knot edges respectively) must occur to justify a split.

# 3  Applying Clustering Maintenance to Maintain Knots

The community graph represents a dynamic trust network that is continuously changing, and therefore, it is time-dependent. At the initialization stage, a clustering algorithm is invoked and the community graph is partitioned into individual clusters, each of which satisfies the required knot properties. Over time, members of the community take part in new transactions and generate new evaluations that lead to the creation of new trust relations, e.g., between members who had no comparable experience before. These changes can be summarized as changes in MTM between vertices. These changes can be summarized as changes in the MTM values between vertices, and they can, in turn, lead to possible violations of the strength and stability properties of the desired knot. Any violation of these properties should elicit the running of a cluster maintenance algorithm.

The term maintenance in this paper refers to the update activity performed by the clustering maintenance algorithm, an activity that results in the modification of knots structures. An important part of preserving updated values of trust and reputation, is periodic maintenance of knot structure that helps both to prevent collusion and to discourage members from acting maliciously. The maintenance operation updates the trust value of each member in the community based on the members recent behavior, thereby increasing the reliability of the reputation mechanism. In addition, the role of clustering maintenance is to rene knots clustering whenever community behavior changes. In this sense, renement corresponds to restoring the strength and stability of a clustering in which the values for those two parameters have decreased. In other words, the refinement process improves the quality of a clustering to obtain more precise reputation values.

## 3.1  Clustering Maintenance Prerequisites

A maintenance clustering algorithm should operate only when there is a high probability that a better clustering exists and in accordance with a community policy. The goal is to carry out maintenance actions with minimum overhead, in the process allowing members to join and leave a knot without perturbing the trust relations of the knot and preserving the current knot structure as much as possible. Our maintenance policy is motivated by several objectives. The first objective is to minimize the number of invocations of the algorithm since executing the maintenance algorithm is computationally intensive, and it should only be performed when signicant changes have occurred in MTM values. The maintenance module schedules periodic evaluations of the extent of changes in trust that have occurred in the system. Increases above a certain threshold in the amount of new information invokes the maintenance algorithm. The second objective is to maintain knots that are stable and strong by collecting and preserving a large amount of aggregated MTM. The maintenance procedure thus aims to track changes in the MTM values of edges, in the process identifying within knot edges whose MTM values have decreased or increased beyond a predened trust threshold level. To that end, we analyze the nature of changes in the community graph with respect to the elapsed time and the number of new members ratings that have been accumulated.

**Definition 1.** A Maintenance Interval(MI) *a period of time during which the members ratings are monitored and analyzed by the maintenance function, is dened as:*

$$MI^{t_i} = [t_i - \beta; t_i] \qquad (1)$$

*where $t_i$ is the scheduled time for the maintenance action and $\beta$ represents the length of the time slot in which members' interactions are taken into account for analysis. $\beta$ represents the sensitivity of the community to changes. A large (small) $\beta$ represents how much (little) a community is concerned with preserving the structure of its knots inspite of changes in its members' ratings.*

**Definition 2.** *An R-level of the maintenance mechanism is the total number of new ratings collected during a maintenance interval above which the maintenance algorithm is invoked. Let $N_r$ be the number of new ratings obtained during $MI^{t_i}$. A maintenance action will be invoked if $N_r$ is greater than the R-level.*

**Definition 3.** *A Trust Expert List of member A at maintenance interval $MI^t$, denoted $TEL^t(A, x_1, x_2, \ldots, x_n)$ stores the updated information of direct trust that member A has in each expert $x_i, i = 1..n$. The trust in expert $TE(A, x)$ is calculated based on all ratings provided by A upon each transaction with $x$, while taking into account the time at which the transaction, (old transactions weigh less than new ones).*

Consider the following observations regarding the effects of changes in the trust values between two members caused by new ratings. Assume the edge weights are calculated using the weighting function discussed in section 2.2. The term *inter-cluster* edge refers an edge connecting two nodes hosted in two different knots, while *an intra-cluster* edge refer to an edge connecting two nodes of the same knot.

**Observation 1.** *Decreases in the strength and stability of a clustering due to inter-cluster edges can only be caused in two cases:*

1. *by negative edges whose weights increase and they become positive.*
2. *by positive edges whose weights increase.*

*Negative inter-cluster edges whose weights decrease, or positive edges whose weights decrease can only improve cluster correctness.*

**Observation 2.** *Decreases in the strength and stability of a clustering due to intra-cluster edges can only be caused in two cases:*

1. *by negative edges whose weights decrease, or positive edges whose weights decrease can only improve cluster correctness. whose weight decreases.*
2. *by positive edges whose weights decrease and become negative.*

*Positive intra-cluster edges whose weights increase or negative edges whose weights increase can only improve cluster quality.*

Based on these observations we now define two maintenance policies.

*Correctness Policy*: Maintenance should be conducted in the case of either observation 1 or observation 2 carried out . This policy is not tolerant to a decrease in clustering correctness.

*Relaxed Policy*: Maintenance should be conducted only in the case of observation 2. This policy is tolerant to a decrease in clustering correctness due to observation 1,since it does not affect the quality of the connections within the clusters,and therefore, the contribution of intra-knot members to each other remains basically about the same (the strength of the knot). so that basically the contribution of intra-knot members to each other remains basically about the same (the strength of the knot).

Under the assumption of honest members we can be more biased toward stability (low sensitivity). For example - if an honest member's rating of an expert differs from that of overall knot opinion, that members rating should be considered a contribution to knot opinion rather than dishonesty, and that member should be allowed to remain in the knot . Under the assumption of malicious or dishonest participants, we should be more biased toward correctness (high sensitivity). For example  if an attackers rating of an expert differs from that of overall knot opinion, that attackers rating is strictly considered to be damaging to knot opinion, and the attacker should be removed from the knot.

## 4    The Knot Maintenance Algorithm

In this section, we present our knot-aware management policy, which uses a scheduled reputation maintenance algorithm to evaluate the changes that have taken place in the trust relations of community members. The algorithm identies decreases in knot correctness and acts to exclude the members that have caused this decrease (i.e., they are evaluated as unsuitable for the knot). It then applies the hierarchical approach for re-clustering the semi-clustered graph in which the excluded nodes are singleton clusters.

Before invoking the maintenance procedure (see Algorithm 1), it is important to describe the process of updating the weights on the graph edges. During a maintenance interval MI, new ratings are accumulated and the TEL is modified accordingly. The MTM values between a vertex and its neighbors are then calculated in accordance with the updated TEL. Finally the weighting function and the threshold value TTL are applied and the new edge weights are calculated. For existing edge weights, the results may comprise an increase, a decrease, or no change, and for a newly created edge, the results will be its initial weight.

The maintenance algorithm is executed in four phases. In the first phase, during the MI the new ratings are accumulated. At the scheduled time of maintenance, the information that has been accumulated is analyzed. If the number

---

**Algorithm 1.** Maintenance Algorithm

**Input**

$G = <V, E>$: Community graph, $V$: the set of vertices, $E$: the set of $MTM$ edges

$C_G$: A clustering of $G$.

$WF$: Weight function.

$MTM$: Mutual Trust Member relation function.

$\kappa$: Maximum allowed TCL.

$\alpha$: Community TTL.

**Output**

$C$: An updated clustering of $G$.

---

```
 1: /* Second Phase */
 2: CalculateTEL(RatingsList, V)
 3: E' = WF(MTM(E', α))
 4: G_new = <V, E'>
 5: C = C_G
 6: /* Third phase */
 7: clustersList = {} /*The list of clusters for the re-clustering phase*/
 8: for all e = (v_i, v_j) ∈ E' do
 9:     /* process intra-cluster edges */
10:     if cluster(v_i) = cluster(v_j) then
11:         if (WF(v_i, v_j)_old ≤ 0∧WF(v_i, v_j)_new ≤ 0∧WF(v_i, v_j)_new ≤ WF(v_i, v_j)_old)∨
            (WF(v_i, v_j)_old ≥ 0 ∧ WF(v_i, v_j)_new ≤ 0) then
12:             clustersList.addVertexAsSingletonCluster(v_i)
13:             clustersList.addVertexAsSingletonCluster(v_j)
14:             C ← reconstructCluster(C, v_i)
15:     /*process inter-cluster edges */
16:     if cluster(v_i) ≠ cluster(v_j) then
17:         if ((WF(v_i, v_j)_old ≤ 0) ∧ (WF(v_i, v_j)_new ≥ 0)) ∨ (WF(v_i(WF(v_i, v_j)_old ≥
            0 ∧ WF(v_i, v_j)_new ≥ 0 ∧ WF(v_i, v_j)_new ≥ WF(v_i, v_j)_old) then
18:             clustersList.addVertexAsSingletonCluster(v_i)
19:             clustersList.addVertexAsSingletonCluster(v_j)
20:             C ← reconstructCluster(C, v_i)
21:             C ← reconstructCluster(C, v_j)
22: /* Fourth phase - re-clustering */
23: candidatePairs ← allPositiveMCCPairs(clustersList, C)
24: while candidatePairs ≠ ∅ do
25:     Extract the cluster (c_i, c_j) ∈ candidatePairs whose MCC is maximal;
26:     if ∀u, v ∈ (c_i ∪ c_j)|TCL_{c_{ij}}(u, v)| ≤ κ then
27:         ∀c ∈ {c_i, c_j}
28:         if c ∈ C then
29:             C.remove(c)
30:         else
31:             clustersList ← clustersList − {c}
32:         C ← C ∪ merge(c_i, c_j)
33:         candidatePairs ← getPositiveMCCPairs(clustersList, C)
```

**Table 1.** Summary of Maintenance Policy

| Split action | Member position | Old WF(i,j) | New WF(i,j) |
|---|---|---|---|
| Ignore | Intra-knot | $WF(i,j)_{old} \leq 0$ | $WF(i,j)_{new} \leq 0$ <br> $WF(i,j)_{new} \geq WF(i,j)_{old}$ |
| Ignore | Intra-knot | $WF(i,j)_{old} \leq 0$ | $WF(i,j)_{new} \geq 0$ <br> $WF(i,j)_{new} \geq WF(i,j)_{old}$ |
| perform | Intra-knot | $WF(i,j)_{old} \leq 0$ | $WF(i,j)_{new} \leq 0$ <br> $WF(i,j)_{new} \leq WF(i,j)_{old}$ |
| Ignore | Intra-knot | $WF(i,j)_{old} \geq 0$ | $WF(i,j)_{new} \geq 0$ <br> $WF(i,j)_{new} \geq WF(i,j)_{old}$ |
| Ignore | Intra-knot | $WF(i,j)_{old} \geq 0$ | $WF(i,j)_{new} \geq 0$ <br> $WF(i,j)_{new} \leq WF(i,j)_{old}$ |
| perform | Intra-knot | $WF(i,j)_{old} \geq 0$ | $WF(i,j)_{new} \leq 0$ <br> $WF(i,j)_{new} \leq WF(i,j)_{old}$ |
| Ignore | Inter-knot | $WF(i,j)_{old} \leq 0$ | $WF(i,j)_{new} \leq 0$ <br> $WF(i,j)_{new} \geq WF(i,j)_{old}$ |
| perform | Inter-knot | $WF(i,j)_{old} \leq 0$ | $WF(i,j)_{new} \geq 0$ <br> $WF(i,j)_{new} \geq WF(i,j)_{old}$ |
| Ignore | Inter-knot | $WF(i,j)_{old} \leq 0$ | $WF(i,j)_{new} \leq 0$ <br> $WF(i,j)_{new} \leq WF(i,j)_{old}$ |
| perform | Inter-knot | $WF(i,j)_{old} \geq 0$ | $WF(i,j)_{new} \geq 0$ <br> $WF(i,j)_{new} \geq WF(i,j)_{old}$ |
| Ignore | Inter-knot | $WF(i,j)_{old} \geq 0$ | $WF(i,j)_{new} \geq 0$ <br> $WF(i,j)_{new} \leq WF(i,j)_{old}$ |
| Ignore | Inter-knot | $WF(i,j)_{old} \geq 0$ | $WF(i,j)_{new} \leq 0$ <br> $WF(i,j)_{new} \leq WF(i,j)_{old}$ |

---

**Algorithm 2.** reconstructCluster

```
1: function reconstructCluster(clustering C,vertex v)
2:     cluster ← cluster(v)
3:     cluster.RemoveVertex(v)
4:     if ∃u, w ∈ cluster s.t. |TCL(u, w)| ≥ κ then
5:         clustersList.addAllVerticesOfCluster(cluster)
6:         C.remove(cluster)
7:     return C
```

of total community ratings is above R-level, we continue to the next step of the
maintenance algorithm; otherwise, there is not enough information to justify
maintenance.

The second phase updates the MTM values and the edge weights using the
weighting function. Calculating new MTM values based on the updated TEL is
performed using an edge matrix $M_{new}^{MTM} = \{x_{ij}|i,j = 1,\ldots,|V|\}$ which holds
the MTM value of each pair of vertices of the community graph, where $x_{i,j} = 0$
for $MTM(v_i, v_j) = 0$ when $v_i$ and $v_j$ have no comparable ratings and $x_{i,j} \neq 0$
for $MTM(v_i, v_j) \neq 0$ when $v_i$ have a number of comparable ratings with $v_j$.

After the nal edge weights are determined, we apply WF to each pair of
vertices in the $M_{new}^{MTM}$ matrix to convert it to the $M_{new}^{WF}$ matrix.

The third phase entails analyses of changes in members' behavior and of
changes in edge weights that have occurred in existing trust relations, or it
evaluates new relations that have been created. The changes can be tracked by
comparing values of the $M_{new}^{WF}$ matrix with the values of the previous community
graph weight matrix $M^{WF}$. The algorithm behaves differently for inter-cluster
vs. for intra-cluster edges. The exact operations of this phase are detailed in
Table 1. Each entry in the table corresponds to the changes that occur in the
weights between any two nodes. The decision may be either to extract the node
from its current node, or to leave it as is. The purpose of this strategy is to
exclude from a knot members whose opinions are different from those of the rest
of the knot members and to perform a re-clustering action in predened cases.

The fourth phase of the algorithm is the re-clustering of the singleton clusters
using the original hierarchical clustering of [3], wherEach entry in the table
corresponds to the changes that occur in the weights between any two nodes.
The decision may be either to extract the node from its current node, or to
leave it as is. The purpose of this strategy is to exclude (from a knot) members
whose opinions are is different from those of the rest of the knot members and
to perform a re-clustering action in predened cases.e the pair of clustered to be
merged is the pair with the highest MCC value.

The algorithm is depicted in detail in Algorithm 1. Only the third phase,
which is the central focus of this paper, is described in detail and follows the
rules described in Table 1. If the exclusion of a node from a cluster result in trust
chains of length higher then $\kappa$ the cluster is split according to Algorithm 2. The
clustering that result from the third phase is the input for the fourth phase.

## 5    Evaluation Results

We evaluate the maintenance algorithm in light of our goal to reduce the need
to perform complete re-clustering operations after changes have occurred in the
community trust graph by instead conducting local modications to the knot clustering of the graph. Therefore, we evaluate the performance of our maintenance
algorithm in terms of knot strength and stability and in terms of the quality of
the clustering as a classication algorithm.

For the purposes of evaluation, we use a set of community graphs, each constructed using the same set of members and a different set of members ratings.

For each simulation, we randomly generated over 5000 ratings meant to simulate the ground true knowledge regarding of an existing clustered structure. For each experiment, ratings were constructed with a different level of noise ranging from 10% to 30% (noise is a signicant change in members' rating proles that may cause deviations from the original knot structure).

Each simulation begins by applying the knot clustering, the results of which can vary from clearly identfied knots to an arbitrary partitioning of the knots in accordance with the existing trust levels. Next, at each scheduled maintenance time ti, the maintenance algorithm is invoked if the total number of ratings collected during the maintenance interval is above the R-level. New ratings can result either in new edges in the graph or in modifications of the trust values (edge weights) between existing members represented by nodes.

The goal of the maintenance algorithm is to track signicant changes in edge values that violate clustering structure, remove the corresponding vertices from existing knots, and then apply partial re-clustering to obtain an optimal set of knots. The resulting set of knots is compared with the alternative of repeatedly conducting knot clustering. Therefore, each time a maintenance event is performed, we execute knot clustering on the full data set of ratings. For input, maintenance re- clustering requires the last clustering and the set of ratings collected by the last maintenance interval. For the knot clustering operation, the input is the community graph, including the ratings collected by all maintenance intervals. The experiments are repeated for graphs with different levels of clear cluster structures and for different levels of noise.

Fig. 1 demonstrates the results of the experiment by comparing the performances of the maintenance algorithm and the knot clustering algorithm at different phases of maintenance time and for different noise levels. In each panel of Fig. 1, the x-axis represents the points in time at which maintenance operation was conducted. The two lines represent the quality of the result clustering as obtained by the maintenance algorithm and by the knot algorithm in terms of strength, stability, and F-score. Fig. 1(a) depicts strength results under conditions of 20% noise. As expected, the strength of the clustering by the maintenance algorithm is lower than that by knot clustering. However, the difference between the two algorithms in the first maintenance event is relatively small. Moreover, the results indicate that the difference becomes much smaller for higher levels of noise, as shown by the better performance of the maintenance algorithm in the first maintenance event at a 30% noise level (Fig. 1(b)). This can be explained by the nature of the first maintenance event, in which the effects of changes are less global. From the second maintenance phase, the strength of the clustering knots created by the maintenance algorithm is, as expected, lower than that of the clustering created by knot clustering. Fig. 1(d), presents the stability results of the same experiment with 30% noise. Although the stability of the clustering created by the maintenance algorithm is better in the first and second maintenance phases than that of the clustering created by knot clustering, that changes over time. The reason for that outcome is also explained by the local changes that are being applied by the maintenance algorithm to preserve stability. The F-Score, which is defined as

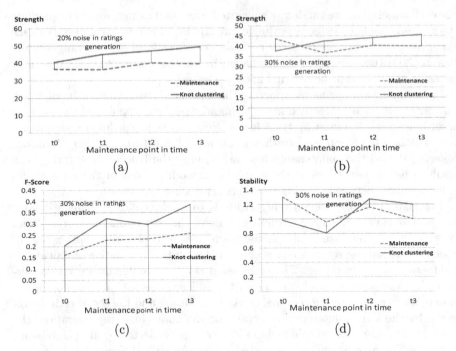

**Fig. 1.** Performances of maintenance algorithm in different noise levels

the harmonic mean of precision and recall, examines the quality of the resulting clustering as a classier ( and where the error is defined as a node belonging to a different cluster than its original cluster.) All the experiments show that the results of the knot algorithm are better than those of the maintenance algorithm, but a comparison of error shows that relative to the knot algorithm, that of the maintenance algorithm is less than 0.15. These results show that the maintenance algorithm, which is more efficient in terms of computational overhead, could replace the knot clustering algorithm for early maintenance events, especially to preserve the original knot structure.

Our next experiment simulates the attack scenario. We evaluate algorithm performance in the event of a slander- attack aimed to decrease the reputation of an expert in a virtual community network. In slander attacks, one or more members falsely give low ratings to an expert. The effect of a single slandering member is minor, especially if the system limits the rate at which negative ratings can be produced. However, slander attacks may become serious if they involve the collusion of several members. Our goal was to demonstrate that the maintenance algorithm can be used as a defense technique that identies malicious members in an effort to prevent the false ratings of a slander- attack. To simulate the attack scenario, we rst apply the initial clustering, and for the next phase of maintenance we use a set of low ratings of an expert given by fraudulent members of the same knot vs. other the opinions of other members, who gave the same expert high ratings. Our maintenance mechanism demonstrates a high

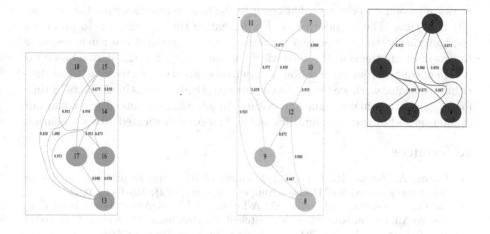

**Fig. 2.** Knot structure before a slander attack

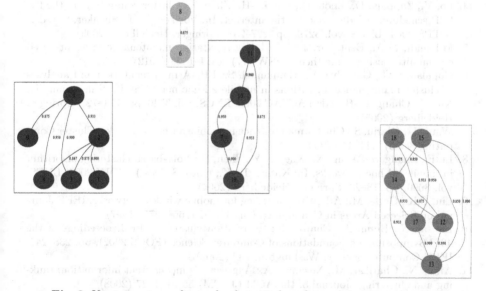

**Fig. 3.** Knot structure after a slander attack and a maintenance operation

sensitivity to false ratings and reacts accordingly by removing the fraudulent attackers from the knot. This is clearly shown in 2 and 3, in which slandering users are moved from their original knot and inserted into their own, new knot.

# 6    Concluding Remarks

We have introduced a clustering maintenance algorithm for a dynamic trust network based on the properties of knot clustering. The algorithm is edge-centric and works in response to changes that occur in the trust relations within the community over time. The key motivation for presenting this algorithm is to provide a good alternative to the expensive process of knot clustering that is run in response to new trust information obtained within a community. The simulation based experiment confirms our expectations and demonstrates the effectiveness of the algorithm. In future work we intend to further investigate the optimal points in time for triggering the maintenance procedure. In addition, we intend to extend our evaluation and further examine different and more sophisticated attack scenarios.

# References

1. Jøsang, A., Ismail, R., Boyd, C.: A survey of trust and reputation systems for online service provision. Decision Support Systems 43(2), 618–644 (2007)
2. Gal-Oz, N., Gudes, E., Hendler, D.: A Robust and Knot-Aware Trust-Based Reputation Model. In: Karabulut, Y., Mitchell, J., Herrmann, P., Jensen, C.D. (eds.) IFIPTM 2008. IFIP, vol. 263, pp. 167–182. Springer, Boston (2008)
3. Gal-Oz, N., Yahalom, R., Gudes, E.: Identifying knots of trust in virtual communities. In: Wakeman, I., Gudes, E., Jensen, C.D., Crampton, J. (eds.) Trust Management V. IFIP AICT, vol. 358, pp. 67–81. Springer, Heidelberg (2011)
4. Lo, V., Zappala, D., Zhou, D., Liu, Y.-H., Zhao, S.: Cluster computing on the fly: P2P scheduling of idle cycles in the internet. In: Voelker, G.M., Shenker, S. (eds.) IPTPS 2004. LNCS, vol. 3279, pp. 227–236. Springer, Heidelberg (2005)
5. M'hamdi, M.A., Bentahar, J.: Scheduling reputation maintenance in agent-based communities using game theory. JSW 7(7), 1514–1523 (2012)
6. Gopalan, S.G., Gayathri, V., Emmanuel, S.: FPGA implementation and analyses of cluster maintenance algorithms in mobile ad-hoc networks. In: Srikanthan, T., Xue, J., Chang, C.-H. (eds.) ACSAC 2005. LNCS, vol. 3740, pp. 714–727. Springer, Heidelberg (2005)
7. Wang, L., Olariu, S.: Cluster maintenance in mobile ad-hoc networks. Cluster Computing 8(2-3), 111–118 (2005)
8. Li, F., Zhang, S., Wang, X., Xue, X.-Y., Shen, H.: Vote-based clustering algorithm in mobile ad hoc networks. In: Kahng, H.-K., Goto, S. (eds.) ICOIN 2004. LNCS, vol. 3090, pp. 13–23. Springer, Heidelberg (2004)
9. Lin, C.R., Gerla, M.: Adaptive clustering for mobile wireless networks. IEEE Journal on Selected Areas in Communications 15(7), 1265–1275 (1997)
10. Bansal, N., Blum, A., Chawla, S.: Correlation clustering. In: Proceedings of the 43rd Symposium on Foundations of Computer Science (FOCS 2002), pp. 238–247. IEEE Computer Society, Washington, DC (2002)
11. Ailon, N., Charikar, M., Newman, A.: Aggregating inconsistent information: ranking and clustering. Journal of the ACM (JACM) 55(5), 1–27 (2008)
12. Kinateder, M., Baschny, E., Rothermel, K.: Towards a generic trust model – comparison of various trust update algorithms. In: Herrmann, P., Issarny, V., Shiu, S.C.K. (eds.) iTrust 2005. LNCS, vol. 3477, pp. 177–192. Springer, Heidelberg (2005)
13. Guha, R., Kumar, R., Raghavan, P., Tomkins, A.: Propagation of trust and distrust. In: Proceedings of the 13th International Conference on World Wide Web (WWW 2004), pp. 403–412. ACM (May 2004)
14. Edachery, J., Sen, A., Brandenburg, F.J.: Graph clustering using distance-k cliques. In: Kratochvíl, J. (ed.) GD 1999. LNCS, vol. 1731, pp. 98–106. Springer, Heidelberg (1999)
15. Ward, J., Hook, M.: In: Application of an Hierarchical Grouping Procedure to a Problem of Grouping Profiles 23(1), 69–82 (1963)

# On the Tradeoff among Trust, Privacy, and Cost in Incentive-Based Networks

Alessandro Aldini[1], Alessandro Bogliolo[1], Carlos Ballester Lafuente[2], and Jean-Marc Seigneur[2]

[1] Department of Base Science and Fundamentals, University of Urbino, Italy
[2] Institute of Services Science, University of Geneva, Carouge, Switzerland

**Abstract.** Incentive strategies are used in collaborative user-centric networks, the functioning of which depends on the willingness of users to cooperate. Classical mechanisms stimulating cooperation are based on trust, which allows to set up a reputation infrastructure quantifying the subjective reliance on the expected behavior of users, and on virtual currency, which allows to monetize the effect of prosocial behaviors. In this paper, we emphasize that a successful combination of social and economic strategies should take into account the privacy of users. To this aim, we discuss the theoretical and practical issues of two alternative tradeoff models that, depending on the way in which privacy is disclosed, reveal the relation existing among trust, privacy, and cost.

## 1 Introduction

A growing trend towards autonomic user-centric architectures is giving rise to community-scale initiatives with the purpose of sharing services, among which personal hotspot and peer-to-peer are two representative examples. Members of these communities may share access to the Internet as well as network resources and user-generated contents and applications. User-centricity is reshaping the Internet value chain, and its success depends strongly on the attitude to cooperate of each actor involved [2]. Intrinsic motivations to be cooperative, such as sense of community and synergy, do not suffice to contrast typical obstacles like selfishness and, even worse, cheating. They must be integrated with extrinsic incentives, especially for communities in which users behave as *prosumers*, i.e., they combine the roles of service producers and consumers. Extrinsic motivations can be analyzed from social and economic perspectives.

From a social viewpoint, it is well-recognized that computational notions of trust support the estimation of user's trustworthiness as perceived by the community [8]. On one hand, the reputation resulting from user's behavior shall be viewed as an enabling factor for accessing the best services at the most favorable conditions. On the other hand, reputation is related to identity, thus contrasting the idea of privacy, which represents another social value that may keep the user from taking part in some kind of interaction. However, the lower the attitude to expose sensitive information is, the higher the probability of being untrusted.

J. Zhou et al. (Eds.): IFIPTM 2014, IFIP AICT 430, pp. 205–212, 2014.
© IFIP International Federation for Information Processing 2014

Trading privacy for trust is thus a way for balancing the subjective value of what is revealed in exchange of what is obtained.

From an economic viewpoint, the capability of monetizing the effects of cooperative and prosocial behaviors is fundamental whenever trust does not represent a sufficient incentive. This is the case, e.g., of wireless communities, the highly dynamic nature of which hinders the establishment of a stable reputation infrastructure, which suffers the frequent renewal of the community members. Moreover, reputation may not provide guarantees of reciprocity, according to which the attitude to cooperation is strengthened by the perspective of future mutual interactions. While reciprocity is not perceived as an incentive in classical models based, e.g., on client-server architectures, it represents a pillar of cooperation in user-centric environments, in which community members behave as prosumers. Monetization provides a framework where virtual credits play the role of commodity money used to purchase services [7], thus replacing (or complementing) the role of trust during negotiation. While using virtual currency in place of trust can be beneficial, the maximum benefits deriving from these orthogonal incentive mechanisms are obtained when they are combined in a mixed strategy [1,17]. In other words, among the favorable conditions that can be obtained during negotiation by a trusted user (in terms, e.g., of amount of resources and, more in general, quality of service), it is quite natural to include the service cost. The relation is dual, as an effect of the marketplace is that the cost applied by a user providing a service may have an impact on her/his reputation as perceived by the buyers of the service.

In this paper, we investigate the tradeoff existing among the three dimensions that characterize the incentive strategies resulting from the discussion above, namely trust, privacy, and cost. To this aim, we discuss the theoretical benefits and the implementation issues of two models that differ for the way in which privacy is managed and traded with respect to trust and cost.

## 2   Incremental vs. Independent Release of Privacy

According to an established view of privacy management, sensitive information is disclosed incrementally. Whenever a user requires access to a service, a certain portion of user's identity is exposed depending on the amount of her/his personal information disclosed, while the related reputation is employed to negotiate transaction and cost to pay. The basic assumption behind the incremental model is that the amount of privacy released is irrevocable, meaning that once different pieces of sensitive information are linked and exposed by a user, it is not possible to break anymore such a link. In fact, the case in which user's identity is revealed all at once represents a limiting scenario of this model.

As an example, suppose that Alice uses a pseudonym to ask for a service without revealing to be Alice. To this aim, she discloses some information, e.g., a piece of evidence associated to the pseudonym, which is trusted enough to obtain the service at a certain cost. For privacy reasons, in order to negotiate other services with different users, Alice may use several pseudonyms, each one characterized by its own reputation level. At a certain point, if Alice requires a service with high trust threshold, she may need to expose the link between two of her pseudonyms in order to benefit of the related reputation combination, thus revealing that the same identity is behind them. Hence, linking more evidence is a way to grant a request at the cost of increased privacy loss. However, from now on, such a link is irrevocable, in the sense that Alice cannot spend one of the two pseudonyms without spending also the other at the same time.

As opposite to this policy, we envision a model with a higher degree of freedom in the management of privacy, in which the privacy disclosure is independent of the information released in previous interactions, by breaking the irrevocability that characterizes the incremental model. Such a flexibility would allow the user to choose which (and how much) information to disclose depending solely on the service trust threshold and on the cost she/he is willing to pay for the service, without any constraint deriving from the privacy released in the past.

With respect to our example, this means that after having linked two different pseudonyms, somehow Alice would be able to break such a link in future interactions, in which she may use only one of the two separately from the other. The need for this capability could be motivated, e.g., by the fact that only one of the two pseudonyms is sufficient to negotiate certain services, or because Alice may prefer to maintain separation of identity by using two unrelated pseudonyms in two different social environments.

## 2.1   Theoretical Aspects

Before discussing the design of the independent model, which is the novel contribution of this paper, it is worth analyzing from the theoretical standpoint the potential benefits of this model with respect to the incremental one, in order to motivate its implementation. This is done by verifying whether the achieved flexibility of privacy influences positively the tradeoff with trust and cost.

The efficacy of mixed cooperation strategies has been demonstrated through formal methods, like game theory [12,13], and model checking [1,11]. For our purposes, we have conducted a preliminary verification based on the analysis of a real-world cooperation system for user-centric networks [3], which has been modeled and analyzed through the model checker PRISM [4]. Such a system entails a cooperation process balancing trustworthiness with service cost and is based on irrevocable *all-at-once* identity disclosure. Hence, our formal model extends this system by including the capabilities of the two different models of privacy release, in order to evaluate for each of them how trading privacy for trust influences access to services and related costs.

To summarize the comparison results, we observe that the major freedom degree of the independent model allows the user to obtain access to the same services by saving up to 30% of private information disclosure. If the objective is not only trading privacy for trust, but also cost optimization, it is worth comparing cost functions that depend on trust in different ways [3,17]. Preliminary results show that in many cases the independent model ensures lower costs when the same average level of privacy release is considered and that such a model never induces higher costs than the incremental model.

## 2.2   Implementation Issues

As far as the design of the two models of privacy management is concerned, we notice that the incremental model can employ known techniques, while the independent one represents a novel approach requiring non-standard mechanisms.

The pseudonyms model by Seigneur and Jensen [14] obeys the principle of incremental release of privacy, as it is based on irrevocable linkability of pieces of evidence. In order to implement a mechanism balancing trust with privacy, they allow users to freely create pseudonyms identified by the *crypto-id*, i.e., the hash of the public key of a locally generated asymmetric cryptography key pair. Then, depending on the context, one or another pseudonym could be used to carry out actions logged as events signed with the private key of the pseudonym. If needed, one or several pseudonyms could also be linked together in order to increase the number of known actions and potentially increase the trust in the linked entity assuming that all these actions had a positive outcome.

In the following we present a technique for the independent model. As for the pseudonyms model, we use the notion of virtual identity generated by means of the crypto-id. As a crucial assumption, reputation and each trust association are mapped to pieces of the crypto-id rather than to the crypto-id as a whole.

Whenever issuing a service request, the sender chooses a bitmask $B$ that is applied to her/his crypto-id through the bitwise AND operator in order to extract $n$ bits of the crypto-id to be revealed to the request receiver. We use $C_B$ (and the term *chunk*) to denote the result of this operation. Hence, a chunk represents a set of $n$ bits of the crypto-id, of which we know value and position. The calculated chunk is transmitted to the receiver and represents a portion of the identity of the sender. Notice that the negotiated transaction is not associated to the sender directly, but is related to the chunk extracted from sender's crypto-id, which could be shared by several different users.

*Example 1.* The bitmask 01110000 identifies the same chunk for the crypto-ids:
$$K_1: 10010100 \qquad K_2: 00010010$$
while the bitmask 00001110 does not. Now, assume that the user with crypto-id $K_1$ uses bitmask 00010010 for a certain interaction. If in a future interaction with the same receiver she/he employs the bitmask 00010000, thus revealing less information, then the receiver cannot link the two interactions to the same identity, as they could be related to different crypto-ids.                    □

Since a user can spend different chunks in different transactions and can also combine chunks previously used in order to exploit a combination of their reputations, in a limiting scenario we may envision a reputation for every bit of the crypto-id. Hence, the reputation associated with a chunk is given by the contribution of the reputations of each bit forming the chunk. In the following, without loss of generality, we adopt such an assumption and we present a reputation system in the centralized setting.

User crypto-ids are stored in a non-public repository managed by a trusted, central authority (CA). When a user issues a service request linked to a chunk, she/he sends to the receiver an encryption (through receiver's public key) containing the chunk, a cryptographic proof allowing the CA to validate the request while preserving sender's anonymity, and transaction specific information avoiding replay attacks. Then, the receiver forwards the chunk and the proof to the CA, which performs the validity check and transmits to the receiver the reputation of the chunk. Afterwards, the objective of the CA is to update the reputation of the crypto-ids from which the chunk could be generated on the basis of the feedback reported by the receiver at the end of the transaction.

Ideally, the overall reputation associated with a crypto-id shall result from a combination of the reputations cumulated by every bit of such a crypto-id spent to expose a chunk in some interaction. However, as previously shown, a chunk is potentially shared by several different crypto-ids. Therefore, when the receiver transmits a chunk and the evaluation resulting from the transaction, the CA could not be able to infer from which crypto-id the chunk is actually originated. For this reason, we assume that the CA distributes the result of receiver's evaluation among the bits of the chunk for every crypto-id matching the chunk. Let us explain the feedback mechanism through an example.

*Example 2.* Let us assume that the central repository includes crypto-ids $K_1$ and $K_2$ of the previous example and the following crypto-ids:

$$K_3: 01110111 \qquad K_4: 11011011$$

The four crypto-ids are associated to users $U_1$, $U_2$, $U_3$, and $U_4$, respectively. Even if in principle any reputation metric could be applied, to simplify calculations we report receiver's evaluations as unitary reputation variations and we assume that initially the reputation of each bit of every crypto-id is 0.

Firstly, $U_1$ negotiates a service by using the chunk identified by the bitmask 01110000, for which the receiver provides a positive feedback at the end of the transaction. Since the related chunk is shared by $U_1$ and $U_2$, reputations are changed by the CA as follows:

$$rv(K_1): [01110000] \qquad rv(K_2): [01110000]$$

where $rv(K)$ denotes the vector of the reputations of the bits forming the crypto-id $K$. Secondly, $U_3$ uses bitmask 00011100 and, again, feedback is positive. The related chunk is shared by $U_3$ and $U_1$, for which reputations change as follows:

$$rv(K_1): [01121100] \qquad rv(K_3): [00011100]$$

Thirdly, $U_1$ requires another service for which $U_1$ exhibits a chunk formed by two bits with high reputation, e.g., through the bitmask 01010000. If receiver's evaluation is positive, the CA changes the reputations as follows:

$$rv(K_1): [02131100] \qquad rv(K_2): [02120000]$$

Notice that users are stimulated to use chunks of bits with high reputation in transactions in which they behave honestly. As a consequence, all the users who share these chunks and contributed to their high reputation benefit from this virtuous circle. Finally, consider a transaction with negative feedback conducted by $U_4$ by using bitmask 00000011. Hence:

$$rv(K_3): [000111\text{-}1\text{-}1] \qquad rv(K_4): [000000\text{-}1\text{-}1] \qquad \square$$

By following the considerations concerning the uncertainty of the chunk origin, in case of a request accompanied by chunk $C_B$, the calculation of $C_B$'s reputation results from a combination (e.g., through the arithmetic mean) of the reputations of such a chunk within every crypto-id matching $C_B$.

With abuse of notation, we write $C_B \leq K$ to express that chunk $C_B$ can be extracted from crypto-id $K$. Let $rep(C_B, K)$ denote the reputation of chunk $C_B$ of the crypto-id $K$, which is calculated by combining the reputation of each bit of $K$ contributing to $C_B$. Moreover, let $|C_B|$ denote the number of crypto-ids matching $C_B$. Then, the reputation of $C_B$ is as follows:

$$rep(C_B) = \frac{1}{|C_B|} \cdot \sum_{C_B \leq K} rep(C_B, K)$$

*Example 3.* With reference to the previous example, let us consider the situation just before the third transaction, in which $R_1$ spends the chunk $C_B$ identified by the bitmask $B = 01010000$. Such a chunk is shared by $R_1$ and $R_2$. The reputations of the involved bits are $1, 2$ for $R_1$ and $1, 1$ for $R_2$. Denoted by $f$ the function used to combine the reputation of each bit of the chunk, we obtain $rep(C_B) = \frac{1}{2} \cdot (f(1,2) + f(1,1))$ (e.g., if $f$ is summation then $rep(C_B) = 2.5$). $\square$

As a side effect of chunk sharing, the reputation of a chunk is the result of the behavior of all the users with crypto-ids consistent with such a chunk. In other words, the crypto-ids matching the same chunk actually benefit from the reputation (or pay the mistrust) associated to such a chunk. This aspect is crucial for the requirements of the independent model of privacy release and can be viewed as an incentive to take prosocial and honest decisions, as a high number of trustworthy chunks contribute to increase the probability of obtaining services at a reasonable cost by preserving the desired level of privacy.

Another important aspect of this model is the choice of the chunk size. If privacy is privileged and, therefore, chunks of small size are chosen, then the probability that their reputation values are influenced by a high number of community members increases, thus leading to a worse approximation of the actual reputation of the user exposing a small chunk. On the other hand, if accuracy of reputation is privileged, then the user is motivated to use chunks with a high number of bits, thus sacrificing more privacy. Therefore, a tradeoff exists between the amount of sensitive information the user is willing to invest and the accuracy of her/his reputation estimated by the request receiver in order to negotiate the transaction and the related parameters, including service cost.

The proposed implementation differs from the pseudonyms model by Seigneur and Jensen [14] since a user's pseudonym, here represented by a chunk, may also be controlled by another user. Then, actions may be carried out by several different users, without every user being able to know which other user has also control over the same chunk $C_B$. As shown above, it may be beneficial for the chunk if all users controlling it are trustworthy, but if at least one of them is very untrustworthy and carries out at least one illegal action linked to $C_B$, then the chunk becomes untrustworthy and useless for all other users. In addition, if

$C_B$ is untrustworthy then it may also impact the trustworthiness of any chunk $C_{B'}$ refining $C_B$, i.e., such that $C_B \leq C_{B'}$, as one may wonder whether the user exposing $C_{B'}$ is (or is not) the same untrustworthy user who used $C_B$ in a malicious way. This negative side effect, which can be serious in case $C_B$ is a small chunk, can be mitigated in an implicit way by using mixed cooperation strategies based on trust and cost, or explicitly by reducing the influence upon trust of actions linked to small chunks. This can be done by weighting both the reputation calculation and the feedback evaluation by a discounting factor inversely proportional to the size of the chunk used, in order to reflect that the amount of sensitive information that is exposed in a transaction is proportional to sender's trustworthiness. An alternative, effective but severe solution consists of resorting to a CA capable of revoking blindness in case of suspicious behaviors by some chunk, in order to isolate dishonest users and repair the reputation of the chunk involved.

## 3   Related and Ongoing Work

The main objective of this work has been showing that trust and cost can be effectively combined while also considering privacy as a third dimension. To the best of our knowledge, such an analysis has never been conducted by joining all these aspects in the same framework. In the literature, Automated Trust Negotiation is known to have not fully resolved privacy issues [16]. Wagealla et al. [15] use trustworthiness of an information receiver to make the decision on whether private information should be disclosed or not, which is another way to envisage the relation between trust and privacy. However, it may be difficult to evaluate trustworthiness in first place without enough evidence linked with the receiving entity. The work on modelling unlinkability [10] and pseudonymity [6,9] is valuable towards founding privacy/trust trade. Moreover, the Sybil attack [5], which challenges the use of recommendations, is also worth keeping in mind when providing means to create virtual identities at will without centralized authority. Finally, the trust-privacy tradeoff can be optimized in data-centric ad-hoc networks by using incentive mechanisms [13].

The theoretical analysis conducted on a real-world case study motivates the implementation of the independent model, the applicability of which has been shown through a mechanism based on the splitting of crypto-ids into chunks and on a centralized reputation system. Since chunk sharing is the main principle behind this mechanism, we point out that, as an alternative approach, the model by Seigneur and Jensen [14] may also be turned into a scheme allowing for the sharing of a pseudonym among $n$ users. The private key associated to a pseudonym generated by user $n$ would be sent to the other $n-1$ users encrypted with their public keys. Anyway, this approach raises issues related to the key exchange protocol and to the choice of the $n$ users sharing a pseudonym.

To integrate our reputation system, we plan to design a trust model for both centralized and distributed systems. The idea is to equip every user with a structure collecting information on the set of chunks associated to completed transactions. Such a structure is then used to manage trust towards every chunk under the assumption that the user is not aware of the set of crypto-ids from which chunks are originated.

# References

1. Aldini, A.: Formal Approach to Design and Automatic Verification of Cooperation-Based Networks. Journal On Advances in Internet Technology 6, 42–56 (2013)
2. Aldini, A., Bogliolo, A. (eds.): User-Centric Networking – Future Perspectives. Lecture Notes in Social Networks. Springer (2014)
3. Bogliolo, A., Polidori, P., Aldini, A., Moreira, W., Mendes, P., Yildiz, M., Ballester, C., Seigneur, J.-M.: Virtual Currency and Reputation-Based Cooperation Incentives in User-Centric Networks. In: 8th Int. Wireless Communications and Mobile Computing Conf (IWCMC 2012), pp. 895–900. IEEE (2012)
4. Chen, T., Forejt, V., Kwiatkowska, M., Parker, D., Simaitis, A.: PRISM-games: A Model Checker for Stochastic Multi-Player Games. In: Piterman, N., Smolka, S.A. (eds.) TACAS 2013. LNCS, vol. 7795, pp. 185–191. Springer, Heidelberg (2013)
5. Douceur, J.R.: The Sybil Attack. In: Druschel, P., Kaashoek, M.F., Rowstron, A. (eds.) IPTPS 2002. LNCS, vol. 2429, pp. 251–260. Springer, Heidelberg (2002)
6. Goldberg, I.: A Pseudonymous Communications Infrastructure for the Internet, PhD Thesis, University of California at Berkeley (2000)
7. Greengard, S.: Social Games, Virtual Goods. Communications of the ACM 54(4), 19–22 (2011)
8. Jøsang, A.: Trust and Reputation Systems. In: Aldini, A., Gorrieri, R. (eds.) FOSAD 2007. LNCS, vol. 4677, pp. 209–245. Springer, Heidelberg (2007)
9. Kobsa, A., Schreck, J.: Privacy through Pseudonymity in User-Adaptive Systems. ACM Transactions on Internet Technology 3(2), 149–183 (2003)
10. Steinbrecher, S., Köpsell, S.: Modelling unlinkability. In: Dingledine, R. (ed.) PET 2003. LNCS, vol. 2760, pp. 32–47. Springer, Heidelberg (2003)
11. Kwiatkowska, M., Parker, D., Simaitis, A.: Strategic Analysis of Trust Models for User-Centric Networks. In: Int. Workshop on Strategic Reasoning (SR 2013). EPTCS, vol. 112, pp. 53–60 (2013)
12. Li, Z., Shen, H.: Game-Theoretic Analysis of Cooperation Incentives Strategies in Mobile Ad Hoc Networks. IEEE Transactions on Mobile Computing 11(8), 1287–1303 (2012)
13. Raya, M., Shokri, R., Hubaux, J.-P.: On the Tradeoff between Trust and Privacy in Wireless Ad Hoc Networks. In: 3rd ACM Conf. on Wireless Network Security (WiSec 2010), pp. 75–80 (2010)
14. Seigneur, J.-M., Jensen, C.D.: Trading Privacy for Trust. In: Jensen, C., Poslad, S., Dimitrakos, T. (eds.) iTrust 2004. LNCS, vol. 2995, pp. 93–107. Springer, Heidelberg (2004)
15. Wagealla, W., Carbone, M., English, C., Terzis, S., Nixon, P.: A Formal Model of Trust Lifecycle Management. In: Workshop on Formal Aspects of Security and Trust (FAST 2003) (2003)
16. Yu, T., Winslett, M.: A Unified Scheme for Resource Protection in Automated Trust Negotiation. In: IEEE Symp. on Security and Privacy, pp. 110–122 (2003)
17. Zhang, Y., Lin, L., Huai, J.: Balancing Trust and Incentive in Peer-to-Peer Collaborative System. Journal of Network Security 5, 73–81 (2007)

# Reputation-Based Cooperation in the Clouds[*]

Alessandro Celestini[1], Alberto Lluch Lafuente[2], Philip Mayer[3],
Stefano Sebastio[2], and Francesco Tiezzi[2]

[1] Istituto per le Applicazioni del Calcolo, IAC-CNR, Rome, Italy
[2] IMT Institute for Advanced Studies, Lucca, Italy
[3] Ludwig-Maximilians-Universität München, Germany

**Abstract.** The popularity of the cloud computing paradigm is opening
new opportunities for collaborative computing. In this paper we tackle
a fundamental problem in open-ended cloud-based distributed computing platforms, i.e., the quest for potential collaborators. We assume that
cloud participants are willing to share their computational resources for
shared distributed computing problems, but they are not willing to disclose the details of their resources. Lacking such information, we advocate to rely on reputation scores obtained by evaluating the interactions
among participants. More specifically, we propose a methodology to assess, at design time, the impact of different (reputation-based) collaborator selection strategies on the system performance. The evaluation is
performed through statistical analysis on a volunteer cloud simulator.

## 1 Introduction

Cloud computing has gained huge popularity in recent years. This is mainly due
to the progress in virtualization technologies and the transfer of data centers to
low-cost locations. This emergent paradigm meets many of today's requirements
like the need of elaborating big volumes of data or the necessity of executing
applications of which only the front-end is able to run on a mobile device. Next
to the presence of traditional cloud computing platforms built running in propri-
etary data centers, another trend that is gaining popularity is the use of volunteer
resources offered by institutions or ordinary people for, e.g., scientific computations. These collaborative environments can effectively be seen as cloud computing platforms where participants take advantage of virtualization techniques
to share their computational resources for distributed computing applications,
like the execution of tasks. Differently from grid computing, we cannot expect
volunteer participants to guarantee a certain level of performance in terms of
shared resources or online availability. On the other hand, volunteer clouds offer the unique opportunity of letting participants find their collaborators in the
entire volunteer network. The quest for collaborators is one of the key aspects
in such platforms.

[*] Research partially supported by the EU through the FP7-ICT Integrated Project
257414 ASCEns, STReP project 600708 QUANTICOL, and the Italian PRIN
2010LHT4KM CINA.

J. Zhou et al. (Eds.): IFIPTM 2014, IFIP AICT 430, pp. 213–220, 2014.
© IFIP International Federation for Information Processing 2014

The contribution of the paper is twofold: (1) a reputation-based approach to the collaborator selection problem, and (2) a methodology to assess, at design time, the impact of the selection strategies on the system performance. We focus on a peer-to-peer cooperative environment on top of which a cloud platform offers a task execution service. The aim of the platform is to maximize the number of successfully executed tasks. We consider a cloud platform with an integrated reputation system, where a reputation score is associated to each node denoting the trustworthiness of the node. Reputation scores are computed on the basis of the rating values released by other nodes. These ratings evaluate the behavior of the node in past interactions. Specifically, we exploit the concept of reputation as an indicator of the likelihood that a node will successfully execute the task, i.e., the higher the reputation the higher the probability that the task will be successfully executed. We assume that tasks have an associated Quality of Service (QoS) requirement given by a deadline, after which the task execution is considered unsatisfactory.

The reputation-based node selection strategies provide *loose coupling* and *self-adaptivity*, since the nodes take their decisions based on the reputation learning mechanism. Overall, the system is able to autonomously adapt the load of nodes during system execution while avoiding to interact with nodes to check their current status. This is in particular useful in platforms that are *dynamic*, where nodes can join and leave the system continuously over time, and *heterogeneous*, since participants with different computational resources are rated with the same mechanism but can customize their strategies according to their needs.

As a reference case study for experimenting with the proposed reputation-based approach, we have used the SCIENCE CLOUD [10,3]. In particular, we have modeled this cloud platform with DEUS [1] and carried out a number of experiments considering different configuration scenarios. The obtained results show the benefit of the use of reputation-based approaches. Our experimental analysis shows that a probabilistic reputation-based strategy (compared to both reputation based and random approaches) is more robust to the workload variation, offering the best performance at a reasonable communication overhead.

The SCIENCE CLOUD [10,3] is a volunteer P2P Platform-as-a-Service (PaaS) system developed within the European project ASCENS [2] with the aim of creating a decentralized platform for sharing computational resources in scientific communities. Participants contribute with their desktops, mobile devices, servers, or virtual machines by running platform nodes on them. Nodes may be *heterogeneous*, i.e., they may offer different virtual resources (CPU, disk, memory) and also highly *dynamic*, i.e., they may enter or leave the system at any time, and their load as well as their resources may change. The SCIENCE CLOUD provides distributed application execution as its main functionality. Applications may range from batch tasks to more sophisticated human-interactive applications. We focus here on task-based scenarios where, for each task, one *initiator* node is chosen as being responsible for processing the task (not necessarily executing the task itself). This node needs to be secure against failures, i.e., if it goes down another node needs to take its place. The initiator may choose to execute the task itself, but may also choose to delegate to a collaborator node. Whoever finally executes the task is called the *executor*. We assume that a deadline is associated with each task and that a task is successfully executed if the deadline is met. Moreover, each task requires only one executor node. Since the SCIENCE CLOUD is a cooperative environment, we consider scenarios without malicious nodes: nodes accept a task only if they satisfy the resource requirements of the task and if they estimate that they are able to execute it. These estimations assume that the node will remain always connected. However, nodes are not aware of their online/offline times and thus, it may happen that a node accepts a task but, before finishing its execution, goes offline. When a node goes offline it loses all the tasks in its queue regardless of the time in which it will return online. An offline node that returns online will maintain its identifier; this is indispensable to describe the node behavior.    Our goal in such scenarios is to maximize the overall number of tasks executed, which is to be achieved by selecting, for each new task, the node most likely to successfully execute the task.

## 2   Node Selection

We suggest and discuss here some reputation-based strategies based on the Beta reputation system [9] for addressing the node selection problem. Each strategy consists of a *node ranking schema* and a *node selection strategy*.

First, we briefly describe (see Fig. 1) the underlying architecture and the protocol that nodes follow to implement the reputation-based strategies: (1) the initiator node sends a request to the reputation system asking for a list of potential executor nodes ordered according to the node selection strategy; (2) the reputation system provides the desired answer to the initiator node; (3) the initiator node starts contacting the potential executor nodes using the obtained list; (4) the contacted nodes send their response to

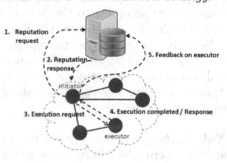

**Fig. 1.** Finding a collaborator

the initiator, either rejecting the request or accepting it (and eventually communicating the completion of the task execution); (5) the initiator node provides feedback to rate its interaction with the contacted executor nodes.

*Reputation Systems.* A reputation system associates a reputation score to each node, denoting the trustworthiness of the node, i.e., the higher the reputation, the more trustworthy the node. The reputation score of each node is computed on the basis of the rating values released by other nodes. Such ratings correspond to evaluations of the behavior of the nodes in past interactions, which in our case can have only two possible outcomes: 'satisfactory' (i.e., the task was executed and its QoS was satisfied) or 'unsatisfactory' (the task was not executed or its QoS was not satisfied). In other words, we consider *binary* ratings. In our approach, the reputation of a node is an indicator of the probability that the node will successfully execute the task. We consider the termination deadline as the QoS parameter and we assume that missing a deadline makes the task completion useless.

In this work, we focus on *probabilistic trust* systems [7,8] which use probability distributions to model the behavior of a node. The goal of such systems is to provide an estimation of the distribution's parameters modeling the node behavior on the basis of past interaction outcomes, i.e., the ratings. This estimation is indeed the reputation score of the node and is used to compute the probability of future interaction outcomes with it.

For the definition of our strategies we exploit the Beta reputation system [9]. The name of this system is due to the use of the Beta distribution to estimate the posterior probabilities of binary events. In the Beta system, the behavior of each node is modeled as a Bernoulli distribution with success probability $\theta \in [0,1]$. This means that, when interacting with a party whose behavior is (determined by) a given $\theta$, the estimated probability that a next interaction will be satisfactory is $\theta$. The reputation computed by the system is then an estimation $\tilde{\theta}$ of the node's behavior $\theta$. Specifically, to compute the reputation of a given node, the Beta reputation system takes as input the number $\alpha$ of past satisfactory interactions with the node and the number $\beta$ of past unsatisfactory interactions. The reputation $\tilde{\theta}$ of the node is given by the expected value of a random variable $\vartheta$ distributed according to the Beta distribution $Beta(\alpha + 1, \beta + 1)$, with $\alpha \geq 0$, $\beta \geq 0$, that is defined as $\tilde{\theta} = \mathrm{E}[\vartheta] = \frac{\alpha+1}{\alpha+\beta+2}$.

Summing up, in our case the reputation of a node denotes the likelihood that the node, if selected, will not disconnect before completing the task and that it will accept the task because it is not overloaded, i.e., it can meet the deadline. Thus, nodes with high reputation should be able to successfully execute a task with higher probability.

*Node Ranking Schema.* The interactions we aim at evaluating in our systems are: (i) **accept**, the selected node accepts the task; (ii) **reject**, the selected node rejects the task, since it cannot meet the deadline; (iii) **complete**, the selected node successfully completes the task execution, i.e., it meets the deadline and does not go offline during the execution; (iv) **fail**, the selected node fails in executing the task because it goes offline during the execution.

Notably, we assume that the executor nodes are truthful: they are able to accurately predict the task completion time and accept a new task *iff* they are principally able to execute it within the task deadline. However, nodes do not know their online-offline cycles a priori. It is thus possible that a node misses a task it has accepted by going offline.

Each action can be evaluated by the nodes as satisfactory (+), unsatisfactory (−) or nothing (0), which corresponds to giving a positive, negative or no rating, respectively. The ranking schema is defined by the value assigned to each individual interaction which in our case is **accept** (0), **reject** (−), **complete** (+) and **fail** (−). Notably, the negative rating assigned to the action **fail** is given for each task whose execution was not successful. Notice also that no rating is given in case of task acceptance.

*Node Selection Strategies.* Reputation scores are used by the initiator node for the selection of an executor. We consider the following node selection strategies: **Random (R)**: a node is chosen randomly using an uniform probability distribution over the node pool (i.e., reputation is not taken into account). **Reputation-based (RB)**: the node with the highest reputation score is chosen. If more than one node exists with the same score, the choice is arbitrary (i.e., random). **Probabilistic reputation-based (PRB)**: a node is chosen randomly using a probability distribution over the node pool. Such a distribution assigns a probability to each node that is proportional to the reputation score of the node, i.e., the higher the node reputation, the higher the probability the node is selected. The idea is to introduce some randomness to avoid congesting nodes with good reputation, and also some fairness by giving nodes with low scores the chance to achieve a higher ranking (again). The probability that a given node $i$ will be selected among $l$ nodes (the node-$i$'s neighbors) according this strategy is defined as $P(select_i) = \frac{\tilde{\theta}_i}{\sum_{j=1}^{l} \tilde{\theta}_j}$.

## 3 Validation

We present here an experimental validation of the proposed approach based on simulations and their analysis. Our simulation model is implemented in DEUS [1], an open-source discrete event simulation tool developed in Java. Our statistical analysis has been performed with MultiVeStA [12,15], a distributed statistical analysis tool that can be integrated with any discrete event simulator. MultiVeStA provides a language (MultiQuaTEx) to express the system properties of interest in a compact fashion, and performs independent distributed DEUS simulation runs until these properties are evaluated with the required accuracy.

The simulator implements the basic machinery to suitably model the scenarios under consideration. In the following we discuss some parameters of the configurations of the simulator that can be taken into account to set up the desired volunteer cloud scenarios.

Tasks are generated by initiators according to some parametric process that determines frequency of task generation, their duration (expressed as CPU cycles) and memory occupation. Tasks are defined by their duration and their deadline. If the deadline expires the task execution is considered to be useless. The deadline offset is defined as 20% beyond the ideal task duration. Thus, if a task that requires t_exec arrives at time t_arrival, the task execution is considered useful if it is completed within time: t_arrival + t_exec + task_exec*20%.

When a node accepts a task execution request coming from another node a communication overhead is evaluated to the simple yet realistic network models described by Saino *et al.* [13].

The nodes realize an exclusive task execution environment where the whole Virtual Machine (VM) is assigned to only one task at a time. Its behavior is modeled by a $M/G/1/+\infty$ queue using the Kendall's notation [4], i.e., Poisson arrival process, general service time distribution with only one VM and infinity queue capacity. A task is accepted by a node only if the node is able to satisfy the requested task deadline, taking into account the tasks already on its queue but without knowing its departure time (i.e., the point in time when it goes offline). Thus, it is possible that a node accepts a task since it is able to satisfy the QoS constraint, but after a while it leaves the network losing the task execution results until that point. In this case the task is lost.

There are executor nodes of two classes: *stable* and *unstable*. Stable nodes are always online. Unstable nodes have two possible states (online and offline) and two transitions (from online to offline and back). Their change of state obeys some parametric, periodic or stochastic model. There are $n$ stable nodes and $m$ unstable nodes created in the initial simulation stage. During the simulation, unstable nodes can leave the network (causing a miss for all the tasks on their execution queue) and reconnect subsequently according to a parameterizable process. When a node comes back online it retains its identifier; in this way the behavior history of unstable nodes is preserved. Nodes are heterogeneous. Disregarding of their class they have computational resources (CPU, RAM) randomly selected in some range (uniformly distributed). The node RAM constitutes a constraint on the task that can be accepted by the node.

In the following we refer to the average results obtained after reaching a 95% confidence interval, with a radius of 0.05, evaluated with the Student's t-test [4]. To evaluate the performance of the proposed strategies we have considered four different measurements to be relevant: the hit rate perceived, the messages spread in the network (total and refused messages), the QoS (Quality of Service) perceived by the task initiators (through the waiting and sojourn times) and the algorithm fairness (considering how well the followed approach is able to equally distribute the task load). For sake of brevity not all the results are reported here. We refer the interested reader to our Technical Report [5].

In our scenarios the arrival processes are Markovian, i.e., the inter-arrival time between two consecutive tasks can be modeled as an exponential random variable with a mean value equal to 750 ms or 1000 ms in the comparing workload. Also, the unstable node departure and reconnection times are modeled with Markovian processes with a mean value equal to 72 seconds. The simulated time is 7 hours, and the temporal analysis considers a granularity of 200 sec. The tasks are described by a deadline of 20% of its duration, a task duration uniformly distributed in a range of [0...24] minutes and a memory requirement in the range of [0...512] MB.

In the low-load situation, analyzing the hit rate $(H+R)$ (Fig. 2) almost all the approaches behave similarly. When the node load increases, it is the PRB approach that obtains the best performance, since it is able to spread the load on more nodes in comparison to the RB and the R approaches. At the same time, the PRB approach is able to take into account the information gained on the evaluation of the node's behavior through the reputation scores, and does not stop on a local minimum. From the rate of refused requests (not shown here), we have observed that both reputation-based approaches (RB and PRB) are able to identify the stable nodes and redirect the load towards them. The strategies that implement a random choice (i.e., R and PRB) are able to spread the load more uniformly among the nodes.

Fig. 2 shows the benefits of using different node selection strategies. It is worth observing that the RB approach is more sensitive to the increase in system load; indeed its performance on the $H+R$ rate decreases quickly. The PRB approach instead is the more stable under the change of workload. The task distribution among nodes shows that the RB approach tends to direct the load to few nodes.

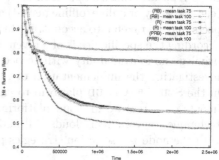

**Fig. 2.** $H+R$ rate

Concluding, the node selection process done through a reputation-based mechanism can be an effective way to select an executor node. Using only the reputation score, it is possible to observe a degradation on the performance when the task load is high, since the reputation initially leads to a redirection of all tasks to a few nodes that soon get overloaded and consequentially lose their score due to task rejections. The mix of the two approaches, realized in the PRB approach, seems to be the more effective way to use the knowledge acquired with the reputation scores, and at the same time avoids getting stuck in a performance local minimum. This is because the PRB approach allows some degree of exploration of the nodes that do not currently have high scores.

## 4    Concluding Remarks

In this paper, we have investigated the problem of task distribution in voluntary, peer-to-peer cloud computing environments where nodes are willing to share their resources to other nodes. We have proposed a solution based on (1) a reputation-based approach to the collaborator selection problem, and (2) a methodology to assess, at design time, the impact of the selection strategies on the system performance.

Some similar works to ours are the trust management framework proposed by Mishra et al. [11] for the sake of trustworthy load balancing in cluster environments, and the reputation-based approach to discovery and selection of reliable resources in P2P Gnutella-like environments, proposed by Damiani et al. [6].

We have shown that reputation-based systems can be beneficial in cases where available node resources are unknown, or where nodes deliberately do not want to disclose their status (e.g., current load) or their resources (e.g., CPU, memory). In our experiments, the reputation score calculated through the evaluation of node interactions has been used as the main criteria for selecting nodes for task execution. Our simulation results shows how the task performance parameters are affected by the use of three different strategies.

Currently, we are calculating reputation scores by considering all aspects of the behavior of a node in a uniform way, i.e., all (satisfactory or unsatisfactory) ratings have the same weight. We plan to extend our analysis with more sophisticated reputation-based approaches, where separate behavioral aspects of a node (e.g., capacity or online/offline period) are rated differently and where further aspects may be taken into account. In this way, we can tune the selection strategies according the specific needs of a given cloud application, which for example may privilege node availability with respect to other features. Furthermore, we are investigating the implementation of reputation-based node selection strategies in the SCIENCE CLOUD platform to validate the simulation results with experiments on a real-world cloud platform. We are also evaluating an ACO-based technique for volunteer clouds [14] and we are investigating how to combine it with the node *pre*-selection strategies proposed in this paper.

# References

1. Amoretti, M., Picone, M., Zanichelli, F., Ferrari, G.: Simulating mobile and distributed systems with DEUS and ns-3. In: HPCS (2013)
2. European integrated project ASCENS, http://www.ascens-ist.eu/
3. The science cloud platform, http://svn.pst.ifi.lmu.de/trac/scp/
4. Bolch, G., Greiner, S., de Meer, H., Trivedi, K.: Queueing Networks and Markov Chains, 2nd edn. Wiley (2006)
5. Celestini, A., Lluch-Lafuente, A., Mayer, P., Sebastio, S., Tiezzi, F.: Reputation-based cooperation in the clouds. Technical report, IMT Lucca (2014), http://eprints.imtlucca.it/2191/
6. Damiani, E., di Vimercati, D.C., Paraboschi, S., Samarati, P., Violante, F.: A reputation-based approach for choosing reliable resources in peer-to-peer networks. In: CCS (2002)
7. Despotovic, Z., Aberer, K.: A Probabilistic Approach to Predict Peers' Performance in P2P Networks. In: Klusch, M., Ossowski, S., Kashyap, V., Unland, R. (eds.) CIA 2004. LNCS (LNAI), vol. 3191, pp. 62–76. Springer, Heidelberg (2004)
8. Gambetta, D.: Can We Trust Trust? In: Trust: Making and Breaking Cooperative Relations, ch. 13, pp. 213–237. Basil Blackwell (1988)
9. Jøsang, A., Ismail, R.: The beta reputation system. In: The 15th Bled Electronic Commerce Conference (2002)
10. Mayer, P., Klarl, A., Hennicker, R., Puviani, M., Tiezzi, F., Pugliese, R., Keznikl, J., Bureš, T.: The Autonomic Cloud: A Vision of Voluntary, Peer-2-Peer Cloud Computing. In: SASO AWARENESS Workshop, pp. 1–6 (2013)
11. Mishra, S., Kushwaha, D., Misra, A.: A cooperative trust management framework for load balancing in cluster based distributed systems. In: Recent Trends in Information, Telecommunication and Computing (ITC), pp. 121–125 (2010)
12. MultiVeStA website, http://code.google.com/p/multivesta/
13. Saino, L., Cocora, C., Pavlou, G.: A toolchain for simplifying network simulation setup. In: SIMUTOOLS (2013)
14. Sebastio, S., Amoretti, M., Lluch-Lafuente, A.: A computational field framework for collaborative task execution in volunteer clouds. In: 9th International Symposium on Software Engineering for Adaptive and Self-Managing Systems (SEAMS) (2014)
15. Sebastio, S., Vandin, A.: MultiVeStA: Statistical model checking for discrete event simulators. In: 7th International Conference on Performance Evaluation Methodologies and Tools (VALUETOOLS) (2013)

# Introducing Patient and Dentist Profiling and Crowdsourcing to Improve Trust in Dental Care Recommendation Systems

Sojen Pradhan and Valerie Gay

University of Technology Sydney (UTS)
Sydney, Australia
{Sojendra.Pradhan,Valerie.Gay}@uts.edu.au

**Abstract.** Healthcare blogs, podcasts, search engines and health social networks are now widely used, and referred as crowdsources, to share information such as opinions, side effects, medication and types of therapies. Although attitudes and perceptions of the users play a vital role on how they create, share, retrieve and utilise the information for their own or recommend to others, recommendation systems have not taken the attitudes and perceptions into considerations for matching. Our research aims at defining a trust dependent framework to design recommendation system that uses profiling and social networks in dental care. This paper focuses on trust derived in direct interaction between a patient and a dentist from subjective characteristics' point of view. It highlights that attitudes, behaviours and perception of both patients and dentists are important social elements, which enhance trust and improve the matching process between them. This study forms a basis for our profile-based framework for dynamic dental care recommendation systems.

**Keywords:** Health social networks, Social communications, Crowdsourcing, Recommendation systems, Trust, Reviews and ratings.

## 1 Introduction

It is part of the human nature to share experiences, and to turn to our peers to get support, recommendations and answers on all aspects of our life. This feature has been adopted online, and it is done through various channels such as blogs, micro blogs, wikis, forums, social networking sites (SNSs). The source of information is gradually moving from friends, families, radio and television to the Internet. Web users check specific websites before making decisions about their everyday activities (what to buy, where to eat, which movie to watch, which professionals to choose). Social networks such as Amazon, eBay, IMDb, Eatability, TripAdvisor, Epinion, Elance, and also Health social networks (HSNs) such as PatientsLikeMe, CureTogether, Health-Line, DailyStrength, WebMD are providing recommendations to the users.

One of the evolving features of the online world is 'reviews' and 'ratings' on any product or service. Crowdsources have been influencing the users in making daily

J. Zhou et al. (Eds.): IFIPTM 2014, IFIP AICT 430, pp. 221–228, 2014.

decisions to choose a particular product or service, beyond the traditional form of instructions from experts or local peers or health professionals [1,2]. These reviews and ratings are shaping and influencing public views on health issues such as vaccines, breast implants and dental implants. Thus, sources of health information is shifting online. Moreover, HSNs are promoting a sense of community and providing variety of services such as emotional support, self-tracking, Physician Q&A and clinical trial access [3], to win trust from the web users.

Trust is a complex phenomenon that is used in many aspects of our daily life. Whenever a truster interacts with a trustee, a level of trust is inherently present regardless of simple or complex types of interactions [4]. The level of trust means the level of confidence of a truster in the trustee to act or carry on the action in a given situation. In this paper, we are focusing on how a level of trust changes with different types of people with their personality, attitude, taste and perception [5] and how it can be captured within a HSN environment. Our research aims at designing a framework for dynamic recommendation systems in dental care by including social elements of trust from patients' and dentists' profiles. Trust on the recommendation system as an information provider for patients, would be increased.

This paper is organised as follows; Section 2 discusses a shift of social communication and rise of recommendation systems. It is followed by a study of the complex nature of trust in Section 3. Section 4 proposes a framework for dental care recommendations systems based on trust enhanced by profiling both patients and dentists. Trust measurement through patients and dentists profiles are further elaborated in section 5. We conclude this paper outlining future works to validate the framework.

## 2     Social Communications and Recommendation Systems

Some studies [6,7] highlighted the fact that we live in a 'small world', and demonstrated that two people in the US are connected by less than 'six degrees of separation'. With the rise of social media, a study claims that the degrees of separation have reduced to four [8]. In addition to the use of social media, pervasive and ubiquitous computing and mobile networks have also dramatically increased the speed of communication. It also has revolutionised the access to healthcare information. In result, patients are sometimes not accepting doctors' or dentists' recommendations without doing their own research online [2], to find a trustworthy source. Indeed, if patients fail to have their needs (questions, diagnosis, and understanding) fulfilled through direct communication with doctors or dentists, they would search in Internet [9,10]. It has become a better source of information than the traditional healthcare providers. The attitude and behaviour of patients has changed due to ubiquitously available online information [11,12]. A survey indicated 81% of adult users have used Internet for health information and acknowledged that the Internet is the most widely used source for health information ahead of doctors, friends and families [13].

However, is the online data accurate? Search engines cannot provide answers to this question [13]. Not only the content but the source of the information is also critical while measuring trust. Classifying the information based on trust is one of the methods to overcome the colossal problem of information overloading in the Internet. Recommendation systems have been gaining popularity to do so. Traditionally two popular methods, content-based filtering (CB) and collaborative filtering (CF) are used. CB analyses description of items or individuals that have been rated by the user. A good example of this method is matchmaking sites, through which list of potential dates will be suggested based on the preferences chosen in the profile. However, the recommendation system like Amazon is not only using CB method but they analyse the users' similarity based on ratings and their profile (demographic information, history of buying etc.) and recommends products based on other users' behaviour. This method is known as collaborative filtering (CF). Both methods have limitations, CB does not consider the target users' similarity information whereas CF does not explicitly consider the content [14]. CF is one of the most popular methods used in recommendation systems, but has many challenges [14-16]. *Cold start problem* emanates when a new item or individual is added to the system and no user ratings exist in the initial phase. *Scalability problem* arises when the number of users and items rises exponentially. *Shilling attacks* are caused by biased behaviours such as making positive comments on own items and negative remarks to others. *Data Sparsity* is caused due to high volume of items/goods to recommend. *Gray sheep* symptom is when a user's preference is isolated and not similar to any other users in the system.

Main goal of recommendation systems is to suggest a list, based on knowledge extracted from consumers' previous behaviours. Recommendation systems have been using both CF and CB methods, referred as hybrid method. In this research, we will use hybrid method by analysing subjective characteristics of both patients and dentists. Trustworthiness is a critical factor while choosing a dentist due to the nature of invasive treatment.

# 3    Trust and Personalisation from User Profiling

Trust is an important sociological concept which depends on many factors such as past experiences, beliefs, values, tastes, personalities, opinions, rumours, influences and so on. It is defined and researched in various areas such as psychology, sociology, business, science, philosophy [17]; with many different meanings (contexts). In almost all contexts, trust is implied as a judgment in precarious situation that trustee will act in the best interest of truster [18]. Information which is useful and trustworthy in one context may not be useful in another context [5].

In dental treatment, trust emerges from an experience of interaction between patients and dentists; therefore the source of trust is an actual experience, referred as *direct* trust [17]. When the experience is transcribed in the web, it takes another form. It becomes a part of *social trust*, presented as a collection of experiences of many patients together. Trust usually can be looked at from two different aspects: *functional* (trust in performance) and *referral* (trust in recommendation) [19, 20]. Two patients may have different opinion about the trustworthiness of a dentist, despite the same behaviour and treatment by the same dentist. Therefore, personalisation of trust from subjective characteristics is important in social network environment, and it has been overlooked [5, 21]. This research focuses on subjective characteristics from user profiles to personalise the level of trust and match patients with suitable dentists, which will eventually increase trustworthiness in the recommendation system.

Traditional cues such as body language, tone of voice, facial expression and postures are present in face to face communications. But they are missing in the online communication, therefore, pertinent user profiling with subjective characteristics is critical to measure a level of trust precisely. In this research, we postulate that more accurate the profiles of both patients and dentists are, the greater chance to match a suitable dentist within a given time and place.

## 4     Proposed Framework

The proposed trust dependent framework for dynamic dental care recommendation system is shown in Figure 1.

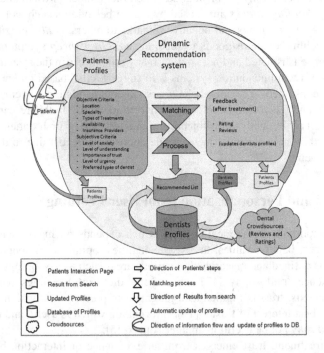

**Fig. 1.** Proposed profile-based trust framework for dentists recommendation system

Initially, patients will choose objective criteria such as location, specialist, treatment, availability and insurance providers. Subjective criteria such as attitudes, feelings, and perceptions would be determined by widely available standard personality tests. Based on the criteria, the system would provide a list of dentists (recommended list) available in the location with a number of reviews and aggregated ratings from the crowdsources. From the recommended list, the patient will choose a dentist for their treatment. After the treatment, patient will rate and write reviews about the interaction with the dentist. This information would update dentist's profile. Updating the information in real-time environment, for both patients and dentists, would benefit many other potential patients in future for the system.

For the purpose of this research, we have crawled dental reviews and ratings information from popular dental reviews sites: DrOogle[1] and Yelp[2] in the US. Separate reviews files are created for major cities in the US, for example, New York, Los Angeles, Chicago, and so on. The reviews for the dentists are analysed, by using text mining techniques to determine types of dentists.

## 5    Trust Measurement from User Profiling and Crowdsources

Trust plays a dynamic role in what people do in their daily activities. With an increased use of Internet, trust has been perceived in the form of security, privacy, credibility of source, quality of information, quality of systems and many more. Majority of trust related studies have been focusing on trends of behaviour and less on human factors such as personality, attitudes and perception. In this research, we focus on subjective characteristics of both patients and dentists to derive a level of trust.   Majority of HSNs allow users to create, share and retrieve information and retain personal data online.   Subjective characteristics such as attitude or perception of users are not available on the sites. Not only retrieving subjective characteristics of patient is challenging but privacy provision and anonymity adds even more complexity.

In this research, we source subjective characteristics of patients by asking directly to them. Based on ontology, natural way of being, people's attitudes, behaviours and perceptions have been studied from a very long time. In 1928, William Marston described that people show their emotions through attitudes and behaviours, using mainly four types of behaviour: Dominance (D), Inducement (I), Submission (S), and Compliance (C), referred as DISC personality test in modern days.   Furthermore, extensive list of behaviours which fall into the categories of DISC are listed here [22].

- Dominance (D): direct, outspoken, decisive, assertive, competitive, ambitious and time-conscious.
- Inducement (I): influencer, friendly, talkative, expressive, attention-seeking, optimistic, outgoing and people-oriented.
- Submission (S): stable, consistent, good listener, patient, team player, need time to adjust, peacemaker and family-oriented.
- Compliance (C): competent, compliant, logical, analytical, perfectionist, organised, data driven, observant and detail-oriented.

DISC personality test is one of the methods to determine subjective criteria for patients and used in this study. There are many other methods available and the system will cater to use other methods as well. Analysing and finding out a type of patient and dentist is a critical process while matching for the recommendation systems.

---

[1] www.doctoroogle.com
[2] www.yelp.com

For example, dental educator, Cathy Jameson [23] stated that qualification and expertise of dentist would be important for D type of patient and they would not like socialising as much, whereas, I type of patient would prefer discussing in a friendly manner.

The online survey we conducted in early stage of this research showed quality, reliability and even personality of dentist is important while choosing a dentist as shown in the figure 2 below. In this research, we have now taken the terms patients use to describe their dentists, as trust elements for dentists.

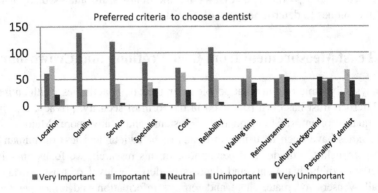

**Fig. 2.** Preferred criteria to choose a dentist

Question is "What combination of trust elements does the most trusted dentist constitute for a particular 'type of patient'?" Although different measuring criteria for ratings are used amongst different dental review sites [24], most of the sites allow patients to provide reviews about their experience after the dental visits. From two top US dental reviews sites: DrOogle and Yelp, we have analysed terms used to describe their dentists when the patients are satisfied or not satisfied. The terms are listed in the table 1 below. Based on the frequencies of terms used by patients for a typical dentist, type of dentist is determined. For example, if a term 'friendly' is used by many patients to describe a specific dentist, the dentist would be classified as a 'friendly' dentist.

**Table 1.** Trust elements affecting positively and negatively to dentists

| Trust elements affecting positively to Dentists | | Affecting negatively |
|---|---|---|
| Friendly | Explains well | Rude |
| Caring | Recommended by many | Rushed |
| Professional | Quality of service | Poor manner |
| Experienced | Reliable | Aggressive |
| Knowledgeable | Good personality | |

To determine the best combination of trust elements for a type of patient, an online survey and focus group will be conducted. Many researchers in dental area have identified and mentioned that caring, compassion, thoughtful and supportive dentists are preferred by patients [25, 26]. Some others [27, 28] pointed out importance of expertise and knowledge sharing from dentists to the patients. These terms are also used to describe the patients in the reviews.

## 6    Conclusion and Future Work

This paper highlights that trust elements derived from subjective characteristics such as personality, attitudes, and perception of both patients and dentists, can enhance the suitability of matching while recommending a dentist to a patient. It proposes profile-based trust dependent framework for dynamic dental care recommendation systems. This framework could also be used in other domains as trust derived from different personality, attitude and perception, plays a vital role in dynamic recommendations systems. In the dental care, recommendation systems are still in their infancy and social elements of trust are not incorporated in the existing dental review sites. By integrating subjective characteristics, the effectiveness of recommendation systems would be increased and would provide benefits to the dental society. Collective intelligence from dental crowdsources is a major source for recommendations, but adding subjective criteria for patients and dentists, will enhance the matching process. In the near future, matching rules would be drawn through online questionnaires to general public (as a patient to a dentist) and dentists. The methods of online survey and focus group as well as analysis of dental reviews data will be explored further in the future. A recommendation tool has been developed to test the matching rule with a real reviews data available from the popular dental reviews sites. Eventually, the recommendation system would be a trusted source to find a suitable dentist.

## References

1. Bhuiyan, T., Xu, Y., Josang, A.: State-of-the-Art Review on Opinion Mining from Online Customer's Feedback. In: The 9th Asia-Pacific Complex Systems Conference, Tokyo, Japan, November 4 -7 (2009)
2. Ratzan, S.C.: Our New "Social" Communication Age in Health. Journal of Health Communication 16(8), 803–804 (2011)
3. Swan, M.: Emerging patient-driven health care models: an examination of health social networks, consumer personalized medicine and quantified self-tracking. International Journal of Environmental Research and Public Health 6(2), 492–525 (2009)
4. Lilien, L., Bhargava, B.: Trading privacy for trust in online interactions. Idea Group (2008)
5. Jøsang, A., Quattrociocchi, W., Karabeg, D.: Taste and trust. In: Wakeman, I., Gudes, E., Jensen, C.D., Crampton, J. (eds.) Trust Management V. IFIP AICT, vol. 358, pp. 312–322. Springer, Heidelberg (2011)
6. Gray, E., Seigneur, J.-M., Chen, Y., Jensen, C.: Trust propagation in small worlds. In: Nixon, P., Terzis, S. (eds.) iTrust 2003. LNCS, vol. 2692, pp. 239–254. Springer, Heidelberg (2003)
7. Shu, W., Chuang, Y.H.: The perceived benefits of six-degree-separation social networks. Internet Research: Electronic Networking Applications and Policy 21(1), 26–45 (2011)
8. Barnett, E.: Facebook cuts six degrees separation to four. In: The Telegraph (November 22, 2011),
http://www.telegraph.co.uk/technology/facebook/8906693/
Facebook-cuts-six-degrees-of-separation-to-four.html (2012)

9. Hou, J., Shim, M.: The Role of Provider–Patient Communication and Trust in Online Sources in Internet Use for Health-Related Activities. Journal of Health Communication 15(S3), 186–199 (2010)

10. Tustin, N.: The role of patient satisfaction in online health information seeking. Journal of Health Communication 15(1), 3–17 (2010)

11. Pickens, J.: Attitudes and perceptions. In: Borkowski, N. (ed.). Organizational Behavior in Health Care, ch. 3, Michael Brown, USA, pp. 43–76 (2005)

12. Ferguson, M.J., Bargh, J.A.: Beyond the attitude object: Automatic attitudes spring from object-centered-objects. In: Wittenbrink, B., Schwarz, N. (eds.) Implicit Measures of Attitudes, pp. 216–246 (2007)

13. Moturu, S., Liu, H.: Quantifying the Trustworthiness of Social Media Content: Content Analysis for the Social Web. LAP Lambert Academic Publishing (2010)

14. Su, X., Khoshgoftaar, T.M.: A Survey of Collaborative Filtering Techniques. Hindawi Publishing, Advances in Artificial Intelligence (2009)

15. Walter, F.E., Battiston, S., Schweltzer, F.: A model of trust-based recommendation system on a social network. Auton Agent Multi-Agent System 16, 57–74 (2008)

16. Lopez-Nores, M., Blanco-Fernandez, Y., Pazos-Arias, J.J., Diaz-Redondo, R.P.: Property-Based Collaborative Filtering: A New Paradigm for Semantics-Based, Health-Aware Recommender Systems. In: Fifth International Workshops on Semantics Media Adaptation and Personalization (2010)

17. Dokoohadi, N., Matskin, M.: Personalizing Human Interaction through Hybrid Ontological Profiling Cultural Heritage Case Study. In: International Workshop on Semantic Web Applications and Human Aspects (SWAHA), Collocated with 3rd Asian Semantic Web Conference (ASWC), pp. 133–140 (2008)

18. Goudge, J., Gilson, L.: How can trust be investigated? Drawing lessons from past experience. Social Science & Medicine 61(7), 1439–1451 (2005)

19. Victor, P., De Cock, M., Cornelis, C.: Trust and Recommendations. In: Ricci, F., Rokach, L., Shapira, B., Kantor, P.B. (eds.) Recommender Systems Handbook, 1st edn. (2011)

20. Josang, A., Pope, S.: Semantic constraints for trust transitivity, pp. 59–68. Australian Computer Society, Inc. (2005)

21. Golbeck, J.: Computing and applying Trust in web-based Social Networks, University of Maryland, Maryland, USA (2005)

22. DISC Insights, http://www.discinsights.com

23. Meyer, E.: Meeting the needs of difficult dental patients, clear communication and careful preparation can help moderate stressful situations. Inside Dental Assisting 10(5) (September/October 2012)

24. Pradhan, S., Gay, V., Nepal, S.: Social Networking and Dental Care: State of the Art and Analysis of the Impact on Dentists, Dental Practices and their Patients. In: BLED 2013 Proceedings, Paper 22 (2013)

25. Sbaraini, A., Carter, S.M., Evans, W., Blinkhorn, A.: Experiences of dental care: What do patients value? BMC Health Services Research 12, 177 (2012)

26. Yarascavitch, C., Regehr, G., Hodges, B., Haas, D.A.: Changes in Dental Student Empathy During Training. Journal of Dental Education 73(4), 509–517 (2009)

27. Merijohn, G.K., Bader, J.D., Frantsve-Hawley, J., Aravamudhan, K.: Clinical decision support chairside tools for evidence-based dental practice. Journal Evid. Base Dent. Pract. 8, 119–132 (2008)

28. Mettes, T.G., van der Sanden, W.J.M., Mokkink, H.G., Wensing, M., Grol, R.P.T.M., Plasschaert, A.J.M.: Routine oral examinations in primary care: Which predictors determine what is done?, A prospective clinical case recording study. Journal of Dentistry 36, 435–443 (2008)

# Abstract Accountability Language*

Walid Benghabrit[1], Hervé Grall[1], Jean-Claude Royer[1], Mohamed Sellami[1],
Karin Bernsmed[2], and Anderson Santana De Oliveira[3]

[1] Mines Nantes, 5 rue A. Kastler, F-44307 Nantes, France
`{firstname.lastname}@mines-nantes.fr`
[2] SINTEF ICT, Strindveien 4, NO-7465 Trondheim, Norway
`Karin.Bernsmed@sintef.no`
[3] SAP Labs France, 805 avenue du Dr Donat Font de l'Orme
F - 06250 Mougins Sophia Antipolis, France
`anderson.santana.de.oliveira@sap.com`

**Abstract.** Accountability becomes a necessary principle for future computer systems. This is specially critical for the cloud and Web applications that collect personal and sensitive data from end users. Accountability regards the responsibility and liability for the data handling performed by a computer system on behalf of an organization. In case of misconduct (e.g. security breaches, personal data leaks, etc.), accountability should imply remediation and redress actions. Contrary to data privacy and access control, which is already supported by several concrete languages, there is currently no language supporting accountability clauses representation. In this work, we provide an abstract language for accountability clauses representation with temporal logic semantics.

## 1 Introduction

On-line processing of personal data requires privacy assurance and transparency on how data protection principles imposed by regulatory frameworks are being implemented by service providers. In addition, data owners need to have means to legally hold service providers accountable for their data processing and usage. Accountability for computer systems, as defined in [1], can be viewed as a general posteriori control to ensure the enforcement of some announced promises. In the following, the term "clauses" refers to theses promises. Setting up an accountable system faces many challenges. First, there is no adequate language for accountability clauses representation; such clauses are generally stated in natural language, making it hard for computer programs to assert whether or not service providers are respecting their clauses. There is also a lack of automated assurance necessary to assert that a service provider's clauses are being carried out (for instance, the collection of events showing who created a piece of data, who modified it and how, and so on). In addition, effective and profitable use of on-line services relies on data transfer and storage across different services.

---

* This work has been partly funded from the European Commissions 7th Framework Programme (FP7/2007-2013) under grant agreement no: 317550 (A4CLOUD).

J. Zhou et al. (Eds.): IFIPTM 2014, IFIP AICT 430, pp. 229–236, 2014.

These services may be hosted at heterogeneous environments and using different representations for their accountability clauses. This heterogeneity makes it difficult to check clauses compliance in an automated way and the data-owner has no means to verify that her/his preferences are being respected.

Different machine readable representations of privacy obligations have already been proposed [2,3,4]. However they only cover the preventive aspects of accountability and do not offer constructs to represent the other aspects (i.e. auditing and rectification). Despite some formal work, like [5,6,7,8], there is not yet a concrete formal language close to legal or contractual texts for data privacy obligations. To express accountability clauses we propose in this paper an Abstract Accountability Language (AAL), which is devoted to expressing accountability clauses in an unambiguous style and which is close to what end-users need and understand.

The content of this paper is as follows : Section 2 presents background on accountability and related work. The syntax and semantics of AAL are presented in Section 3. We show the expressiveness of AAL in Section 4. Finally, we discuss our results and present directions for future work in Section 5.

## 2     Background on Accountability

In [1], the authors argue that the usual "hide-it-or-lose-it" perspective on information is dominating but not adequate in a world where information should be communicated to third-parties. Classic privacy means and access control are insufficient to guarantee the protection of privacy since the data can be duplicated on the Web and it is possible to infer accurate details from public information.

In the context of the EU A4Cloud project[1], we consider that accountability concerns data stewardship regimes in which organizations that are entrusted with personal data may be responsible and liable for collecting, sharing, storing and otherwise processing the data according to contractual and other legal requirements from the time the data are collected until when the data are destroyed. Legal accountability is a subset of accountability and covers accountability clauses imposed by laws and regulations. In this paper we use the term *clause* to denote anything an actor is required to do because of a promise coming from a contract or the legislation. This refers to a legal duty that the actor is forced to perform and it implies some sanctions for neglecting it.

The analysis of accountability done in the A4Cloud project identifies four roles related to the creation, storing and processing of data. These roles are already present in current regulations like "Directive 95/46/EC". *Data subject*: this role represents any end-user which has data privacy concerns. Thus the data subject is the original creator of a data and express preferences about the future management of his data. *Data controller*: it is legally responsible to the data subject for any violations of its privacy and to the data protection authority in case of misconduct. *Data processor*: this role is attributed to any computational actor which processes some personal data. It should act under the control of a

---

[1] www.a4cloud.eu

data controller. *Auditor*: it represents data protection authorities which are in charge of the application of laws and directives related to data privacy.

As said before, several languages for specifying privacy preferences and policies. Despite the fact that they provide means for expressing formal and verifiable clauses, they are not readable by lawyers or privacy officers who may be involved in an accountable system. In addition, as far as we know, there are neither tool nor method to assist the design and the analysis of an accountable system proposed with these models. This makes it difficult for end-users to evaluate the compliance of a set of clauses (i.e. policy) with a given data privacy regulation or to compare two policies. In the previously cited research, authors also propose an approach to validate the correctness of their clauses, which is inadequate for non software verification specialists.

This paper presents a language for accountability clause representation that is: *i) Close to natural language:* to be adequate to end-users who do not necessarily have skills in a certain policy language, *ii) Machine understandable:* to be enforceable and to offer means for implementing audit functionalities required for violations detection and evidence collection within an accountable system. *iii) Expressed in a formal language:* to promote its automatic compliance checking and verification, and *iv) Abstract:* to act as a pivot model between different accountability clauses representation models and as such promotes the interoperability of heterogeneous systems.

AAL is only the top part of the design of an accountable system; in [9] we present an end-to-end framework for accountability from natural clauses to concrete policy enforcement relying on our AAL language.

## 3 Abstract Accountability Language

To represent accountability clauses, we adopt the point of view of [10] with minor modifications. We consider that an accountability clause to be a triplet $(uc, aa, rc)$. The informal meaning of such clause is: *"Do the best to ensure the usage control (uc), and if a violation of the usage is observed by an audit (aa) then the rectification (rc) applies"*. Usage control covers classic access control but also data distribution (or data transfer). The audit part covers the detection, judgment and evidences collection steps[2]. Rectification subsumes punishment[2] and includes also sanction, remediation and compensation functionalities.

In contrast to [10] we consider not only clauses violators but also victims and not only punishment but also remediation and compensation for the victims. We focus here on accountability clauses as expressed in legal directives. To give a formal and rigid description of these clauses we define a formal and abstract language AAL for Abstract Accountability Language. In our abstract approach we assume that there is an implicit secure logging mechanism. These logs should be sufficient to provide effective detection of breaches and identification of violators. Means to secure logs and auditing is out of the scope of this paper, but the

---

[2] As stated in Section 2, prevention, detection, judgment, evidence and punishment are the five steps of accountable system.

interested reader can look at [11]. In the following, we introduce the syntax of
AAL in Section 3.1 and its associated semantics in Section 3.2.

## 3.1   Syntax

We present in Listing 1.1 the syntax of a minimal AAL kernel.

```
1   AALprogram    ::= Declaration* Clause*
2   Declaration   ::= AgentDec | ServiceDec | DataDec
3   AgentDec      ::= AGENT Id TYPE'('AgentType*')' RS'('service*')' PS'('service*')'
4   ServiceDec    ::= SERVICE Id TYPE'('Type*')' [Purpose]
5   DataDec       ::= DATA Id TYPE'('Type*')' SUBJECT agent
6   AgentType     ::= "Subject"|"Controller"|"Processor"|"Auditor"
7   Clause        ::= CLAUSE Id ':' Usage [Audit Rectification]
8   Usage         ::= [Quant Variable]* ActionExp
9   Audit         ::= AUDITING [Usage THEN] agent.audit'['agent']' '()'
10  Rectification ::= IF_VIOLATED_THEN Usage
11  ActionExp     ::= Action | NOT ActionExp | Modality ActionExp |
12                    Cond | ActionExp (AND|OR|THEN|ONLYWHEN) ActionExp
13  Exp           ::= Variable | Constant | Variable.Attribute
14  Cond          ::= [NOT] Exp | Exp ['=' | '!='] Exp | Cond (AND|OR) Cond
15  Action        ::= agent.service ['['[agent']']'] '('Exp')' [Time] [Purpose]
16  Quant         ::= FORALL | EXISTS
17  Variable      ::= Var ':' Type
18  Modality      ::= MUST | MUSTNOT | MAY | ALWAYS
19  Type, Var, Attribute, Id, agent, Constant, Purpose ::= literal
```

**Listing 1.1.** AAL Syntax

An AAL program is divided in two parts: declarations and clauses. The declaration part allows users to declare system agents (with theirs types, actions
that they can performs called *provided* services PS() and actions they can uses
called *required* services RS() (line 3)), services (defined by a name Id, arguments
Types, and optionally a purpose specifying the context of their usage Purpose
(line 4)) and data (with their types (line 5)). We use a first-order type system supporting sub-typing for the data types declaration[3]. The clauses part, as
mentioned before, an accountability clause (line 7) is a triplet (*uc, aa, rc*).

- Usage control *uc*, is a combination of actions[4] and conditions applied on
  variables that can be quantified (line 8). We represent actions in the following form: agent1.action [agent2](args) (line 15) where: agent1 (resp.
  agent2) is the agent using (resp. providing) the action and args the needed
  arguments. Optionally we can add a purpose and time[3]. The keyword THEN
  is used in the sense of implication, exp1 THEN exp2 means that when *exp1*
  occurs then *exp2* must also occurs. The exp1 ONLYWHEN exp2 construction
  means that *exp1* occurs only if *exp2* has been realized in the past.
- Audit actions *aa* are introduced by the AUDITING keyword and are expressed
  as agent1.audit[agent2]() (line 9) where: agent1 is an auditor auditing
  agent2's logs. Such an audit operation can be more complex therefore we
  extends it by adding usage control [Usage THEN].
- Rectification *rc* is introduced by the keyword IF_VIOLATED_THEN (line 10)
  followed by an usage expression, that represents the actions to perform when
  the audit detects that the usage control *uc* has been violated.

---

[3] Due to space limitations, we do not detail it in this paper.

[4] Actions are prefixed by modalities : MUST for obligation, MUSTNOT for prohibition
and MAY for permission.

## 3.2   Semantics

In order to interpret the language AAL, we resort to temporal logic [12]. Linear-time temporal logic (LTL) is a modal logic with modalities referring to time. Indeed we focus on an extension with quantified data, known as first-order temporal logic [13]. Precisely, the grammar is defined in Table 1. Note that $\varphi$ ranges over any set of propositions defined over the set of events: this set is assumed to be given, as well as the interpretation of each proposition as a subset of events.

**Table 1.** Temporal Logic: Syntax

formula   $\psi ::=$ **true** | **false** | $\neg\psi$ | $\psi \vee \psi$ | $\varphi$   (propositional formulas)
    |   $\exists x.\psi$                     (first-order formulas)
    |   $\mathtt{X}\psi$ | $\mathtt{G}\psi$ | $\mathtt{F}\psi$           (temporal formulas (future))
    |   $\mathtt{X}^{-1}\psi$ | $\mathtt{G}^{-1}\psi$ | $\mathtt{F}^{-1}\psi$      (temporal formulas (past))

We will now describe the temporal operators. Assume that a finite sequence of events is given, as well as a position in the sequence. $\mathtt{X}\psi : \psi$ is true in the next position (in the sequence of events), $\mathtt{X}^{-1}\psi : \psi$ is true in the previous position, $\mathtt{G}\psi :$ for next positions, $\psi$ is always true. Its dual (with respect to negation) $\mathtt{F}\psi : \psi$ will be true at some time. Symmetrically, $\mathtt{G}^{-1}\psi$ means that for previous positions, $\psi$ has always been true; its dual (with respect to negation) $\mathtt{F}^{-1}\psi$ means that $\psi$ has been previously true.

*Instantiation and Extension for Accountability.* In order to instantiate the general framework presented in the preceding paragraph, we need to define the set of events and the set of atomic predicates. The set of events is defined as the set of messages exchanged. A message is a structure with four components: source (emitter), target (receiver), the service name and a data (the content). Such a message is written as: *source.service[target](data)*. The atomic predicates over the set of events are defined with patterns (terms with free variables) or with logical predicates (equalities, comparisons). Given a pattern $\varphi$, a message $e$ and a valuation $\sigma$ assigning closed terms to the free variables in $\varphi$, $\varphi(e)$ is satisfied if the term $\varphi[\sigma]$ is equal to message $e$. A predicate $\varphi$ equal to a disjunction $\vee\varphi_i$ of patterns $\varphi_i$ can be extended to a sequence of message in order to define a projection: if $\pi$ is a sequence of messages, then $\varphi(\pi)$ is the sub-sequence of $\pi$ containing all the messages $e$ in $\pi$ such that $e$ satisfies some $\varphi_i$ for some valuation, and only these messages. We add a new modality for accountability :

formula   $\psi ::= \dots$
    |   $\mathtt{Acc}(\varphi : \psi)(\varphi : \psi)$   (Accountability)

Intuitively, a sequence $\pi$ satisfies proposition $\mathtt{Acc}(\varphi_1 : \psi_1)(\varphi_2 : \psi_2)$ at position $p$ if the sequence before $p$ satisfies $\neg\psi_1$ when projected with $\varphi_1$ and the sequence after $p$ satisfies $\psi_2$ when projected with $\varphi_2$. More formally, given a sequence $\pi$ and two positions $p$ and $q$ such that $(0 \leq p \leq q < |\pi|)$, we denote the subsequence of $\pi$ starting at $p$ and terminating at $(q - 1)$ by $\pi^{p,q}$.

$$(\pi, p) \vDash \texttt{Acc}(\varphi_1 : \psi_1)(\varphi_2 : \psi_2) \overset{\text{def}}{\Leftrightarrow}$$
$$\big((\varphi_1(\pi^{0,p+1}), p) \vDash \neg\psi_1\big) \Rightarrow \big((\varphi_2(\pi^{p+1,|\pi|}), p) \vDash \psi_2\big)$$

*Interpretation.* We give the main elements for the interpretation of AAL accountability clauses. Let $(uc,\ aa,\ rc)$ an AAL clause with its three parts, the accountability clause is translated using the $\texttt{Acc}$ modality $G(aa \implies \texttt{Acc}(\varphi_1 : uc)(\varphi_2 : rc))$. Actions are represented by messages : $source.service[target](data)$. The Boolean operators ($\texttt{NOT}, \texttt{AND}, \texttt{OR}$) and quantification ($\texttt{FORALL}, \texttt{EXISTS}$) are translated in a straightforward manner : $\texttt{NOT}\ \neg$, $\texttt{AND}\ \wedge$, $\ldots$ . The operator $\texttt{MUST}$ is translated in $F$, $\texttt{ALWAYS}$ in $G$ and $\texttt{MUSTNOT}$ translated in $G\neg$. The operator $\texttt{THEN}$ is translated as an implies $\implies$. The $\texttt{ONLYWHEN}$ operator is used for past and translated in $=> F^{-1}$. The $\texttt{MAY}$ operator is interpreted as a conjunction of $\texttt{MUSTNOT}$ with the idea that what is not permitted is forbidden. For instance, if $Required$ is the set of required actions for agent $a$, and $act \in Required$ then $\texttt{MAY}\ a.act$ is translated as $\bigwedge_{b \in Required \wedge \neg b = act} G\ \neg b$.

## 4   Validation : The Health Care Use Case

To validate the expressiveness and adequacy of AAL for accountability clauses representation, we extract clauses from a realistic use case documented in [14] and illustrate their representation in AAL. This use case concerns the flow of health care information generated by medical sensors in the cloud. Patients will be connected to wireless sensors that monitor their vital signs (e.g., movement, temperature, etc.). The sensor data will be transmitted to the cloud where they will be further processed and stored. Figure. 1 represents a component diagram for the use-case. In this design, involved actors are represented as interconnected components. The interactions between the components are made via interfaces representing the different services offered and used by the actors. In the following we present three accountability clauses and their representation in AAL.

*Clause 1: The data subject's right to access, correct and delete personal data.* This clause is statically ensured by the $\texttt{AccesRightInterface}$ (noted $\texttt{ARI*}$ in Figure. 1) interface. However, this preventive means cannot be sufficient since for instance the actor Y might not implement actions properly. Thus the hospital clause should be written in AAL, making explicit the audit step and the rectification that applies in case of violation.

```
EXISTS p:Patient EXISTS d:Data
   (d.subject = p) THEN (MAY p.read(d) OR MAY p.write(d) OR MAY p.delete(d))
AUDITING DPA.audit[hospital]()
IF_VIOLATED_THEN MUST DPA.sanction[hospital](...)
```

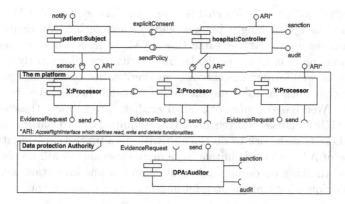

**Fig. 1.** Component diagram for the health care use case

*Clause 2: The data subject's informed consent.* Data subjects must consent to the processing of their personal data, before any personal data is collected about them. We assume that the hospital defines a specific protocol to get the explicit consent. In a first time the hospital sends its policy to the patient (**sendPolicy**) which then replies to the hospital with its consent or not (**explicitConsent**).

```
EXISTS p:Patient EXISTS d:Data
((p = d.subject) THEN MAY p.sensor[X](d)
    ONLYWHEN d.subject.explicitConsent[hospital]("true"))
AND (MAY p.explicitConsent[hospital](b:Boolean)
    ONLYWHEN hospital.sendPolicy[p]("processing policy and purpose"))
AUDITING DPA.audit[hospital]()
IF_VIOLATED_THEN MUST DPA.sanction[hospital](...)
```

*Clause 3: The data controller must notify the data subjects of security or personal data breaches.* In case of a security or privacy incident that is related to the patients' personal data, Cloud providers X and Y must notify m platform, m must notify the hospital and the hospital must notify the patients. We assume that the hospital has been informed (or has detected) a violation with the **violation** action. The usage clause is below.

```
EXISTS p:Patient EXISTS d:Data
(MUST hospital.violation(d) AND (p = d.subject))
        THEN MUST hospital.notify[p]("data breach")
```

The three clauses presented above shows that AAL is capable of expressing the accountability requirements for all actors involved in the use case.

## 5   Conclusion

Accountability makes clear the responsibilities of data controllers, in particular in the case of data breaches, reinforcing trustworthiness in the cloud. We propose for the first time a domain specific language (DSL) to express rules close to sentences in laws, data directives and contracts. This language is equipped with a formal logical background and is the first stone towards clauses enforcement trough accountable design and verification. We demonstrate the expressiveness of AAL on a use case that includes real examples of clauses from data protection legislation. Our proposal defines conditions and event sequences which are relevant to express complex chains of actions. The syntax of AAL is simple and abstract enough making it human readable and such it can easily be used by non specialist users. At the same time, AAL is based on a temporal logic semantics making it machine readable. Such semantics allows early expression simplifications, well-formedness checking and verification of expected properties. We start such a work in [15] using the mCRL2 model-checker. We are currently developing a Web based framework called AccLab [5], to support these concepts.

Accountability clauses written in AAL are quite close to natural language. However, there is still work to fill the gap with data protection legislation. The exact shape of AAL is not definitive since more experiments will be needed. We have started thinking on design and verification but one important aspect is to develop techniques for manual and automatic clauses enforcement.

# References

1. Weitzner, D.J., Abelson, H., Berners-Lee, T., Feigenbaum, J., Hendler, J., Sussman, G.J.: Information accountability. Commun. ACM 51(6), 82–87 (2008)
2. DeYoung, H., Garg, D., Jia, L., Kaynar, D., Datta, A.: Experiences in the logical specification of the HIPAA and GLBA privacy laws. In: WPES 2010, pp. 73–82 (2010)
3. Le Métayer, D.: A formal privacy management framework. In: Degano, P., Guttman, J., Martinelli, F. (eds.) FAST 2008. LNCS, vol. 5491, pp. 162–176. Springer, Heidelberg (2009)
4. Piolle, G., Demazeau, Y.: Representing privacy regulations with deontico-temporal operators. Web Intelligence and Agent Systems 9(3), 209–226 (2011)
5. Etalle, S., Winsborough, W.H.: A posteriori compliance control. In: Lotz, V., Thuraisingham, B.M. (eds.) SACMAT 2007, pp. 11–20. ACM (2007)
6. Jagadeesan, R., Jeffrey, A., Pitcher, C., Riely, J.: Towards a theory of accountability and audit. In: Backes, M., Ning, P. (eds.) ESORICS 2009. LNCS, vol. 5789, pp. 152–167. Springer, Heidelberg (2009)
7. Feigenbaum, J., Jaggard, A.D., Wright, R.N.: Towards a formal model of accountability. In: NSPW, pp. 45–56. ACM (2011)
8. Zou, J., Wang, Y., Lin, K.-J.: A formal service contract model for accountable saas and cloud services. In: SCC 2010, pp. 73–80 (2010)
9. Benghabrit, W., Grall, H., Royer, J.-C., Sellami, M., Önen, M., Oliveira, A.S.D., Bernsmed, K.: A cloud accountability obligations representation framework. In: CLOSER (2014)
10. Feigenbaum, J., Jaggard, A.D., Wright, R.N., Xiao, H.: Systematizing "accountability" in computer science. Technical Report TR-1452, University of Yale (2012)
11. Vaughan, J.A., Jia, L., Mazurak, K., Zdancewic, S.: Evidence-based audit. In: IEEE 25th Computer Security Foundations Symposium, pp. 177–191 (2008)
12. Fisher, M.: Temporal representation and reasoning. In: Handbook of Knowledge Representation, pp. 513–550. Elsevier, Amsterdam (2008)
13. Hodkinson, I.M., Wolter, F., Zakharyaschev, M.: Decidable fragment of first-order temporal logics. Ann. Pure Appl. Logic 106(1-3), 85–134 (2000)
14. Bernsmed, K., Felici, M., Oliveira, A.S.D., Sendor, J., Moe, N.B., Rübsamen, T., Tountopoulos, V., Hasnain, B.: Use case descriptions. Deliverable, A4Cloud (2013)
15. Benghabrit, W., Grall, H., Royer, J.-C., Sellami, M.: Accountability for Abstract Component Design. In: EUROMICRO DSD/SEAA 2014, Verona, Italy (August 2014)

---

[5] http://www.emn.fr/z-info/acclab/

# Trust Assessment Using Cloud Broker

Pramod S. Pawar[1,2], Muttukrishnan Rajarajan[1], Theo Dimitrakos[2],
and Andrea Zisman[3]

[1] City University London, London EC1V 0HB, United Kingdom
r.muttukrishnan@city.ac.uk
[2] British Telecommunications, Adastral Park, Ipswich IP5 3RE, United Kingdom
{pramod.s.pawar,theo.dimitrakos}@bt.com
[3] The Open University, Walton Hall, Milton Keynes MK7 6AA, UK
andrea.zisman@open.ac.uk

**Abstract.** Despite the advantages and rapid growth of Cloud computing, the cloud environments are still not sufficiently trustworthy from a customer's perspective. Several challenges such as specification of service level agreements, standards, security measures, selection of service providers and computation of trust still persists, that concerns the customer. To deal with these challenges and provide a trustworthy environment, a mediation layer may be essential. In this paper we propose a cloud broker as a mediation layer, to deal with complex decision of selecting a trustworthy cloud provider, that fulfils the service requirements, create agreements and also provisions security. The cloud broker operates in different modes and this enables a variety of trust assessments.

**Keywords:** cloud trust, cloud broker, multi-cloud, reputation.

## 1 Introduction

Despite the advantages and rapid growth of cloud computing, most organizations still continue with their concerns about trust and security of cloud providers. Several challenges [1] such as specification of SLAs, standards, security measures, selection of service providers and computation of trust still persists, implying that the cloud environments are still not sufficiently trustworthy from customer's perspective. To deal with the challenge of identifying dependable cloud service providers for the service, cloud marketplaces are gaining popularity and allow consumers to select providers that best match their requirements. However, their complex requirements and the numerous choices available to the consumer make it difficult to decide on a provider to host their service. In addition, their concern about the trustworthiness of the providers remains unanswered. The cloud characteristics [2] such as elasticity and the complex deployment models like multi-cloud and federated clouds create major challenges in trust assessment of cloud providers. A unanimous trust assessment across all deployment architecture may not be suitable, this creates a compelling requirement to have a suitable separate trust assessment for every deployment architecture.

J. Zhou et al. (Eds.): IFIPTM 2014, IFIP AICT 430, pp. 237–244, 2014.

The assessment of the cloud computing environment leads to crucial requirements which are essential to evaluate the cloud provider's trustworthiness and they are: a) An independent mediation layer capable of performing variety of trust assessment to evaluate the cloud providers b) An evaluation framework that is trusted enough such that malicious providers cannot manipulate the evaluation process c) An evaluation of cloud providers based on fine-grained QoS parameters together with consumer feedbacks, recommendations and additional distinguishing parameters that relate to the cloud computing environments [1]. Due to the complexity of service requirements and difficulty of trustworthiness evaluation of the cloud providers, third parties like cloud brokers can play an important role to assist the consumer in selecting an appropriate provider and also assist in deployment of the service.

The work presented in this paper was developed under the FP7 EU-funded project called OPTIMIS [3]. This paper, proposes the trust evaluation of the cloud providers with the use of OPTIMIS Cloud Broker (CBR) as a mediation layer. As a first step towards integration of trust and reputation systems in cloud environment, a set of parameters beyond QoS are identified that includes: SLA, Compliance, interoperability, geographical location of data centers, deployment models, security measures, user recommendations and feedbacks[1]. The trust model[4], [5]   cohesively works with the cloud broker in different modes using SLA and cloud characteristic parameters for evaluating the trustworthiness of the providers, and is robust against malicious group of entities performing reputation based attacks. The OPTIMIS cloud broker supports SLA, compliance with data protection and locations, multi-cloud and federated cloud deployments, security as value additions and integrates trust model enabled with SLA monitoring and user ratings in terms of feedback for the service used.

The remaining paper is structured as follows. Section 2 describes the different modes of operation of cloud broker. Section 3 describes type of trust in each of the cloud broker modes. Section 4 provides trust evaluation using cloud broker. Section 5 provides the related work and finally, section 6 provides the concluding remarks.

## 2    Cloud Broker Service

This paper considers the OPTIMIS Cloud Broker (CBR) [3] for assessing trust of the Infrastructure Providers(IP). The OPTIMIS Cloud Broker (CBR) as shown in Fig. 1

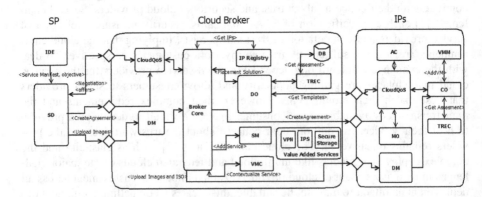

**Fig. 1.** High level component architecture of the Cloud Broker

has architecture that enables multi-cloud deployment, provisions value added service for the consumer's service deployed via cloud broker and also performs Trust, Risk, Eco-efficiency and Cost (TREC) assessment. Details of the components and the multi-cloud deployment process is available from the OPTIMIS toolkit website[6].

## 2.1    Cloud Broker Modes of Operation

The OPTIMIS cloud broker has the capability to operate in four different modes:  a) *cloud service recommendation* b) *cloud service intermediation* c) *cloud service aggregation* and d) *cloud service arbitrage*. Cloud broker used in *cloud service recommendation* mode enables the user to get recommendations from the cloud broker about the most suitable cloud infrastructure provider for hosting their service, based on the degree of Trust, Risk, Eco-efficiency and Cost (TREC). The cloud broker as a *recommender* reduces the effort from the consumer to identify a suitable cloud service provider for its service. However the actual deployment of the service to the cloud infrastructure is performed by the consumer after obtaining deployment solution from the cloud broker.  Cloud broker used as *cloud service intermediation* provides management functionalities like *Value Added Services (VAS)* that are cloud provider specific, which may be essential for the consumer's service that is deployed in the cloud provider environment. As an *intermediary*, the cloud broker also takes complete responsibility of the consumer's/user's services to identify the most suitable IP based on TREC, then performs the deployment on the selected IP, and then manages smooth functioning of the service during its operational stage. The use of cloud broker as *cloud service aggregation* provides management functionalities for *multi-cloud* deployment and operation of a service by combining services from multiple cloud infrastructure providers.  The cloud broker also provides VASs that are independent of cloud providers.  Cloud broker used as *cloud service arbitrage* can be considered as dynamic aggregation wherein the multi-cloud deployment of consumer service is dynamically decided based on the service requirements. In this mode of operation, the cloud broker system decomposes the service requirements at component level and negotiates with multiple cloud providers for each of the service components to formulate an optimized deployment solution taking into account the basic service requirements as well as additional requirements such as TREC, compliance and security.

## 3     Trust Assessment Using Cloud Broker

This section describes the trust assessments performed using the different modes of cloud broker. Table 1 summarizes the feature provided by cloud broker in different modes of operation. Analysis of the summary information reveals that cloud broker in *cloud service recommendation* mode is only responsible to provide the deployment solution which determines that a standard trust model with cloud specific characteristics is sufficient for trust assessment of the cloud providers. Cloud broker as *cloud service intermediation* additionally provides value added services like security service and as for a comprehensive trust assessment it is essential to evaluate security reputation of the cloud provider. The cloud broker as *cloud service aggregation/arbitration* additionally provides support for multi-cloud deployment that compels the requirement of trust assessment for a group of cloud providers.

**Table 1.** Features for cloud broker used in different modes

|  | Deployment Solution | Deployment of Service | Provider specific VAS | Provider Independent VAS | Static Multi-cloud deployment | Dynamic multi-cloud |
|---|---|---|---|---|---|---|
| Recommender | X |  |  |  |  |  |
| Intermediary | X | X | X |  |  |  |
| Aggregator | X | X | X | X | X |  |
| Arbitrage | X | X | X | X | X | X |

### 3.1    Cloud Broker as Cloud Service Recommendation

In this mode of operation the consumer interacts with cloud broker only for getting the deployment solution to identify the trustworhty cloud providers and takes the responsibility of deployment. In this mode the cloud broker uses the trust model as proposed in Pawar et al.[4], [7]. The *Trustworthiness* of an cloud Infrastructure Provider (IP) is modelled using *opinion* obtained from three different computations, namely (i) *compliance of SLA parameters (SLA monitoring)*, (ii) *service provider satisfaction ratings (SP ratings)*, and (iii) *service provider behaviour (SP behaviour)*. The SP behaviour is defined in terms of the credibility for each of the SP based on the feedback provided. In addition to the credibility, the trust model is complimented with early filtering to reduce the impact of malicious feedback providers [7]. The cloud broker uses this trust model to provide recommendations about the cloud providers. The *trustworthiness (T)* of an IP is modelled as below:

$$T = \text{Expectation} (W_{(SPB \otimes SPR) \wedge SLA}) \qquad (1)$$

$$W_{(SPB \otimes SPR) \wedge SLA} = (W_{SPB} \otimes W_{SPR}) \wedge W_{SLA} \qquad (2)$$

where $W_{SLA}, W_{SPR}, W_{SPB}$ are opinions obtained from the SLA monitoring (SLA), SP ratings (SPR), and SP behavior (SPB) values, respectively. The symbol $\wedge$ is the *conjunction operator* used to combine the opinions, and $\otimes$ is the *discounting operator* used as the recommendation operator.

### 3.2    Cloud Broker as Cloud Service Intermediation

The cloud broker in the intermediary mode of operation, have capabilities to provision value added services such as security services. In this mode, the cloud broker inherits and expands on the role of security auditor, enabling the cloud broker to obtain access to security events due to the high value of trust placed, which may not be possible with the wider community. The cloud broker provisions the consumers with security reputation of cloud IP based on their security requirements. The reputation of a cloud IP [5] is calculated in terms of its *trustworthiness(T)* using opinion obtained from computations, namely i) *Incidence Monitoring(M)*: Security incidence events received from monitoring ii) *Enterprise User Rating(EUR)*: Ratings provided by the enterprise user for satisfaction of the security features provided by cloud service providers. The *trustworthiness (T)* of cloud IP is given as:

$$T = \text{Expectation} (W_M \wedge W_{EUR}) = \text{Expectation} (W_{M \wedge EUR}) \qquad (3)$$

Where $W_{M \wedge EUR} = (b_{M \wedge EUR}, d_{M \wedge EUR}, u_{M \wedge EUR}, a_{M \wedge EUR})$.

### 3.3  Cloud Broker as Cloud Service Aggregation/Arbitration

The cloud broker used as *cloud service aggregation/arbitration* is capable of devising multi-cloud deployment solution based on user requirements. This enables the cloud broker to perform trust assessment for a group of providers. Consider that the deployment solution provided contains two target cloud providers. Let $T_1$ and $T_2$ be the trust computed for the first and the second cloud provider. The individual trustworthiness $T_1$ and $T_2$, of the cloud provider are computed based on the parameters, *SLA monitoring, SP rating* and *SP behavior*, as described in Section 3.1. The global trust or the group trust for the cloud provider computed by the broker is as follows:

$$T_{12} = (W_1/(W_1 + W_2)) \, T_1 \; + \; (W_2/(W_1 + W_2)) \, T_2 \qquad (4)$$

Where W1 and $W_2$ are weights assigned for trust computed for each of the cloud providers such that $W1 + W_2 = 1$.

## 4  Evaluation

This section evaluates the trust assessment performed using cloud broker as a cloud service recommendation. The Trust model is evaluated using a simulation with a typical simulation run of 250 iterations, a total of 100 SP nodes and one cloud broker node trying to evaluate a single IP. This paper uses categorized groups of malicious feedback provider and two metrics as considered as in [8]. The malicious groups are: *complementary, exaggerated positive* and *exaggerated negative*. The SP nodes are tagged with one of the four categories: normal group (G1), exaggerated positive group (G2), exaggerated negative group (G3) and complementary group (G4). The experiments use different ratios G1:G2:G3:G4 of SP nodes. The remaining section is as follows: Section 4.1 demonstrates the trust model robustness due to credibility use in trust model. Section 4.2 demonstrates sensitivity of the model to uncertainty.

### 4.1  Average Credibility Decreases with Time

The purpose of the credibility parameter is to ensure that the feedback provided by malicious nodes be weighted less to reduce the influence of malicious nodes and thus to correctly model the reputation of the trustee. In this experiment, the ratio of nodes G1:G2:G3:G4 is given as 70:10:10:10. After the cloud broker node performing transaction with the IP, it computes difference between the feedback provided and the real QoS provided by the IP. This enables cloud broker to compute the current credibility of feedback providers i.e. SPs. In each iteration, credibility of SPs are updated considering its previous credibility and then the average credibility is computed for each group G1, G2, G3 and G4. The result in Fig. 2 shows that the average credibility for the malicious node groups G2, G3 and G4 decreases drastically within a few iterations and then remains low throughout rest of the iterations. This result indicates that malicious node achieve low credibility with time and that the feedbacks provided by the malicious nodes will have a low influence on the reputation computation since the feedbacks provided by these malicious nodes are weighted less.

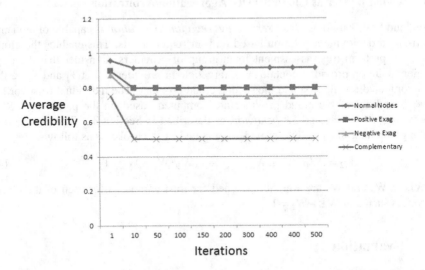

**Fig. 2.** Average Credibility for different groups of SPs. G1:G2:G3:G4 is 70:10:10:10.

## 4.2   Sensitivity to Uncertainty

It is important to consider the feedback providers confidence in their feedback about trustee. The aim of this experiment is to check if the confidence value of the feedback provider has any impact on robustness of the model. For this experiment, keeping the reliability trust provided by feedback provider constant, it is executed for two cases of

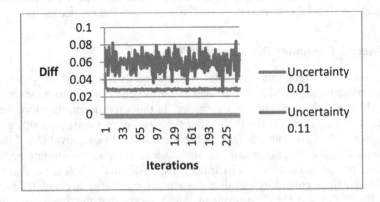

**Fig. 3.** Diff for different levels of uncertainty by the feedback providers

uncertainty for the feedback provided. In the first case a high uncertainty is maintained as u=0.11, while for the second case the uncertainty is reduced to 0.01. In both cases the malicious nodes ratio of 70:30:0:0 is considered for the experiment. It is observed from Fig. 3 that the trust model is sensitive to uncertainty in the feedback value provided. Smaller the uncertainty, the corresponding *diff* value would be small. This result validates that with increase in evidence available, uncertainty in the feedback value reduces and the system robustness increases.

## 5    Related Work

Trust and reputation have been the focus of research for several open systems and the rapidly growing cloud computing technology also appreciates the importance of trust in the cloud computing environment. This is partially observed through the trust and reputation systems that have being discussed in [3], [4], [7], [9]. In OPTIMIS [3], trust is one of the core component used by SP, along with risk, eco-efficiency and cost for evaluating the IP for their service.   Alhamad *et al.* [9] proposes a trust model for cloud computing based on the usage of SLA information and provides a high level architecture capturing major functionalities required. Pawar et al.[4][7]   include SLA compliance information to model trust and also proposed a trust model based on cloud characteristics supported with credibility and early filtering mechanism to reduce the impact of malicious feedback providers.   Significant research exists in the area of brokers used in various areas of computer science. Cloud brokers [1], [10] are also gaining popularity to identify dependable cloud service providers.   The importance of cloud brokerage is also emphasized   by Gartner research [11], which defines different types of brokerage. In line with Gartner research [11], Nair et al.[10] propose the use of cloud broker as 1) *cloud service intermediation* 2) *cloud service aggregation* and 3) *cloud service arbitrage* and provide an abstract architecture for the brokerage.   The OPTIMIS cloud broker architecture, is in line with the concepts defined in [10] and [11]. In addition, it supports trust assessment, matching of consumer requirements, establishing agreements and also provides value added services such as security.

## 6    Conclusion and Final Remark

This paper communicates that a unanimous trust assessment across the cloud computing environment may not be suitable and exploits the use of OPTIMIS cloud broker and its various modes to perform variety of trust evaluations of the cloud providers. This paper uses the opinion based trust model to perform trust assessment of cloud providers to provide recommendations, security reputation and a group reputation in the different modes of cloud broker.   The paper provides evaluation results for the trust assessment performed by the cloud broker in the recommendation mode and reserves the evaluation of the security reputation and group reputation as future work.

**Acknowledgement.** This work has been partially supported by the EU within the 7th Framework Programme under contract ICT-257115 - Optimized Infrastructure Services (OPTIMIS).

# References

1. Habib, S.M., Ries, S., Muhlhauser, M.: Cloud Computing Landscape and Research Challenges Regarding Trust and Reputation, pp. 410–415 (2010)
2. Mell, P., Grance, T.: The NIST Definition of Cloud Computing. Httpcsrcnistgovpublicationsnistpubs800-145SP800-145pdf (September 2011)
3. Ferrer, A.J., Hernández, F., Tordsson, J., Elmroth, E., Ali-Eldin, A., Zsigri, C., Sirvent, R., Guitart, J., Badia, R.M., Djemame, K., Ziegler, W., Dimitrakos, T., Nair, S.K., Kousiouris, G., Konstanteli, K., Varvarigou, T., Hudzia, B., Kipp, A., Wesner, S., Corrales, M., Forgó, N., Sharif, T., Sheridan, C.: OPTIMIS: A holistic approach to cloud service provisioning. Future Gener. Comput. Syst. 28(1), 66–77 (2012)
4. Pawar, P.S., Rajarajan, M., Nair, S.K., Zisman, A.: Trust Model for Optimized Cloud Services. In: Dimitrakos, T., Moona, R., Patel, D., McKnight, D.H. (eds.) IFIPTM 2012. IFIP AICT, vol. 374, pp. 97–112. Springer, Heidelberg (2012)
5. Pawar, P.S., Nair, S.K., El-Moussa, F., Dimitrakos, T., Rajarajan, M., Zisman, A.: Opinion Model Based Security Reputation Enabling Cloud Broker Architecture. In: Yousif, M., Schubert, L. (eds.) CloudComp 2012. LNICST, vol. 112, pp. 103–113. Springer, Heidelberg (2013)
6. OPTIMIS Toolkit I Home - Cloud, but better, http://www.optimistoolkit.com/ (accessed: April 15, 2014)
7. Pawar, P.S., Rajarajan, M., Dimitrakos, T., Zisman, A.: Trust Model for Cloud Based on Cloud Characteristics. In: Fernández-Gago, C., Martinelli, F., Pearson, S., Agudo, I. (eds.) IFIPTM 2013. IFIP AICT, vol. 401, pp. 239–246. Springer, Heidelberg (2013)
8. Jia, C., Xie, L., Gan, X., Liu, W., Han, Z.: A Trust and Reputation Model Considering Overall Peer Consulting Distribution. IEEE Trans. Syst. Man Cybern. Part Syst. Hum. 42(1), 164–177 (2012)
9. Alhamad, M., Dillon, T., Chang, E.: SLA-Based Trust Model for Cloud Computing. In: 2010 13th International Conference on Network-Based Information Systems (NBiS), pp. 321–324 (2010)
10. Nair, S.K., Porwal, S., Dimitrakos, T., Ferrer, A.J., Tordsson, J., Sharif, T., Sheridan, C., Rajarajan, M., Khan, A.U.: Towards Secure Cloud Bursting, Brokerage and Aggregation. In: 2010 IEEE 8th European Conference on Web Services (ECOWS), pp. 189–196 (2010)
11. Gartner, "Cloud Services Brokerage: The Dawn of the Next Intermediation Age"

# Author Index

Printed in the United States
By Bookmasters